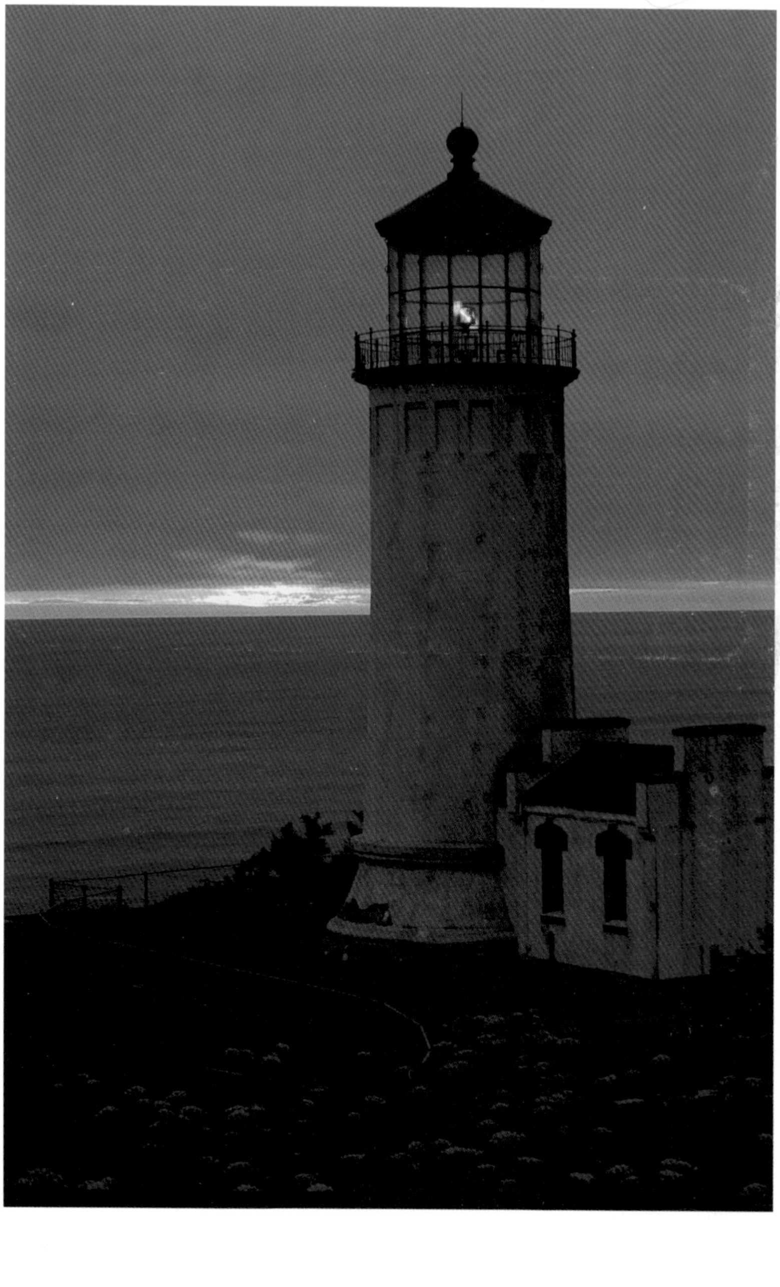

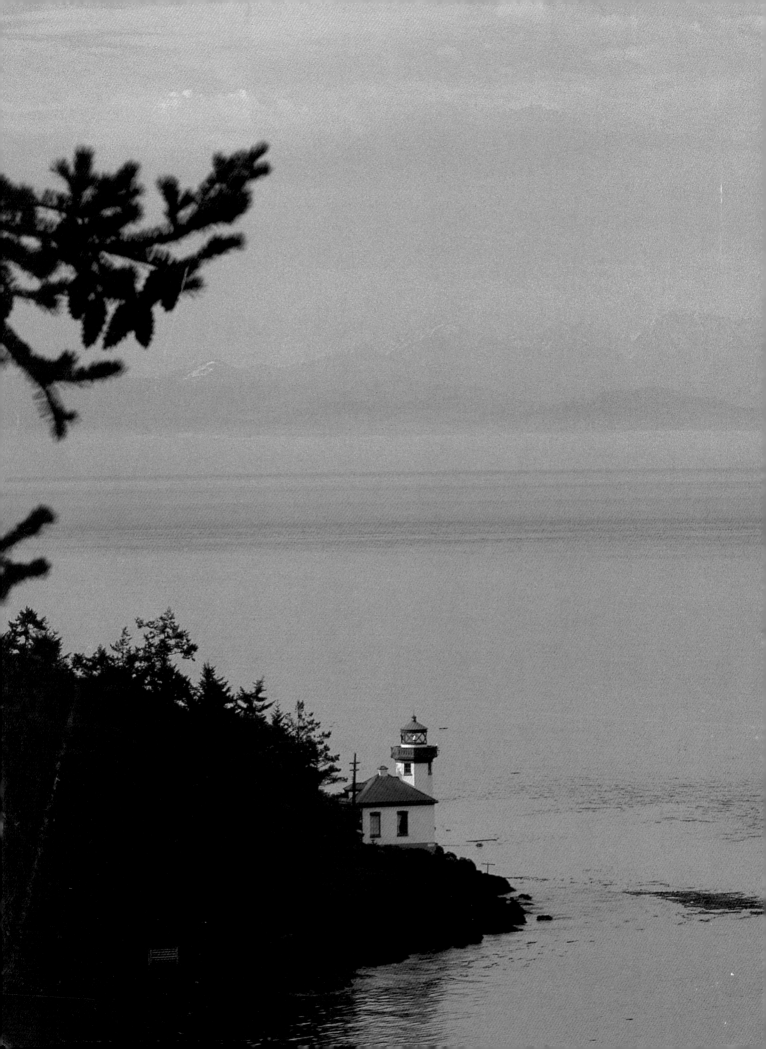

Lighthouses OF THE Pacific Coast

Your Guide to the Lighthouses
of California, Oregon, and Washington

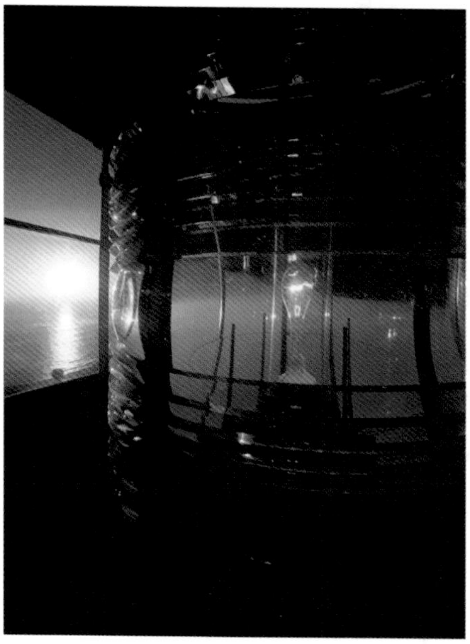

Text by Randy Leffingwell & Pamela Welty
Photographs by Randy Leffingwell

Voyageur Press

JACKSON COUNTY LIBRARY SERVICES
MEDFORD, OREGON 97501

First published in 2000 by Voyageur Press, an imprint of MBI Publishing Company, 400 First Avenue North, Suite 300, Minneapolis, MN 55401 USA

Text copyright © 2000, 2010 by Randy Leffingwell and Pamela Welty
Photographs copyright © 2000, 2010 by Randy Leffingwell
Hardcover edition published 2000. Softcover edition 2010

All rights reserved. With the exception of quoting brief passages for the purposes of review, no part of this publication may be reproduced without prior written permission from the Publisher.

The information in this book is true and complete to the best of our knowledge. All recommendations are made without any guarantee on the part of the author or Publisher, who also disclaims any liability incurred in connection with the use of this data or specific details.

We recognize, further, that some words, model names, and designations mentioned herein are the property of the trademark holder. We use them for identification purposes only. This is not an official publication.

Voyageur Press titles are also available at discounts in bulk quantity for industrial or sales-promotional use. For details write to Special Sales Manager at MBI Publishing Company, 400 First Avenue North, Suite 300, Minneapolis, MN 55401 USA.

To find out more about our books, visit us online at www.voyageurpress.com.

ISBN 978-0-7603-3650-2

The Library of Congress has cataloged the hardcover edition as follows:

Library of Congress Cataloging-in-Publication Data

Leffingwell, Randy, 1948–
Lighthouses of the Pacific coast : your guide to the lighthouses of California, Oregon, and Washington / text by Leffingwell & Pamela Welty ; photographs by Randy Leffingwell.
p. cm. — (A pictorial discovery guide)
Includes index.
ISBN 0-89658-429-1
1. Lighthouses—California. 2. Lighthouses—Oregon. 3. Lighthouses—Washington (State). 4. Pacific Coast (Calif.)—History. 5. Pacific Coast (Or.)—History. 6. Pacific Coast (Wash.)—History. I. Welty, Pamela, 1967– II. Title. III. Series.
VK1024.C2 L44 2000
387.1'55'0979—dc21
00-026342

Edited by Michael Dregni
Designed by Kristy Tucker

Printed in China

Dedication
This book is dedicated to today's lighthouse keepers, the women and men of the United States Coast Guard Aids-to-Navigation Teams

On the endsheets: *Cape Flattery light station marked the contiguous United States's northwestern-most point. (Photo courtesy Columbia River Maritime Museum)*

Page 1: *North Head light station near Ilwaco, Washington, was first lit in May 1898.*

Pages 2–3: *Lime Kiln light station on San Juan Island, Washington, marks a shipping route to Vancouver, British Columbia.*

Page 3 inset: *Old Point Loma's long-deactivated third-order Fresnel still shines dimly over San Diego harbor.*

Facing page: *Point Bonita lighthouse, at the mouth of the Golden Gate, now sits 124 feet above sea level. This light was first lit in 1855 atop the high bluffs where it was often hidden in fog. In 1870, the Lighthouse Board relocated the light and fog signal to this lower rock. Afternoon coastal fog continues to prove the wisdom of the Board's decision.*

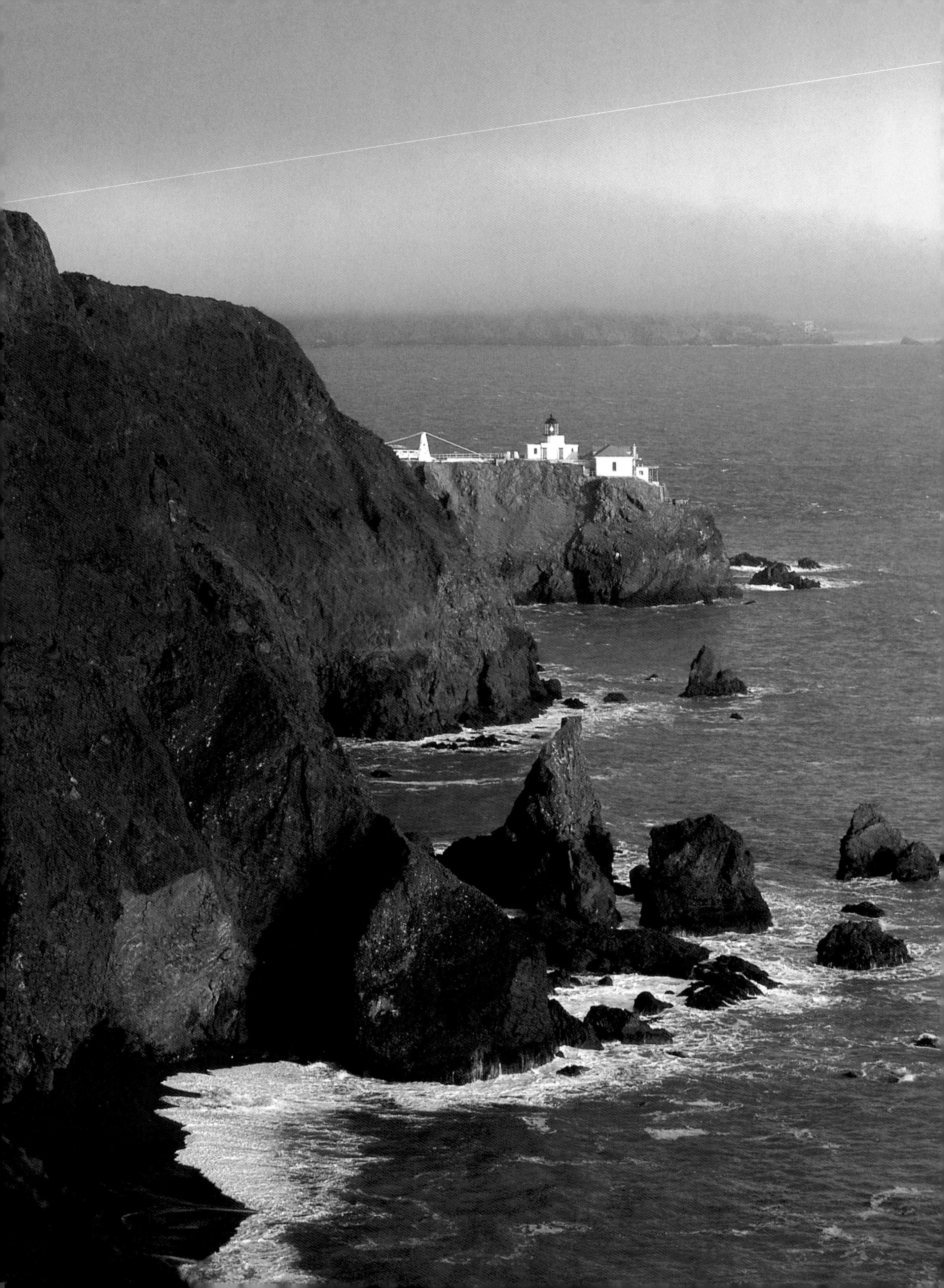

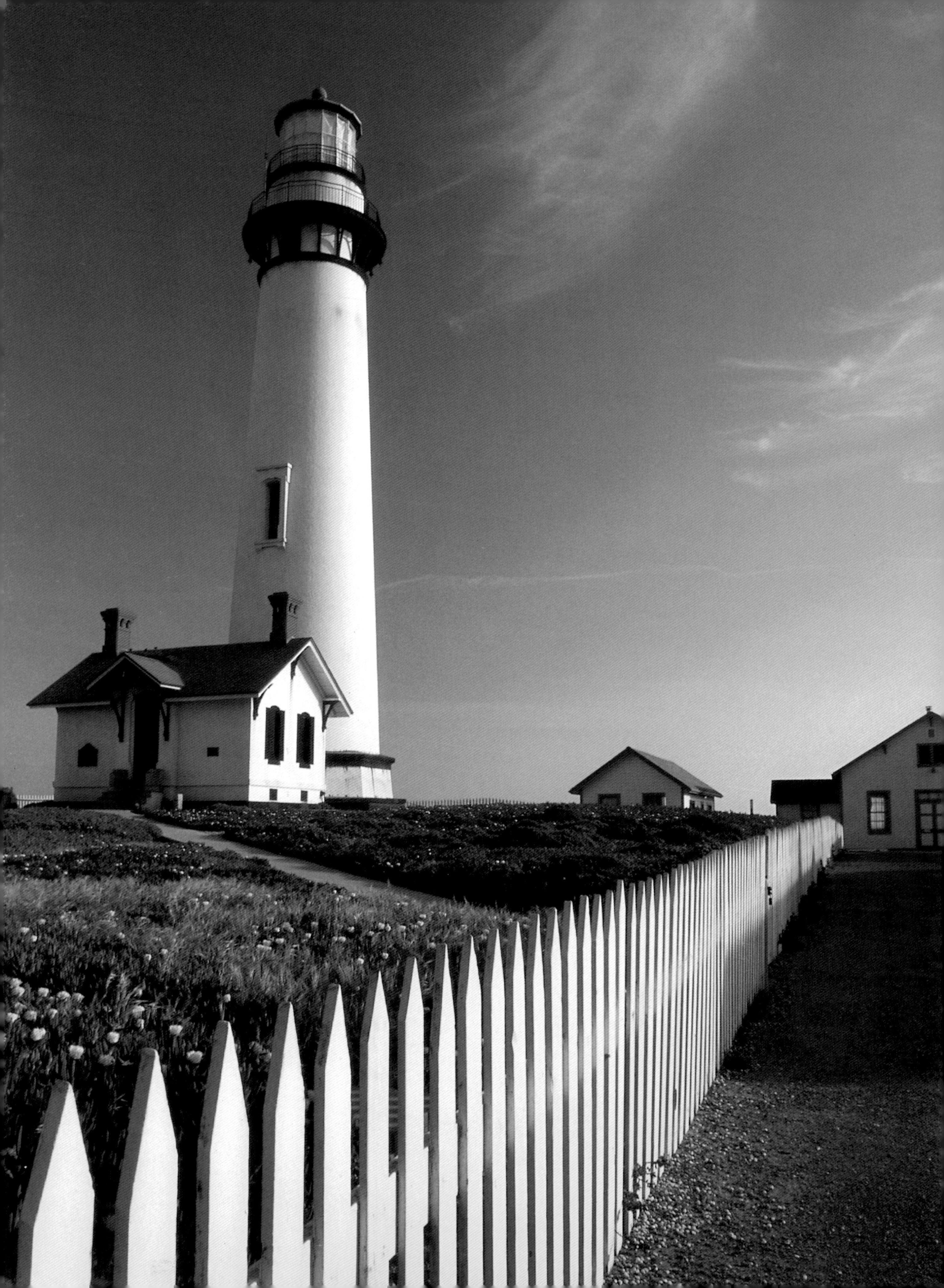

Contents

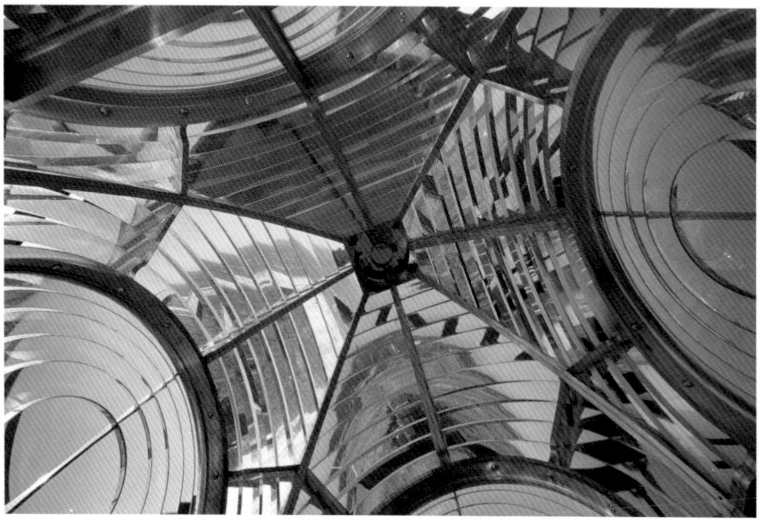

Acknowledgements

Although many organizations control lighthouses throughout the United States, the Coast Guard operates nearly all active lights. Chief Warrant Officer Alex Worden at the Motion Picture–TV Liaison Office in Los Angeles arranged and coordinated the great access that made many of these photos possible.

Coast Guard Aids-to-Navigation Teams maintain the lights. The following members were most generous with their time and assistance: Station Chiefs J. A. Franklin, Astoria, Oregon; Dave Heye, Coos Bay, Oregon; Eric Foster, San Francisco; J. J. Jones, Channel Islands, Port Hueneme, California; John Hurst, Los Angeles; and Sean Thompson, San Diego. EM3 Jeb Wheeler, DC2 Erik Wiard, and MT2 Eric Arwood taught us many lessons in lighthouse keeping while at Cape Flattery; Coast Guard Auxiliarist Eric Castrobrun, Redondo Beach, California, was most informative and helpful. Roy S. Clark, Environmental Division, Coast Guard Civil Engineering Unit, Oakland, California, and Petty Officer Chuck Stercks, Channel Islands, Port Hueneme, California, opened several additional doors. In addition, Ensign Michael Rasch, Air Operations Astoria, Oregon, taught us airlift technology and terminology.

The U.S. Lighthouse Society maintains fascinating archives at its San Francisco headquarters. We are most grateful to founder Wayne Wheeler for his generous help.

David Pearson, curator of the Columbia River Maritime Museum in Astoria, Oregon, made available records and logs of Oregon's lighthouses. Tim Thomas, director of programs and exhibit content at the Maritime Museum of Monterey, California, similarly provided access to stories of California keepers' lives.

The Coast Guard Museum Northwest, Pier 36, Seattle, has an incredible archive of written and photographic materials as well as drawings and blueprints. Captain Gene Davis and Larry Dubia were extremely helpful and encouraging.

Dozens of individuals helped us, gently bending rules, moving barriers, or providing information. We are grateful to the following people:

In California: Superintendent Terry DiMattio and Park Collections Manager Mary Beth Vygralla, Cabrillo National Monument/Point Loma lighthouse; State Parks Film Permit Coordinator Katie Kujawa, California Film Commission, Hollywood; Robert S. Vessely and Andrew G. Merriam, Point San Luis Lighthouse Keepers Association, San Luis Obispo; Bob Lane, Friends of Piedras Blancas, Cambria; Supervising Ranger Linda Rath, Point Sur State Historical Park; Lyn Ann Rose, Central Coast Lighthouse Keepers Association, Point Sur; Captain Bill Kennedy and Helga Boynton, Pacific Grove Police Department; Director Stephen Bailey, Pacific Grove Museum; docent Jerry McCaffery, Point Pinos lighthouse; Park Interpretive Specialist Nelson Morosini, Pigeon Point State Historic Park; Public Affairs staff member Suzanne Summers, Golden Gate National Recreation Area, Alcatraz Island and Point Bonita lighthouse; Ranger Cathy Petrick, Golden Gate National Recreation Area, Point Bonita lighthouse; innkeepers Ann Selover and Gary Herdlicka, East Brother Light Station, Point Richmond; Special Park Uses Administrator Linda Hahn and Ranger Lynda Doucette, Point Reyes National Seashore, Point Reyes lighthouse; John Sisto, Point Arena Lighthouse Keepers Association; Resident Site Manager Lisa Weg and Office Manager Rosanna Torrielli, North Coast Interpretive Association and Point Cabrillo Reserve; Ginny Frundt, head of the Point Cabrillo light-

Page 6: **Pigeon Point light station**
One of California's later lights, Pigeon Point was first illuminated in 1872. It carries on the strongly New England design characteristics of the West Coast's early lights, even to its great height of 115 feet, reached by way of 147 steps. Its fog signal building and 1950s keepers' quarters are now a youth hostel offering overnight accommodation.

Page 7: **Point Cabrillo light station**
Point Cabrillo's restored third-order Fresnel, produced by Chance Brothers of London, shines brilliantly in afternoon sunlight.

house restoration project volunteer organization, and volunteers Ron Eich and Hal Hauck; President Lynn Morris, Del Norte County Historical Society and the Crescent City Museum; Nancy and Larry Schnider, Battery Point Lighthouse resident keepers/curators; President Guy Towers and Vice President Bob Robles, St. George Reef Lighthouse Preservation Society.

In Oregon: Outdoor Recreation Planner John Harper, Bureau of Land Management, Coos Bay, Cape Blanco; Lt. Andrew Dutton, Lt. Matthew Weller, and Aimee Weller, Cape Arago; innkeepers Carol and Mike Korgan, Heceta Head lighthouse; Executive Director Randall Nowalke, Yaquina Lights, Yaquina Bay and Yaquina Head lighthouses; John Arroyo, Bureau of Land Management, Newport, Yaquina Head Lighthouse; Robert Reed, Friends of Cape Meares Lighthouse and Wildlife Refuge; Public Relations staff member Mary Davis and visitor guide Russ Bean, Columbia River Maritime Museum, Astoria, at *Lightship Columbia*.

In Washington: Jeanne Copland, Special Uses Permission, at Washington State Parks and Recreation Commission; Larry Chapman, Fort Canby State Park, North Head lighthouse; Director Bill Hanable, Westport Maritime Museum, Gray Harbor lighthouse; Education Coordinator Robert Steelquist, Olympic Coast National Marine Sanctuary, Port Angeles; Dr. Robert Paine, Zoology Department and Dr. Julia Parrish, Biology Department, University of Washington, Seattle; Park Manager Jim Farmer, Fort Worden State Park, Port Townsend, Point Wilson lighthouse; Park Manager Mike Zimmerman and volunteers Judy and Dale Russell, Fort Flagler State Park, Marrowstone Point Lighthouse; Rick Fackler, Hansville City Parks and Recreation, Point No Point lighthouse; Rod Tucker, Vashon Island City Park, Point Robinson lighthouse; Chris Quidotti, Lime Kiln State Park, Lime Kiln lighthouse; Karen Martinelli, Friday Harbor, and true Friday Harbor local hero Larry Hartford; Rick and Lauri Bethke; Sedro Wooley; Chris and Ron Wilson, Mukilteo Historical Society; volunteer Ellen Koch, Mukilteo lighthouse; Al Simpkins and Eric Henriksson, New Dungeness Chapter, U.S. Lighthouse Society; keepers Richard and Mona Jenkins and family, and Milton Freewater, New Dungeness lighthouse; Chief Park Ranger Ken Hageman, Admiralty Head lighthouse.

Further thanks go to Professor Matie Roig and Dr. Laura Procedo-Choudhury, Broward Community College, Davie, Florida; Mick Batt, Edmund, Oklahoma; Ned Preston, Federal Aviation Administration, Washington, D.C.; Bernard Ricciardi, Wall, New Jersey; Mike Feher, Howell, New Jersey.

A special thanks goes to Bob Allison, Current Enterprises, Redlands, California, and Sharyl Fortune, Everett, Washington, for their exceptional generosity and help during our week at Cape Flattery.

We are grateful to Eric Frischer, Rand McNally Publishing Group, Skokie, Illinois, for the user-friendly GPS program; David Cramer, Manchester, New Hampshire, for further technical support; Robert Cumming, Garden Grove, California; and to Adel, Barbara, and Dave Welty, Santa Cruz, California.

Finally, our deep personal thanks to Fred Larimer, Garden Grove, California, for his patience, assistance, and support.

Randy Leffingwell, Ojai, California
Latitude/Longitude: 34°25.9'N/119°18.8'W
Pamela Welty, Garden Grove, California
Latitude/Longitude: 33°45.5'N/117°57.1'W

Photographic Notes

Because accurate color rendition, great sharpness, and fine grain were crucial for this book, Randy Leffingwell used Fuji's ASTIA film. Its lower contrast and generous latitude proved essential for holding the ranges of light he encountered. Covering some 11,000 miles over eight months, he shot nearly 600 rolls of ASTIA. A&I Labs in Hollywood, California, did his film processing.

He used Nikon F4 cameras and Nikkor lenses from 15mm through 600mm, shooting most everything using a heavy Gitzo tripod, often sandbagged against the winds. Supplemental lighting, used often, ranged from Nikon's dedicated strobes on reduced-power matrix-fill mode, to four Norman battery-powered strobes and four Lowell quartz lights into or through umbrellas.

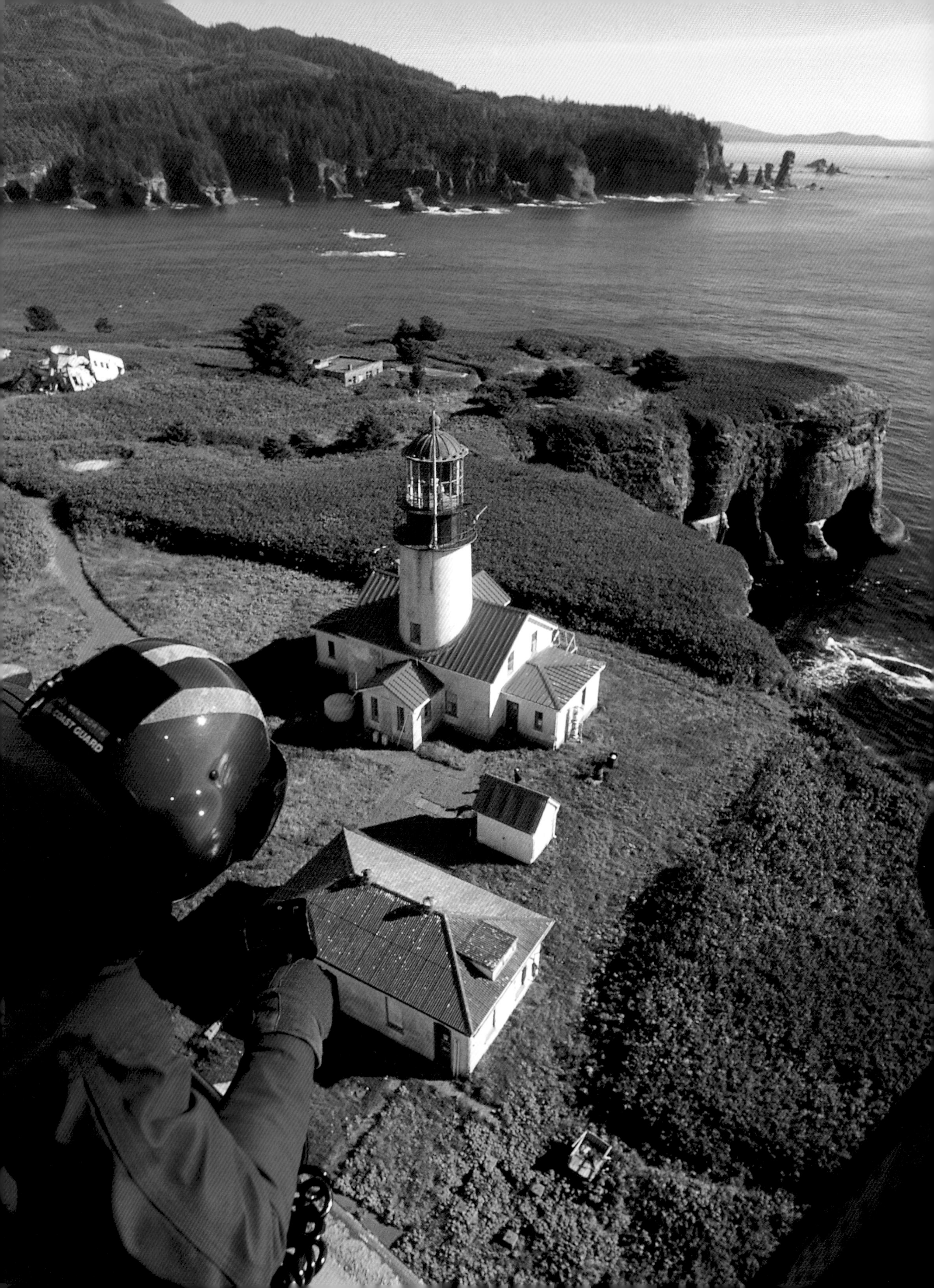
COAST GUARD

Lux Aeterna—Eternal Light

"Easy right. Easy right. Hold."

Chief Flight Mechanic Phil Wentworth was on his stomach, stretched across the floor of U.S. Coast Guard Sikorsky HH-60J Jayhawk helicopter 6003. He peered out the open cargo door, and watched an 1,800-pound load of timber wrapped in a huge cargo net suspended below. Wentworth served as the eyes of pilot Lieutenant Commander Mark Reynolds, who was hovering the Jayhawk sideways, inching toward Cape Flattery Light Station, on Tatoosh Island at the tip of Washington State's Olympic Peninsula.

"Hold position," Wentworth said calmly. "The load is thirty feet above the deck. Down thirty. The load is twenty feet above the deck. Down twenty." The helicopter gently descended. "Down five. Down two. Easy down." Reynolds let the airship sink slowly. The timber settled onto the tall grass.

In all, helicopter 6003 made six ten-minute round trips from the Coast Guard station at Neah Bay, Washington to the 142-year-old lighthouse. It ferried 13,000 pounds of supplies, tools, and food as well as six contracted workers, a cook, and the three-member Coast Guard Aids-to-Navigation Team, or ANT team. The crew's orders were direct and difficult: Renovate portions of the Cape Flattery lighthouse in a quick, five-day time period.

The U.S. Light House Establishment commissioned construction of the Cape Flattery light in 1849. The station was built in 1857 by the Lighthouse Board using a standardized Cape Cod design. The original structure was a duplex, but it had been added onto several times, with additions of kitchens on the east and west ends and a keeper's office behind the tower on the ground floor. The light had been de-staffed about seventeen years ago, and was now fully automatic—but it still got routine servicing, called PMS, or Preventative Maintenance Service, as it bore the brunt of the Pacific Ocean's weather.

The Cape Flattery renovation work was part of the U.S. government's ongoing and increasing commitment to preserve lighthouses. Funding from the Coast Guard's budget and nearly $2 million from the U.S. Interior Department paid for the Cape Flattery work and the repositioning of North Carolina's Cape Hatteras lighthouse. In 1995 and 1996, the Coast Guard also spent $325,000 to repair and renovate California's Anacapa Island light.

The civilian renovation crew had a twenty-eight-point list of essential repairs they needed to perform. These tasks would leave the lighthouse looking little changed from the outside but substantially preserved under its old skin.

The work needed to be done on a tight schedule because the light's automatic fog signal had to be shut off while the crew was on the job, putting ships at risk. Because Cape Flattery is surrounded by fog more often than not, its SA232-02 electronic fog signal operates around the clock every day. It blasts a 124-decibel midrange howl that would cause severe eardrum damage if you were too close when it sounded. The Coast Guard issued a Broadcast Notice to Mariners: The fog signal would not operate until further notice. This allowed the crew to work around the lighthouse—and sleep there at night as well.

For Bob Allison, whose company was contracted for $80,000 of repair work on Cape Flattery over the next few days, the renovation was the largest logistical effort of his four years working with the Coast Guard. He first visited the light in April 1999 with members of the ANT team and staff from the Coast Guard's Facilities Design & Construction Center (FD&CC) in Seattle. Allison needed to see the lighthouse before bidding on the work; he returned in June for another evaluation. Allison then gathered six specialists, including two finish carpenters, from nearly 1,500 miles away. A pair from his crew spent

Cape Flattery light station
Flight Chief Phil Wentworth watches the sling load below his helicopter as it passes Cape Flattery. He directs pilot Mark Reynolds down foot by foot to set the load on the ground.

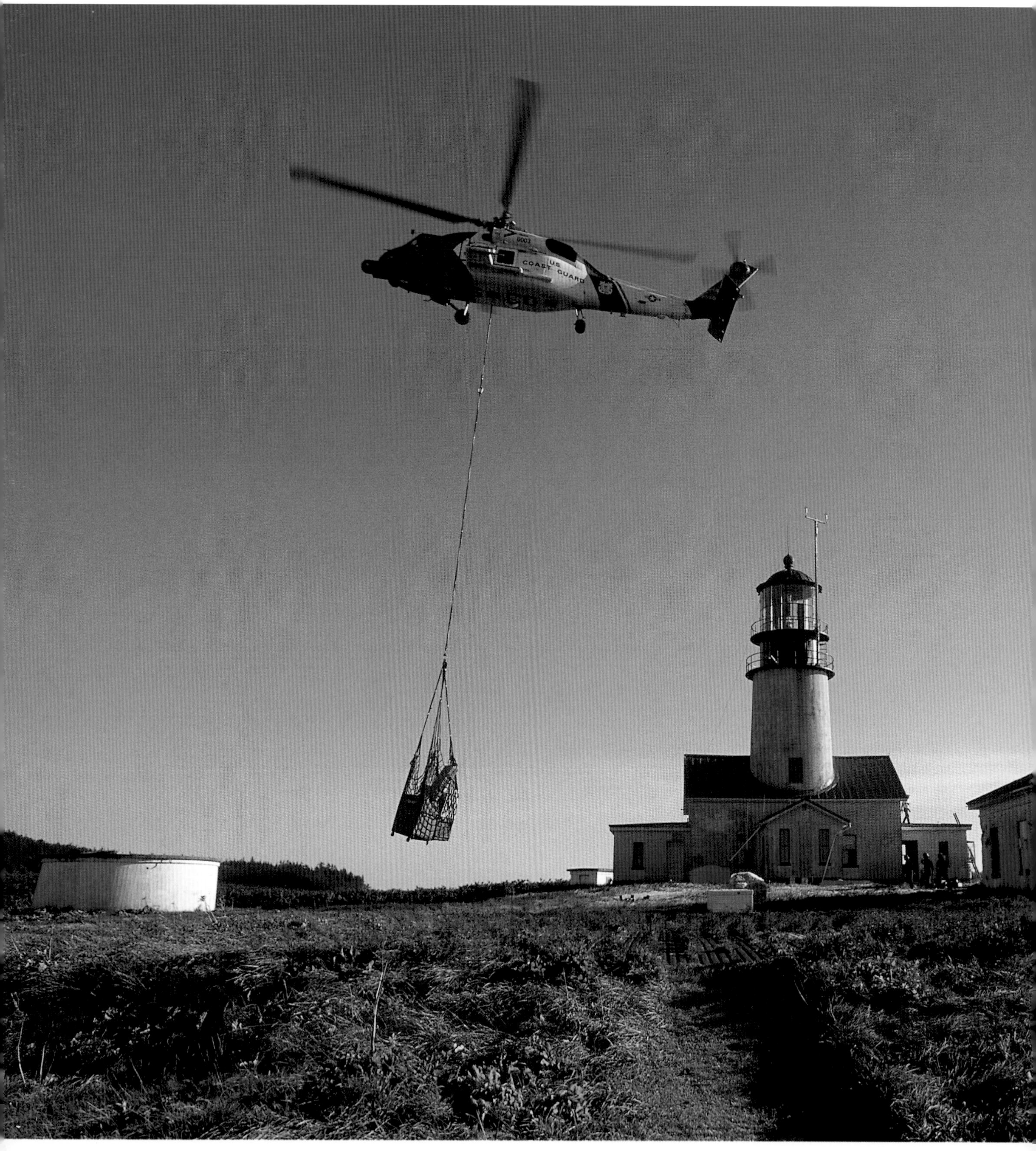
US
COAST GUARD
6003

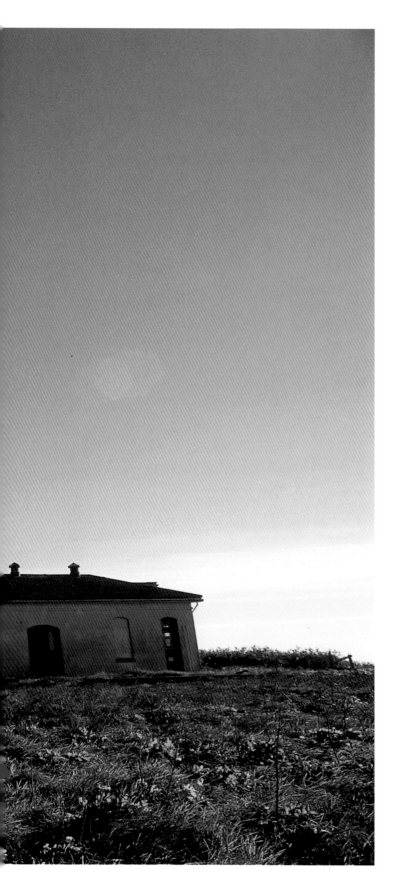

more time at work suspended from bridges than walking on solid land.

The Jayhawk began hauling in the crew and materials on September 13, 1999, despite delays due to fog. The ANT team brought equipment to service the lighthouse lamp and repair the fog signal, two fifty-five-gallon drums of diesel generator fuel, and lumber to build a fence. The "Coasties" also brought thirteen cots and began sorting out sleeping arrangements for all who would share the seven-bedroom keeper's house.

As the final flight with the last two contractors and equipment reached Tatoosh Island in the evening, the other four workers already had begun. No one unpacked clothes; they simply dug their tool belts out and started the job. They took rain gutters and downspouts off the building and lifted ladders to remove the fascia boards.

Allison's finish carpenters, Dan Knobloch and Troy Taylor, attacked the first leaky upstairs bedroom window. All four window frames on the second floor were rotted. To slow the effects of moisture inside the house, Coast Guard Damage Control personnel had installed metal-frame fixed windows as a stopgap solution several years ago. Now Cape Flattery was listed as a National Historic Landmark; repairs and renovations had to recreate the architectural style of the original building.

Resting only long enough to admire the sunset, the contractors set up yellow worklights at dusk and kept going. At 8 P.M., Allison gave the call for dinner. Reasoning that six people preparing food three times a day wasted too many hours, he hired a friend, Sharyl Fortune, to cook for the hungry crew. While his builders ate, Allison introduced the ANT team, which conducted a safety meeting, and set out guidelines for working, eating, sleeping, and bathing on the island.

The lighthouse originally had rainwater catch basins, or cisterns, under and around the house. These were fed by redwood gutters and downspouts that had long since been scrapped. The crew would replace existing gutters with an aluminum version that resembled the redwood style. However, the basement cistern has be-

CAPE FLATTERY LIGHT STATION
Coast Guard helicopter 6003 delivers its fourth sling load out of six, totaling 13,000 pounds of tools, supplies, and equipment for work at the lighthouse. The Sikorsky HH-60J Jayhawk carries about 2,200 pounds of gear at the end of the sixty-foot "pendant."

gun to leak several years earlier, another problem to be repaired. In the meantime, the ANT team set up a 500-gallon catch tank outside the house to hold rain runoff for the water heater for shower, kitchen, and bathroom needs.

The lighthouse light and fog signal got power from solar-panel-recharged storage batteries housed in the duplex. Electricity for the station came from a three-cylinder Lister diesel-powered generator chugging away in the 1872 fog-signal building. With a 10,000-watt output, this diesel would run worklights and power tools. But the house's circuitry could only handle either the hot water heater or the stove, not both at the same time. Some things would have to be done in shifts.

ANT team leader Erik Wiard outlined the Coasties's work for the next few days and told the contractors the Coasties would stay out of their way. Wiard also described features of the island they should try to see. However, since Tatoosh is still Makah Indian land, its north island and a large rock on the west side are hallowed ground, not to be disturbed.

With dinner over and ground rules established, the contractors returned to work. By 3:30 A.M., when the last worklight was turned out, the entire red metal roof had been recaulked, rotted beams in the basement cut out, and ten new three-foot-tall concrete footings were formed and poured. One window was completely out on the second floor and another was ready for removal at first light. Cleaning out rotted wood took the window frame back to the limestone walls. The workplace was covered with a heavy plastic tarp all night and the prevailing northwest wind rattled the plastic like thunder, keeping the exhausted workers awake when they had hoped for sleep.

Day Two

At first light, work began again. The sun was gone, replaced by Cape Flattery's more typical misty gray skies and temperatures in the mid-50s Fahrenheit. Allison set a schedule that provided breakfast at 8 A.M., which gave his crew time to work before they ate, and kept them focused on the job. The ANT team's schedule was similar, but the aroma of hot coffee and fresh-baked blueberry muffins drew everyone into the house.

ANT teams are jacks of all trades. These modern-day lighthouse keepers take two or three days to perform routine servicing that earlier keepers did daily before the Coast Guard started automating stations in the mid-1950s. On each scheduled quarterly visit, ANT teams service fog signals and lighthouse lamps, mow lawns, and do structural repairs, including repairs similar to those that Allison's groups were doing now.

The lineage of lighthouse keepers runs deep, and among its other chores at Cape Flattery, the ANT team planned to rebuild a fence around a keeper cemetery near the light. Located at the island's southeast corner, the small cemetery was the burial site of two children, Mary Margaret Mize, who died in 1908, and Francis Tisdale, who died in 1917. Both succumbed to diseases for which medical treatment was available on the mainland but not on Tatoosh.

The renovation work going on around them placed the ANT team in an awkward position. The Coasties were quite capable of doing the repairs Allison's crew was doing, given sufficient time. But time was a consideration and ANT-team energies were better spent keeping navigation aids functioning. Electrician's Mate Third Class Jeb Wheeler attacked the ailing fog signal that civilian mariners had reported was not working. From inside his waterproof equipment case filled with tools and testing devices, Wheeler pulled out what he needed to get inside the dual speaker tower. When he got inside, he discovered the problem was a cracked resonator tube on the lower horn. A pump inside the signal mechanism forced air against a large diaphragm at the speaker's narrow end. The hairline crack allowed air to leak out the tube rather than vibrate the diaphragm. Fifteen minutes later, his repair was complete, and he screwed the control boxes back in place.

When the lights went out at Cape Flattery at 2:30 A.M. on the second day, the contractors had each worked nearly twenty-nine hours. They had replaced the other westward window, re-plastered some of the house interior, installed smoke detectors, and repaired some

Cape Flattery light station
Work began on the 1857 lighthouse as soon as the crew landed. By sunset, gutters and fascia boards were coming down and one of four windows was already out of the second floor. The cold, moist conditions on the island had taken their toll on the lighthouse, which sees much more fog than sunlight.

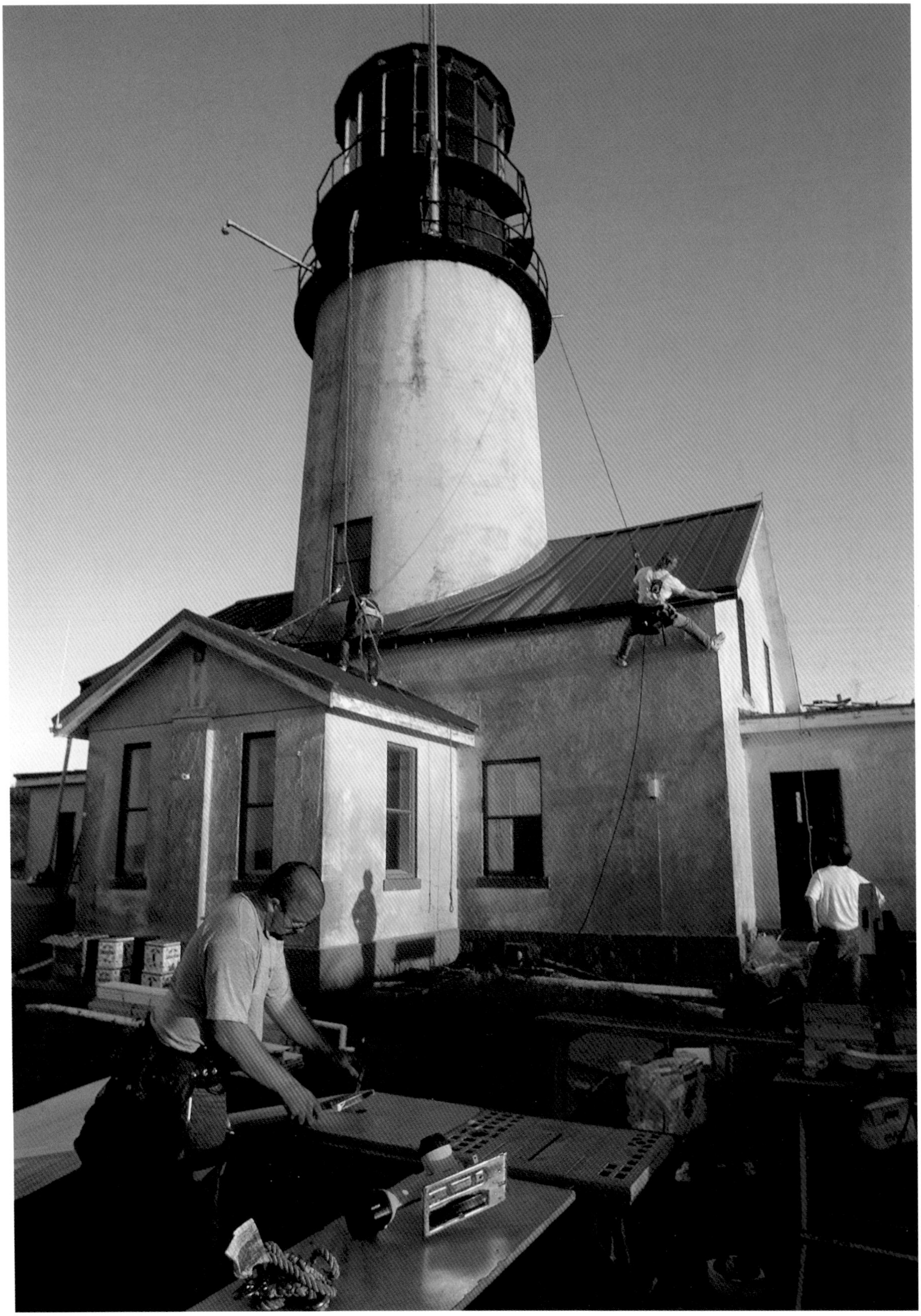

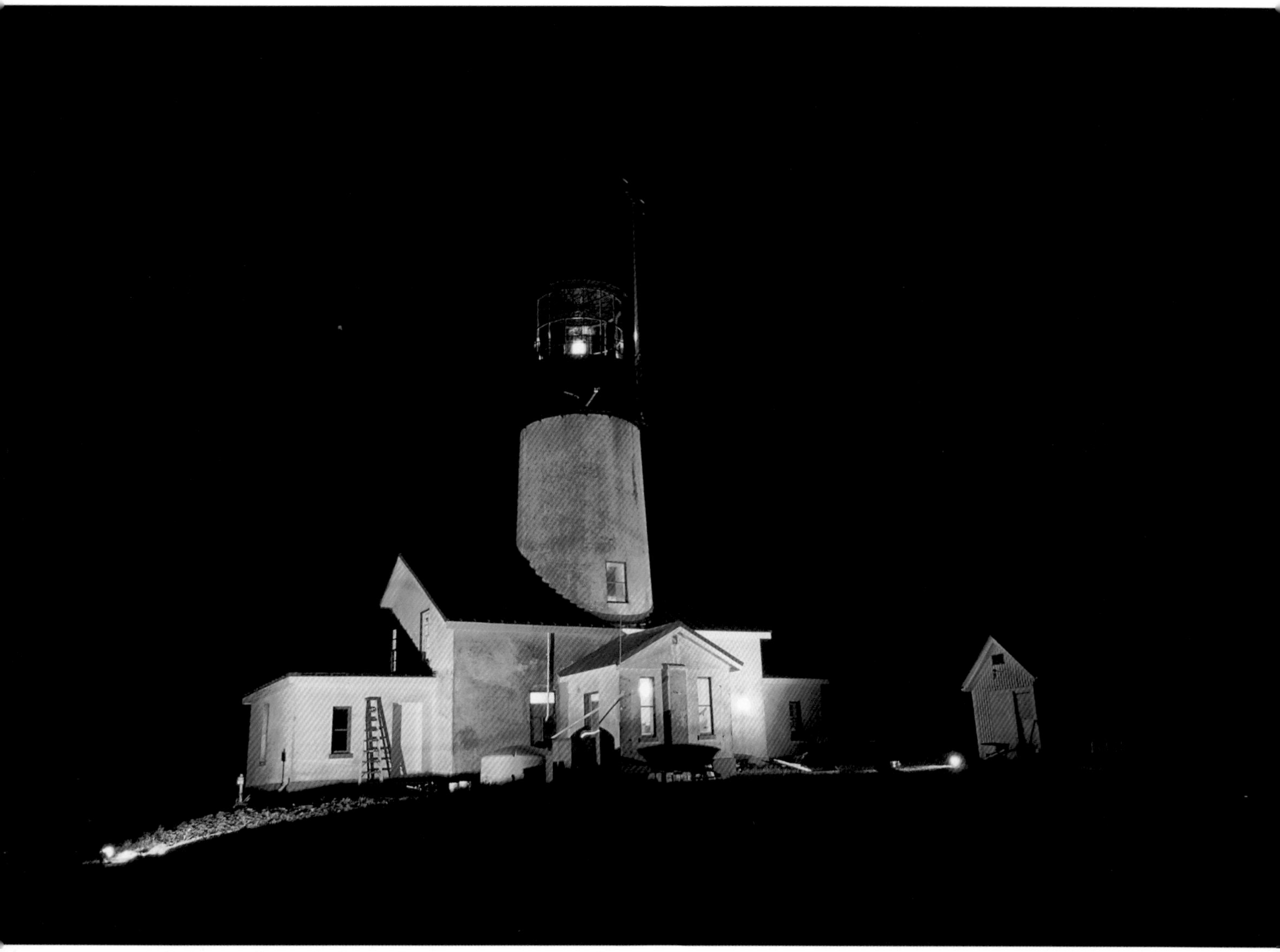

Cape Flattery light station

Cape Flattery followed the architectural plans of the first sixteen West Coast lights, a Cape Cod–style cottage with the light tower rising from the center. This house, like many, was a mirror-image duplex. The low room in back, a keeper's office, and the two kitchen additions on either end, were added in the early 1900s. In the 1880s, Cape Flattery held more than 100 inhabitants. Three lighthouse keepers and their families joined two more assistant keepers who tended the steam (and later diaphone) fog signal. The U.S. Signal Corps set up a weather reporting station there in 1883.

interior light wiring. It is impossible for the Coast Guard—or any budget-strapped government agency—to pull six ANT teams to one site and demand they perform a week-and-a-half's work in four days. Worse, during the time the ANT teams would take to save Cape Flattery, other navigational aid problems would pile up. Yet this kind of commitment is exactly what civilian contractors willingly bring to ambitious projects. Allison put it simply: "There was no problem getting people [to come work at Cape Flattery]. When I told them how much work there was, how little time we had, how much I could pay, how tough the conditions could be, how bad the weather might be, and that they would have to fly in a helicopter to get to the site, and sleep in a lighthouse where they would work, I had no problem at all."

Day Three

As work resumed on the house, the Coasties returned to the cemetery to finish the fence. They set it solidly in concrete and fitted it with diagonal braces to stand against the high winds that hammer the island during winter storms. All three ANT team members are married and have small children. The impact of what they were doing hit them at the same time.

"I wonder if any of the family of Mary Margaret Mize or Francis Tisdale ever come out here," Wheeler said. "This looks pretty good now and it would be really nice for them to see it."

Wiard wondered how they could even reach the island. It is true that private boats have landed on the beach on rare occasions when the sea is calm. But could the workers even find the cemetery if they got here?

"Is there even anyone left that knows about them?" Machinery Technician Second Class Eric Arwood asked.

That question hung in the air. For whom were they doing this? Why had they built this fence so strong? Why, in fact, were Allison's men working so hard to save a building that only ANT teams will see just four times a year. ANT team supervisor, Chief J. Franklin in Astoria, Oregon, had told his group their top priority this trip was to replace the fence. Even after realizing that it was virtually impossible for any Mize or Tisdale to come back to see where grandparents had worked and lived and lost a child, the Coasties continued the job, carefully sweeping the grave sites in the tiny yard on a distant corner of the island.

Later, Wheeler and Arwood began the PMS lighthouse service. When the Coast Guard automated Cape Flattery in 1977, it made the station self-powered and self-contained. This was critical here, as well as at Washington's Destruction Island lighthouse and other stations where maintaining a shore-power electric connection was impossible due to tides, storms, and marine life attracted to the flavor of insulation coatings. The Coast Guard fitted high-efficiency solar panels across the lighthouse's south face that would deliver a modest charge even on the darkest day.

What had originally been a duplex's parlor was now the battery room, and the ANT teams replaced the windows with vented metal panels to allow battery vapor to escape. While Wheeler recorded data, Arwood measured voltage and tested specific gravity of the six Exide E lead-acid batteries that are the light and fog signal's primary power.

Automated lights have full backup systems. At Cape Flattery, the primary system is supported by a ten-cell NiCad rechargeable system. A control box manages distribution of electricity and also notifies the ANT team if any systems malfunction, lantern bulbs fail, or batteries switch over from the primaries.

Meanwhile, Allison's crew was also at work. Carpenter Knobloch put a third coat of paint on the four new windows while Taylor, Garth Kuykendall, Jon Vevik, Shannon King, and Carl Carlson climbed up to the lantern room and began stripping window seals and recaulking the glass. Wearing mountaineering and bridge-building safety harnesses, Kuykendall and Vevik hung off the hand-holds originally placed there by the lighthouse architects for just that reason. After they caulked the windows, the crew cleaned each pane of glass inside and out, which relieved the ANT team of another routine chore.

Then Kuykendall and Vevik roped up and dropped off the gallery railing to repair the seal around the tower's base. After dinner, all six began to replace false ceilings and started to hang the t-bars and tiles. Three hours later, they finished in the kitchen. To silence their grumbling stomachs, the cook made microwave popcorn and fired up two more pots of coffee. The six contractors and three Coasties sat for a moment.

It was clear that they could go home on Friday: All their work would be completed. Everyone agreed that Tatoosh Island was beautiful, but it was not somewhere they wanted to spend their weekend. At midnight, energized with popcorn and sweet coffee, Kuykendall and King headed out to hang gutters.

Day Four

Wheeler resumed the PMS while Wiard and Eric Arwood serviced the diesel generator. Wheeler inspected the New Zealand–built Vega Rotating Beacon VRB-25 to be sure it was level. Each lighthouse has two "certified-to-be-true" levels, and one is mounted on the rotating light's base. If an earthquake shakes the tower, the light's focus and range may be affected if the lens is knocked off level.

Wheeler checked the focus next, using a target placed in the bulb holder at the beacon's center. At battery-powered stations, the beacons rotate twenty-four hours a day even though the bulb lights only when it becomes dark. This keeps motor bearings from seizing and prevents sunlight from melting the optical-grade plastic Fresnel lenses. Vega beacons cost $6,000 each, whereas Fresnels cost $3,500 to $7,000 in the 1850s, about $70,000 to $140,000 at today's inflation rate.

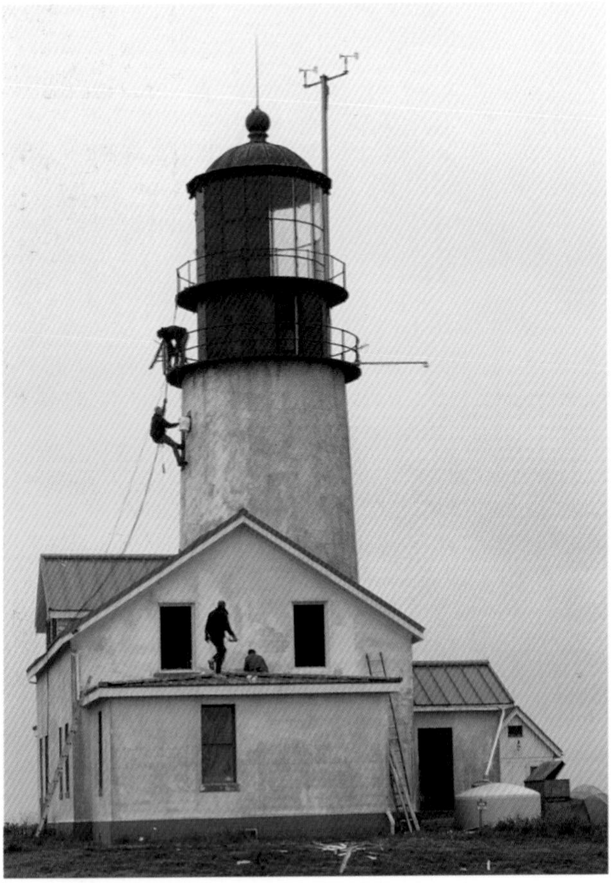

Finally, Wheeler cleaned and refitted all six bulbs in the automatic changer. The light at Cape Flattery uses fifty-watt quartz-iodine bulbs, similar to those in automobile accessory driving lights. The lenses of the Vega beacons are of such high quality that the Coast Guard reports a range of seventeen to nineteen nautical miles from these small bulbs. ANT team procedure is to replace the bulb currently in use. Wheeler found the changer in the second bulb spot, meaning the first bulb had burnt out and the first spare had been rotated into position. He pulled the bulb from third spot into first, from fourth into second and so on, fitting new bulbs into the fifth and sixth positions.

His final test checked the secondary beacon, an older-style Tideland 250-mm lantern. This lantern does not rotate but duplicates the effects of spinning Fresnels by flashing on and off. Electronic circuitry will light the lantern within ninety seconds of the Vega's failure. He shut it off. Its six-bulb changer cycled through the five spares, waiting five seconds between each, the solenoid-activated changer making a loud metallic sound. At eighty-seven seconds, the light came on. A minute later, Wheeler switched it off, the Vega beacon recycled noisily into first position, and he set everything back to standby. The ANT team's work on Cape Flattery was complete.

Outside, things were eerily quiet. The contractors were also finished; they knew if they got their tools packed, they had time to explore the island. Each had done almost fifty-six hours of work in three-and-a-half days. Now they wanted to see the cemetery and explore the island.

Throughout the week, they had heard about the history of Cape Flattery, stories of the hundred or more people who lived here in the early 1920s when it was not only a lighthouse but also a U.S. Weather Service reporting station. There had been a school, post office, and general store on Tatoosh Island. They'd heard how hellish the storms were and how tough life was.

The crew had done fine work. Never once did they

Cape Flattery light station
Jon Vevik hangs off the watch room gallery to repair a hole in the lighthouse wall's south face. The lantern room above him is blacked out on the shore side to eliminate reflections from the rotating beacon inside. Below the tower, the two east bedrooms get new windows.

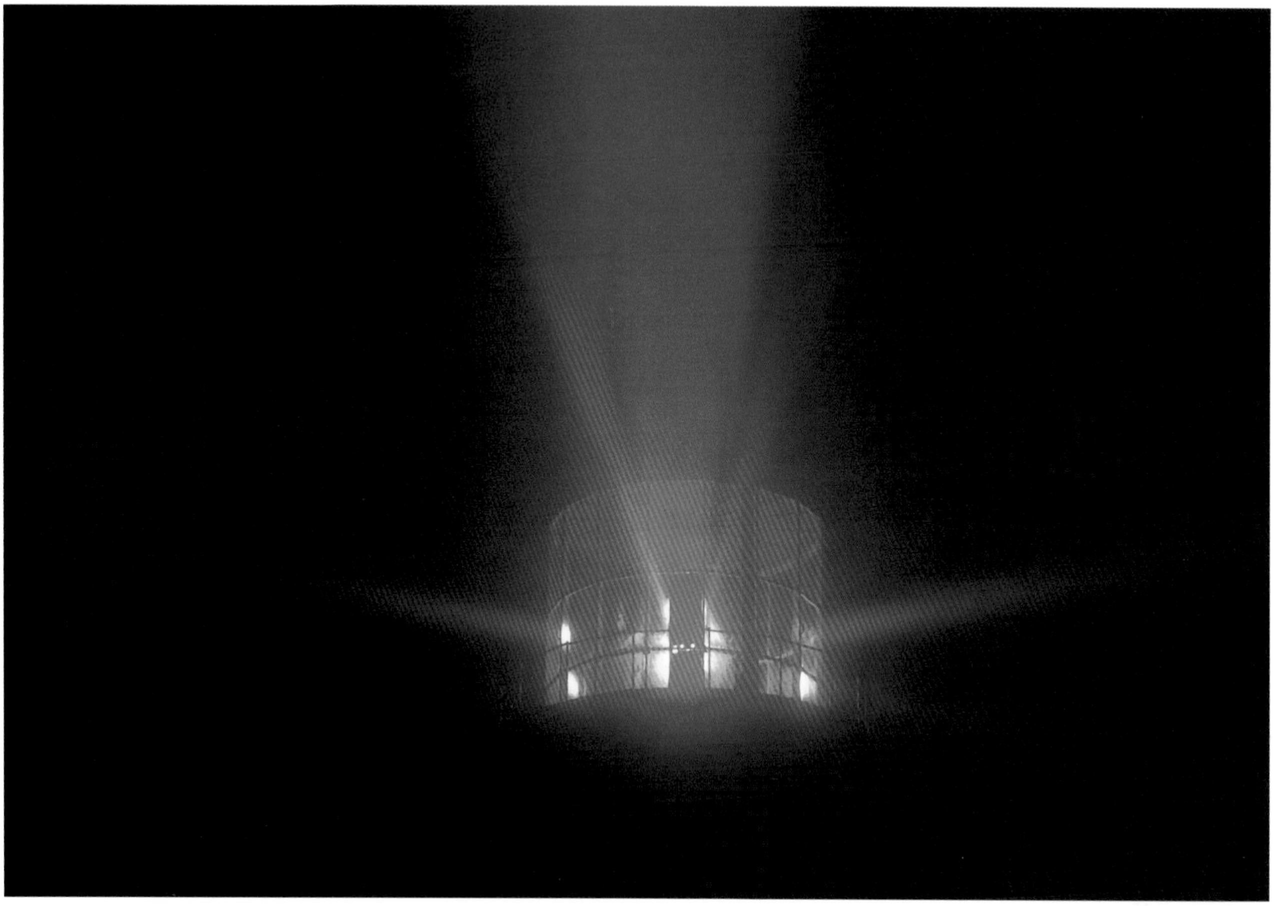

Above: CAPE FLATTERY LIGHT STATION
The red panel warns mariners to steer left or right immediately or risk running aground on Duncan Rock, just north of Cape Flattery. In thick fog, the six beams of the Vega Rotating Beacon appear like spokes of a wheel arcing across the sky. The beacon is 165 feet above sea level, and to mariners at sea, it appears to flash every twenty seconds.

Right: CAPE FLATTERY LIGHT STATION
Cape Flattery sits on Tatoosh Island, a 16-acre, 100-foot high landmass off the far northwest corner of Washington. The lighthouse was one of the first planned for the West Coast, initially proposed in 1848. The tower stands 65 feet tall.

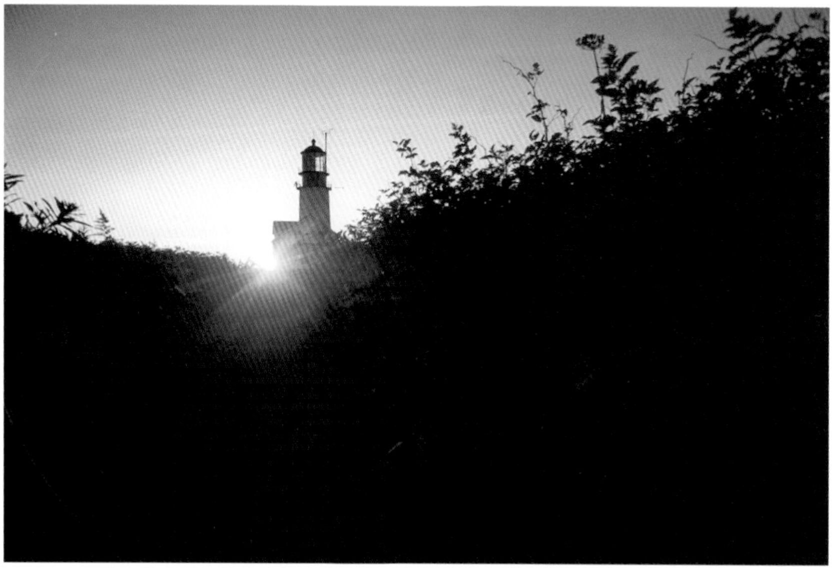

say, "It's good enough." The quality of their work was homage to the lighthouse builders and keepers who came before them.

Kuykendall, a rock climber, ventured onto the top of the lighthouse dome. He clambered back down, amazed by gargoyles cast into the roof as rain spouts and the elegance he saw in a place no one else could see.

"That's all brass," he pronounced. "It's beautiful workmanship. The guys that did this were real artists."

Day Five

The view outside the window was pure white. There should have been a red roof, a green hedgerow, an ocean, a horizon. Instead, thick fog enshrouded Tatoosh. Even the seagulls screamed in frustration.

Everyone crammed into the warm kitchen, sipping coffee, complaining. The smell of fresh-baked cranberry muffins failed to brighten anyone's outlook. Arwood held the Coast Guard cellular phone. "Their plan," he said, "is to be here at eleven to begin sling loads off the island. The wind is supposed to shift and this will break up by noon." This raised spirits in the room even though it failed to budge the fog outside.

Unexpectedly, just before 9 A.M., helicopter 6003 arrived. No one could see it; they could only hear its rotor chop. It sounded too near the 100-foot-high bluffs at the south face of the island. Then it rose up, swung around to the west, moved in slowly over the helo pad and set down, kicking up the wet grass in its rotor wash.

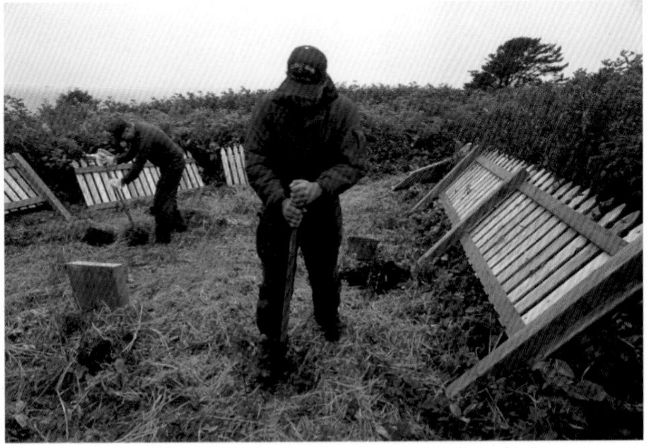

Cape Flattery light station
Coasties Erik Wiard, left, and Eric Arwood finish up new postholes for a cedar fence. Wiard constructed the fence to surround the graves of Mary Margaret Mize, age five, and Francis Tisdale, age seven, children of two former keepers on the island.

Pilot Reynolds and co-pilot Ensign Michael Rasch walked to the lighthouse and told everyone this fog began only a mile south of the island and stopped 300 feet above it. But everywhere north and east, along the Strait of Juan de Fuca, was socked in. This was, Rasch said, a cloud on the ground. It was supposed to lift, and they would fly.

Through lunch and the early afternoon, visibility remained less than the length of the island. Tensions—evident a day before—reappeared. Personalities that survived due to huge workloads, closed in like fog. Personal stories everyone heard the first day grew old when repeated on the fifth. This was the modern-day equivalent of what happened for years at remote, isolated lighthouses.

Everyone here heard about winter storms at Oregon's Tillamook Rock lighthouse that forced enraged silence on all four keepers; they resorted to notes at the dinner table rather than speak to one another. Many times, lighthouse keepers watched supply or relief ships arrive and lay off shore, unable to reach them because of high seas, severe storms, or thick fog. Sometimes, after trying for days to get supplies and relief keepers to the station, the tenders gave up and sailed off. This was why many stations worked three-weeks-on, one-week-off schedules. At distant stations in Alaska, the practice was an incredible two-years-on, one-year-off—with full pay.

At 3 P.M., a decision had to be made: 6003 would take one load of civilians with personal gear only, no sling loads. It would return for the loads and the other people when the weather cleared—Saturday, possibly Sunday; there was no telling exactly when.

Predictably, an hour after the helicopter lifted off with its single load for the day, the wind shifted and fog lifted in huge scoops. Still, there was not time for another flight.

Later, long after dinner, the Coasties went out to check on the generator and sling loads. Thick fog had returned, dense enough to focus the Vega beacon's beams into six shafts. On the lantern room's northwest face, ANT teams had long ago fitted a red panel to alert mariners to Duncan Rock, a mostly submerged hull-ripper about a mile beyond Tatoosh. As a sailor, if all you saw of Cape Flattery was that red flash, you steered left or right immediately or risked shipwreck. In the fog, the red panel shone brilliantly.

Standing in the fog, Wheeler gave Knobloch a riddle

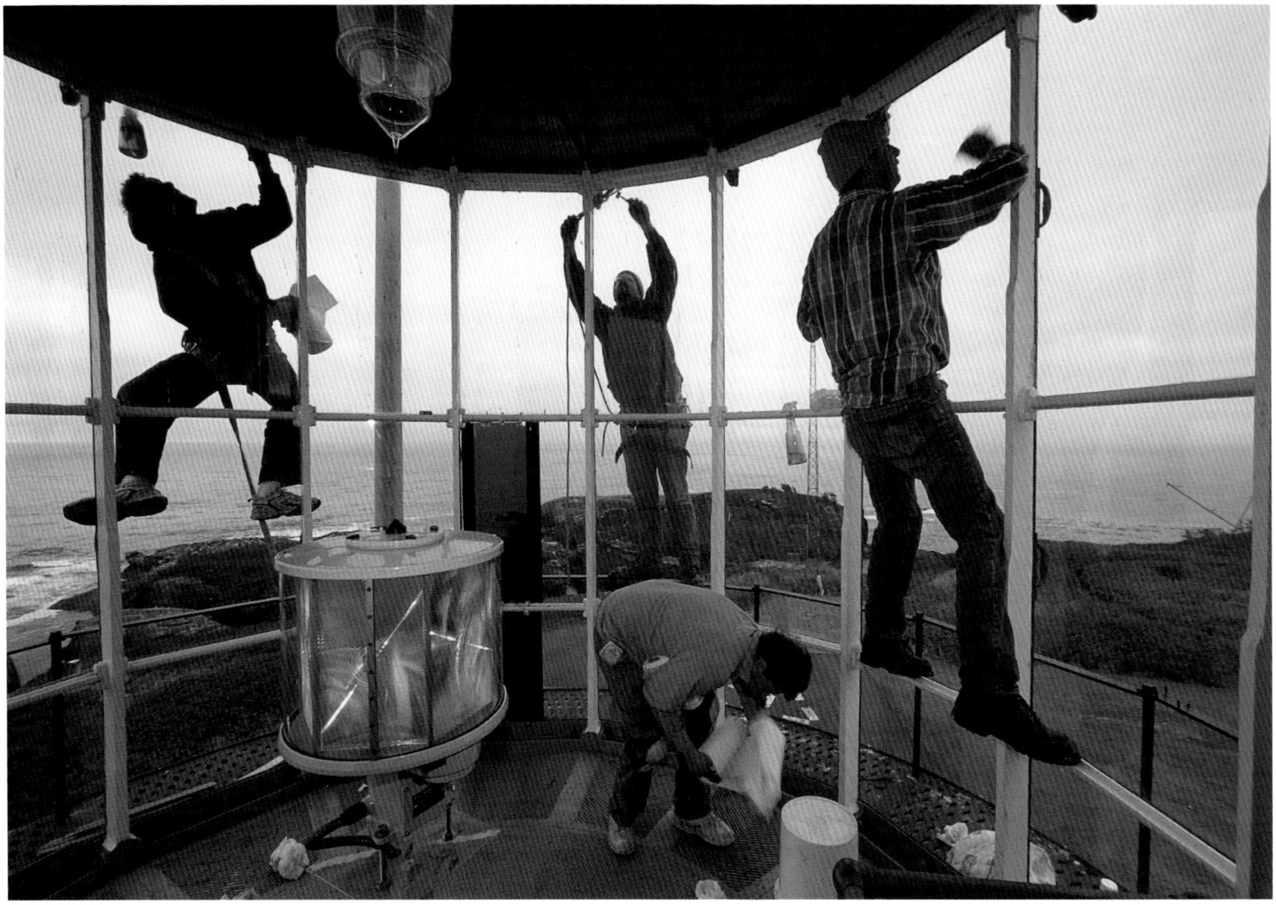

CAPE FLATTERY LIGHT STATION
One task for the contractors was to reseal all the lantern-room windows. Garth Kuykendall, far left, and Troy Taylor, far right, adopt "Wickie" techniques: standing on the slender outside handholds and interior sills around the gallery to gain height. "Wickie" is the nickname given to experienced assistant keepers who trimmed lantern wicks. Jon Vevik, outside, balances on the railing while Shannon King gets ready to clean all the glass.

to think about: "An old man, sitting in his recliner in the dark, is watching television. Outside he hears a crash. He runs up the stairs, looks out, and says, 'Oh my God! I've killed them all.' What happened?"

"The lighthouse keeper let the lamp go out," Wheeler explained. "A ship crashed on the rocks, killing everyone on board."

The Coast Guard had taught him that riddle in Lighthouse Technician School as a lesson in deductive reasoning to solve technical problems—and to reinforce the importance of his job.

Day Six

The sun rose and golden light streamed through the bedroom windows. At 8 A.M., Arwood reported that a Coast Guard Dolphin was on the way to shuttle the last civilians to Neah Bay. The ANT team would fly to Port Angeles, Washington, where a van was waiting to take them home. The sling loads would go "as weather permitted" during the next week.

Just before the helicopter lifted them off, Wheeler was on the phone to ANT headquarters, telling them to issue a new Broadcast Notice to Mariners: The fog signal had resumed. In the brilliant sunlight, it sounded stunningly loud for two seconds, then off for five, on for two, off for fifty-one.

Cape Flattery lighthouse was back in service.

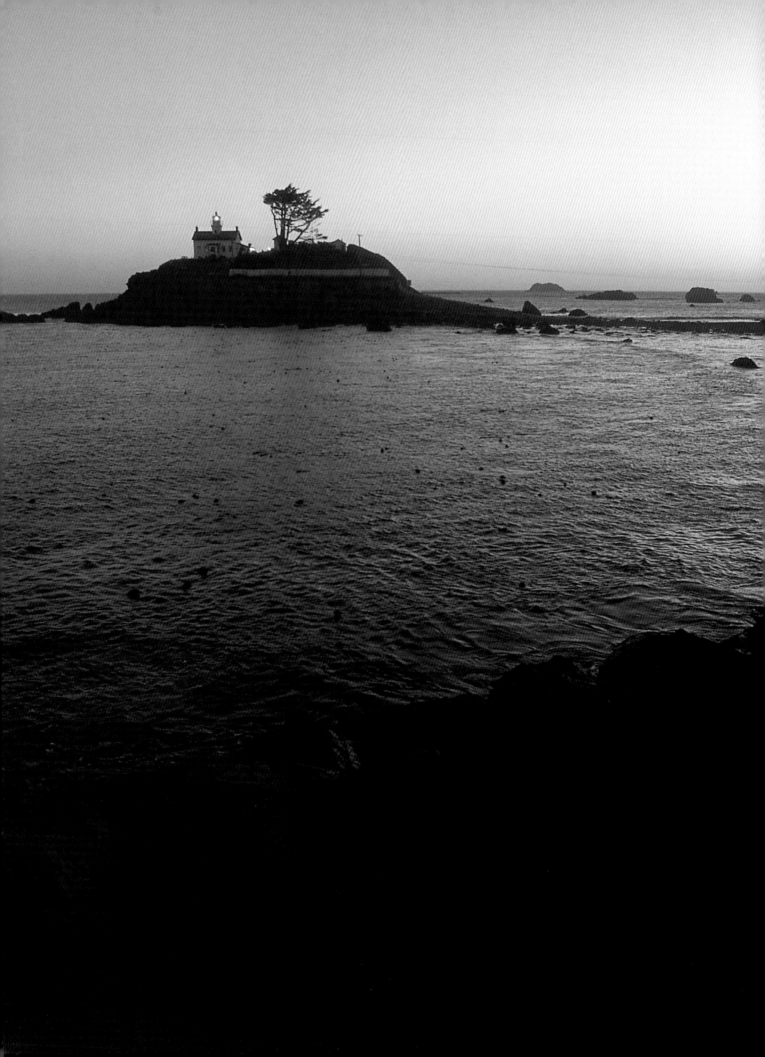

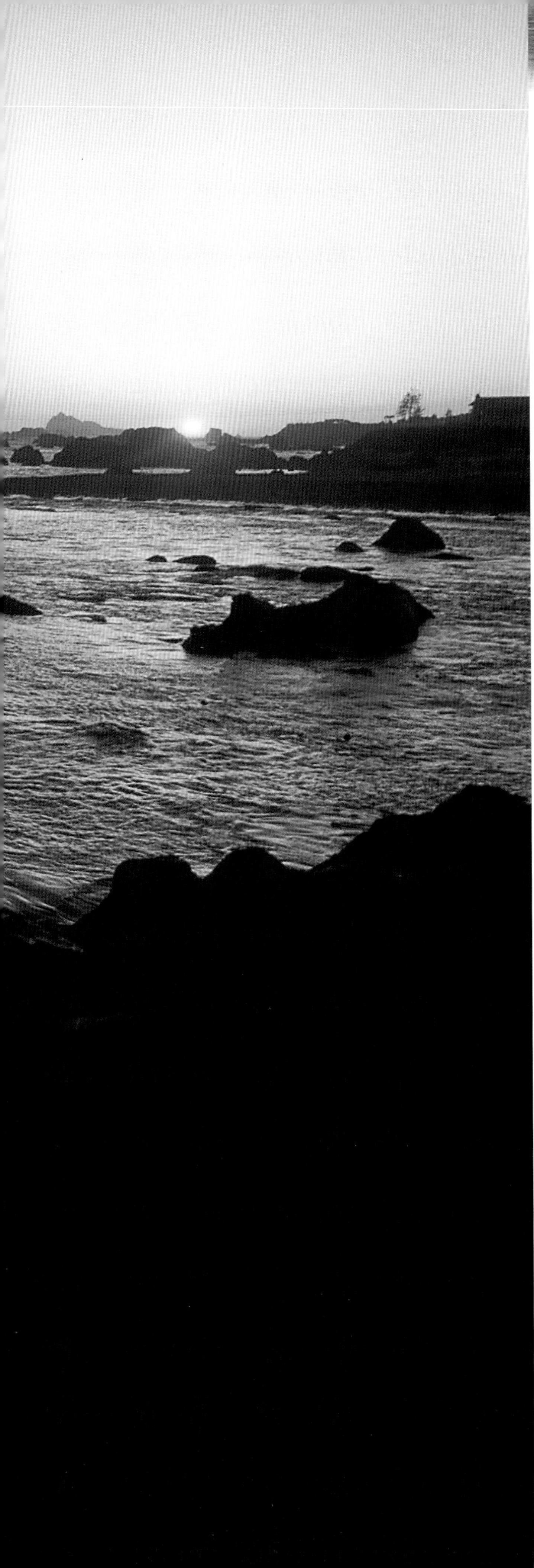

CHAPTER 1

The Lighting of the West

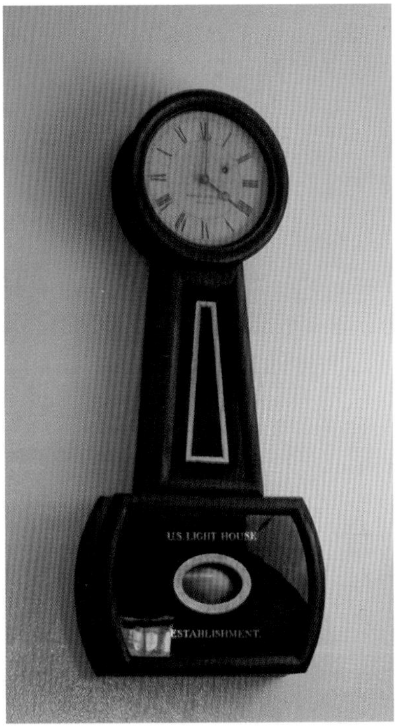

Left: Battery Point lighthouse
"Crescent City [later known as Battery Point] Light Station," the District Inspector wrote in 1914, "is situated on an island which is accessible from the mainland only at times of low tide and during good weather. In stormy weather the station is isolated for days at a time, it being then inaccessible even at times of low water. And at all times during stormy weather it is inaccessible by boat."

Above: Battery Point lighthouse
This Howard & Davis pendulum clock, made in Boston for the Light House Establishment, dates from around 1856.

The long Pacific Coast, stretching some 1,300 miles from Mexico's border with California up to the Canadian border, was a dark and daunting line to mariners in the 1800s. The earth's geology had given the West Coast a dramatically different contour from the Atlantic Coast: Jagged, irregular, high cliffs, and, worse, a sudden, steep drop off the continental shelf that allowed prevailing winds from the west to drive waves onto the shore with incredible speed and power.

In 1848, the United States Congress created the Oregon Territory, and with the same act, appropriated funds for the U.S. Light House Establishment (USLHE) to construct the first two lights on the far northwest coast. The first lighthouse was to be built at Cape Disappointment, near the Columbia River mouth in what would become Washington State; the second on New Dungeness spit, south of the busy port of Nootka on Vancouver Island, which was the Pacific's most active harbor at that time.

Yet, as news spread of the discovery of gold near Sacramento, California, the discovery's consequences became clear to the federal government. The city, bay, and port of San Francisco needed protection. The Army and Navy would fortify the area to ward off invasion; the Treasury Department would build lighthouses to protect the entire West Coast for friendly shipping.

But where on this little-known shore so far from Washington, D.C., should the Light House Establishment put its towers?

Surveying the Pacific Coast

Congress ordered the U.S. Coast Survey to California; these surveyors had earlier sited lights on the Atlantic Coast. The leader was Professor Alexander D. Bache, a physicist from Girard College in Philadelphia, Pennsylvania, who was an expert in magnetism and its effects on navigation. The survey team was to confirm the wisdom of the New Dungeness and Cape Disappointment sites, then to locate as many other sites as they saw fit.

Bache and his team reached San Francisco early in 1849. In the East, the Survey had its own ships commanded by naval officers. However, Bache couldn't find ships in the West available until late that summer, so he had to delay plans. Bache, chief topographer A. M. Harrison, and the surveyors began to map and designate sites to recommend to Treasury Department Auditor Stephen Pleasonton, who oversaw the USLHE. The Coast Survey, meanwhile, dispatched a brand-new brigantine-rigged cutter, the C.W. *Lawrence*, to San Francisco from Washington, D.C., in October 1848.

The task facing Bache and Harrison was enormous. On the Atlantic Coast by this time, the Lighthouse Board was adding bells, buoys, or Fresnel-lens-equipped lighthouses wherever mariners worked new inlets, harbors, or ports that needed illumination. On the virgin Pacific shores, the Coast Survey had a clean slate.

The California, Oregon, and Washington coastlines measured 1,300 sea miles plus another 500 or so miles up into Alaska. Yet there were fewer rivers and inlets than on the East Coast. While the entire Pacific shore was treacherous, there were fewer particularly lethal spots than on the Atlantic. Harrison reported this observation to Pleasonton who promptly reduced his appropriations request.

Following their survey, Harrison told Pleasonton there was need for sixteen lighthouses on the West Coast. In California, the Coast Survey wanted to light Alcatraz Island in San Francisco Bay; Battery Point (later called Fort Point) on the south side of the Golden Gate to San Francisco Bay; Fort Bonita along the bay's north shore; and another on the Farallon Islands that rose unexpectedly out of the Pacific twenty-five miles west of the bay. They wanted a fifth lighthouse at Point Loma to mark San Diego harbor; others at Santa Barbara and Point Conception; and Point Pinos to protect the increasingly busy harbor at Monterey. They recommended two more lighthouses further north, at Humboldt Bay and at Crescent City near the Oregon Territory border.

The long Oregon Territory coastline needed four lights. Harrison recommended one to mark the Umpqua River mouth; lights on Smith Island and at Willapa Bay; and the last at Cape Flattery to mark the entrance to the Strait of Juan de Fuca. Bache reiterated the previous requests for Cape Disappointment and New Dungeness.

The Coast Survey cutter *Lawrence* arrived in San Francisco on November 1, 1849. Throughout 1850, it explored San Diego Harbor, San Pedro Bay south of Los Angeles, Monterey Bay, and San Francisco Bay. The surveyors continued along Oregon's coast and into the Columbia River. Then they traced the Strait of Juan de Fuca and all of Puget Sound. When they were done, they concluded that the convoluted Pacific shoreline with its many large bays measured 8,900 miles, not just 1,300.

Opening the West

The entire Pacific coastline, from Oregon up to Sitka Bay and down the length of Spanish California, was known as the "Maritime West." In the early days of the American union, politicians, merchants, and even sailors held a provincial attitude about the Pacific, looking on it as just the western shore of New England. By 1812, the Russians established a trading center and agricultural community at Fort Ross in California. Russian America continually suffered from severe food shortages, so Russian traders moved down into the Spanish territory beyond the northernmost presidio at San Francisco to find tillable soil and edible game.

Bostonian, English, and Russian trading companies made commercial inroads in California. Atlantic whalers discovered a rich harvest along the Pacific shore in the late 1830s and 1840s, and Honolulu and Maui emerged as the harbors of choice. Some of the largest companies established whaling facilities there, where as many as a ship a day called to process the valuable oil, some of it destined to fuel East Coast lighthouses.

In 1838, the Russian American Company's agricultural and commercial settlement at Fort Ross found itself in competition with a German-Swiss immigrant, Johan Augustus Sutter. Sutter had already visited Sitka and Honolulu, establishing supply and credit lines with every company there. He reached California and eventually convinced Spanish Governor Pio Pico to transfer to him 50,000 acres of fertile land that lay about 100 miles east of the small community of Yerba Buena. He established a community he called New Helvetia, or New Switzerland, at the junction of the Sacramento and American Rivers. (In 1847, Yerba Buena became San Francisco, but from the start everyone called New Helvetia "Sutter's Fort.")

President James K. Polk's policy of Manifest Destiny dictated that all contiguous lands must belong to the United States. In 1846, the British decided not to fight over the wilderness known as the Oregon Territory, which they saw as just trees, mountains, and deserts. The British signed a treaty leaving what would become Washington and Oregon under the United States's control. The British drew their boundary along the forty-ninth parallel, the present-day Canadian border.

Then Polk declared war on Mexico. Following eighteen months of battles, Mexico surrendered. On February 2, 1848, Mexico agreed to set its border at Texas's Rio Grande River and to sell to the United States an additional 1.2 million square miles of land, including Arizona, New Mexico, and upper California territories. Congress paid $15 million for the land and assumed $3.25 million in Mexican debt to U.S. citizens. Polk called the United States "a model and example of free government to all the world." He anticipated that the Maritime West would likely remain a vast unpopulated area. "Who," he asked, "can calculate the value of our glorious Union?"

Polk would have been surprised at the answer if news had traveled faster. Nine days before the U.S./Mexico agreement, at dawn on January 28, James Wilson Marshall, a carpenter from New Jersey, cleaned out the artificial channel that turned his waterwheel. Marshall worked for Johan Sutter, building a sawmill near Sutter's Fort. At the bottom of the ditch, Marshall found gold, a discovery that launched one of history's greatest population shifts—and reevaluations of national worth. By June 1, 2,000 men were digging in the river; that number doubled inside thirty days as local workers and merchants left jobs, shops, and families to head to the American River.

"By early spring of 1848, while mile-long strings of wagons were snaking westward over the trans-Mississippi prairie," one historian recalled, "the shortage of ships in Atlantic and Gulf ports was already acute. Dozens of long-abandoned craft were pulled off the mud, given superficial repairs, sent half[way] around the world, and again shoved up on a mud bank, this time in San Francisco." One report counted 500 ships at anchor and abandoned, some still carrying the cargo that brought them to the port.

That, of course, was contingent upon the ships navigating past rocky shores, treacherous reefs, unexpected islands, and finally the San Francisco bar, a bay mouth plagued with frequent fog, nasty tides, and heavy surf. While Congress increased the Light House Establishment budget to $652,000 for 1848, Polk's Manifest Destiny gave little thought to navigation aids in the distant Maritime West.

Unaware of the riptides surrounding USLHE management, Bache sent regular reports to Pleasonton by mail boat, leaving a month-long lapse from dispatch to delivery, so through 1849 and 1850, the Coast Survey got feedback months late. Mariners and merchants on the West Coast appealed to Bache to do his job quickly as more than a ship a day was sailing into San Francisco Bay—and there were wrecks with alarming regularity. Between 1500 and 1849, just 44 ships sank along the West Coast. In the next ten years, 31 went down within twenty-five miles of Alcatraz Island, and 133 sank between San Diego and Cape Flattery. Passengers perished by the dozens and cargoes sunk—sometimes a hundred tons of food and supplies inbound and a million dollars in gold outbound.

In September 1850, Pleasonton asked for a $53,000 increase in the Oregon Territory lighthouse appropriation to cover Bache's request for a light at Cape Flattery as well as twelve buoys in the Columbia River. Congress gave the USLHE more than $909,000. Pleasonton followed Harrison's recommendations and designated $90,000 for California lights. He also approved $150,000 so the Coast Survey could purchase its first steamer for the West Coast.

In 1851, Congress voted $750,464 for the Light House Establishment, which included $15,000 each for the Humboldt Bay and Umpqua River lighthouses, as well as $5,000 for fog signals at Cape Disappointment, Cape Flattery, and New Dungeness. The U.S. Army Corps of Engineers would supervise construction. Congress approved money for West Coast lighthouses, but work did not start.

California Senator William Gwin demanded to know why. The explanation lay in the busy bureaucracy of the young federal government. The Coast Survey, influential merchants and mariners, mayors and governors, and even insurance adjusters or chambers of commerce could ask senators or representatives for a lighthouse. Once the bill authorizing construction passed, a second proposal requested money to build it. When that was available, Congress transferred the project to the Corps

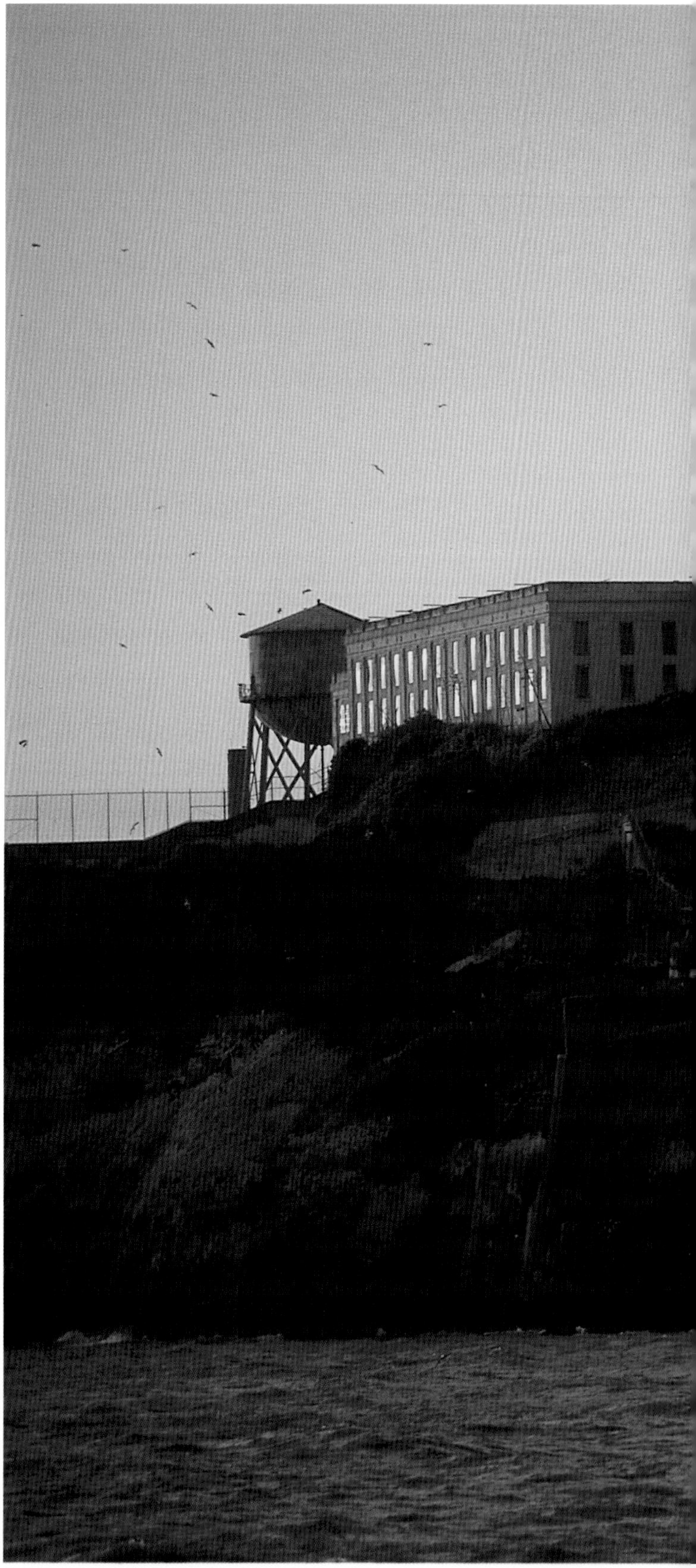

Alcatraz Island lighthouse
Alcatraz Island these days seems peaceful and beautiful following its legendary career as a federal maximum security prison. Alcatraz is now one of America's most popular tourist attractions.

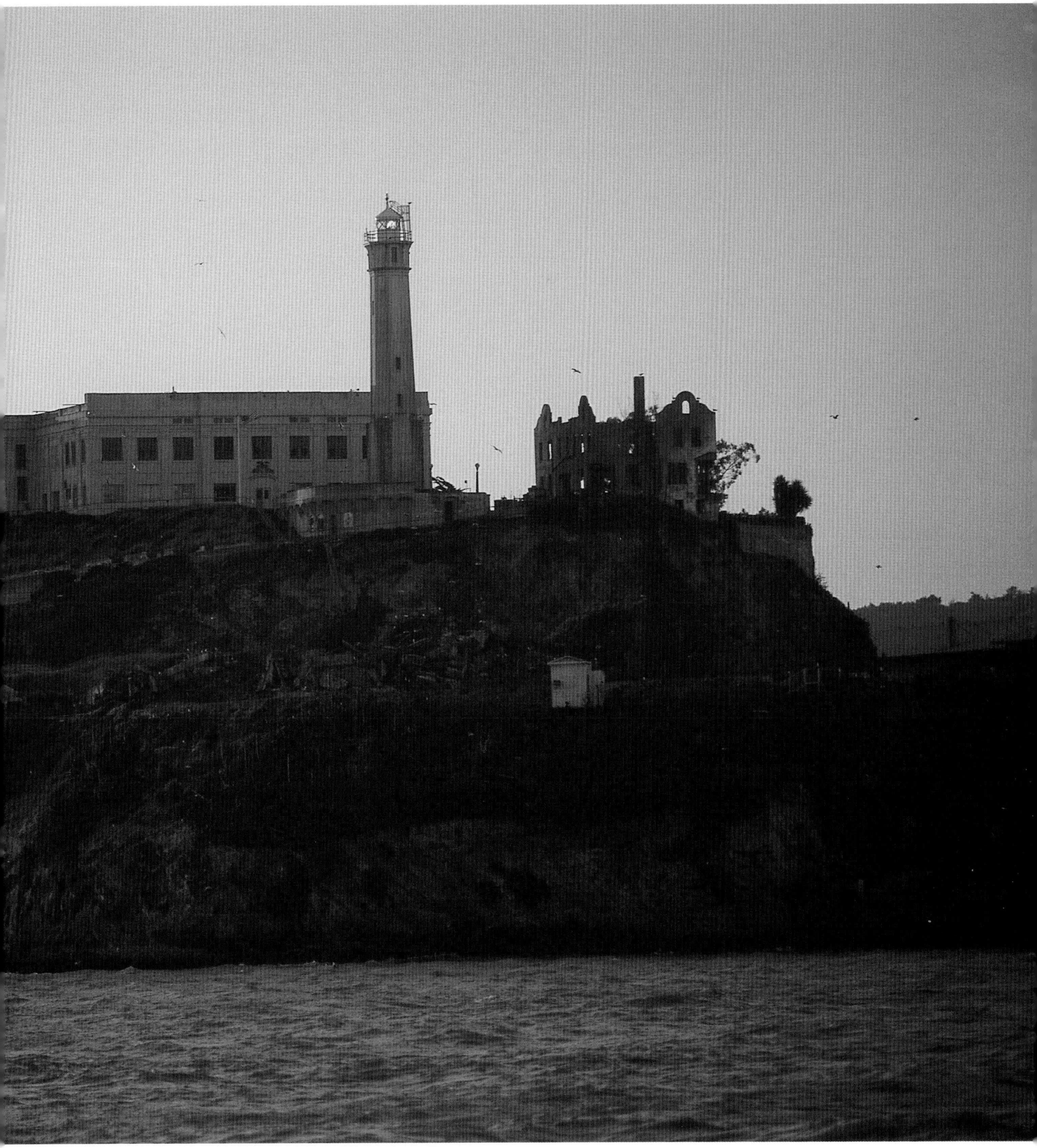

THE U.S. LIGHT HOUSE ESTABLISHMENT

Elbridge Gerry brought up lighthouses first. As a Massachusetts representative, he introduced a "Lighthouse Bill" in the U.S. House on July 8, 1789, to establish and provide for lighthouses in the newly formed United States. President George Washington signed this act in the nation's capital, New York City. It was the country's first public works act and its ninth law of any kind. The law created the U.S. Light House Establishment (USLHE).

In 1820, lighthouse management moved to the Treasury Department where Secretary William Crawford assigned "care and superintendence" of the USLHE to the Fifth Auditor, Stephen Pleasonton. Overnight, the Delaware native found himself in charge of the nation's fifty-five lighthouses.

Pleasonton was diligent but overwhelmed by his new task. He enlisted local customs collectors to supervise lighthouses. They paid keepers, selected sites for future lights, managed construction, and inspected lights annually. Still, Pleasonton controlled the purse strings; nothing happened without his prior approval.

He got his job as auditor because he was a skilled accountant; the job description never called for managing people or projects. In 1837, readers of the *American Coast Pilot* urged publishers Edmund and George Blunt to challenge Pleasonton's competency at managing the lights.

Congressional inspectors reported on December 13, 1838, that most of the lighthouses were in good condition, and manned by dedicated people. However, the general consensus was that the USLHE needed reorganization to operate with tighter discipline, and clearly, all lighthouses needed the new Fresnel lenses made in France.

Between 1822 and 1842, the USLHE built an average of nine new lighthouses a year, increasing the number from 70 to 256 (only two used Fresnel lenses) during that period. They maintained 30 lightships and more than 1,000 buoys. Congressional allocations enlarged lighthouse budgets from $145,000 to nearly $400,000 annually.

Pleasonton's hardest challenge was yet to come, however. Early in 1848, the United States took possession of California from Mexico and immediately after, from Sutter's Fort in the Sacramento Valley, came the fevered cry of "Gold!" For the beleaguered Fifth Auditor, this was not exciting news.

of Engineers, which selected plans and took bids on the job. As the private contractors completed work, Congress launched a third proposal for funding to pay keepers. At any stage, a proposal could stall in a committee or lapse from one session into the next, delaying progress by months. When Congress passed the last bill, the Treasury Department finally transferred funds from one ledger column to the column for diplomatic accounts, audited by Pleasonton.

Changes were looming for the lighthouse administration, however. On March 4, 1851, President Millard Fillmore signed into law House appropriations bill HR 294, removing Pleasonton's authority. Site-determination power on the Pacific and Atlantic went to Coast Survey Superintendent Alexander Bache; for Great Lakes lights, the Topographical Engineers now had authority.

Two final sections of this law promised real change. First, Fresnel lenses were specified for all new lighthouses, and for those existing towers needing replacement lights. Second, Section 8 created the Lighthouse Board to enforce this change and others, study the USLHE, and recommend future Congressional legislation. The Board would include two Navy officers, two Army Corps of Engineers officers, and a civilian. George Mifflin Bache, Alexander Bache's brother and Pleasonton's former Third District inspector, would lead the Board. It all seemed simple enough.

Still, the Coast Survey had been working in California for nearly three years and no lighthouse construction had begun. Ironically, the need for navigation aids was reinforced on November 25, 1851, when the Coast Survey's own cutter, the *C. W. Lawrence*, got caught in fog in the Golden Gate, hit rocks, and sank.

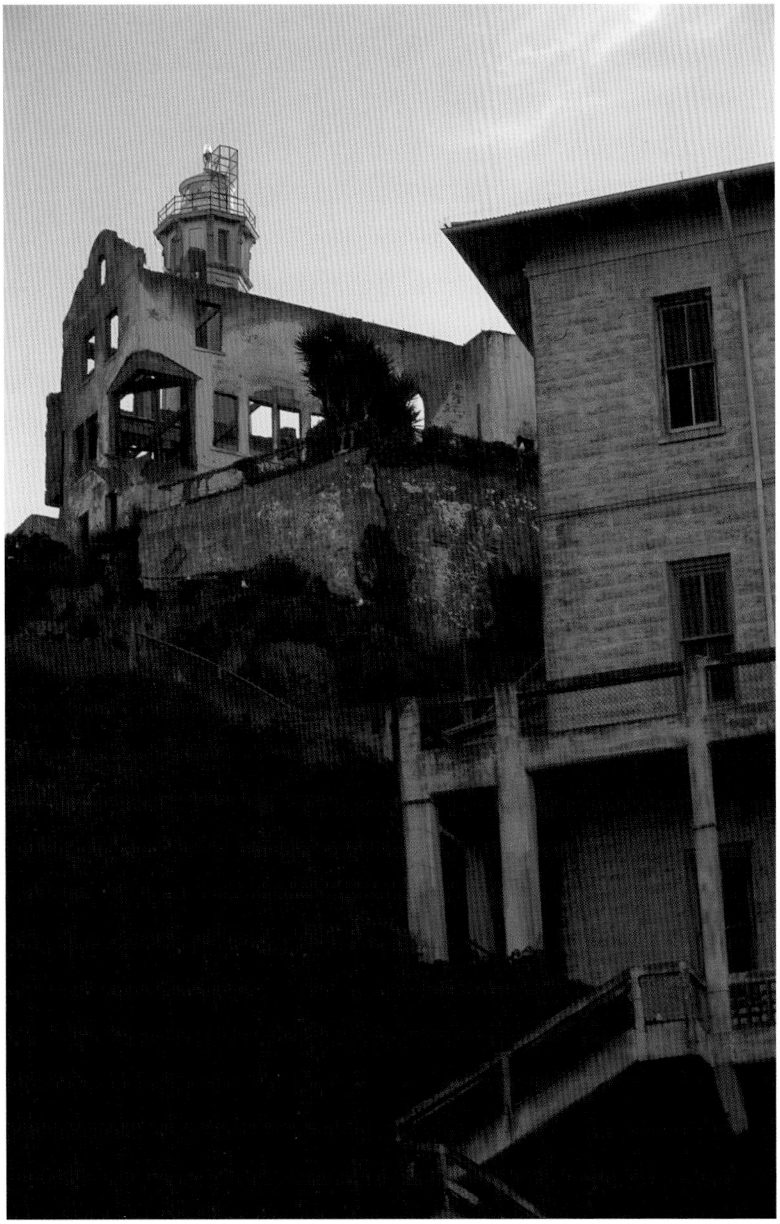

Alcatraz Island lighthouse
Below the lighthouse stand remnants of the warden's residence. The large building (situated along the dock) was the living quarters for guards and their families from 1909 until 1969. The light, a modern Vega Rotating Beacon, sits inside the tower with its backup mounted on the conical roof.

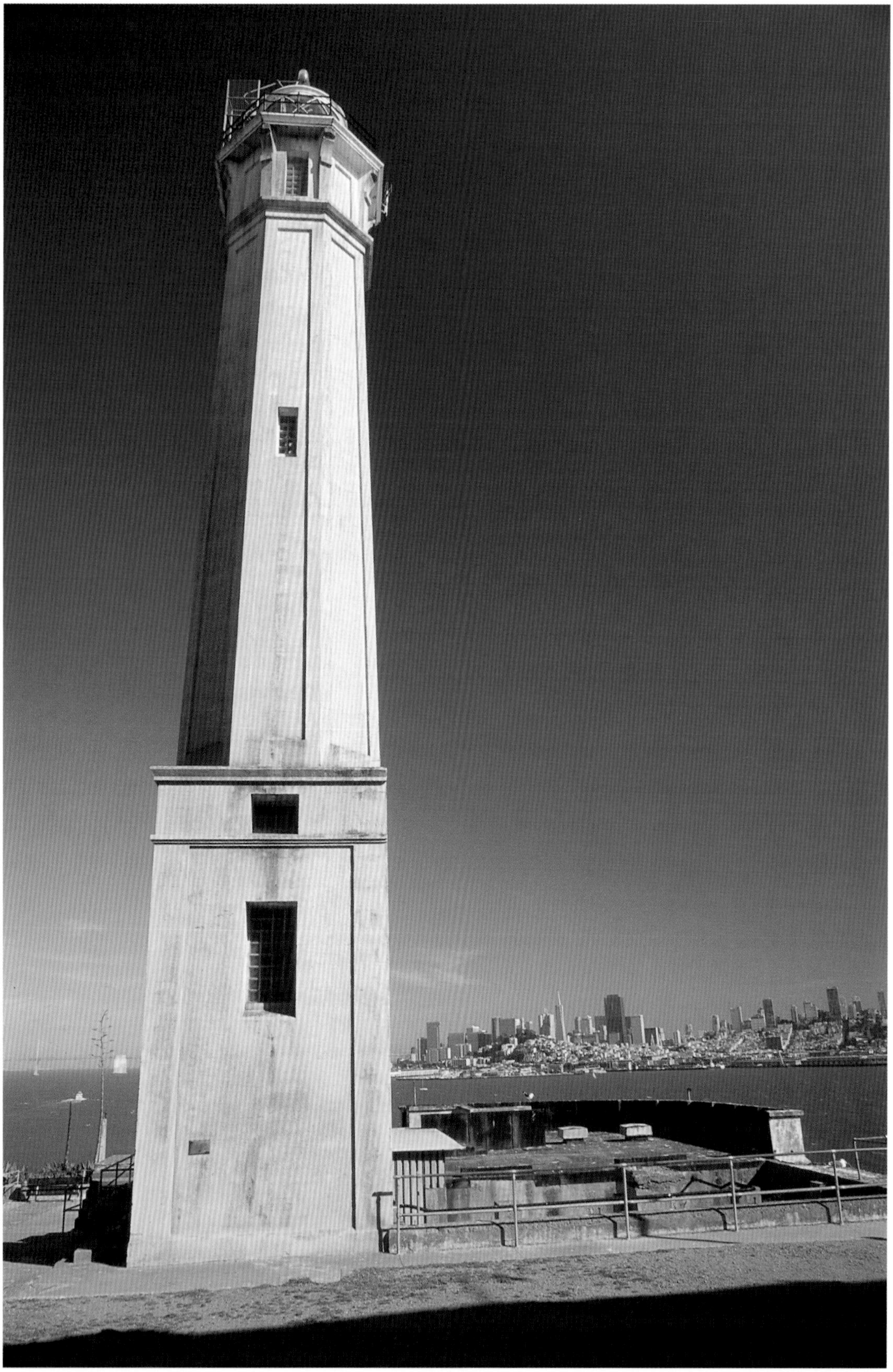

Erecting the First Lights

In 1852, regular shipping service between Los Angeles and San Francisco was established via the fast coastal cutter *Sea Bird*. Backers of the *Sea Bird*, commercial shippers, and others continued to clamor impatiently for navigation aids. Lighthouses had been approved and funded, but before they could be built, scandal rocked the boat.

The Treasury Department's public story was that a contractor who bid on all eight Pacific lighthouses failed to provide the $75,000 security bond and abandoned his bid, delaying the schedule. There was more to the story, however. A Senate Select Committee looking into federal government abuses, bribery, and fraud started investigations on August 14, 1851. It learned that former Treasury Chief Clerk John McGinnis became head of the Bureau of Lighthouses and Marine Hospitals on March 31; McGinnis felt this was a demotion, so he retired. Needing a "pension," he proposed to Treasury Secretary Thomas Corwin that he serve as general West Coast lighthouse contractor, telling Corwin candidly that he anticipated an $8,000 profit, which would see him through his remaining years. Corwin approved, Assistant Secretary William L. Hodge issued the contract, and stashed the appropriation in a desk drawer. But Treasury rules required the bond; McGinnis missed his deadline, and Hodge quickly secured other contractors. The Select Committee questioned all these maneuvers.

The McGinnis scandal forced Congress to act. On August 31, 1852, it gave the Lighthouse Board further decision-making power. Board members included the Navy's Commodore William B. Shubrick and Commander S. F. DuPont, Army brevet Brigadier General James Kearney, Topographical Engineers Corps Brigadier General Joseph G. Totten, Alexander Bache, and physicist and Smithsonian Institution first secretary Professor Joseph Henry. The Board voted to add two more officers and named Shubrick chairman. It wasted little time instituting its recommended changes. By mid-October 1852, it brought order to U.S. lighthouses by providing specific regulations to keepers. To better manage the growing organization around America's shores, the Board divided the East, Gulf, and West Coasts into twelve districts.

Hodge contracted Baltimore, Maryland, builders Francis A. Gibbons and Francis S. Kelly to construct nine West Coast lighthouses within days of McGinnis's default. They had erected several East Coast lights as subcontractors, including Bodie Island near Cape

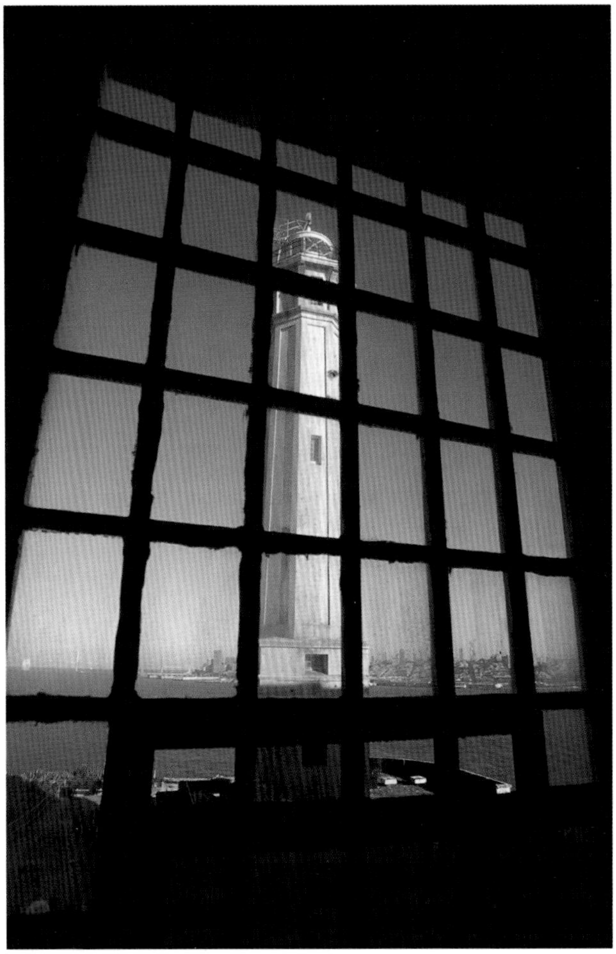

ALCATRAZ ISLAND LIGHTHOUSE
Only inmates with good behavior records could visit the prison cinema on the front of the building's second floor. This was one of their few opportunities to see San Francisco's skyline and the free world outside.

ALCATRAZ ISLAND LIGHTHOUSE
All that remains of the 1909 lighthouse is the eighty-four-foot-tall tower. It was originally attached to a head keeper's residence that was destroyed when Native Americans, claiming treaty rights dating back more than a century, occupied Alcatraz Island beginning in 1969. The 1909 tower replaced the original Cape Cod–style lighthouse that was the West Coast's first lighthouse. That original tower was too low to shine past the newly built federal prison.

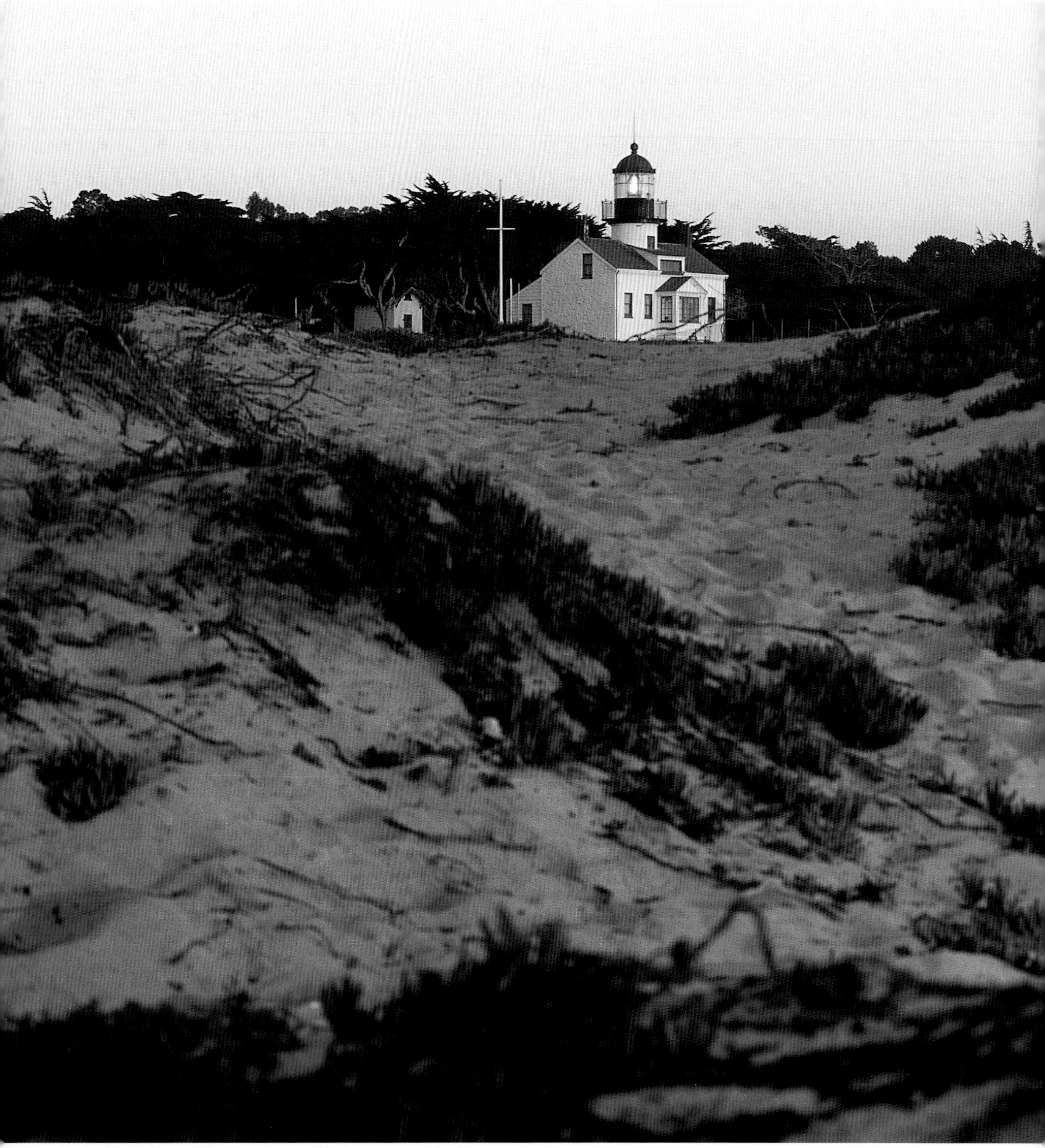

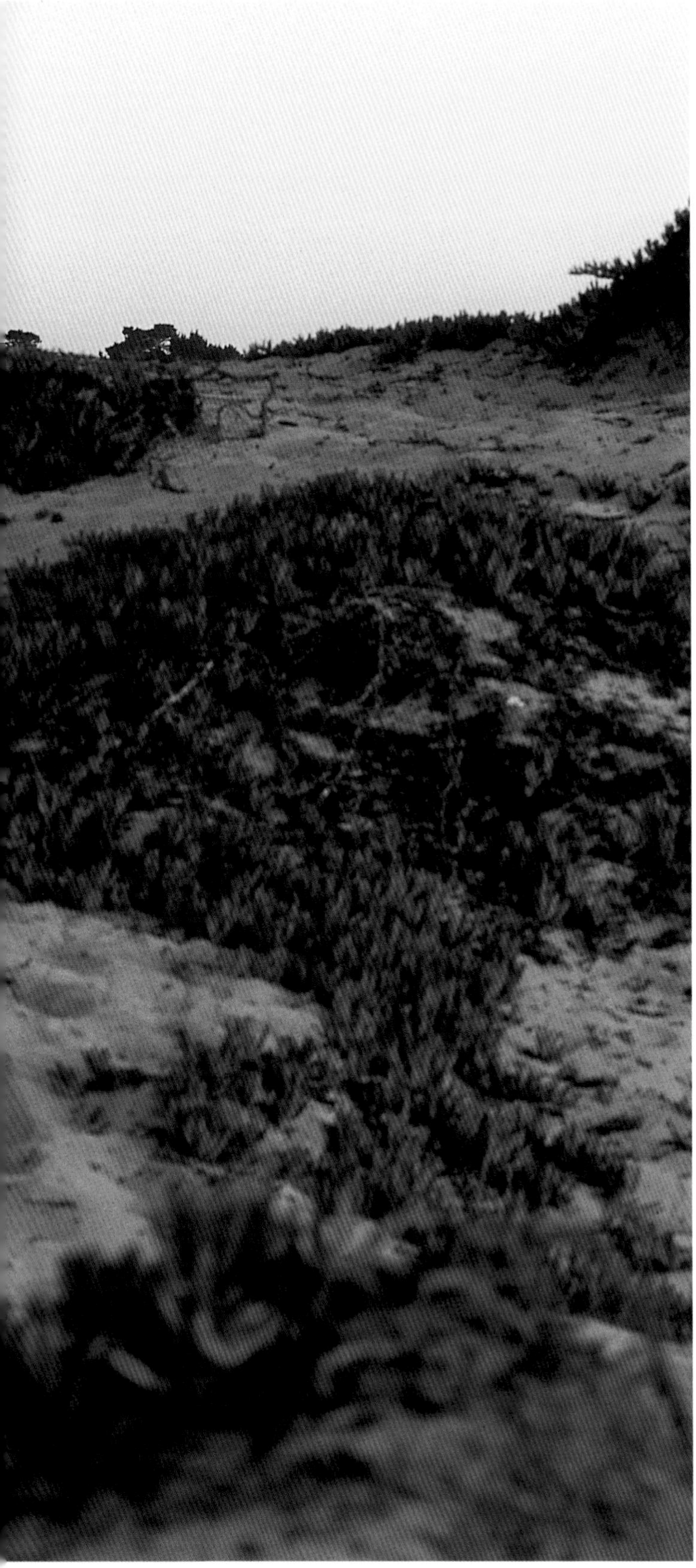

Point Pinos lighthouse
Point Pinos lighthouse sits hundreds of yards back from the ocean it marks. It was not the best placement for a lighthouse, but it was the easiest site for Gibbons and Kelly's construction crew in 1853. The original light station land, on which keepers from Charlotte Layton to Emily Fish raised food and livestock, is now a golf course.

The Battle Between Lewis Lanterns and Fresnel Lenses

Accountant Stephen Pleasonton had neither technical lighthouse knowledge nor maritime experience. But as the Fifth Auditor of the Treasury Department, he was put in charge of lighthouses, and he needed help. Besides relying on local inspectors, he turned to Winslow Lewis. Lewis had years of experience as a sea captain, and eventually turned his hand to inventing parabolic reflecting and magnifying lanterns that became standard in many U.S. lighthouses. Using Swiss inventor Ami Argand's oil lamp with its hollow circular wick, Lewis fitted a reflector around the burning wick, significantly brightening the beam.

In July 1810, a month after he received his patent, Lewis demonstrated his system to Boston customs collector Henry Dearborn at Cape Ann, Massachusetts. Dearborn urged the Treasury Department to buy Lewis's patent. In 1812, the U.S. Light House Establishment (USLHE) paid Lewis $60,000 for his patents (around $1.2 million today, adjusted for inflation). USLHE sweetened the deal further with a contract for him to install and maintain his light systems in all U.S. lighthouses.

Through the years, Lewis's relationship with USLHE auditor Stephen Pleasonton was curious. Pleasonton not only sought Lewis's advice about technology, but he allowed Lewis to bid against others to construct lighthouses. Lewis built his first lighthouse in 1818. Within ten years, he was so integrated into Pleasonton's system that he created only five basic building designs and convinced Pleasonton these would fill all USLHE needs. Other contractors bid against Lewis but rarely won, because he was willing to build at a loss. Lewis knew he would recoup his investment by providing his lights and maintaining them. This meant a financial fortune for Lewis. Records indicate that Lewis constructed more than forty lighthouses for the government, although he bragged he built twice that many.

Across the Atlantic in France, physicist and government road-builder Augustin Jean Fresnel revolutionized European lighthouses by developing a new type of lens in 1822. His complex invention captured 90 percent of the light from a flame. Using reflecting and refracting lenses and prisms, he precisely controlled where the light shined. Fresnel created his cylindrical lenses in five sizes, or orders, with the first being the largest and most powerful. The Fresnel lens, as it came to be known, used only half as much oil as Lewis's parabolic reflectors, and Fresnels created a better light.

The initial price of a Fresnel lens was five to ten times what a Lewis system cost because the French lenses required hundreds of pieces of glass to be precisely ground and intricately assembled. Because of the Fresnel's high price and Lewis's desire to sell and maintain his own systems, Pleasonton (and Lewis) kept the French lenses out of American lighthouses. Pleasonton's lack of knowledge, excessive frugality, and his reliance on Lewis's inferior system badly affected the USLHE.

In 1838, however, the House Committee on Commerce circumvented Pleasonton by appropriating funds outside the USLHE to purchase two Fresnels for tests and evaluation. U.S. Navy Captain Matthew Perry was already en route to England, so Congress detoured him to France. He arrived in Paris on August 19, 1838, and contracted with Henry LePaute, who was the official manufacturer of lenses for the French and English governments, for two lenses and one lantern. Pleasonton rationalized that spending an additional $2,600 for a second lantern was not needed when the one lantern could be copied less expensively in the United States.

Two years later the lenses arrived in New York, accompanied by Louis Bernard, one of LePaute's engineers. The total cost for installing the lenses in the twin lighthouses at Navesink, New Jersey, included: the cost of the lenses, Bernard's fee, reimbursement for a translator, and pay for a large installation crew. It also included $3,930 paid to a New York company that copied the one French lantern, (which ended up costing $1,330 more than if they had bought two lanterns from LePaute). At a total price of $18,975.36, it's easy to understand Pleasonton's perception of Fresnel lenses as "extravagant."

Hatteras, North Carolina, and Egmont Key near Tampa, Florida. They accepted $90,000 for the six California jobs and $31,000 for the Cape Disappointment light. With this money, they were to buy the building supplies and Argand/Lewis parabolic lamps, hire workers, transport crew and equipment to California, build towers, and install lamps. After posting bond, Gibbons and Kelly gathered plans, materials, bricklayers, stonemasons, carpenters, a painter, plasterer, blacksmith, mechanics, and other laborers. Then they hired experienced builders Roger J. Mahon and William A. Timanus to supervise construction.

Five weeks later, as Mahon and Timanus prepared to sail, the Treasury determined it would pay for Fresnel lenses in each lighthouse and deducted $1,055 from each site for removing the Lewis lights. Then, just before the ship sailed, the Treasury enlarged the Cape Disappointment tower diameter. It also decided to thicken the walls of each tower to a three-foot base and two-foot top. This returned $1,000 to each contract.

Gibbons and Kelly chartered two schooners, the *Oriole* in Baltimore and *Tropic* in New York. They refitted both ships and loaded them with yellow pine boards, window and door frames, shutters, cupboards, roofing tin, flooring stone, oil, paint, and glass. Captain L. H. Leutz, who had experience in the Pacific, and twenty-five lighthouse builders set sail on the *Oriole* from Baltimore's Chase's Wharf on August 12, 1852.

Gibbons and Kelly's ships made good time, arriving together in San Francisco on December 4, 1852, just before the Lighthouse Board took over from the Treasury. Workmen started nine days later to prepare a foundation on Alcatraz Island for their first lighthouse.

To eliminate wrong decisions or bad guesses, Gibbons and Kelly provided superintendents Mahon and Timanus with one basic building plan for all their Pacific lighthouses with variations as single-family or duplex residences. Every house would be a traditional story-and-a-half, rectangular Cape Cod–type cottage designed by Treasury Department architect Ammi E. Young. Each measured 20 by 38 feet and stood 40 feet to the steeply angled roof peak. The light tower rose from the house's middle. The keeper's bedroom was a few steps from the tower; a tight spiral staircase led up to the lantern room. The only design freedom Timanus and Mahon had was in tower height to meet Coast Survey specifications for the new Fresnel lens's focal center. Plans gave each lighthouse a basement, and they constructed outbuildings to store flammable oil and other supplies.

The Coast Survey's site was on Alcatraz's southeast end, facing San Francisco and leaving space for the fortress the Army planned. Once the foundation was done, some of the crew started preparing the second site on the Golden Gate's south side at Battery Point.

Timanus hadn't made provisions to store building materials from either the *Oriole* or *Tropic*, nor had he arranged for a work ship. The six-month charter of the *Oriole* ended in February 1853. The San Francisco customs collector, political appointee Beverly C. Sanders, ran day-to-day operations for area lighthouses; he approved chartering the *Oriole* for $3,000 a month, with his office paying the lease. In March, with a few local hands supplementing the Baltimore builders, Timanus's foundation crew sailed the *Oriole* south to start on Point Pinos lighthouse.

As the builders turned their first shovels on Monterey Peninsula, Congress passed a new appropriation. Funds authorized on March 3, 1853, specifically included "large buoys to be placed on sunken rocks in San Francisco Bay, under direction of the Superintendent of the Coast Survey." Congress added $25,000 for a lighthouse at San Francisco's Point Bonita, $10,000 for one at San Pedro Bay south of Los Angeles, and also funded one at Santa Cruz. Agreeing that costs were rising, legislators made an allowance: To complete lighthouses in California and Oregon Territory, Congress provided $120,000 for the Lighthouse Board's anticipated overruns based on Corps of Engineers's surveys outlining construction difficulties. The bill also paid salaries for thirteen keepers and eleven assistants. Shubrick's Board placed an order with French lens maker Henry LePaute for more than forty Fresnel lenses for the new Pacific lighthouses and to improve Atlantic lights.

Suddenly, five years of Congressional and Treasury Department foot dragging gave way to a tidal wave of activity and appropriation.

The First Light Is Lit

A month after the funding floodgates opened, Timanus's crew landed on South Farallon Island to begin a foundation for the West Coast's fourth lighthouse. Excavating the rock of Alcatraz and Battery Point had been challenging, whereas at Point Pinos, they worked on softer ground and had an easier time. At southeast Farallon

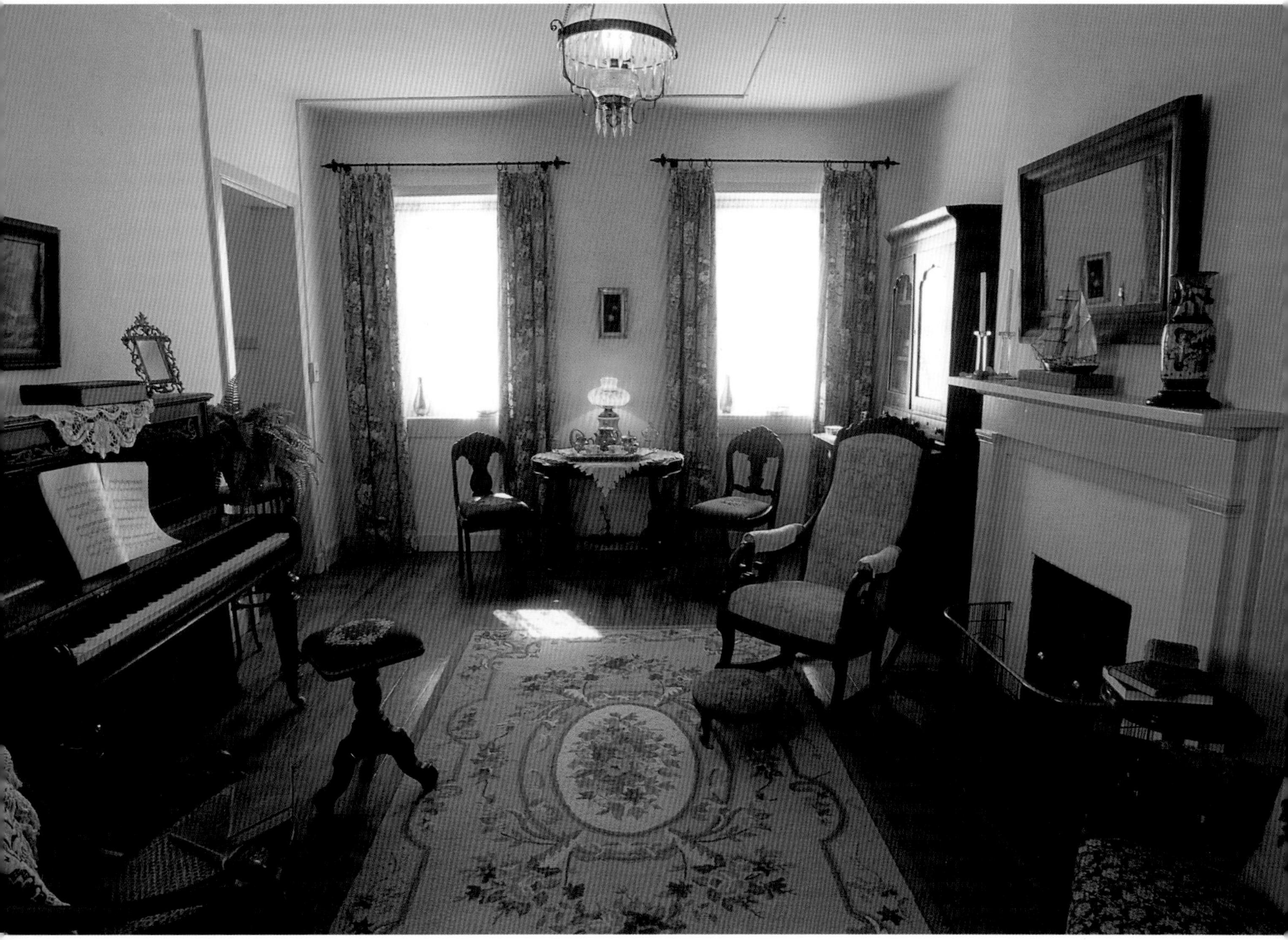

Point Pinos lighthouse

The light's most celebrated keeper was Emily Fish, whose personal lifestyle was as impressive as her dedication to lighthouse duties. Emily became keeper in 1893 and remained until retirement in 1914. The Pacific Grove Museum operates the residence as a living history museum, and often a docent portrays Mrs. Fish, talking about her duties and her life.

Island, the miners encountered an unexpected obstacle.

As early as 1810, trader Alexander Baranov's Russian and Aleut trappers harvested sea lion pelts from the Farallons. They told Baranov about the thousands of sea birds nesting there. Decades later, when gold-rush miners reached San Francisco, they learned eggs were a luxury in short supply. Poachers soon found the Farallons, and in baggy clothes with dozens of pockets to cradle the eggs, they robbed the nests. Some days, the poachers gathered 10,000 eggs, which sold in San Francisco for a dollar each. The price doubled in Sacramento.

When the unarmed lighthouse builders reached the South Farallon Island harbor, they met gun-toting egg harvesters who didn't want a lighthouse to scare birds or attract other harvesters. Boldly claiming they had the license to harvest the island, they ran off the builders.

The Coast Survey's first Pacific steamer had finally reached San Francisco, and it now sailed to Farallon bristling with heavily armed Revenue Marine soldiers who knew there were no government egg-harvesting licenses. The harvesters quickly recognized that lucrative though the poaching was, it was not worth their lives. An edgy truce was established, and the builders made camp at the base of the 300-foot-high rock on which the Coast Survey wanted the light.

Navigating the Pacific Coast also continued to be an obstacle to the lighthouse builders themselves. Loaded with building materials and a new crew of masons and carpenters, the *Oriole* set sail in late spring 1853 from San Francisco north to Cape Disappointment to build the next lighthouse. Captain Leutz planned to enter the Columbia River and anchor in protected waters to unload. But as his harbor pilot steered the ship across the bar on September 13, 1853, the wind died. The current dragged the ship onto rocks, ripping out the bottom within view of the Coast Survey's selected lighthouse site. All hands were saved, but the ship sunk with $10,000 worth of materials for the Cape Disappointment, Umpqua River, and Cape Flattery lights.

Gibbons and Kelly then hired not one but two more ships. Their contract specified completing all lighthouses by March 1, 1854. To meet that date, they sent Mahon north with one group and Timanus south with the other. By July, they had workers at all eight sites and had finished Alcatraz for $14,567.26, some $432 under budget. Yet while it was finished, it was not complete.

Fresnel maker LePaute couldn't keep up with orders from the French, British and U.S. governments. The Lighthouse Board sent Navy Lieutenant Washington A. Bartlett to Paris, where he contracted manufacturer L. Sautter & Cie for two third-order lenses and oil lamps for Alcatraz and Battery Point. Sautter's price of $3,810 per unit included delivery to San Francisco, and the lenses arrived in October 1852. However, by this time, the Board had exhausted its 1852 budget. Worse, while there was money for 1853, the lighthouse blueprints that Gibbons and Kelly used were scaled to fit Lewis reflectors and Argand lamps: Fresnels were taller and wider. Towers had to be enlarged, and while workers rebuilt the structures, the lenses remained in storage for eighteen months.

Finally, on June 1, 1854, Alcatraz keeper Michael Kassin touched a match to the wick and the West Coast's first lighthouse flared to life.

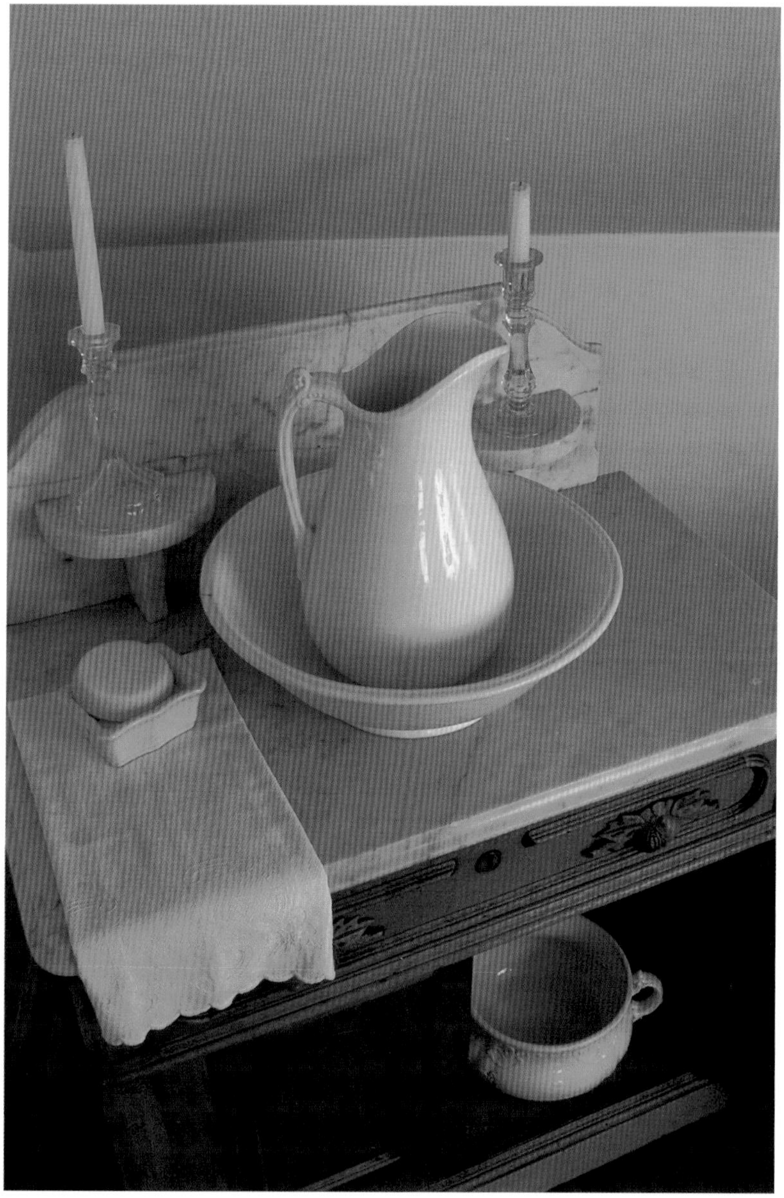

POINT PINOS LIGHTHOUSE
The work was hard and the conditions often were tough, but life and leisure were easy and elegant. Emily Fish's washtable in her bedroom reflects the simple style at the turn of the twentieth century. Wash water was carried into the kitchen or up to this table. A privy stood outside.

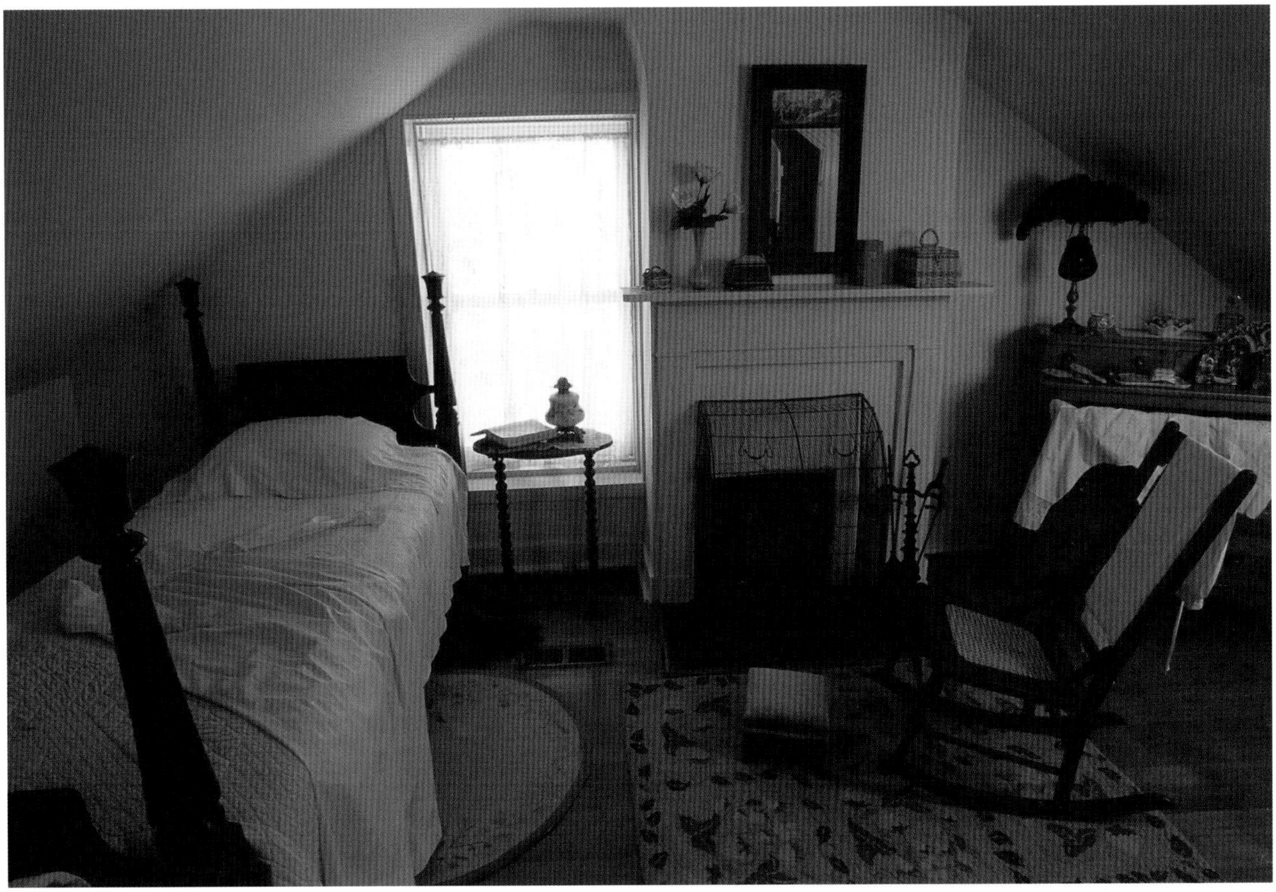

Above: POINT PINOS LIGHTHOUSE
The small Cape Cod–style lighthouses, designed by Washington architect Ammi E. Young, measured just 20 by 38 feet. The second floor contained two bedrooms, separated by the spiral staircase up to the lantern room. While keeper Emily Fish's wealth and her visits to China added to the decor, the lighthouse furnishings were of high quality.

Right: POINT PINOS LIGHTHOUSE
The land side of Point Pinos lighthouse received the open quarter of Henry LePaute's Fresnel lens. This optic was designed for Fort Point light in the middle of the Golden Gate inlet to San Francisco Bay. That lens, with 288 degrees of coverage, was temporarily deactivated to build a fort. It was sent here to the Monterey Peninsula.

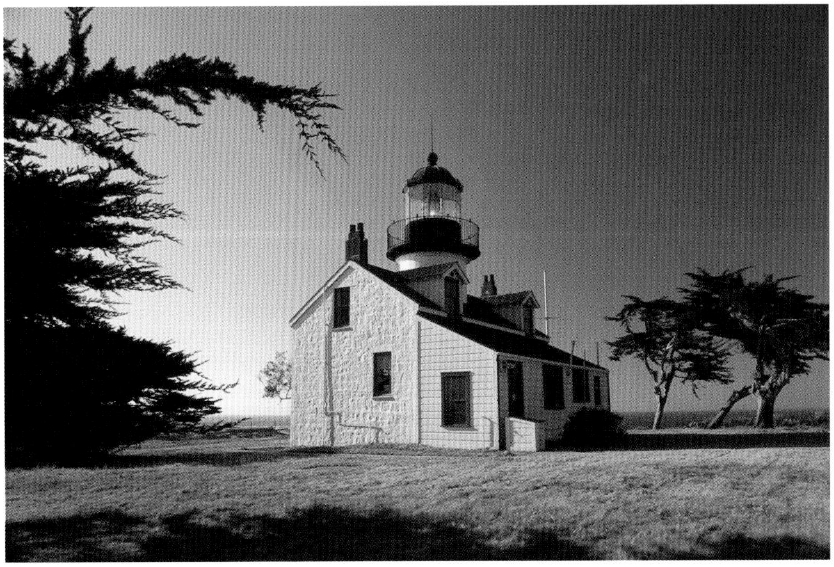

Lighthouse Science

The year is 1856, and Congress has just appropriated funds for a new West Coast lighthouse. The Coast Survey team has established the approximate location of the new light, but there are many decisions to be made before construction can begin. One of the first people assigned to the job is the lighthouse engineer, who is responsible for all preliminary work including setting the site elevation, selecting a lens, choosing a light source, and finally calculating the light's candlepower.

The first step is deciding on the "portee," the approximate distance from which the light should be seen. A headlands light will need a greater portee than one placed on a harbor breakwater, for example. The portee is the determining variable upon which the height of the lighthouse is based. Due to the curvature of the earth, a light placed 100 feet above sea level would be visible from only 13.23 miles, but a light situated at 500 feet above sea level could be seen from 29.5 miles, regardless of the type of lens and light source selected.

Once the elevation is determined, the appropriate lens must be selected. The engineer can choose between seven different lens sizes and two lens styles. The size, or "order," of the lens is determined by its focal distance, which is half the diameter of the apparatus on the focal plane. The largest lens, a first-order, has a focal distance of 36.22 inches; the smallest, a sixth-order, has a focal distance of just 5.91 inches. West Coast lenses are all based on the work of French designer Augustin Fresnel, who created a catadioptric lens assembly that contained as few as several dozen pieces of optical glass and prisms in the smallest lenses, and up to more than 1,000 elements in the largest, first-order optics.

There are two styles of prism alignment. One style places the elements concentrically around a vertical axis, creating a "drum lens." The other is composed of separate elements, formed in segments of rings on a central axis; these feature a large refractor—basically a magnifying glass in the middle—and is called a "bull's-eye lens" as it resembles the shape of a bull's eye target. As the lens rotates, these magnifying bull's eyes swing past the light source, giving the impression of a flash from a distance. The drum-lenses do not rotate, and while the light source (electric bulbs only) may go on and off, it is more subtle than the flash. To flash or not, to go off and on, is referred to as the light's "signature," the characteristics that allow mariners to differentiate one lighthouse from another.

A light source must then be decided upon. The engineer's choice will depend on the source's brightness. Brightness is the luminous intensity of any surface in a given direction, per each unit of projected area of the surface as viewed from that direction. Simply put, a 50-watt searchlight will always appear brighter than a 50-watt flashlight because the searchlight has a larger reflecting surface.

More impressive, perhaps, than the mathematics needed to solve these problems is the fact that Augustin Fresnel, who spent most of his days supervising road construction for the French government, devised this intricate light magnifying, bending, and focusing system in 1822, without hand-held calculators or computer-aided design and manufacturing. The lighthouse engineers had it easy.

Point Pinos lighthouse
The LePaute third-order Fresnel lens now is illuminated by a 1,000-watt quartz lamp, flashing on in a prescribed sequence. These characteristics are known as the light's signature, and each light's signature is unique. This enables mariners to recognize the light and plot their location.

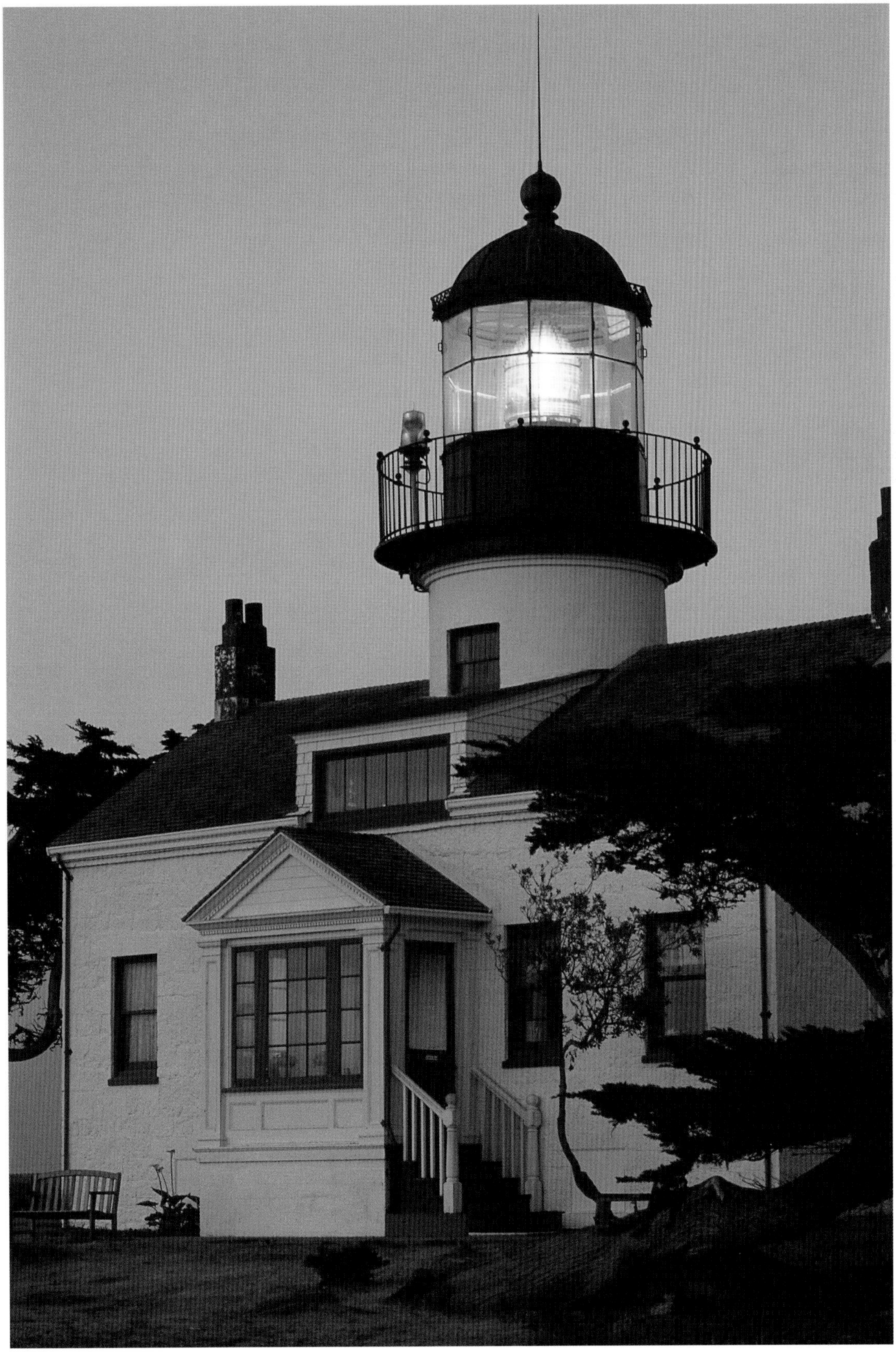

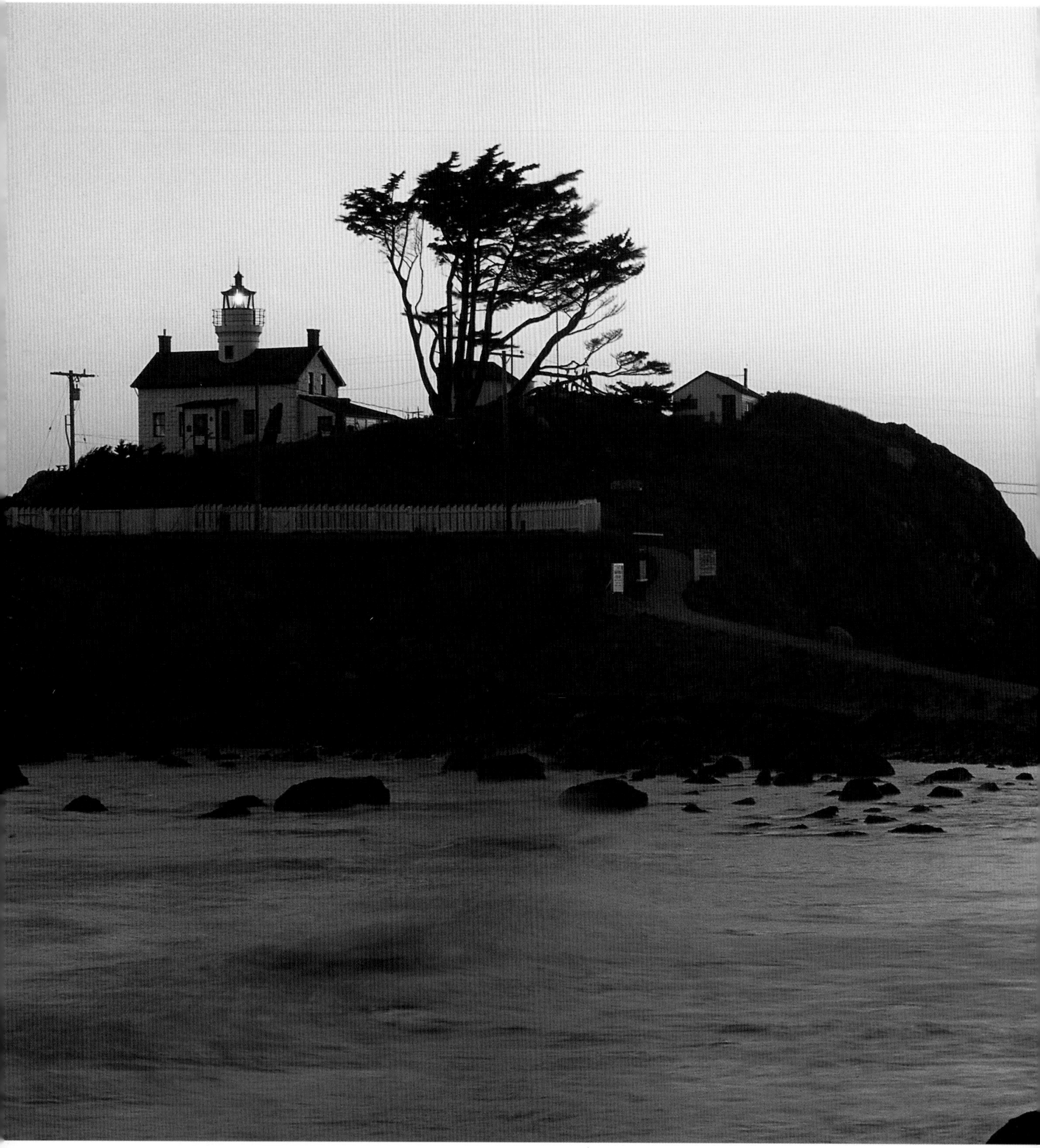

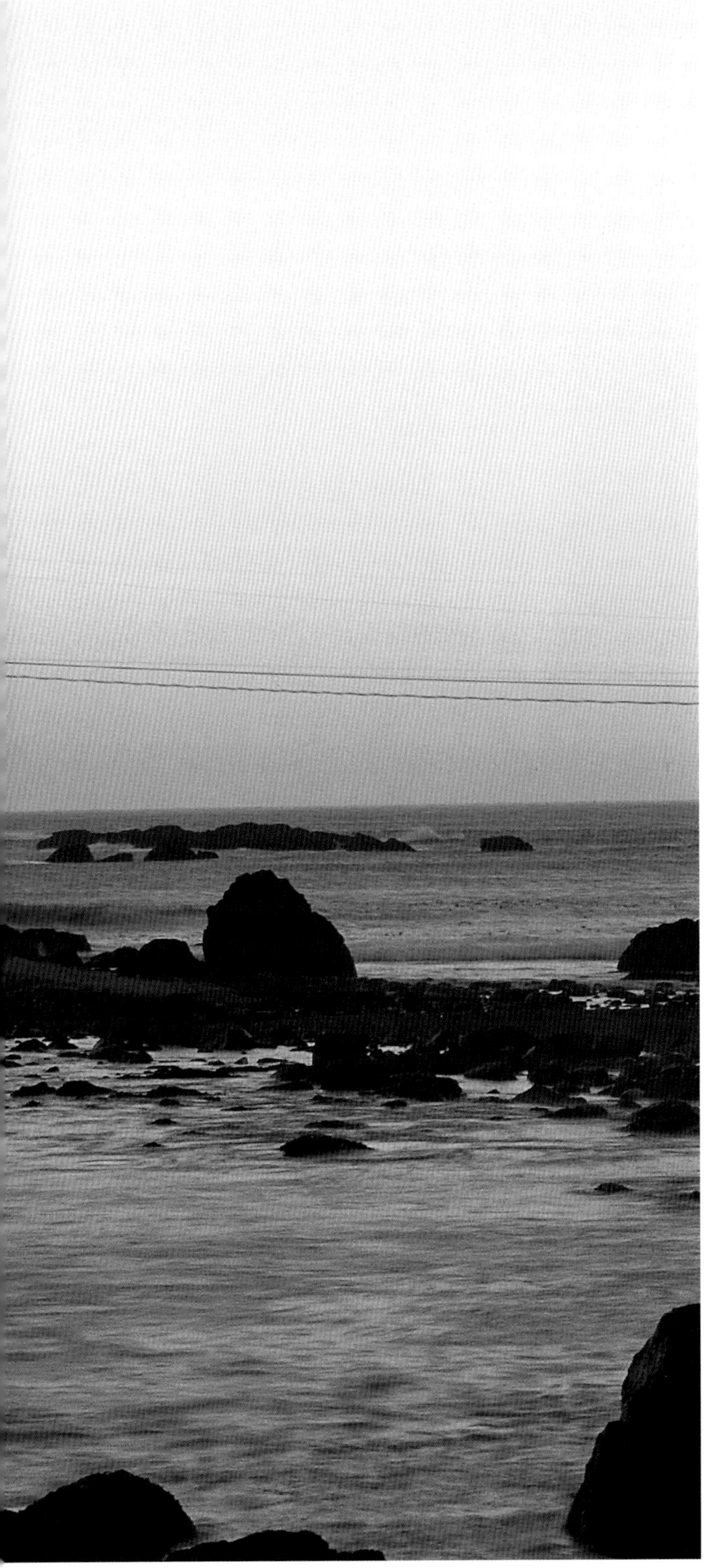

BATTERY POINT LIGHTHOUSE
The Crescent City light at Battery Point is another small Cape Cod with the tower rising up through its center. Its small, fourth-order LePaute Fresnel cost 6,616 French francs in 1856, roughly $20,000 adjusted to inflation today. Its four panels contain 315 individual pieces of glass. Keeper Theophilus Magruder first lit the lens on December 10, 1856.

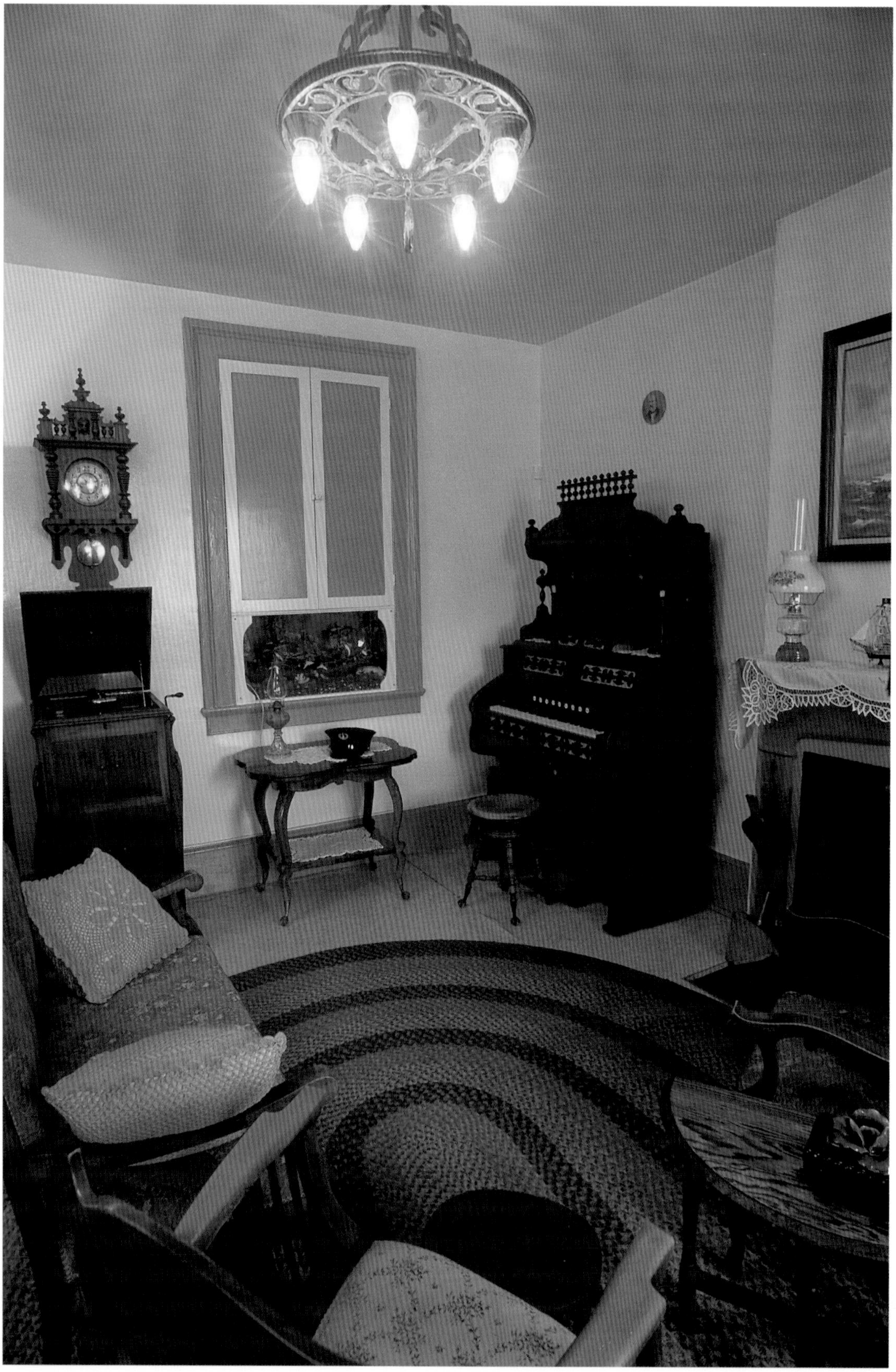

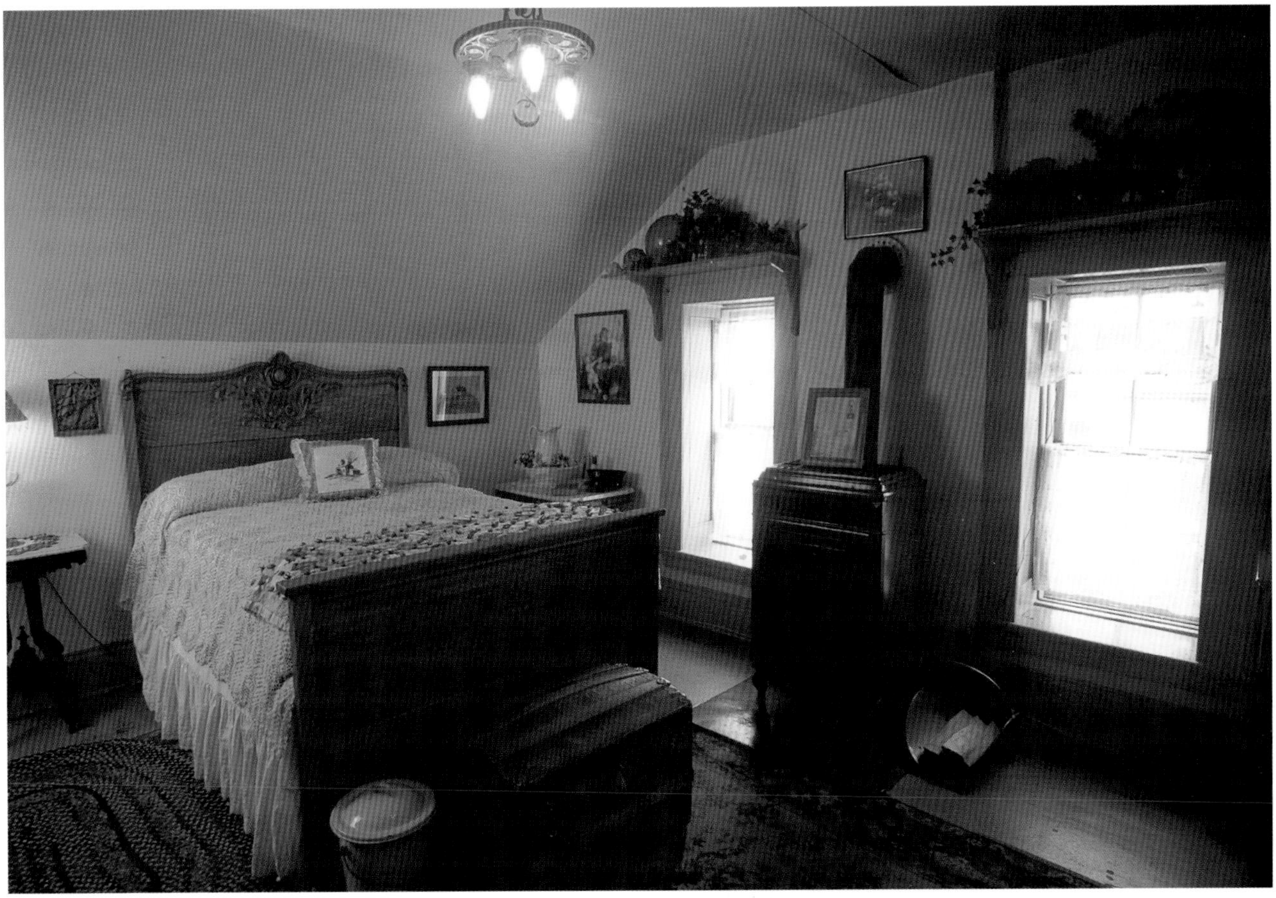

Above: **Battery Point lighthouse**
Battery Point has had fifteen keepers since 1856. The last head keeper was Wayne Piland, who slept in this bedroom with these very furnishings until 1953, when the Coast Guard automated Crescent City using a post light at the end of the breakwater. Del Norte County Historical Society succeeded in reactivating the light as a private navigation aid in December 1982.

Right: **Battery Point lighthouse**
Ammi Young designed kitchens in early lighthouses as one of two ground-floor rooms. But growing families quickly needed that space, so cooking moved to lean-to sheds grafted onto the rear of the houses. This kept cooking smells and the risk of fire outside the house. By the 1920s, most lighthouses moved kitchens back inside solid walls.

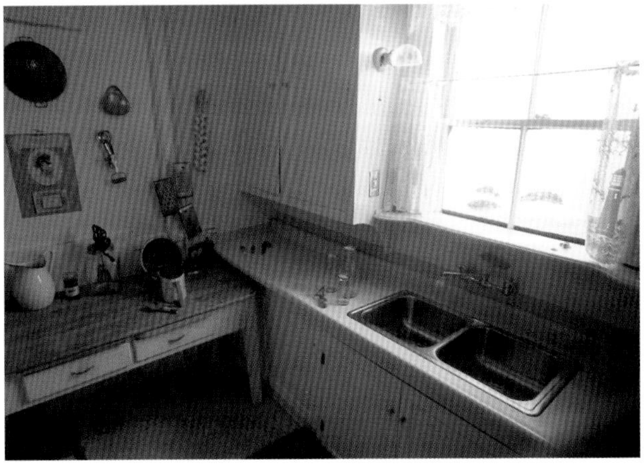

Facing page: **Battery Point lighthouse**
The downstairs parlor now shows a cabinet and built-in aquarium where the original back window was located. The Light House Establishment provided head keepers with five-light ceiling fixtures; first assistants got four lights and the second assistants got three lights. In 1900, head keeper John Jeffrey, a Civil War veteran, earned $804 but paid for his uniform—$8.35 for pants, shirt, and apron.

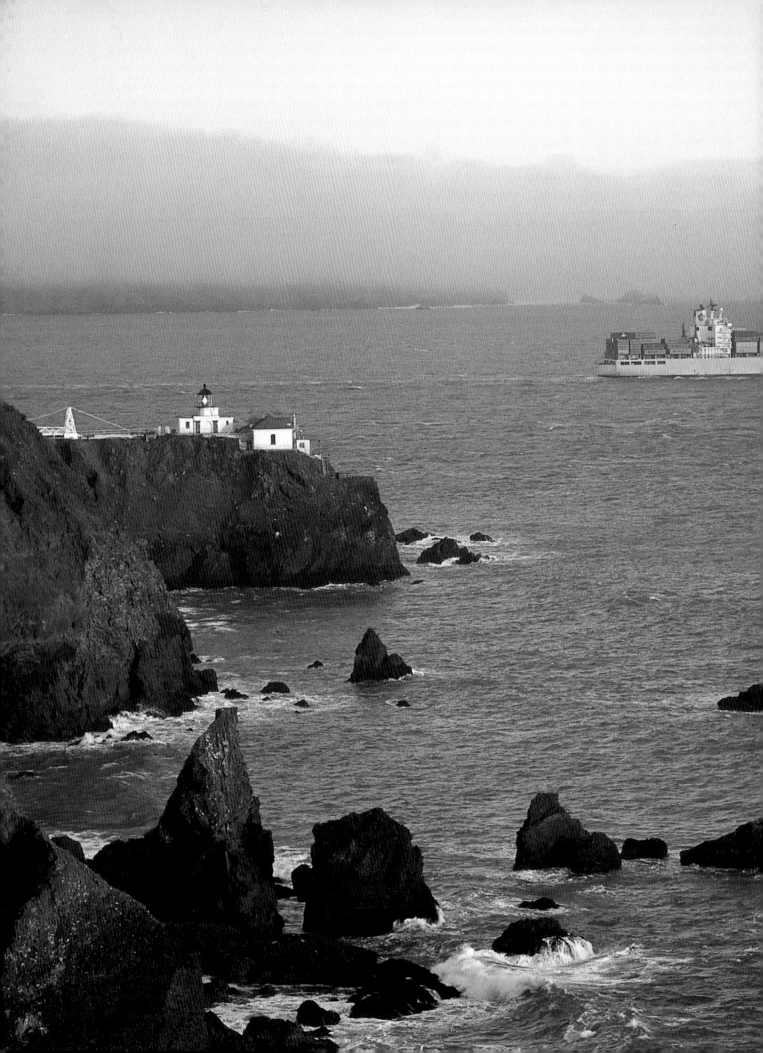

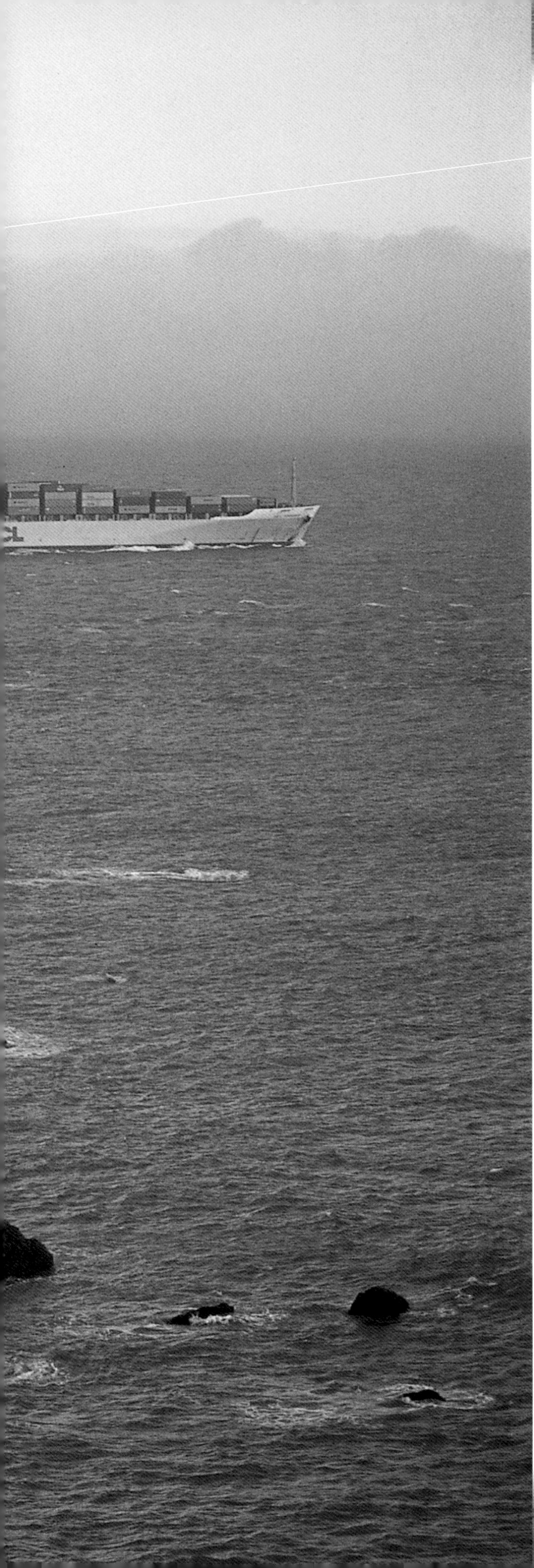

CHAPTER 2

Filling the Dark with Light and Might

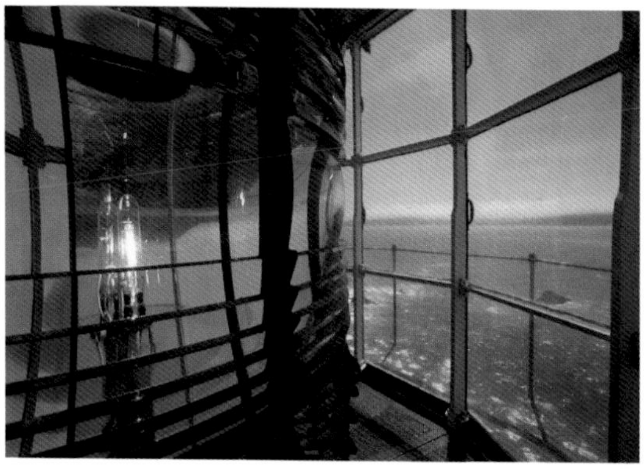

Left: Point Bonita lighthouse
As the guardian and marker of the north shore of the Golden Gate, Point Bonita sees endless shipping traffic, often in seemingly endless fog. The lighthouse, completed in 1877, sits 124 feet above sea level. Its second-order lens is simple and flashes every three seconds through its 125 pieces of glass.

Above: Point Bonita lighthouse
This lens was first lit in April 1855, mounted in the lantern room of a 56-foot-tall brick tower 306 feet above sea level. After relocating it below the fog layer, head keeper John Brown relit the light in February 1877. Visitors today go with Golden Gate National Recreation Area rangers to see the light.

No sooner had the Coast Surveyors written their description of Alcatraz as a barren, inaccessible island than Army Engineers decided it was a perfect defense position. The Army finished its survey by mid-1852, and the next spring began constructing a fort on the rock. By April 1855, not even nine months after keeper Michael Kassin first lit the light, the Army had a battery of ten-inch guns in place.

The Army also found Battery Point appealing for defense purposes. While crews finished the stubby Cape Cod–style lighthouse during summer 1852, the Army took over the site, and the lantern room sat empty as the builders awaited funds to install the new Fresnel. The Army appealed to the Lighthouse Board's Twelfth District inspector, Army Captain Henry W. Halleck, for a favor: It wanted to remove the cottage and build another structure later. The Cape Cod came down in 1853, and in 1854, the Army Engineers began erecting a three-story brick compound called Fort Winfield Scott. Because the strait was a tricky passage for mariners, Halleck struck a bargain: Builders Roger Mahon and William Timanus hastily constructed a thirty-six-foot-tall wooden tower between the fort and seawall.

At Point Pinos, Coast Surveyors gave contractors three site choices. One was a rock that to build on, even at low tide, was too tough a challenge to consider. The second was barely an eighth of a mile inland from the rock but on solid ground. The third was on granite in rolling hills nearby. Unsupervised, the work crews chose the third site, nearest the stone for the house and tower but furthest from the ocean. Five hundred yards of sand and beach grass separated the lighthouse from the rocky coast.

The second-order LePaute Fresnel lens that Washington Bartlett ordered for the Point Pinos lighthouse was caught in the lensmaker's backlog. So, in December 1854, the Board dispatched to Point Pinos the third-order Fresnel lens that was originally made for Battery Point. This lens provided only 288 degrees of coverage because engineers saw no need to light the Golden Gate's high bluffs behind the light and not having those prisms saved money. When workers installed the lens at Monterey, they paid special attention to its configuration and aimed its focused light out to sea.

The Board already had hired keepers for some Pacific lights. Afraid of losing keepers to tempting goldfields, the Board allowed them to occupy the lighthouses even before lenses were installed. English emigrant Charles Layton, his wife Charlotte, and their four children moved into the cottage near Monterey in August 1853, even though he had few duties.

Not only did the Board let Twelfth District keepers move in early, but it also paid them more than they could earn at any other U.S. lighthouse. The Board set annual salaries for most East Coast head keepers at $600, but it found hotel owners in San Francisco, in order to hold on to help, paid housekeepers $1,000 a year, so the Board stretched to find $400 more for its Pacific staff. Layton earned $1,000, as did all the others except those at Alcatraz. There, Michael Kassin received $1,100 as the highest paid U.S. keeper; his first assistant, John Sloan, earned $700, $100 more than any head keeper back East. There's little doubt this was necessary to keep them from venturing up river to Sutter's Fort. The Laytons had prospected for gold from 1849 through 1851—although without much success. Layton was glad to be distracted from gold by a good salary. He inaugurated service at Point Pinos on February 1, 1855, after living in the cottage, maintaining the grounds and buildings, and drawing his salary for eighteen months.

Fresnel Problems

When LePaute's fifth-order Fresnel arrived in San Francisco from Paris, workers installed the small fourteen-inch-diameter lens in the temporary Battery Point tower. Right after technicians put it in place, however, several storms during March 1855 coincided with large tide changes to threaten the wood structure. The Army Engineers rebuilt the seawall, using granite blocks, and for the next several years the light operated on its temporary site.

Problems like these frustrated the Board. District inspectors not only had to observe the lights and review the keepers, but also, in the West Coast's Twelfth Dis-

Point Bonita lighthouse
On a day such as this, it's difficult to see the need to locate the West Coast's first fog signal at Point Bonita. But just a few miles west of the point, the fog waits. Bonita used a twenty-four-pound cannon that retired U.S. Army sergeant Edward Maloney fired every half hour. At one point he worked seventy-two hours without relief.

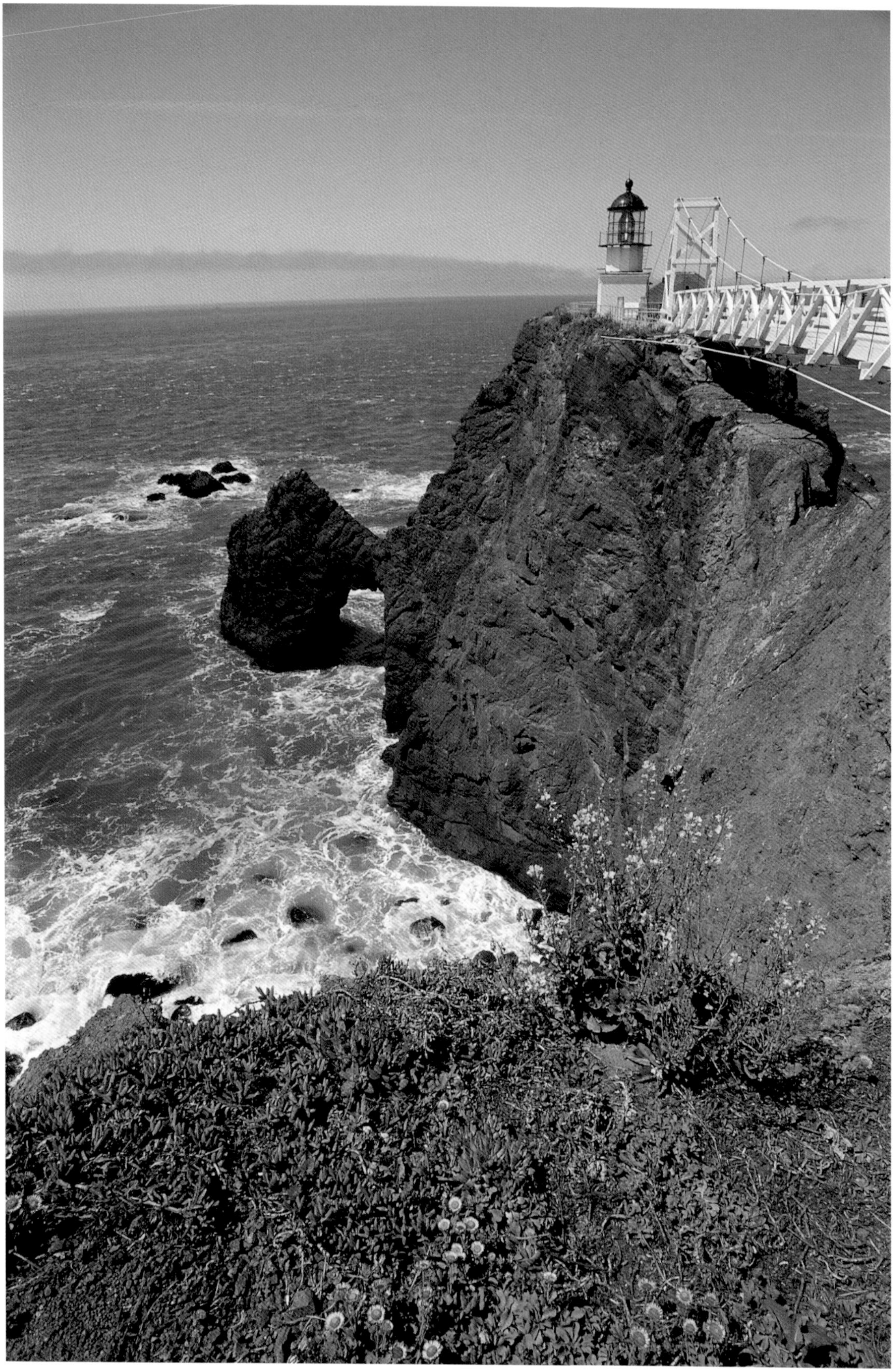

trict, they were construction supervisors. Mahon and Timanus made daily decisions that kept work moving forward. But some of these problems, such as dismantling the original Battery Point light, had to be decided on a higher level. The district inspector—Halleck or his replacement, Captain Campbell Graham—was as high as one got without going to Superintendent William Shubrick in Washington, D.C..

As Mahon and Timanus completed the lights, Graham watched building costs and freight fees aboard ships he was leasing for them. Contractors Francis Gibbons and Francis Kelly in Baltimore continued to ship work crews and timber from the East that were readily available in the West; they did the same with metal that could have been formed or cast in San Francisco. Because of transportation charges for supplies and moving workers from San Francisco, Point Pinos cost $26,000, some $9,000 over budget. Graham immediately started finding materials and labor himself and wrote his first local construction contract, for the Point Bonita light.

Meanwhile, Mahon's crew began work at Cape Disappointment, building the stone light tower on the bluff and constructing wood houses at the cove. A portion of his workers headed south to begin the foundation at Humboldt Bay. Timanus's team started at Point Conception, a location that kept his entire crew busy until the lighthouse was nearly complete. In April 1853, most of the crew continued to San Diego.

The Point Loma location caused Gibbons and Kelly trouble from the start. Their contract called for a light in San Diego that was to be completed by March 1, 1854, the deadline for all West Coast lights. However, the contract did not tell them where the San Diego light was to go. Gibbons and Kelly wrote Shubrick to learn its exact location. The reply came back: Point Loma. To the crew, this sounded like an additional, unexpected light they would have to build.

Gibbons pointed out to Shubrick that Point Loma was some distance from San Diego across a broad bay. It was 400 feet above sea level, could only be reached by land, and required that they build a road eight miles long that would include bridges. While he and Kelly absorbed the loss of the *Oriole* and its materials, Gibbons felt this extra work merited more money. The Board replied that a contract was a contract; this was the San Diego light specifically included in their agreement. So on April 7, 1853, the schooner *Vaquero*, loaded with materials from San Francisco, stopped at Point Conception to board Timanus and his builders. They worked their first thirty-five days below Point Loma creating the access road to get them and their supplies to the site. In mid-May, they began the house and tower.

Water—for drinking and for mixing mortar—was a problem at Point Loma. The rainwater cistern that blueprints called for held 2,700 gallons, which the Board reckoned was a nine-month supply. But it would not fit, so Timanus instead built a smaller cistern of 1,240 gallons, shoehorning it under the house. But it never rained enough at Point Loma to fill even the smaller basement tank; keepers later had to haul fresh water seven-and-a-half miles up the hill on a two-mule wagon that carried eighty gallons.

Crews labored on the last four lighthouses simultaneously and finished all six before September 1854. The third Fresnel lens—a first-order optic for the Farallon Island light—reached San Francisco from France aboard the *St. Joseph* on December 12, 1854. Through early 1855, other lenses and lights came at the rate of one or two monthly. As the lenses reached the lighthouses, however, a discrepancy became clear. Gibbons and Kelly experienced their own version of Murphy's law as they learned that the more physically challenging the lighthouse was to build, the worse was the fit of its Fresnel. Here was another executive decision that only the district inspector could make.

With two different Twelfth District inspectors in the first three years, decisions were not always consistent. The Board had to placate California's vocal Senators John Weller and William Gwin; it needed to respond quickly when problems arose along the Pacific shoreline. In summer 1855, the Board had transferred Topographical Engineer brevet Major Hartman E. Bache from the Fourth District to San Francisco. Replacing Graham, Major Bache arrived on June 30 and promptly sailed off to inspect the coast.

Bache decided that the towers at Cape Disappointment, Humboldt Bay, and Point Loma—and the temporary wood structure at Fort Point, as it was known by then—needed only to be altered for the lenses to fit. But it was not going to be that easy at Point Conception or Farallon Island.

On South Farallon, the crew had quarried the brittle rock and hauled stones up to the site 315 feet above the

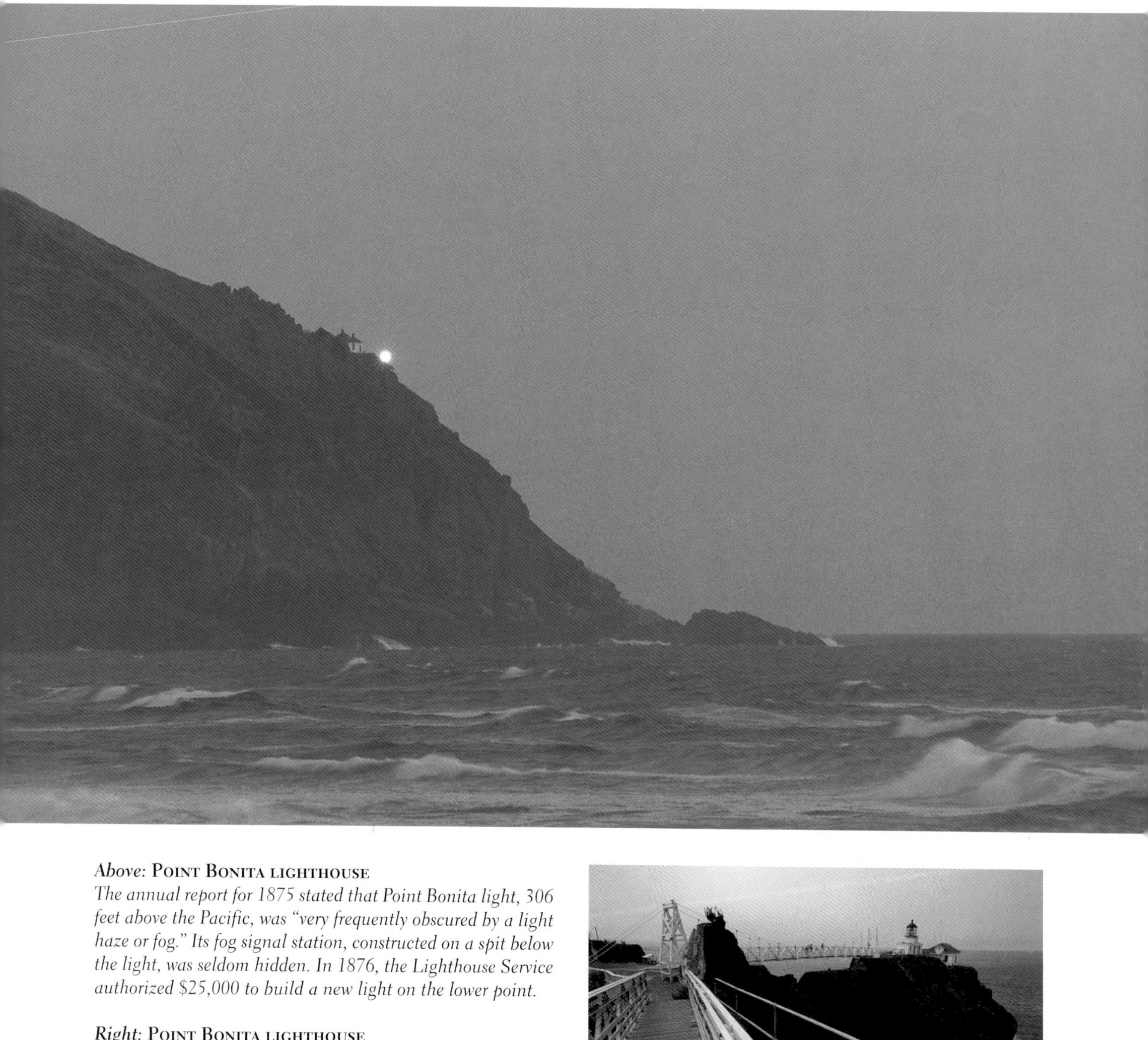

Above: **Point Bonita lighthouse**
The annual report for 1875 stated that Point Bonita light, 306 feet above the Pacific, was "very frequently obscured by a light haze or fog." Its fog signal station, constructed on a spit below the light, was seldom hidden. In 1876, the Lighthouse Service authorized $25,000 to build a new light on the lower point.

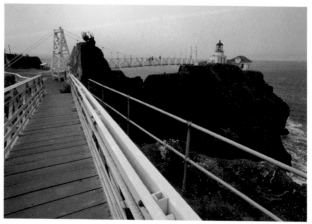

Right: **Point Bonita lighthouse**
Building the Point Bonita lighthouse was one of the West Coast's trickier engineering and building feats. It required flattening a rock, digging a tunnel 118 feet long, and stretching a narrow rock bridge across a chasm to reach the rock. In 1954, the land bridge fell, and the Coast Guard built the suspension bridge.

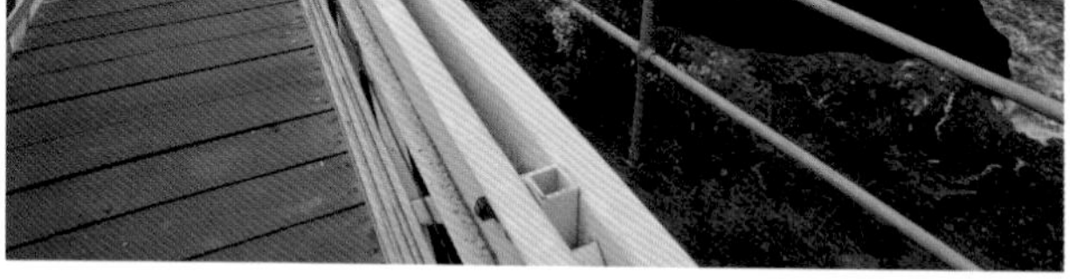

Lighthouse Fuels

Guiding mariners towards safe harbors using the light from a fire is a centuries-old practice. The earliest known "lighthouse," a tower on the Egyptian island of Pharos, reportedly stood 450 feet tall, lasted more than 1,000 years, and burned wood. Due to wood's short burn time, Egyptian light keepers spent most of their time chopping and carrying wood to feed the insatiable fire that led mariners to the city of Alexandria. Historians and archaeologists have found examples of other early lighthouses in Italy and France. Regretfully, the Dark Ages destroyed the vestiges of most of them.

With the dawn of the Middle Ages, sea commerce was re-established and wood-burning lighthouses were reborn. Eventually, however, the wood supply for lighthouse fuel ran short, and technicians were forced to search for a new fuel.

Coal was discovered to burn at a consistent brightness and produce quality light, but problems occurred when the heat generated by the fire melted coal grates. Worse, coal produced so much warmth that in summer rooms became too hot for keepers to tend the fires. The search began for a fuel that would be easy to work with, create a bright light, and put out little or no heat. Theory suggested that liquid fuel was the answer, but the question was, how do you successfully burn a liquid?

In the mid-1700s, John Smeaton found the answer. His lamp used a small bowl of whale oil with a series of wicks rising from the middle. This lamp-and-fuel combination produced quality light and virtually no heat, but it also produced gray smoke and a terrible aroma. Despite these drawbacks, it was used in American lighthouses until 1810.

Swiss inventor Ami Argand improved upon earlier lamps by using a hollow wick that drew oxygen up through it, which produced a virtually smokeless, brighter flame. American Winslow Lewis combined the Argand lamp with his newly patented parabolic reflector and was able to boost a 7-candlepower Argand lamp to 2,450 candlepower.

The whale-oil-burning Argand lamps in Winslow Lewis's reflectors appeared to be an ideal solution: They were easy to use and inexpensive. Unfortunately, the low cost wouldn't last. As supplies of whale oil dropped, prices increased. While the fuel sold for $.55 gallon in 1841, it doubled by 1847 to $1.07. By 1854, the price had reached $1.38.

When William B. Shubrick became Lighthouse Board chairman in 1854, one of his priorities was to solve the fuel problem. He recognized that the cost of whale oil would continue to rise, and in his annual financial report, he recommended that U.S. lights burn colza oil, also known as rapeseed. (Today, colza oil is found in the common canola cooking oil.) If Congress could convince U.S. farmers to grow colza, Shubrick surmised that it would help reduce the government's dependency on foreign markets, and it "would be a great boon to the country as well as a source of profit to the producers." American farmers got the message, and the Board purchased 12,000 gallons of U.S.-produced colza oil in 1862.

Regretfully, U.S. colza production could not keep pace with lighthouse needs, and once again the Board went looking for a new fuel solution. This time it did not have to look far. Board member Joseph Henry had been experimenting with lard oil. He had little success until he pre-heated the oil before trying to light it. The resulting light burned brightly, produced little smoke, and unlike colza, lard was in great supply and was inexpensive. Once again, lighthouses were converted to burn a new fuel: By 1867, all U.S. large-order lenses were fueled by lard.

In its constant search for high-quality fuel, the Board began experiments in 1870 with mineral oil (today called kerosene). Mineral oil is extremely volatile and must be handled and stored with caution. Unlike whale oil, however, mineral oil burns well at all temperatures; unlike lard, it does not need to be preheated. Beginning in 1878, the Board began to exchange lard burners for kerosene lamps in small-order lenses. This conversion process was slow; mineral-oil lamps had to be built, transported to lighthouse depots, delivered to lighthouses, and installed during quarterly inspections by engineers. Five years after the conversion began, the first large lens to receive a kerosene lamp, New Jersey's first-order Navesink lighthouse, was finally lit by mineral oil in 1883.

Lighthouses also tried burning other combustible fuels. In 1803, Cape Hatteras, North Carolina, was authorized to use porpoise oil, and Christina light near Wilmington, Delaware, burned a gas made from rosin in 1844. Researchers also experimented with combustible magnesium obtained by the electrolysis of magnesium chloride, which is found in great quantity in seawater. The resulting flame produced a brilliant white glare but burned up too quickly.

As early as 1880, lighthouse researchers began experimenting with electricity. The lighthouse at Hell Gate, New York, was first switched on in 1884; it cost $11,000 to build and used nine electric lights. The 6,000-candlepower lights were intended to illuminate the dangerous channel, but instead, they blinded ship pilots and created heavy shadows that were mistaken for obstacles. After two years, the light was turned off, and the lighthouse was dismantled and sold for scrap.

The Board had better luck with the Statue of Liberty. On November 7, 1886, the Statue was turned over to the Board for use as a navigational beacon. The nine electric lights in the torch were 305 feet above sea level and could be seen from sea 24.5 miles away. At that height, the light went over most New York Harbor ships and did not blind the captains. Despite its success, it would be several more years before electricity became the staple of America's lighthouses.

water. The rock rose so quickly that its entire ascent was 45 degrees or steeper. The serpentine path to the summit required more than 400 steps that the crew had to chop into the stone. On the summit, they piled stones and mortared them together for the foundation and tower. They hauled bricks out to the island and rowed them ashore. They carried them up to the site four or five at a time, and set them, one layer deep, around the entire stone tower. They followed architect Ammi Young's plans for the tower, but, as they had done at Cape Disappointment, they left the keepers' houses below in the island's only slightly sheltered cove.

The Fresnel arrived in seventy-three cases, and only after technicians began to assemble it at the Farallon tower did they see the problem. The largest Fresnel lenses measured slightly more than six feet wide and twelve feet tall. The workers had built a tower of thousands of carefully placed bricks to house the slightly smaller Lewis parabolic reflectors. The tower was too narrow to provide clearance for the rotating mechanisms of the Fresnel, and its lantern room was too short to fit the lens. It took another year for the builders to dismantle their brickwork and rebuild the tower. To restore morale among the Farallon workers and ease their labor, Bache bought them a mule to haul bricks and mortar up the rock. Shubrick protested the mule's expense but Bache argued him down.

The major reached Point Conception on August 31, a year after Timanus had constructed a stout stone tower meant to withstand winds of more than 100 miles per hour. But like Farallon, it was too small for its Fresnel. Using dimensions Bache derived for the Farallon lens, work crews dismantled the original tower and built a wider one to accommodate the light.

Bache stopped in Santa Barbara to inspect an available site but quickly rejected it because a bluff to the north would block the light. Within a few weeks, the town donated thirty acres beside the harbor for a more suitable location. At San Pedro harbor 150 miles further south, Bache overruled the Coast Survey's recommendation that proposed building on the bluff. Bache relocated the light, at a sixty-foot lens height, on the point that protruded 1,400 feet further out to sea and provided a larger arc of visibility.

He reached Point Loma on September 5, 1855, as Timanus's brick masons were enlarging the tower to fit the Fresnel. But even this concerned him: "The dwelling is of stone," he wrote in his report to Shubrick, "and,

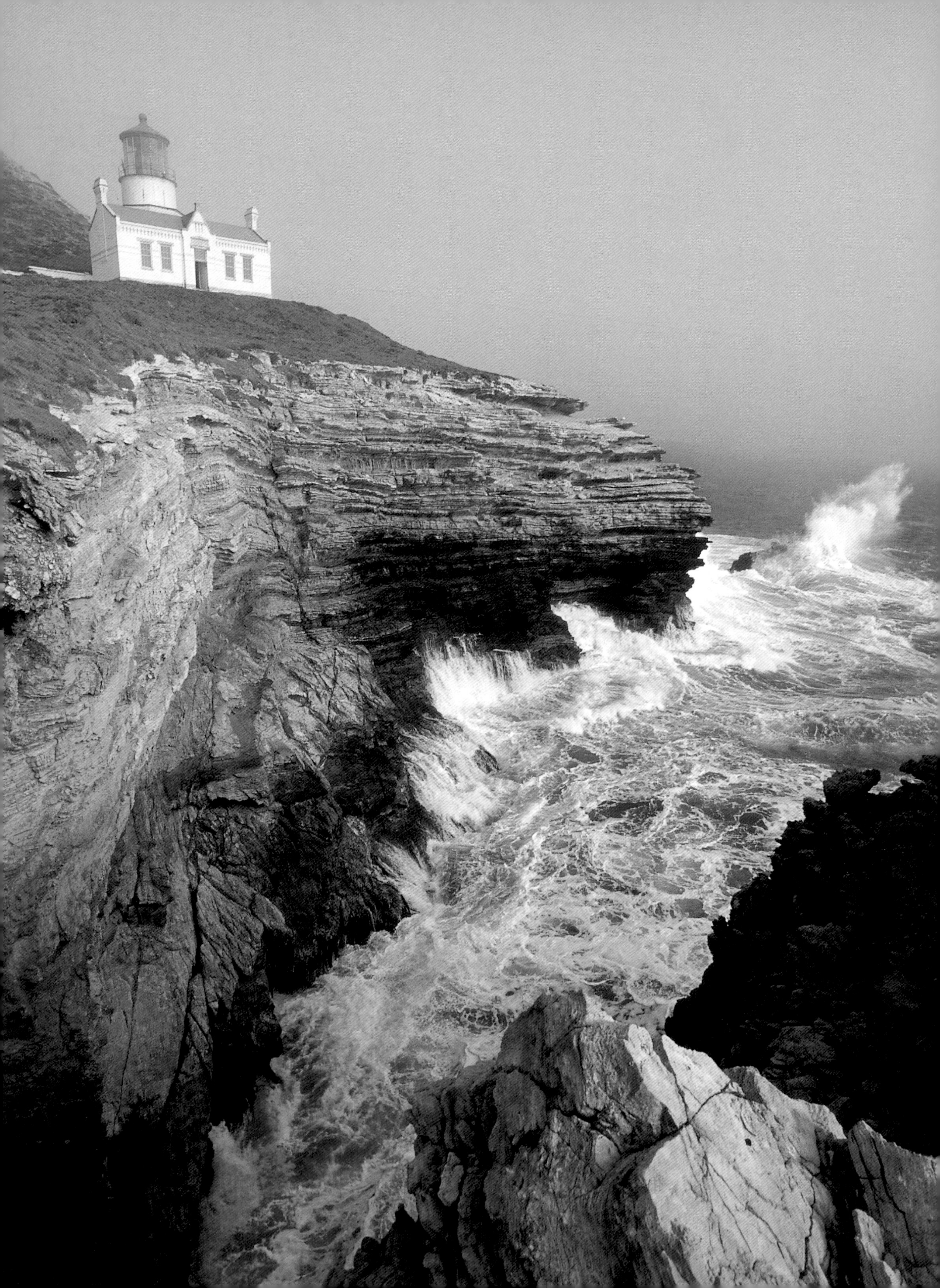

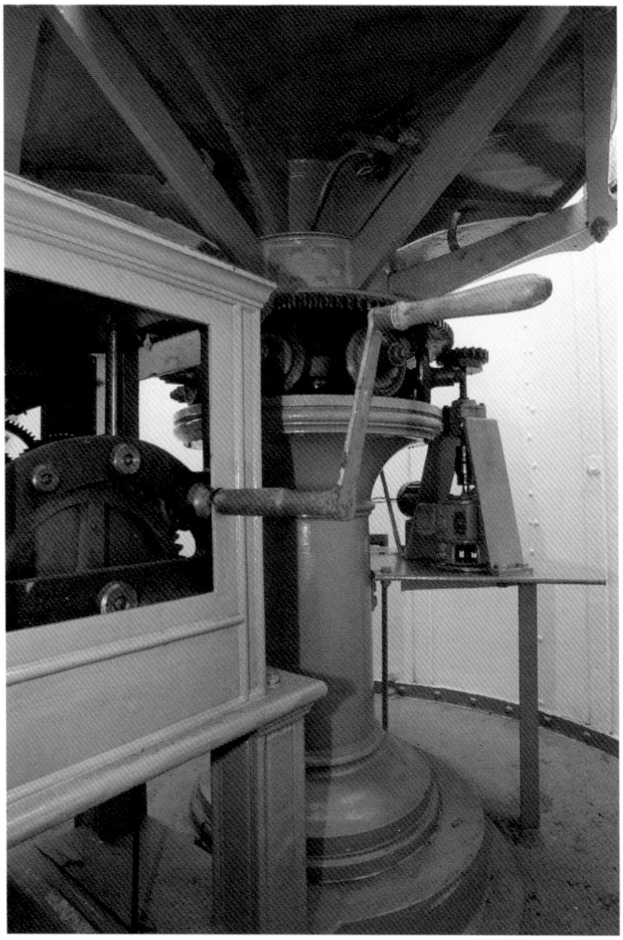

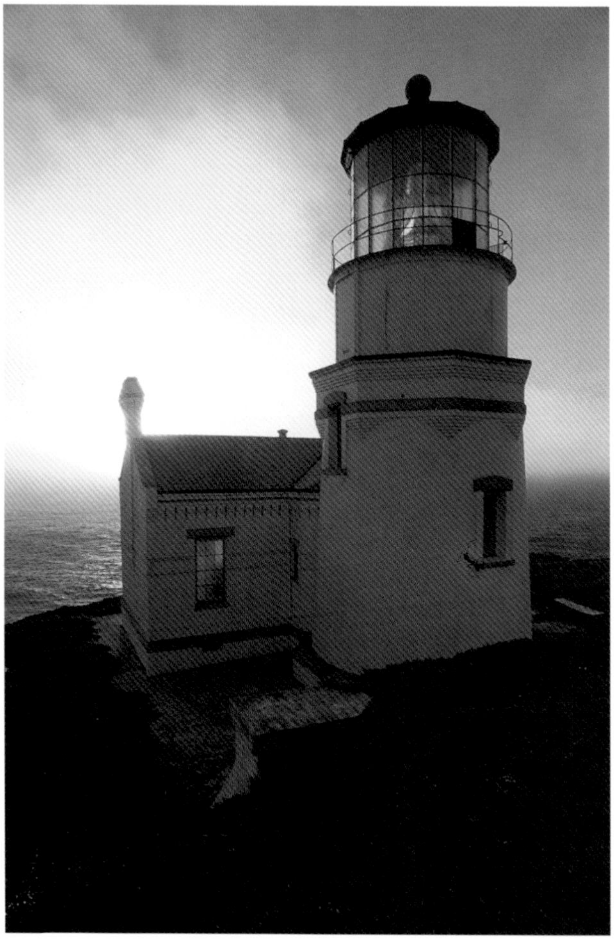

Above, left: Point Conception lighthouse
The original LePaute clockwork mechanism remains in place in the lantern room, with its cable crank nearby to wind the counterweight up to rotate the lens. Behind it is the Coast Guard's 110-volt motor and reduction-gear drive system that turns the lens today.

Above, right: Point Conception lighthouse
Designed for Winslow Lewis's parabolic reflector lights, the original 1854 Cape Cod–style lighthouse was rebuilt to fit its first-order Fresnel. Keeper George Parkinson first lit the LePaute lens in February 1856. The lighthouse was rebuilt again in 1881, replaced with this granite, brick, and stucco building.

Facing page: Point Conception lighthouse
This light is located at the north end of the Santa Barbara channel, where two currents collide and wind and tides combine to create a spot sometimes called the Cape Horn of the Pacific. Point Conception's tower stood 52 feet tall. It still uses its original Henry LePaute first-order Fresnel that sits 133 feet above sea level.

with the exception of the mortar, which is very bad, is quite a creditable piece of work. The tower is of brick. The mortar is not only bad, but the brick itself is of such poor quality, that in places they have wasted away to a depth of a quarter of an inch." Timanus's crew may have been exhausted from the pace of 180-days-straight work, and may have tried to save time by using ocean water for the mortar, although this is pure speculation.

By the time Bache reached Point Loma, Gibbons and Kelly had spent $29,115 to build the structure, and claimed that $13,964 went to the unanticipated transportation and road-construction costs. Now they faced widening the tower to fit the lens, replacing half the bricks and all the mortar. After all its complex construction problems, Point Loma required simple modifications to house its Fresnel compared to other stations. Head keeper James Keating lit its third-order lens for the first time on November 15, 1855.

On his way back to San Francisco, Bache saw Point Pinos in late September 1855. When he realized how far the lighthouse was from the water and that trees and bluffs affected its visibility, he resolved to take part in every lighthouse site selection from then on.

All along the coast, lighthouses went up and lights went on. Point Bonita was Graham's experiment with local services. San Francisco contractors built it using area laborers and materials. The high, windy bluff selected by the Coast Survey suggested to Graham a detached tower, similar to Cape Disappointment and Farallon. He told his contractor to build the houses below the summit to be kinder to the keepers. Construction proceeded on schedule, and on April 30, 1855, John Wolf lit the second-order Fresnel.

Timanus constructed a replacement tower at South Farallon Island. It stood forty-one feet tall, and on January 1, 1856, head keeper Nerva Wines lit the Fresnel there for the first time.

A month after Farallon and a year after Point Pinos, George Parkinson lit his first-order lens at Point Conception on February 1, 1856. Then eight months later, on October 15, John Boyd lit Cape Disappointment, and nine weeks after that, on December 20, D. M. Pierce saw his light first shine from Humboldt Bay.

Building the Second Group of Lights

The number of lighthouses along the Pacific shoreline doubled in 1858. The last of the first eight lighthouses had been lit in 1856; a second group of eight now added their lights to the coastline.

Most of the second group followed the architectural plan that Timanus and Mahon brought west with them, although the duo did not build any more. George D. Nagle constructed the Santa Barbara light, the ninth completed, for a reasonable $8,000. The first keeper, Albert J. Williams, lit the fourth-order light on December 1, 1856.

On December 8, 1856, Theophilus Magruder and his wife moved in to the Cape Cod house at Crescent

Point Conception lighthouse
Two large rooms flank the entry hallway. This workroom contains the original fireplace and a massive bookcase anchored to the lighthouse, and houses the National Oceanographic and Atmospheric Administration (NOAA) weather reporting station, which operates out of a portable computer case.

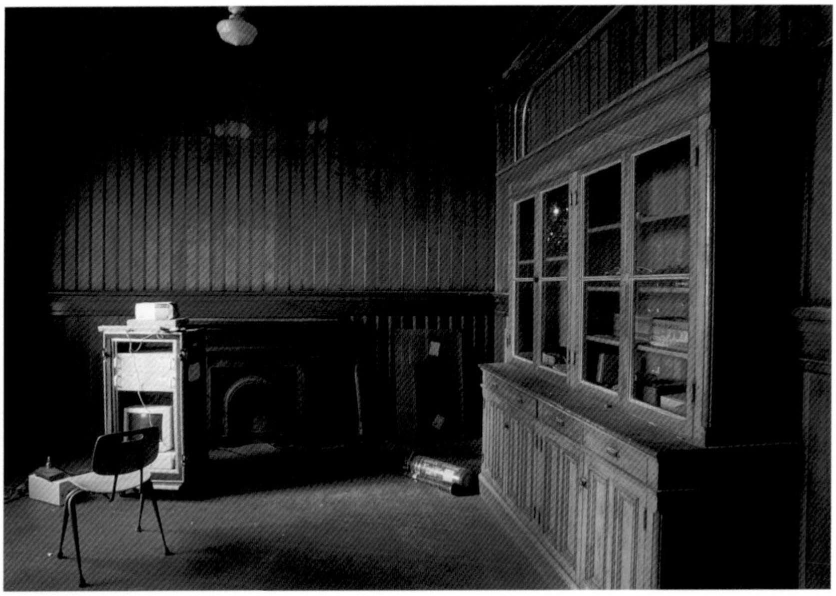

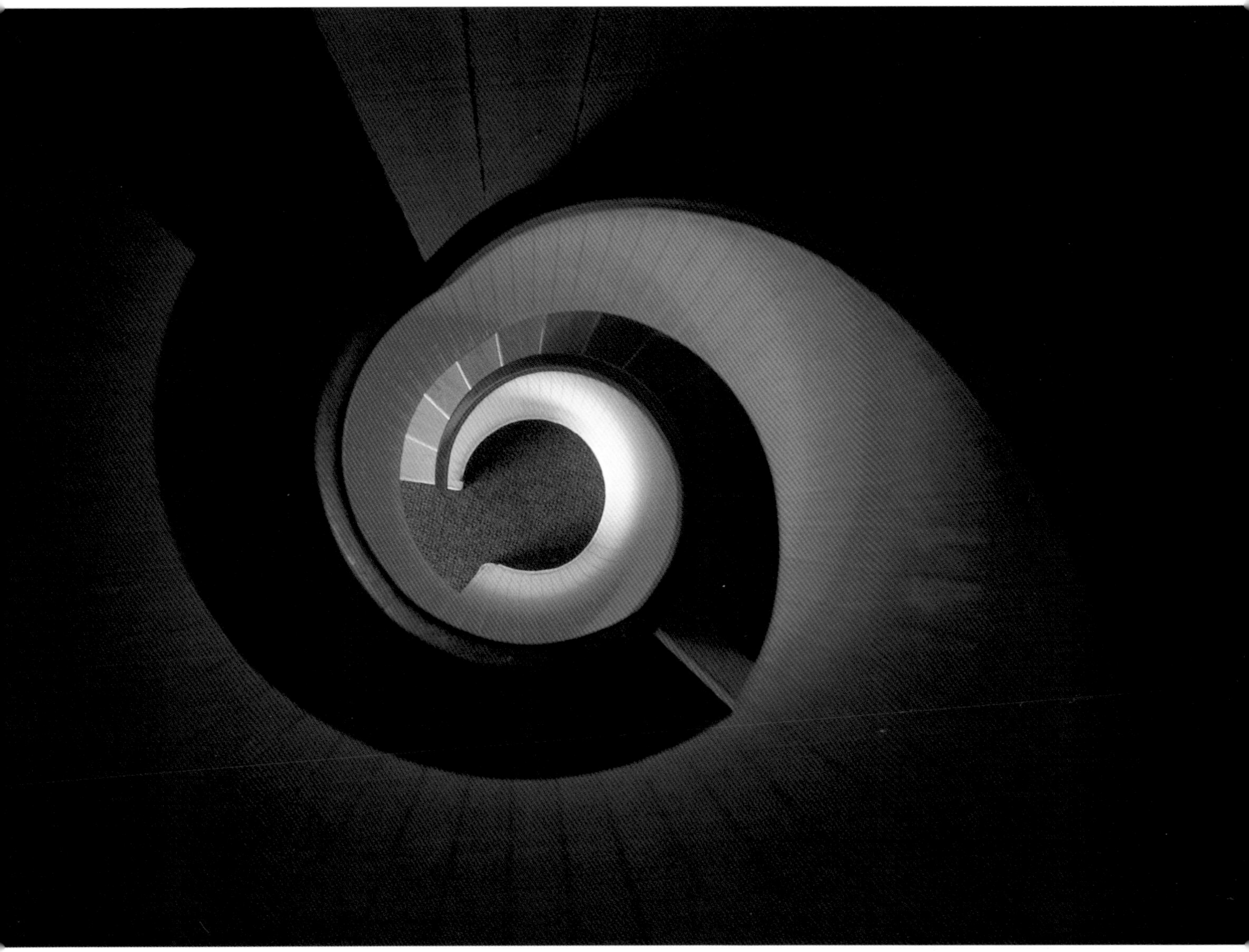

Old Point Loma lighthouse
Architect Ammi Young was an artist, at least in some ways. From this view, the eight-foot-diameter tower stairway resembles the spirals of a nautilus. Each of Young's small Cape Cods used narrow towers to minimize building costs and maximize use of often-cramped building sites.

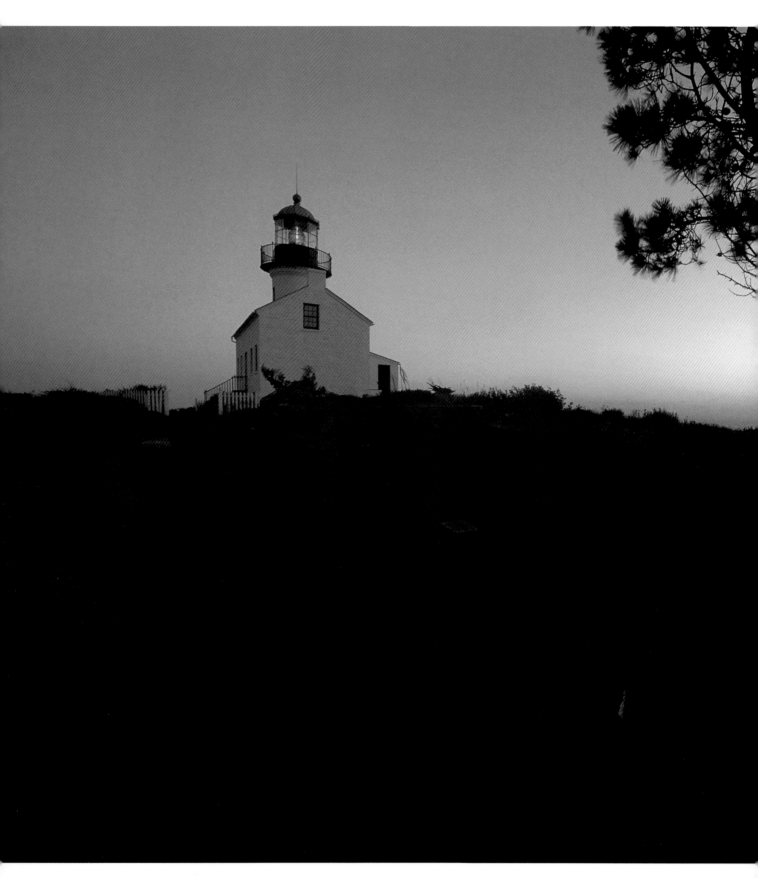

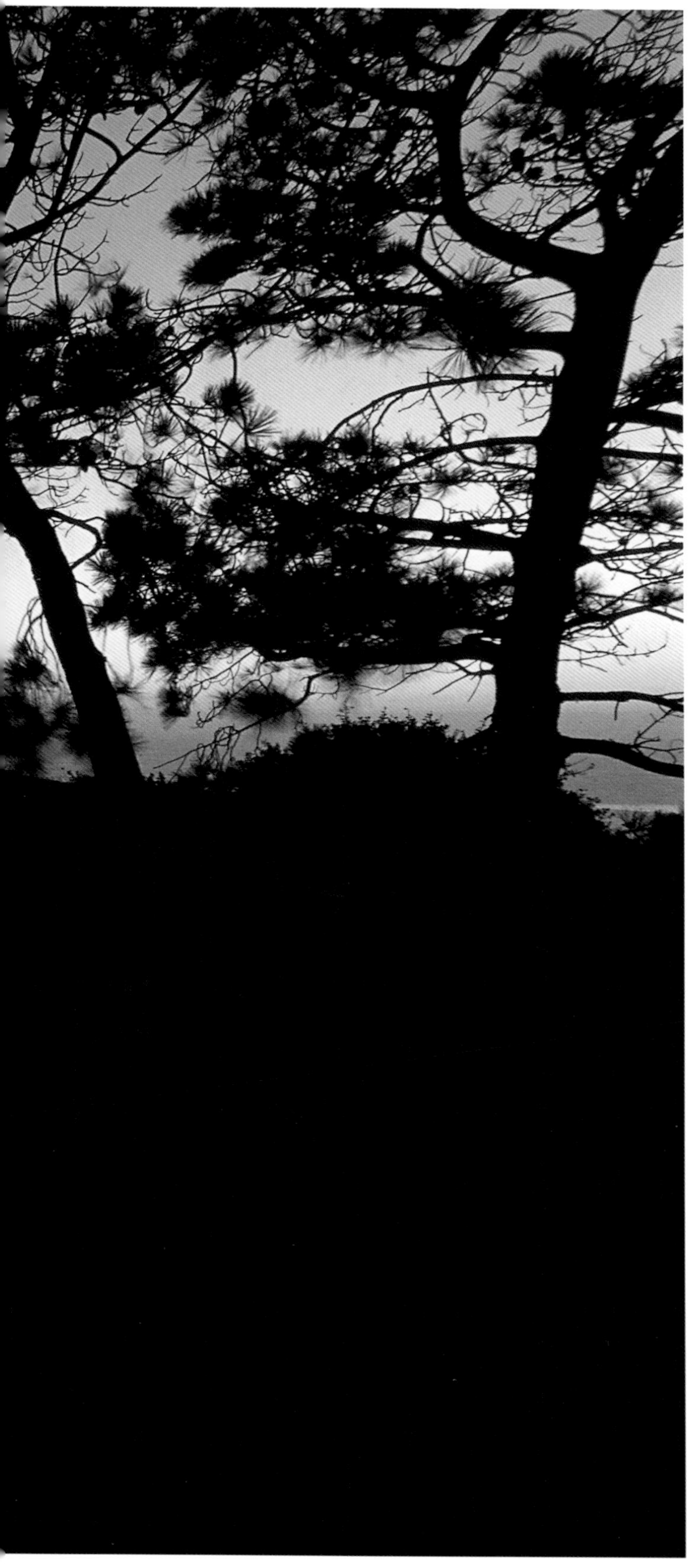

Old Point Loma lighthouse

Old Point Loma lighthouse was another instance where Coast Survey staff misjudged weather conditions—easy to do on an evening such as this one. Normally, the top of the 422-foot rock is shrouded in fog or haze, rendering this lighthouse useless to mariners trying to find San Diego harbor. Operated now as Cabrillo National Monument within the National Park Service, a standard sixty-watt bulb competes with the setting sun.

Lighthouse Costs

A $15,000 lighthouse built between 1850 and 1900 would cost some $300,000 to construct today, based on figures adjusted for inflation. A $3,810 Sautter third-order Fresnel lens in 1855 would be $76,200 today. A LePaute first-order at $6,600, built by French school children making a penny an hour, would cost $132,000 today—if you could find children willing to work for 20 pennies per hour today.

It's fascinating to know what something cost 150 years ago. But unless there's a way to calculate what inflation has done to the dollar, it's only idle speculation. For the purposes of the West Coast lighthouses described in this book, the curious reader can calculate rough modern-day-equivalent prices by multiplying the figures from 1850–1900 by an accepted factor of 20. So, a New York City factory worker making $1 a day in 1848 would earn $20 today, but those harvesting gold from the American River brought out $15 to $16 worth of nuggets and dust each day, worth $300 to $320 per day now.

To understand the history of West Coast lighthouses, it's also informative to see when costs really began to spiral upward. By 1939, when the Coast Guard assumed control of all lighthouses, the factor had changed considerably. A $1,000 automobile in 1939 would cost $11,765 today. By 1950, inflation had rendered a $1 lunch into $6.80 today. So when you read that St. George's Reef Lighthouse was the most expensive built in the United States at $704,000 in 1891, that same project today would cost $14,080,000.

City, California. A native of Washington, D.C., Magruder, came west in 1843 with carpenter James Marshall to find gold. Working as Johan Sutter's contractor to build his mill, Marshall succeeded, while Magruder settled in Crescent City and married. Two days after Magruder occupied the keeper's house, he lit the fourth-order Fresnel, the first in the United States manufactured by Barbier, Bernard & Tirenne of Paris.

Oregon Territorial governor Joseph Lane pushed Congress for a lighthouse at the Umpqua River mouth after the Coast Survey's recommendation in 1849. The river collided with Pacific tides and surf, creating conditions similar to the Golden Gate and Columbia River mouth. Congress authorized $15,000 for an Umpqua light in August 1852 but diverted the money to East Coast projects. A second infusion of nearly $10,000 came in August 1854. The following fall, the $120,000 general appropriation earmarked for lighthouse cost overruns finally got $19,942 to Umpqua, and crews began work in late summer 1856.

Unfortunately, Coast Surveyors never saw the Umpqua at flood stage. Wanting to avoid the Point Pinos error, they set the Umpqua light near the river bank to serve both as a coast light and river marker. As early as 1856, spring runoff from Oregon's Cascade Mountains suggested trouble, however, and fall and winter storms drove ocean breakers onto the riverbanks. Builders worked around the high water, and after a second wet spring and another $5,055 to strengthen foundations and the seawall, they finished the structure. Keeper Fayette Crosby lit the third-order lens on October 10, 1857.

Each storm challenged the Umpqua lighthouse and its niney-two-foot-high tower. On February 8, 1861, a coastal gale coincided with record mountain runoff; the river flooded, backing up against the confused, swirling surf from the ocean storm. This badly undermined the lighthouse foundation, and the house and tower tilted slightly. The light remained in service, but another severe storm in October 1863 did enough additional damage that in late January 1864, the Board ordered the tower abandoned and the Fresnel removed. A week later, literally within hours of clearing out the lens apparatus, the tower shuddered and fell over.

Despite a proven need for a lighthouse at the Umpqua, the Board replaced it with a floating buoy and ordered a new light built at Cape Arago, about twenty-five miles south. It took another twenty-four years to replace the Umpqua light; in 1888, the Board appropriated $50,000 to purchase land farther inland for a new station.

Captain George Vancouver, who explored the Pacific Coast in the late 1700s, named New Dungeness spit because it reminded him of Dungeness Point on England's southeast coast, where a lighthouse was built in 1746. A century later, in 1849, the Coast Survey designated the six-mile-long Oregon Territory spit as a site for a lighthouse.

Funding was appropriated in 1853 and construction began in 1854. A large Cape Cod duplex cottage took shape, its foundation and walls built of sandstone and its 100-foot-tall tower wrapped with a sheath of bricks. As construction neared completion, it became apparent to Seattle's customs collector that the designated first keeper, William Henry Blake, wouldn't reach New Dungeness in time as his departure from San Francisco was delayed until February 1858. The collector temporarily hired Franklin Tucker as head keeper to light the Fresnel on December 14, 1857.

Blake arrived in late February 1858, and established a routine of walking to town for supplies, a sixteen-mile round-trip journey. On one of his trips, he met Mary Ann McDonnell, who lived with her father on the spit's shore end. Blake's walks became more frequent. Following a courtship that lasted nearly four years, Blake married Mary Ann in 1862.

In the late 1780s, Oregon Territory fur trader John Meares visited the island at the Olympic Peninsula's tip, where the Makah tribe's Chief Tatooche entertained him and his sailors. Meares named the island after the chief as it was the summer home to about 150 Makah who fished and harvested whales from a harbor on its east shore.

Coast Surveyor William McArthur recommended sixteen-acre Tatoosh Island for a light in 1849. When Topographical Surveyor George Davidson arrived in 1850 to pinpoint the site, he agreed to a settlement with the Makah for rights to use the island. Surveyors visited the island annually while awaited funding, but when construction supervisor Isaac Smith arrived with his crew in 1855, the Makah had grown impatient. Frustrated by the government's unresponsiveness, tribal members visited Tatoosh Island frequently during the eighteen months it took to construct the lighthouse and other buildings; they often interrupted progress and sometimes took building materials to force payment. Smith's first completed building was a blockhouse he used as a bunkhouse for his crew. He received twenty muskets from the Lighthouse Board, but while the Makah continued to use the island each summer, Smith's crew worked without serious trouble from the natives.

Smith built a Cape Cod house with a sixty-five-foot-tall tower rising from its center, a duplex similar to New Dungeness. This large light required a head keeper and three assistants, who lived in a community Smith constructed. They lit the first-order Sautter Fresnel on December 28, 1857.

Whereas the Santa Barbara lighthouse came in $7,000 under its $15,000 appropriation, the Cape Flattery light on Tatoosh Island was one of the most costly at $36,000—about $720,000 today, adjusted for inflation. This was nearly the entire sum Congress had allocated to build the three lights at Cape Flattery, New Dungeness, and Cape Disappointment.

The first decade of active Pacific navigation aids ended with lighthouses at Oregon's Willapa Bay (also known as Cape Shoalwater) lit on October 1, 1858, and seventeen days later at Smith's Island (formerly called Blunt's Island) at the east end of the Strait of Juan de Fuca.

Sixteen Pacific Coast lights were in place. The ocean that explorer Ferdinand Magellan named *Mare Pacificum* in 1521 had revealed a different personality to mariners who followed in his wake and to lighthouse keepers who marked the way. Magellan's "Peaceful Sea" toppled one lighthouse and wrapped two others in near-perpetual fog.

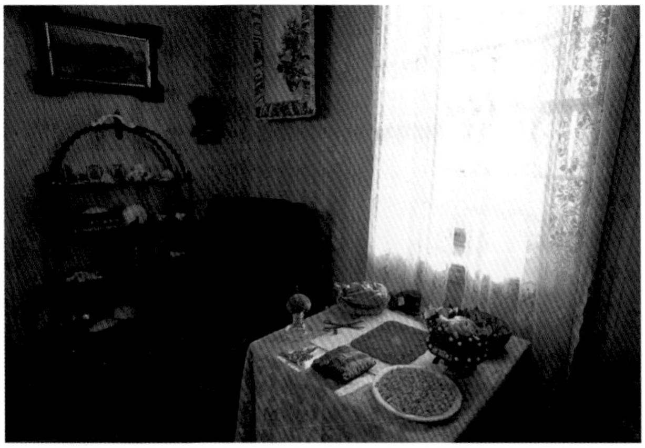

Old Point Loma lighthouse
A bookshelf boasts seashells, starfish, and urchins the Israels' sons and niece found below the lighthouse. Maria Israel used hundreds of smaller shells to decorate picture frames she made and sold in San Diego.

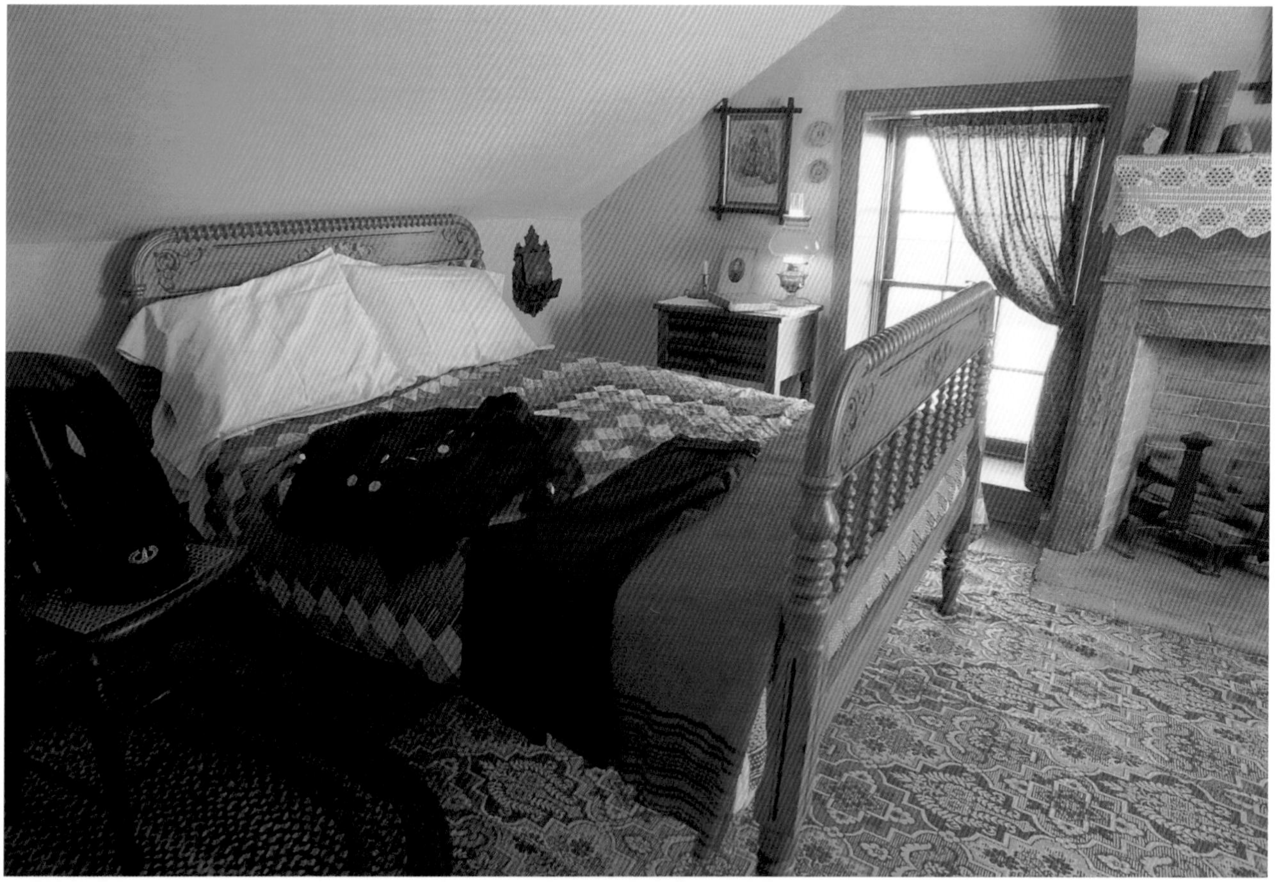

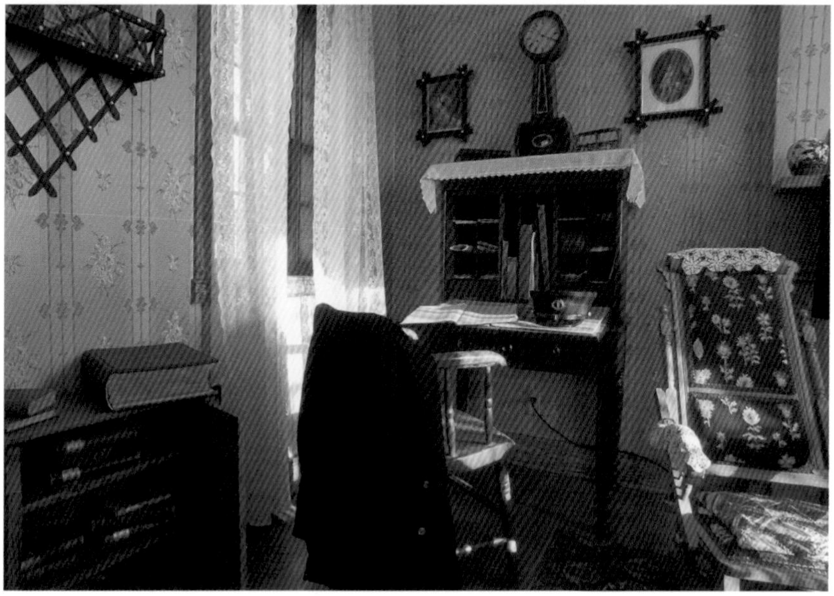

Above: **Old Point Loma lighthouse**
As though ready for work, Robert Israel's head keeper's heavy blue wool uniform lays on his bed. The USLHE provided keepers with most of their furniture, although the families always personalized their homes. Artist Maria Israel created images, some using seashells and others with woven human hair, popular techniques in the late 1800s.

Left: **Old Point Loma lighthouse**
Robert Israel was head keeper in the 1880s. He lived here with his wife, Maria, their two sons, and a niece. Concerned about keepers' boredom, the USLHE circulated forty- to sixty-book libraries in boxes similar to the one in the photo's lower left. Point Loma is now operated by the National Park Service, which carefully restored the 1855 residence to 1880 standards.

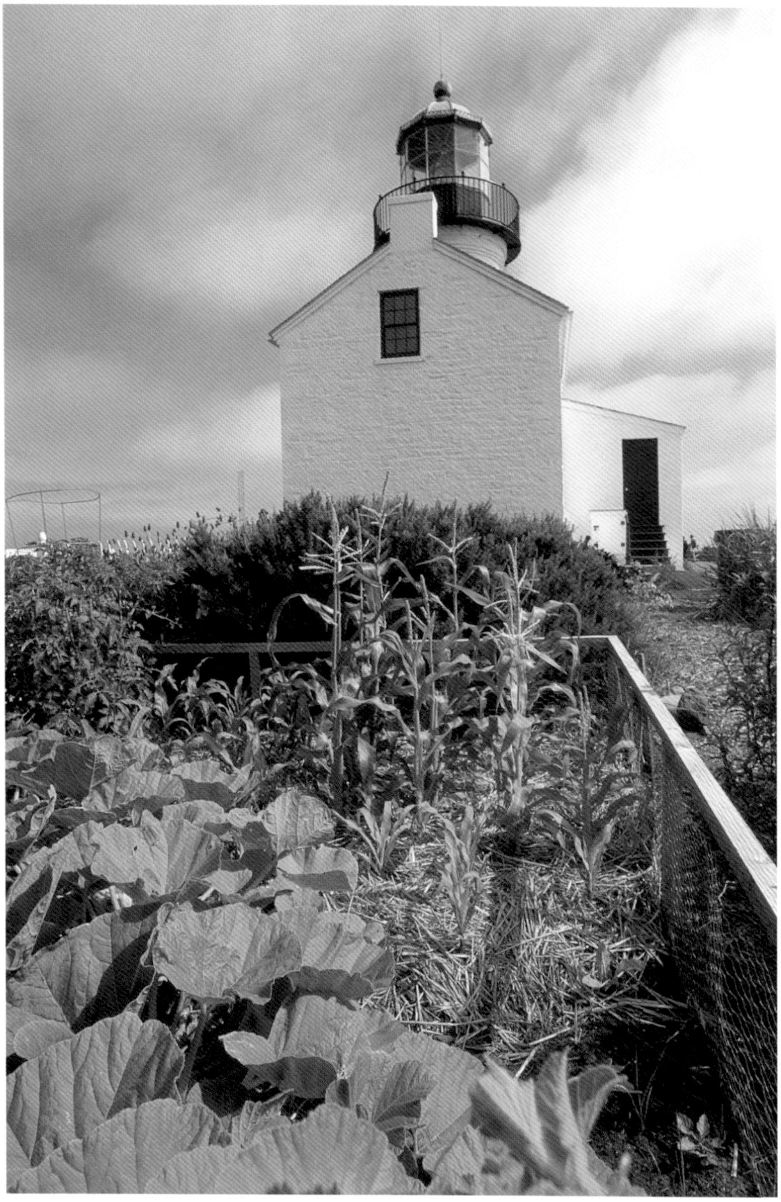

Old Point Loma lighthouse

To some extent keepers were also farmers, or at least on hard rocks like Point Loma, they had to be kitchen-garden tenders. The old light, restored to 1880s standards, boasts a healthy garden of corn, tomatoes, and zucchini.

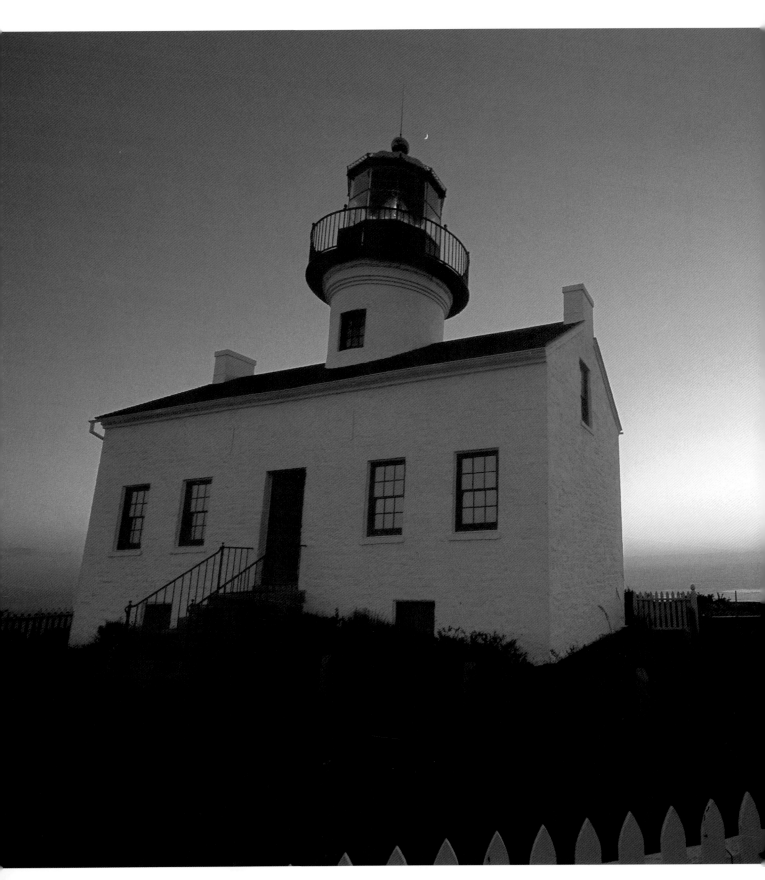

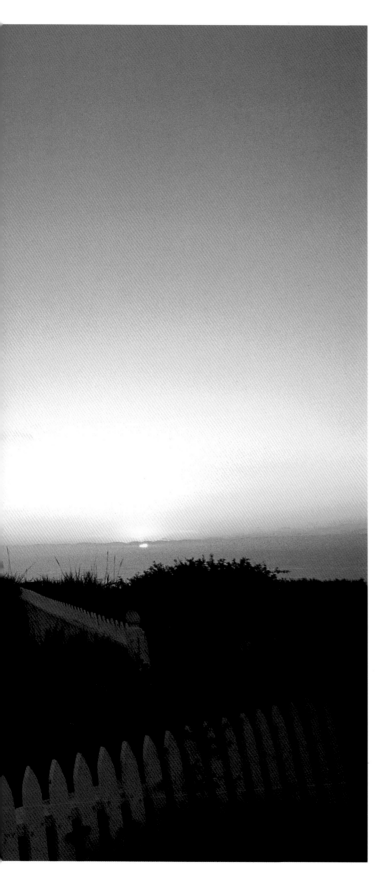

Old Point Loma lighthouse
A crescent moon tops the conical roof of the lighthouse as the sun sets in late summer. Typical of the first sixteen lighthouses built on the West Coast, the architecture is Cape Cod cottage. To keep the job quick and simple for the hurried builders, one standardized design was used.

New Dungeness light station
The old adage is "Red sky at night, sailor's delight; red sky in morning, sailor take warning." Just as there are exceptions to every rule, so was this sunrise over the Strait of Juan de Fuca. Washington's Mount Baker, some ninety miles to the east, looms over New Dungeness Spit's light.

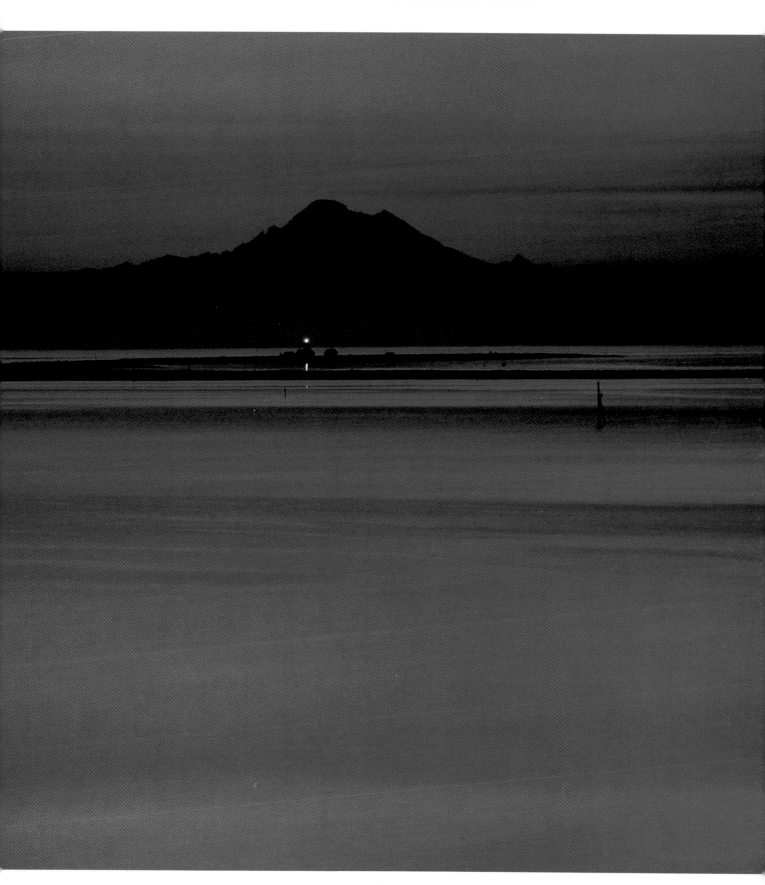

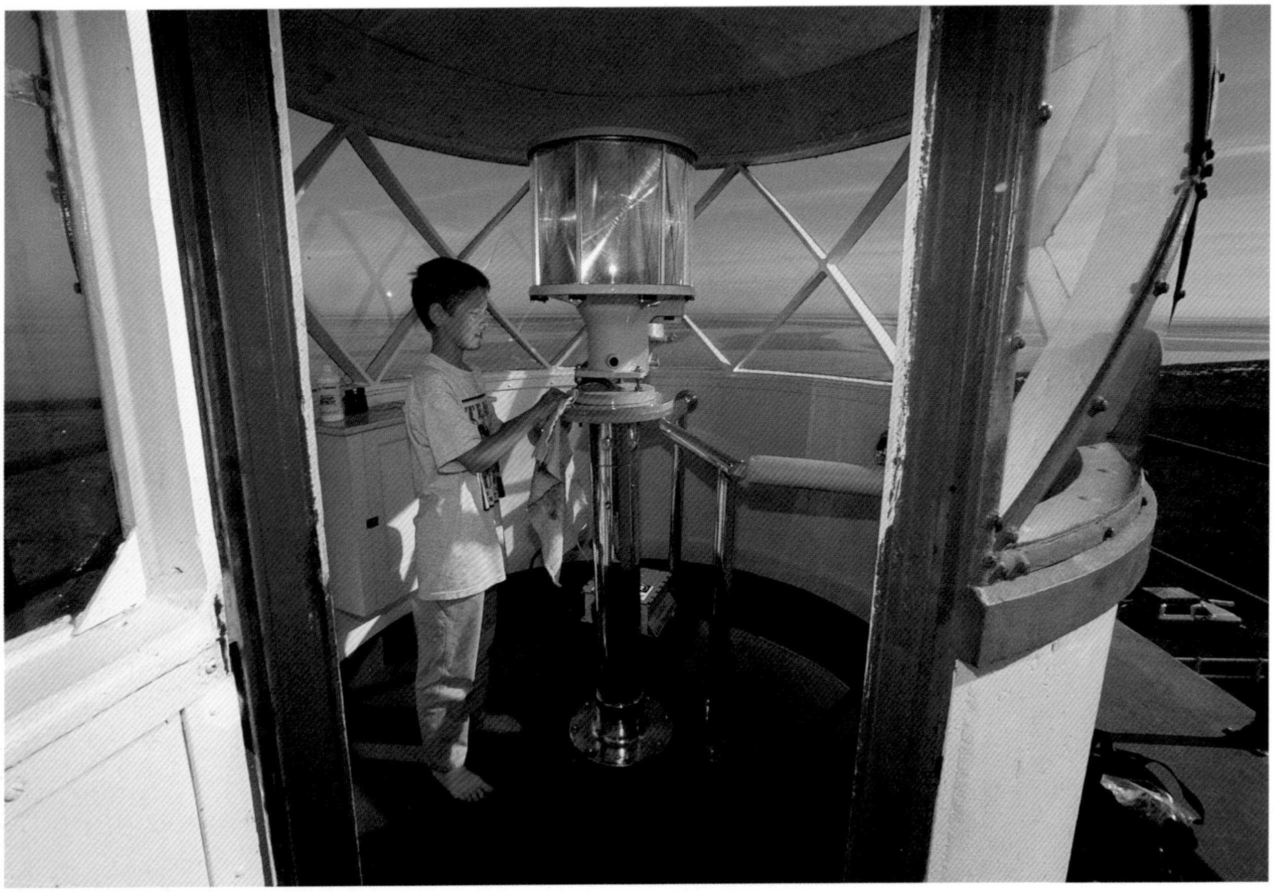

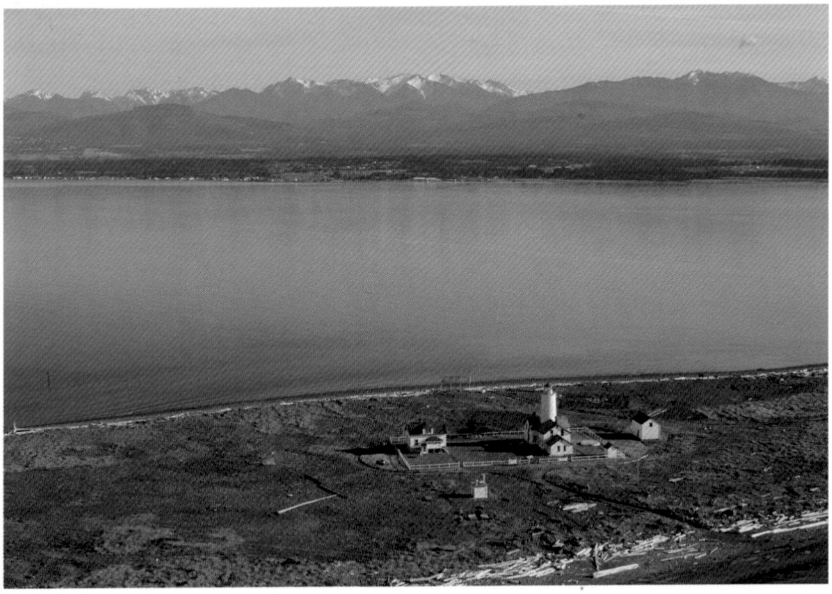

Above: **New Dungeness light station**
Membership has its rewards. U.S. Lighthouse Society members can spend a week at New Dungeness, mowing the lawn, painting walls, or doing other chores. Access is a long walk, six-and-a-half miles out to the light. Ten-year-old Dylan Jenkins, of Crestline, California, joined his grandparents, who assigned him the brass-polishing detail.

Left: **New Dungeness light station**
Located near the northeast end of the long spit, New Dungeness remains an archetypal light station. Seen here from the air, its barn and small oil storage shed behind the light still stand. Behind the head keeper's residence, the fog signal awaits use. Across Dungeness Bay are Washington's Olympic Mountains.

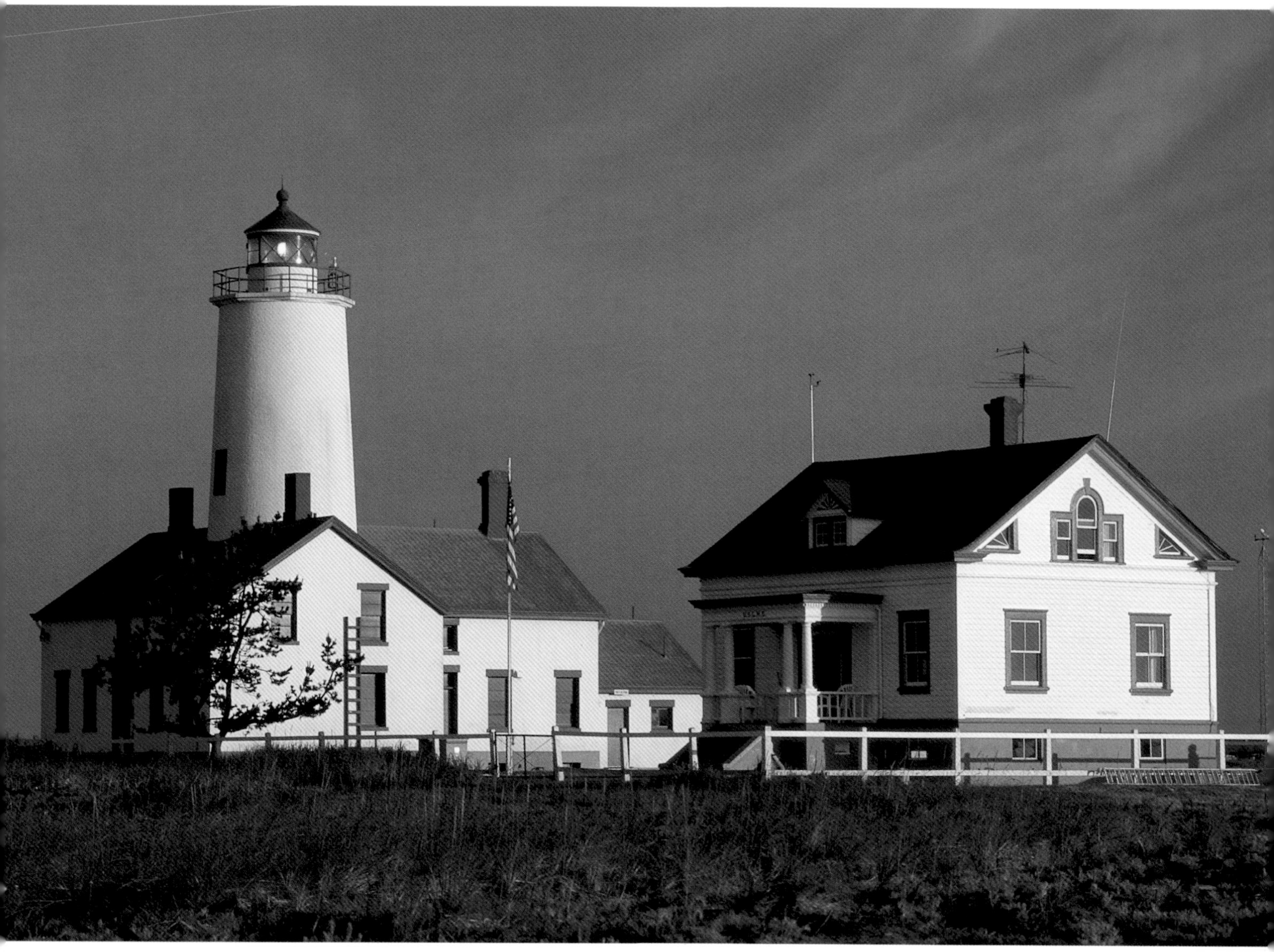

New Dungeness light station
The variation on Ammi Young's architectural plan was this larger duplex lighthouse, similar to the one on Cape Flattery. The duplex lighthouse was completed in 1857, and the head keeper and assistant shared the house until the separate residence was completed in 1904. A typical head keeper's home, it has attic window details missing in the assistant's housing.

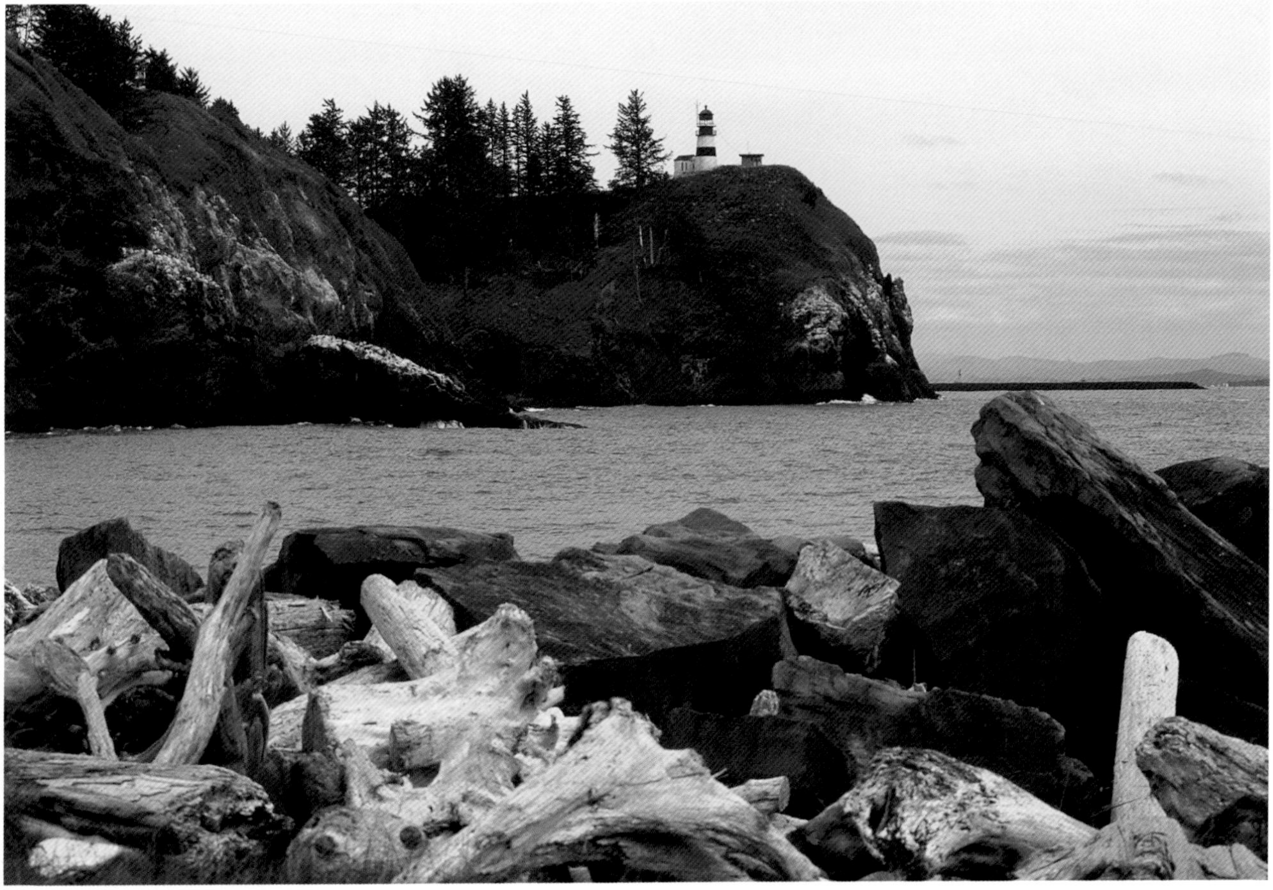

Cape Disappointment lighthouse
Cape Disappointment is the West Coast's only lighthouse with "day markings," the bold black horizontal stripes that are more characteristic of East Coast lights. Because of the high bluff it sits on, its stripes set it off from the frequently white sky behind it and the dark trees surrounding it. Cape Disappointment's evocative name was well earned. In 1775, Portuguese explorer Bruno Heceta searched for the River of the West, a supposed sea route from the Atlantic. He and John Meares, a British navigator sailing in 1788, both believed the Columbia River to be only a large bay. Meares named the high bluff to reflect his frustration.

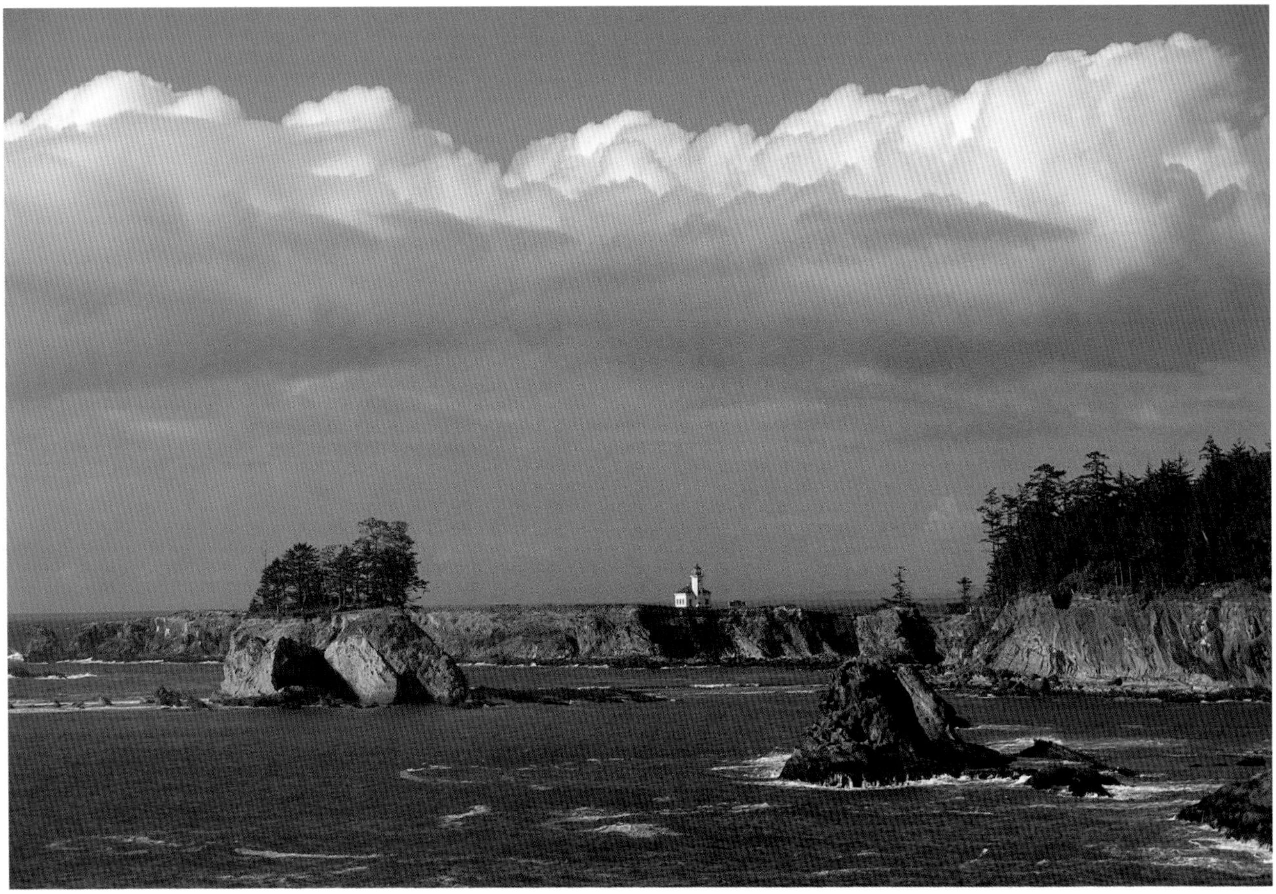

Cape Arago lighthouse
First lit in November 1866, Cape Arago was Oregon's second light, established nine years after Umpqua River—and three after Umpqua collapsed. Commercial shipping had intensified out of nearby Coos Bay, and the USLHE felt this portion of coast needed the light more. The small island proved a challenging site, however.

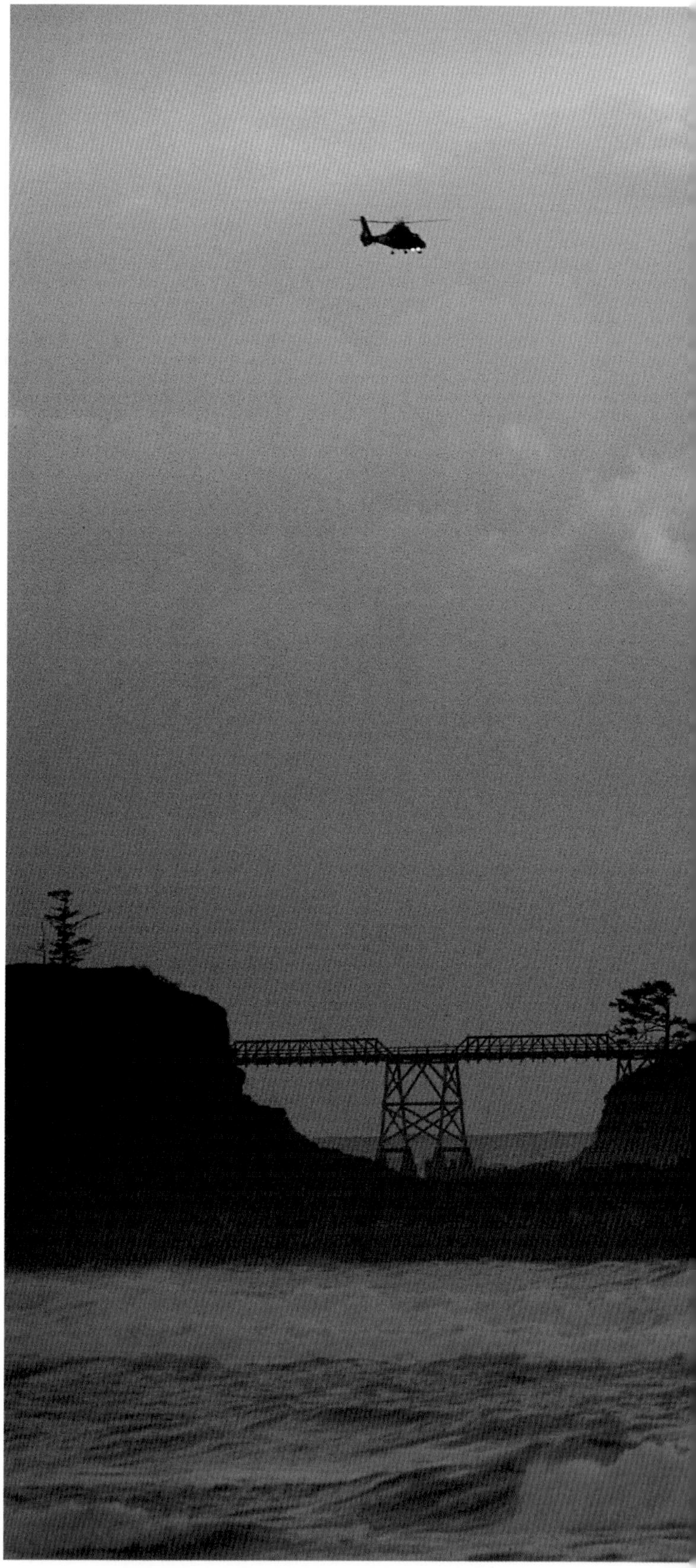

Cape Arago lighthouse
The Coast Guard de-staffed Cape Arago in 1966. Throughout 1993, it repaired and restored the building, removing the original fourth-order Fresnel and replacing it with a Vega Rotating Beacon. High above the light, a Coast Guard Air Operations–Coos Bay helicopter begins a search-and-rescue drill before an approaching storm.

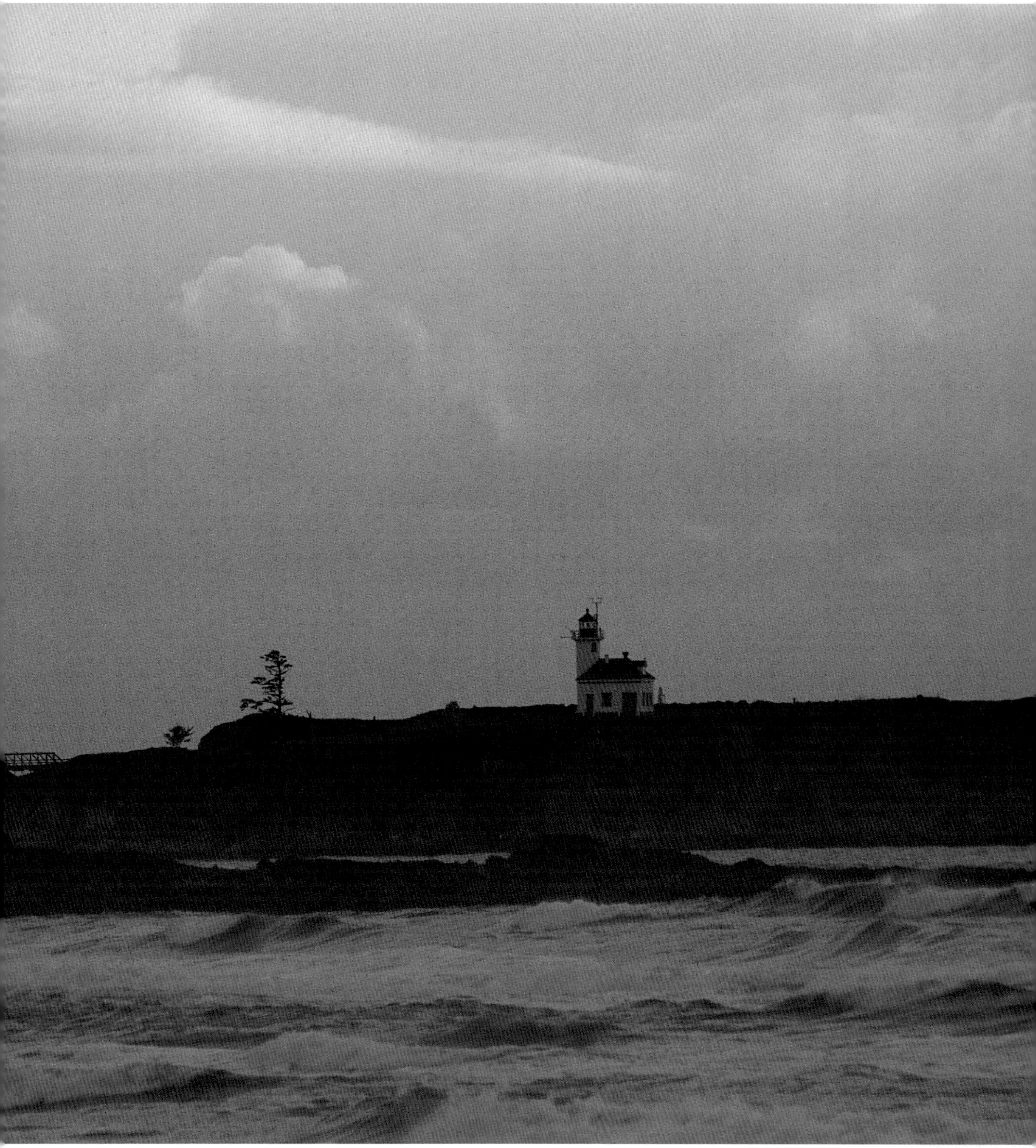

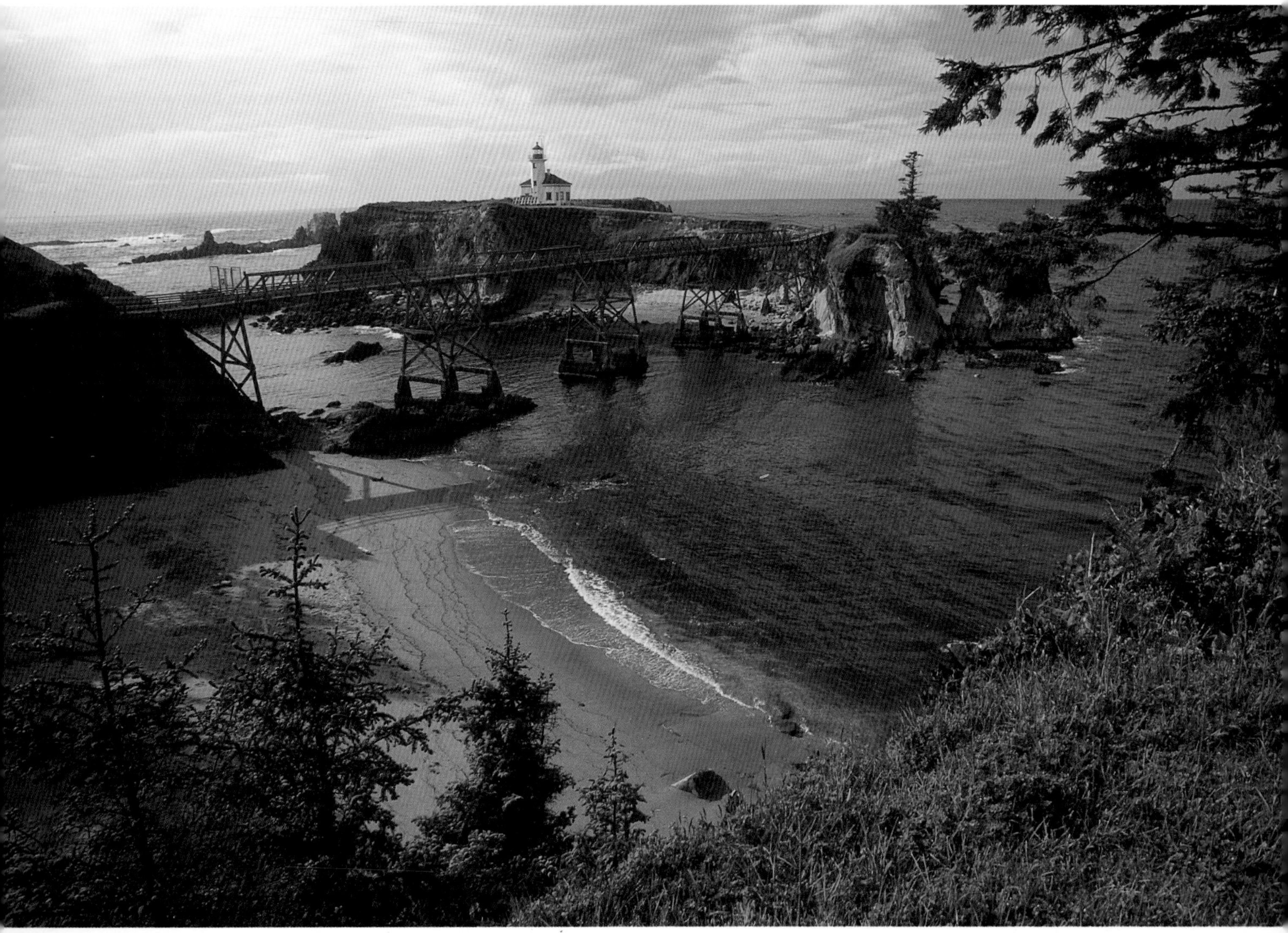

CAPE ARAGO LIGHTHOUSE

This current structure is the third lighthouse on the island, constructed after the high bridge was built in 1898. When the bridge was completed, keepers and staff from a lifesaving station lived on the island. Contractor R. J. Hillstrom, using plans from Puget Sound's Point Robinson light, completed this building in 1934.

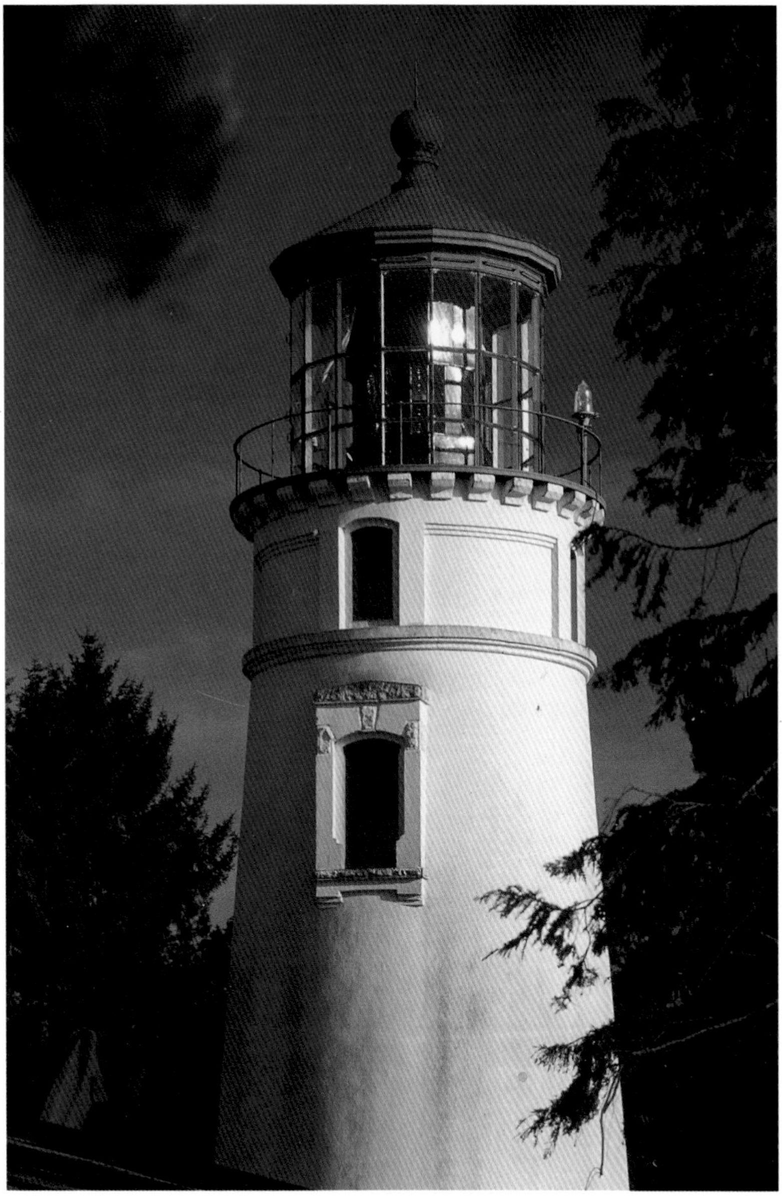

Umpqua River light station
The setting sun glints off the first-order Fresnel, catching its red-glass panel. The signature of the Umpqua River light is red-white flashing alternatively every fifteen seconds. Completed in 1894, the sixyt-foot tower replaced a large Cape Cod duplex with a ninety-foot tower that fell over after spring flooding undermined its foundation.

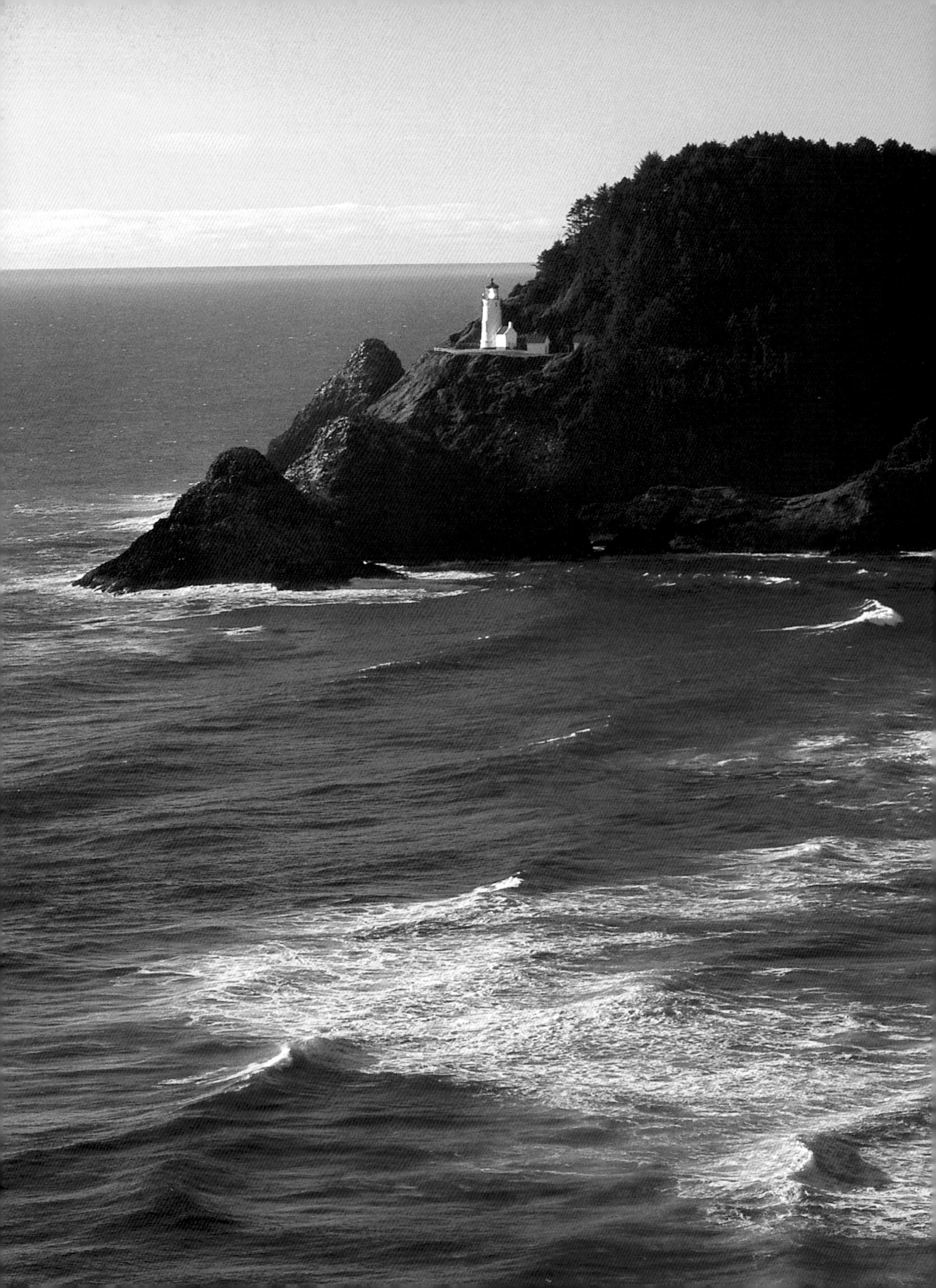

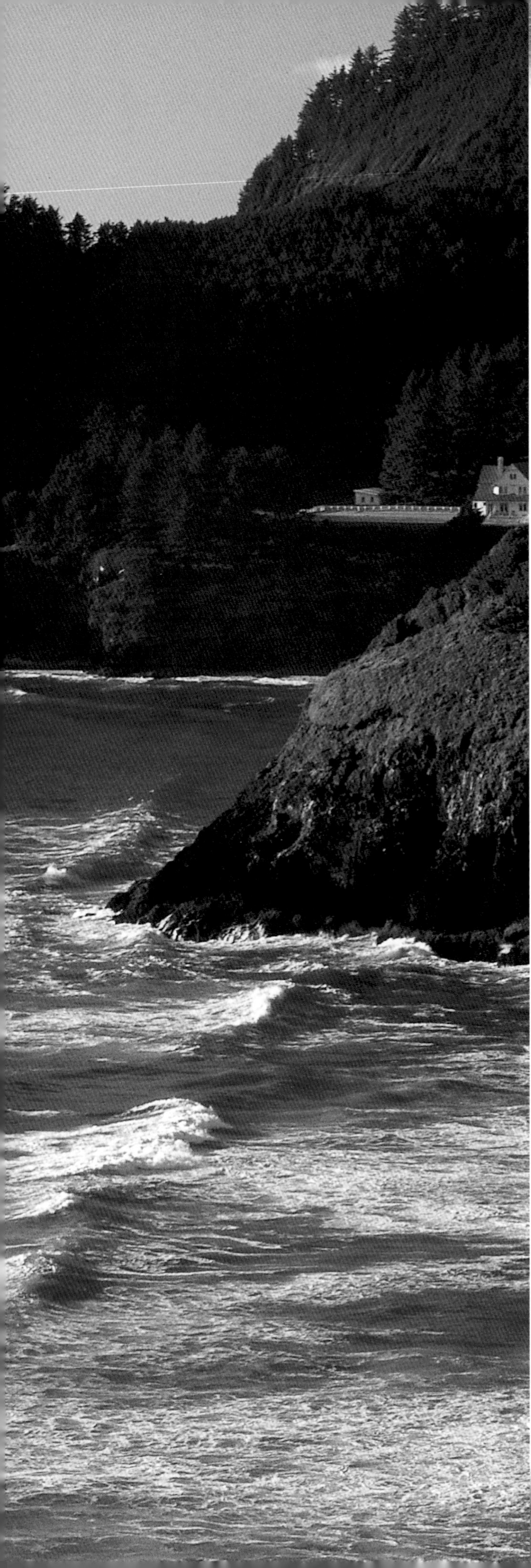

CHAPTER 3

Lives Molded by Isolation and Defined by Simpler Times

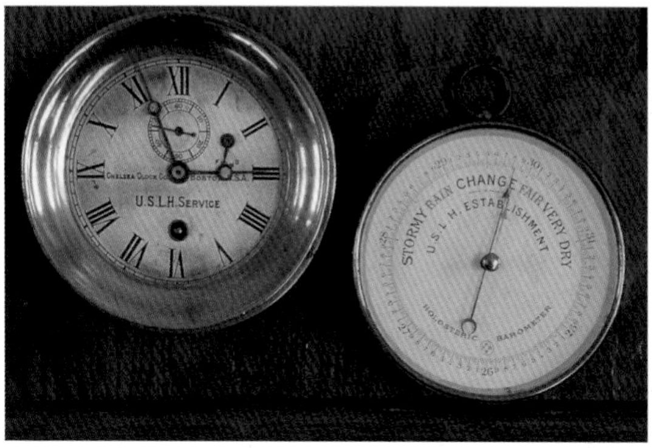

Left: **Heceta Head light station**
Certainly one of the West Coast's most beautiful settings, Heceta Head offers visitors not only the opportunity to visit the light, but also the hospitality of a bed and breakfast by staying in the restored Queen Anne–style assistant keeper's duplex, at right. The first-order Fresnel sits 205 feet above the sea.

Above: **Alki Point light station**
The small museum at Seattle's Alki Point includes these two jewels: an early twentieth-century wind-up clock from the Lighthouse Service and a USLHE barometer from perhaps a century earlier.

Lighthouse duties were a full-time job for keepers and assistants. Stations operating fog signals often had two individuals dedicated to that duty. Daylight was devoted to maintaining the light, its clockwork mechanism that rotated the Fresnel lens, and the station's buildings and grounds.

In years when lamps burned whale oil, rapeseed oil, or kerosene, keepers spent hours wiping Fresnels clean of oil soot. They washed lantern-room windows inside and out. To reach the highest panes of glass, keepers balanced on lantern-room gallery railing (the balcony surrounding the glass) using handholds screwed into the framework to steady themselves. In wet or dry, windy or calm conditions, keepers scrubbed the glass each day.

Every day brought a multitude of duties. Each morning, they trimmed lamp wicks. At dusk, they hauled five-gallon containers of fuel up dozens of stairs. They transferred oil into smaller pitchers to fill lamp reservoirs. They wound up the clockwork mechanisms, a laborious exercise that took twenty minutes or longer of steady cranking at some stations. Just before dark, they drew back the curtains surrounding the Fresnel that kept the sun from discoloring the glass or from starting a fire with the bulls-eye magnifying lenses. They checked every adjustment again, and as darkness fell, they touched a match to the wick. For the next few minutes, they watched the light and swiveled open or closed the vents in the lantern-room windows to improve draft to the flame and brighten its intensity. Satisfied that everything worked as it should, the keeper descended to the watch room, often on the level just below the lantern room.

Paperwork kept them as busy as the physical portion of their jobs. Regulations required daily entries in a logbook, recording weather, work done around the station, and any visitors. In another ledger, they noted the quantities of oil and wick consumed, and often registered at exactly what time they lit and extinguished the lamp.

Mechanization and the arrival of electricity in the first quarter of the 1900s gave keepers slightly more leisure time, even while on duty. The Lighthouse Service provided its keepers with portable libraries of some sixty titles packed in an oak box. These assortments of poetry, history, and popular and classical fiction, rotated among the stations, were carried from one to the next on the quarterly visits of the supply tenders and lighthouse inspectors. Even after the widespread acceptance of wireless radio, reception in many stations was marginal, and reading was the principal form of escape and relaxation during leisure time or long watches.

Jim Gibbs, a well-known West Coast maritime historian and author, served as a young Coast Guard Seaman enlistee and assistant keeper on Tillamook Rock. Soon after he arrived at the station, he discovered a stash of dozens of books, apparently favorites of an earlier keeper reluctant to let go of old friends. Gibbs passed many watches reading by the light of the Fresnel.

Overnight watches generally ran between four and eight hours per keeper. Before electrification, each

Right: **Heceta Head light station**
Heceta Head innkeepers Carol and Mike Korgan operate a bed and breakfast in the former assistant keeper's Queen Anne–style duplex. The inn is renowned for its breakfasts and its comfortable rooms. After dark, Mike occasionally leads guests on a nighttime tour of the light, giving them a view not possible elsewhere in Oregon.

Facing page: **Heceta Head light station**
Along Oregon's coast, Heceta Head commands one of America's most beautiful settings.

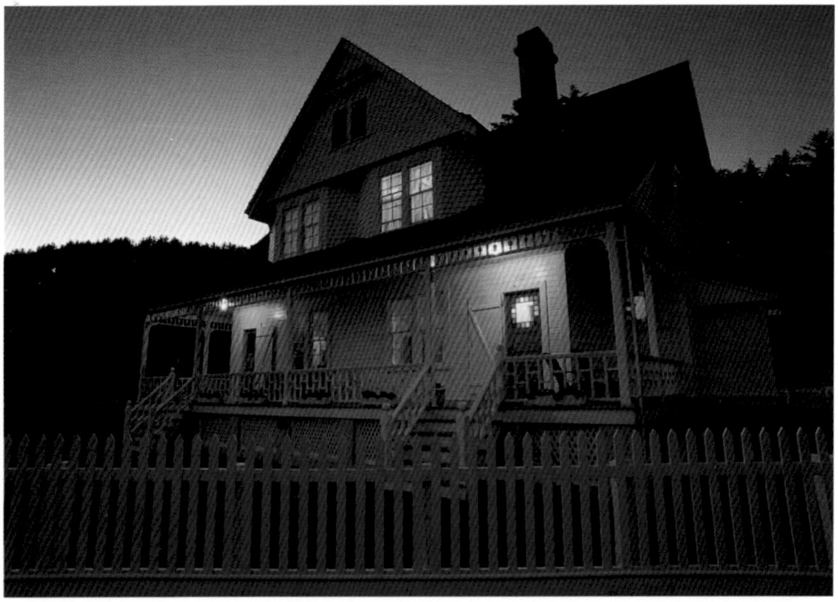

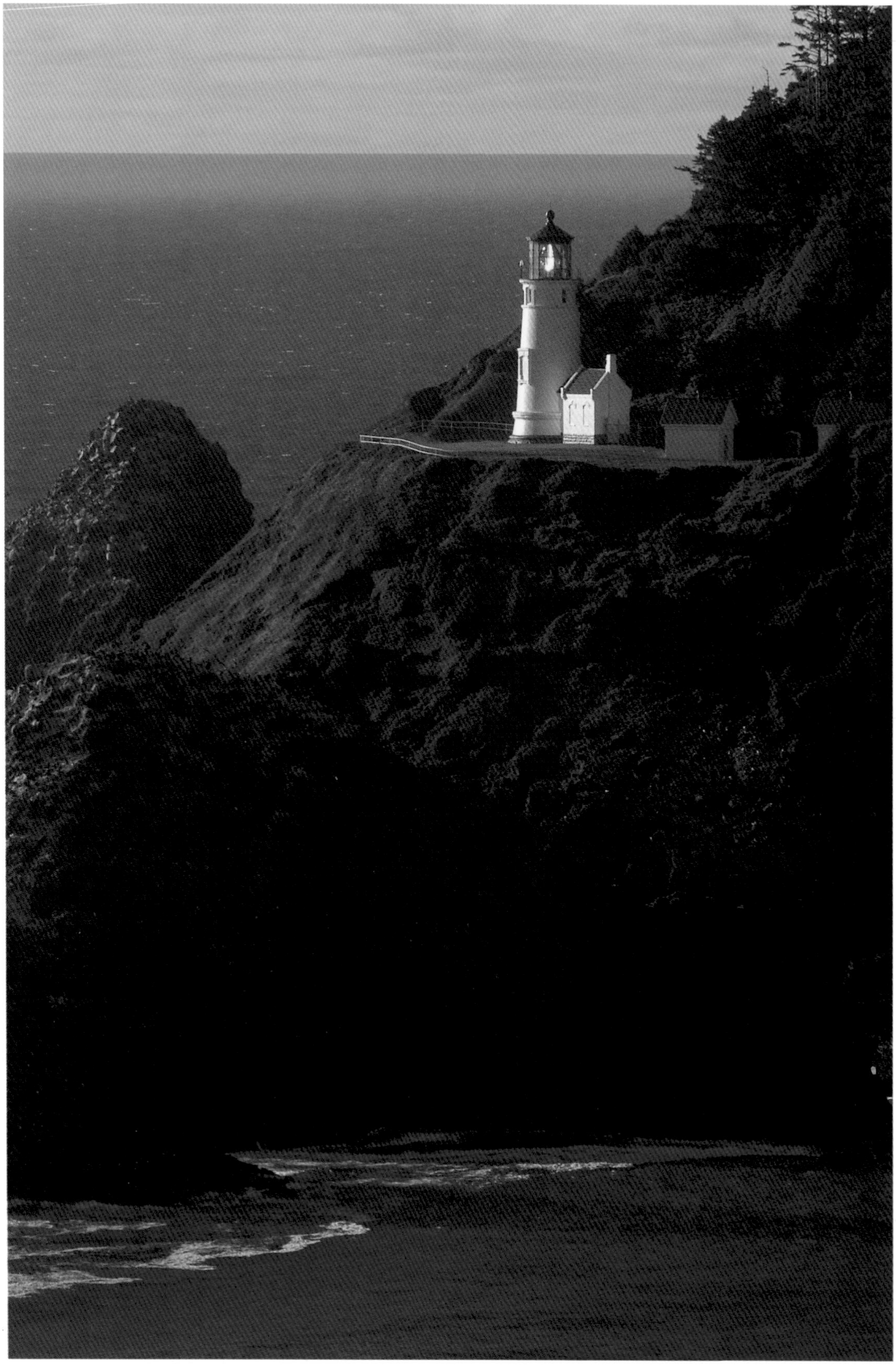

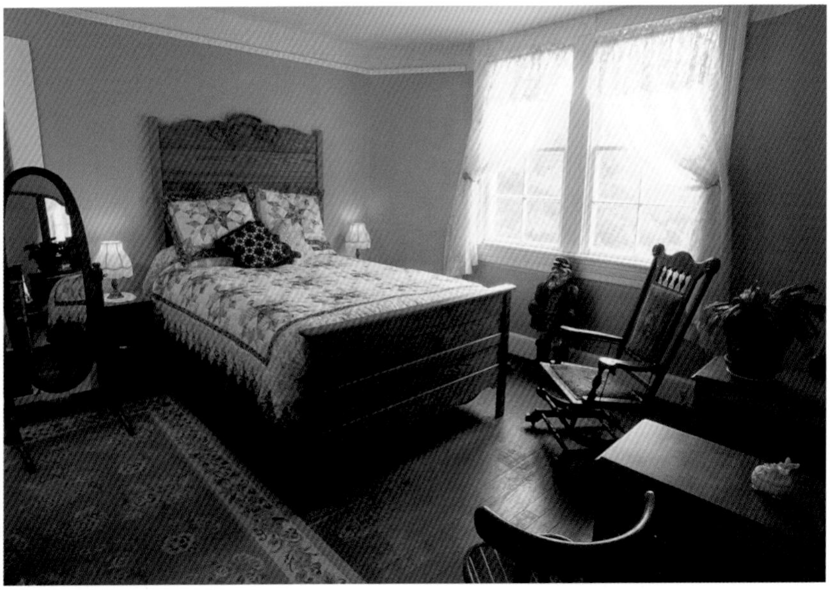

Heceta Head light station
The Mariner's Room overlooks the beach below the light. In 1934, Heceta Head got electricity, which made living and light keeping much easier. The keepers disconnected the light's clockwork mechanism that rotated the Fresnel. Six years later, the station found it no longer needed three keepers, so the head and first assistant shared the duplex.

keeper finished the shift by carrying up more lantern fuel and winding the clockworks before turning over duty. Depending on the light tower's height, many keepers wound the rotating mechanism at least once more during their watch. Many watch rooms had doors to their own galleries, which were welcome on warm nights since lanterns—oil-fired or electric—gave off a large amount of heat. The lanterns' warmth was welcome on cold, damp winter nights inside uninsulated, unheated towers. Many lantern rooms used either iron grillwork or light-gathering prisms in the floor to shine light down to the watch room below. Keepers read or did the paperwork; rules forbade them from sleeping on duty. But there were ways around that.

Often assistants brought a cot for their late-night shifts and placed it in the center of the ground floor. When the clockwork counterweight—some of which were as heavy as 400 pounds—settled onto them, it woke them up. They then dashed up the stairs to rewind the clockwork before the light stopped rotating. This was not officially accepted practice, however.The architecture of many stations made duty manageable in good weather or bad. Head keepers and first assistants often shared duplex houses, or first and second assistants lived in a duplex while the head keeper had a separate residence a few yards away. At New Dungeness near Sequim, Washington, and Cape Flattery, doors to the stairway provided privacy for each keeper's family as the other went up and down during their watch. At smaller houses such as Old Point Loma near San Diego, Point Pinos near Monterey, and Yaquina Bay near Newport, Oregon, the head keeper or an assistant lived in a separate structure and used the house's front door and hallway for access, creeping past closed bedroom doors on their way up. As their four-, six-, or eight-hour duty came to an end, keepers started coffee and cooked breakfast for their relief, usually delivering the wake-up call as well.

At other stations, including Cape Disappointment, Oregon's Heceta Head, and California's Point Bonita, Point Reyes, and Point Conception, keepers lived in houses some distance away from where weather pounded the light. Each made a sometimes perilous climb or descent just to get to work. In severe winter storms, keepers were trapped in watchrooms or fog-signal buildings for a day or more. At all lights, keepers stored the flammable oil in small storage buildings a short distance from the light tower.

In some ways, the lives of keepers were not unlike those of farmers who kept livestock. The light and fog signal needed attention every day without holidays or days off. While keepers could arrange a day each week to go to town, the light still had to be lit each evening and extinguished each morning. Hundreds of times, keepers' wives or children prepared wicks and lit lamps as the keeper fought a heavy tide or was trapped ashore by a sudden unexpected storm and couldn't row home in time.

Connections to the Outside World

The military influence on the Lighthouse Service brought more than improved organization to the lights. It inaugurated inspections as well, giving an edge to otherwise welcome and long-awaited supply ships. The knowledge that vessels which brought food, lamp fuel, and other supplies also carried someone who would scrutinize their logbooks and bedroom dressers with equal intensity made the quarterly visits an event that evoked mixed emotions. The Service devised an award system based on inspection results. Commendations helped when keepers sought a promotion or transfer to more desirable lights that were better locations to raise and educate a growing family.

Mail delivery presented challenges at many stations and was particularly difficult for remote island lights. Long before the Pacific Coast Highway was completed, keepers at Point Sur climbed down from the rock and walked a long mile to the dirt road that passed their station to get mail; the rural route carrier left mail for the entire station in the box at the path head. But if winter storms combined with high tides, Point Sur rock became an island, and mail piled up in the box until the waters receded. A famous story tells of the Point Sur head keeper who ordered early a Thanksgiving turkey from a local butcher, but a late-fall storm rendered the rock inescapable for five days. By the time the keeper could get to the road again, his putrid turkey and mail left little to be thankful for.

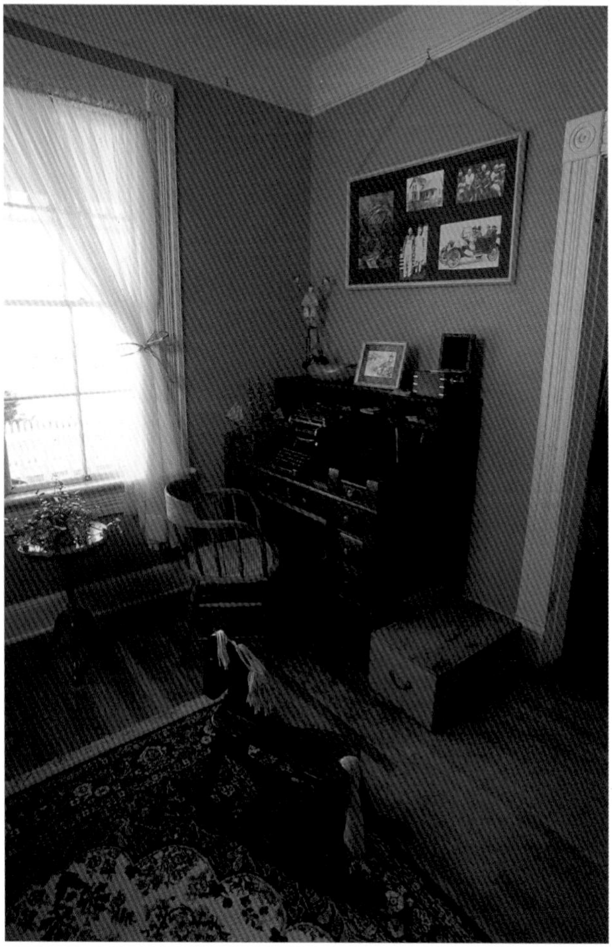

On Tatoosh Island, the government operated Cape Flattery light and beginning in 1883, a weather reporting station. The island's forty residents in the late 1890s relied on a Makah Indian from nearby Neah Bay to deliver mail. As weather permitted, the mail carrier, known as Old Doctor, paddled the seventeen-mile round trip to Tatoosh twice a week in his canoe. Even when he could make it, it required strength, courage, timing, and accuracy: Often Old Doctor threw the mailbag to a keeper who stood on a wave-swept rock to wait for news from the outside world. In those days, carriers were paid by the trip and the distance. Old Doctor generally did pretty well, but three times during his years servicing Tatoosh, he smashed his canoe on the beach rocks.

As late as the 1890s, political shenanigans still controlled keeper appointments. Countless stories exist about the Extinguished Service Check, a government-printed form the size of a personal check that introduced keepers to their unexpected replacements with these words: "You are superseded as keeper of _____ light station on (month, date, year) by _____, the bearer of this note."

Dozens of keepers suddenly found the new political appointee standing at the door, their family in a wagon behind them and furniture towering overhead. This patronage created a system in which keepers were loyal neither to the Lighthouse Board nor the federal government that paid them only $1,000 annually. They were devoted to the senator or representative who had gotten their appointment by twisting arms in back rooms. With job security determined only by the political party in office, inspectors had little authority when disciplining

Heceta Head light station
In the parlor, the desk, typewriter, and medical supply box (beside the desk) date from the Lighthouse Service period. The house was completed in 1893, a year before the fifty-six-foot-tall tower with its first-order Fresnel was first lit.

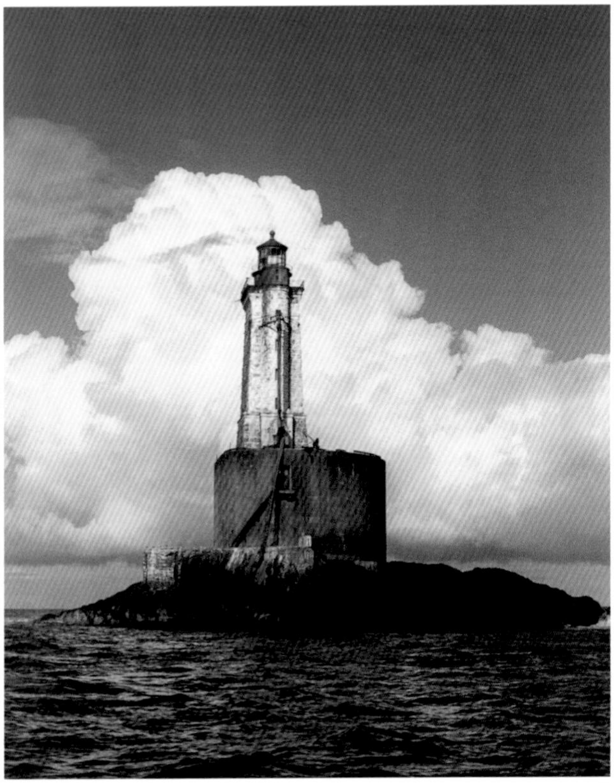

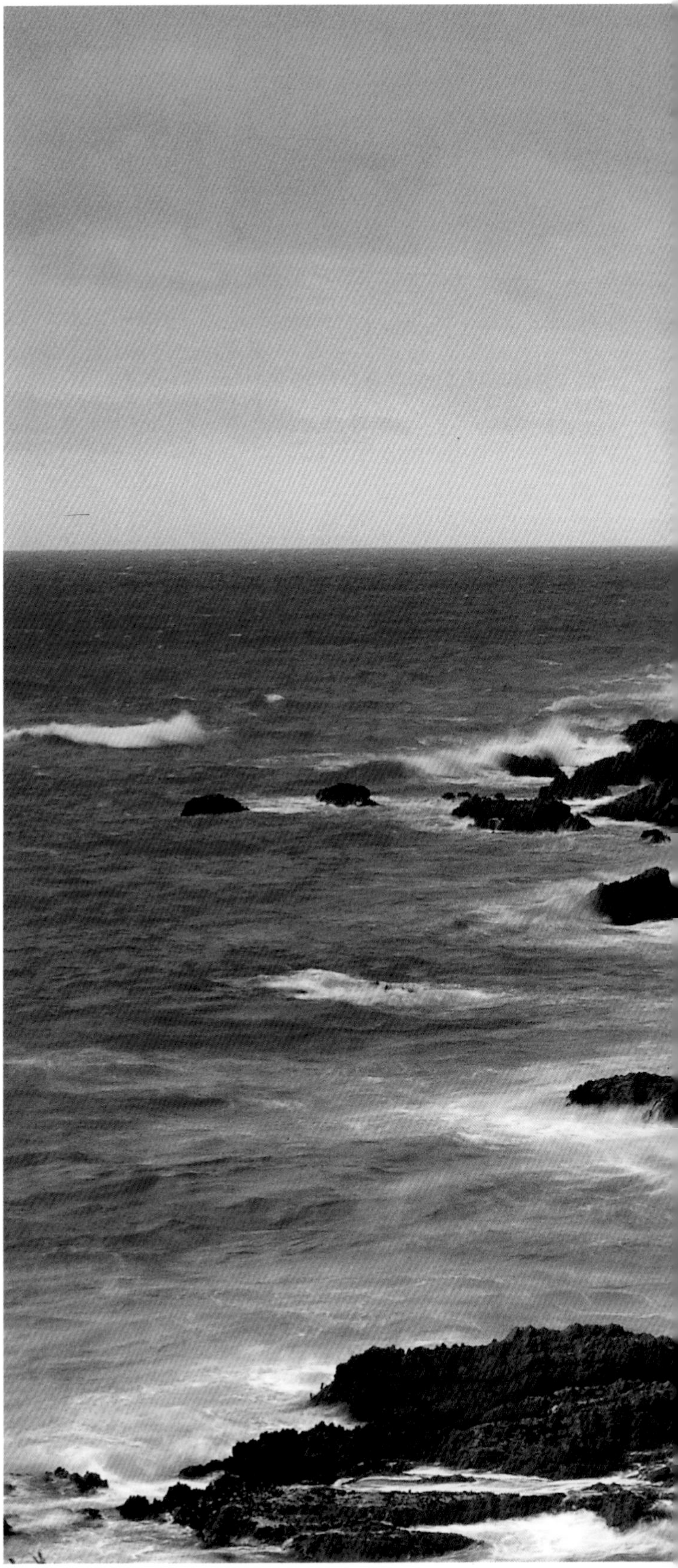

Above: **St. George Reef lighthouse**
This was the most costly lighthouse in the United States to construct—and superlatives continued after it was lit in October 1892. Five keepers worked at the 146-foot-tall tower. During a 1937 winter storm, they were isolated fifty-nine days straight; waves frequently broke over the top of the light. The first-order Fresnel, built by LePaute, has 510 pieces of glass and cost $15,000 in 1892 (about $300,000 today). (Photo © Guy Towers, president, St. George Reef Preservation Society)

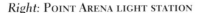

Right: **Point Arena light station**
Point Arena's outside-mounted twin-aero beacon spins day and night. Located about 125 miles north of the Golden Gate, the light was critically affected by the 1906 San Francisco earthquake. The original tower had to be condemned, and a smokestack builder constructed this reinforced concrete tower in 1908.

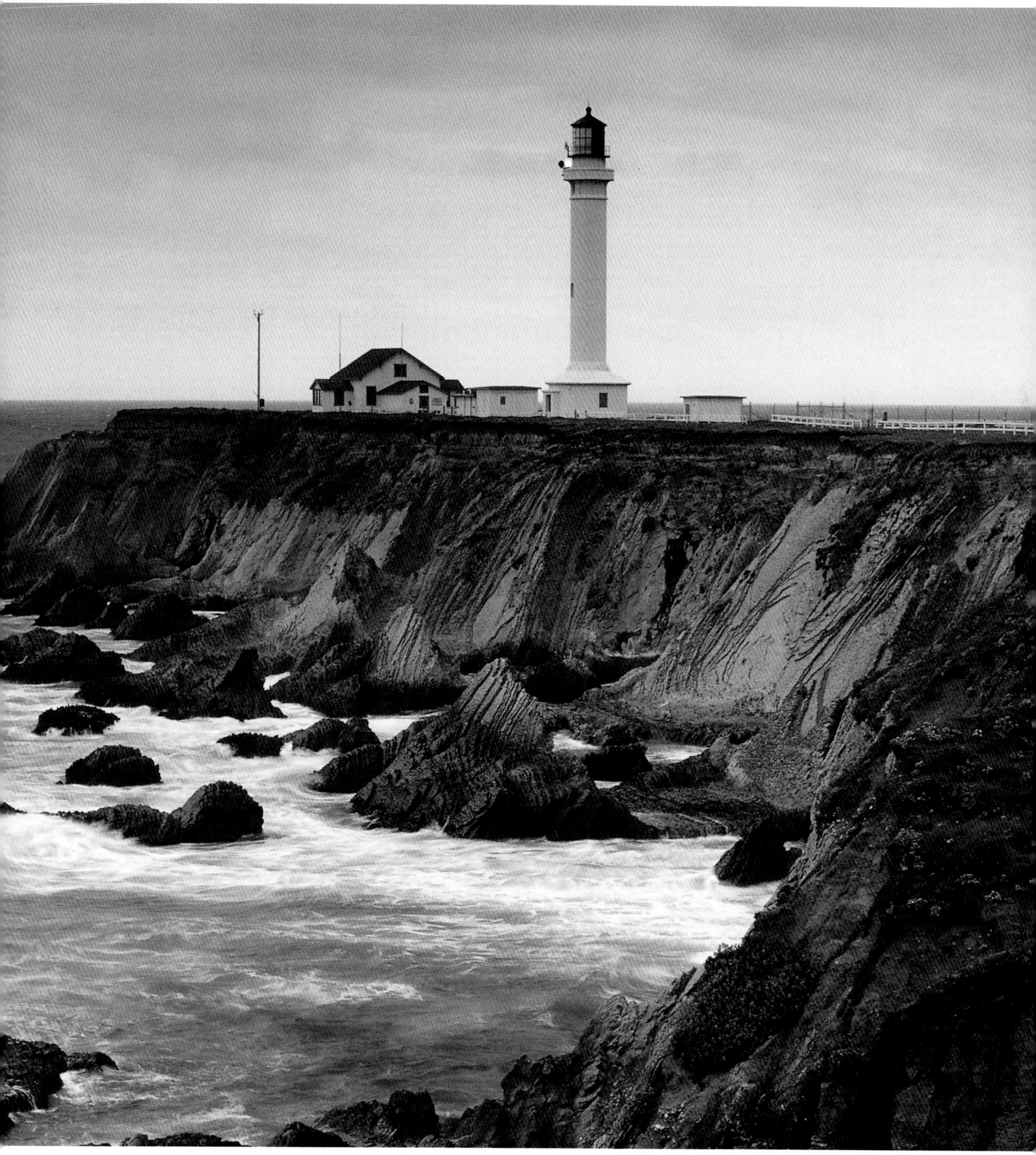

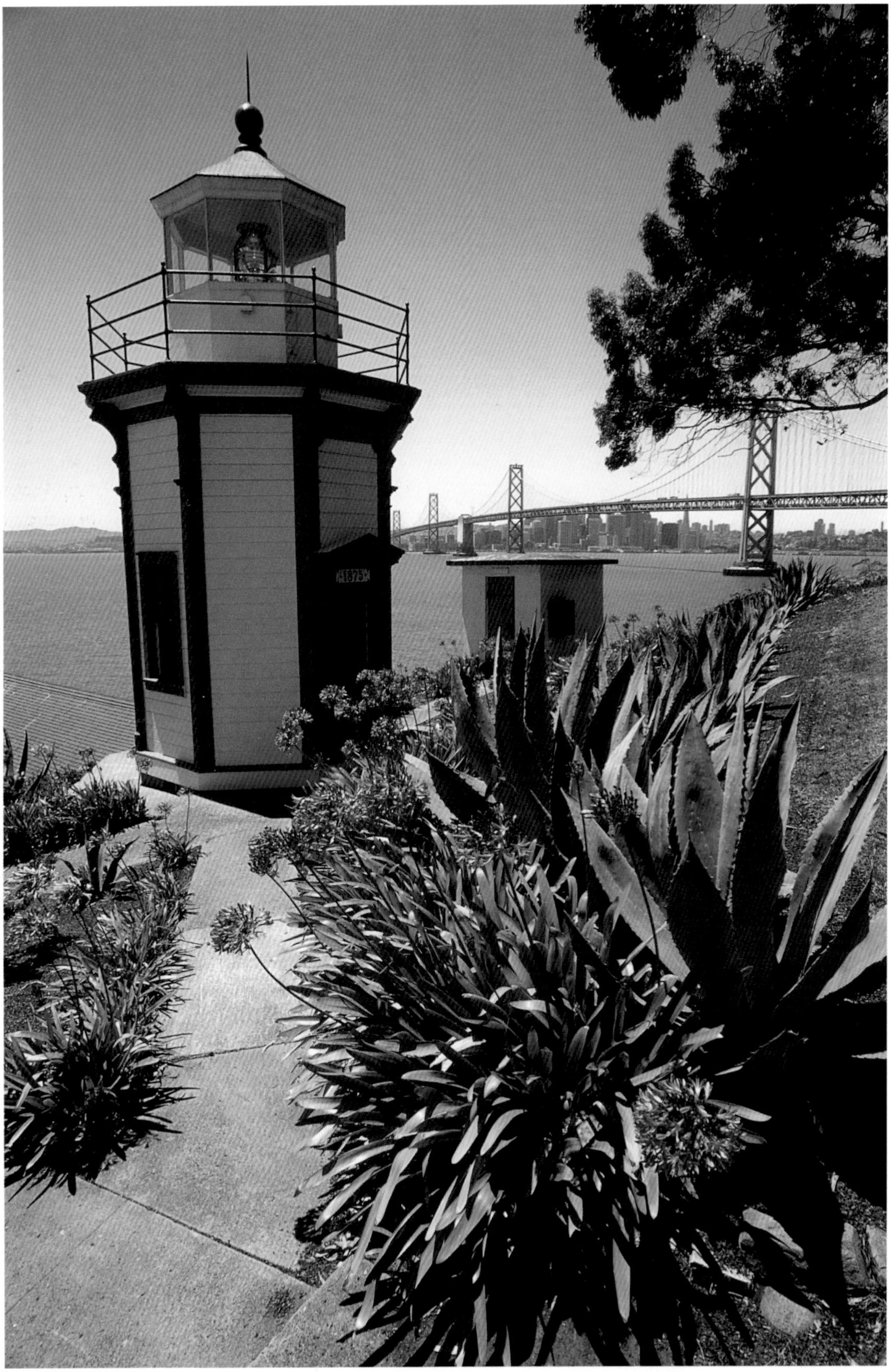
1875

sloppy or careless keepers. As San Francisco satirist Ambrose Bierce wrote, a lighthouse is "a tall building on the seashore in which the government maintains a lamp and a friend of a politician."

President Grover Cleveland extinguished patronage appointments in 1896 when he personally twisted arms to get keepers and others in the Service covered under the government Civil Service Act. After that, the Service required written and verbal examinations to fill positions and adopted a merit system to determine promotions. Keepers served six-month probations before their positions became permanent and they began assignment rotations. Professionalism improved once keepers felt more secure and better appreciated by a system that rewarded good work well done instead of party votes delivered.

The Board preferred married keepers for most stations. While this practice was never written into the rules, it was widespread. However, there were stations where the Board hesitated to assign keepers with spouses and families. It viewed St. George Reef and Tillamook Rock as especially risky lights as the legendary storms these two stations endured challenged the keepers' sanity. Quarters on these rocks were tight and privacy was limited to the closed door of a small sleeping room.

By the same token, on larger rocks where a garden might grow, cows graze, children run and play, and where agitation might be cooled by a walk, lights often had several families in residence. Cape Flattery, Anacapa Island, Point Sur, and Farallon Island all saw children thrive surrounded by wind and water. At all other lights, from isolated Point Reyes and wind-battered Point Conception to Heceta Head and Washington's Grays Harbor, families counted as additional staff. Parents often tethered young children and livestock to keep them from falling off or being blown from precipitous cliffs. But no child who grew up at a lighthouse imagined their life was different from any others. They were molded by isolation and defined by simpler times. Their play, schooling, and chores blended with the seasons and the weather to give them a "normal" childhood in an unusual setting.

Pensions for the Keepers

By the early 1900s, the fifty-year-old Lighthouse Board had become a slow-moving, nine-member decision maker. In an attempt to make the Board answer to a more appropriate parent, Congress transferred it from the Treasury to the Commerce Department in 1903.

While the Treasury administered the Coast Guard, some people in Washington, D.C., and others in private shipping and commerce felt the Board was too military, as its charter specified that seven of its nine members be military personnel. In 1910, the pendulum swung back toward civilian directorship when Congress replaced the Lighthouse Board with a Bureau of Lighthouses. Within

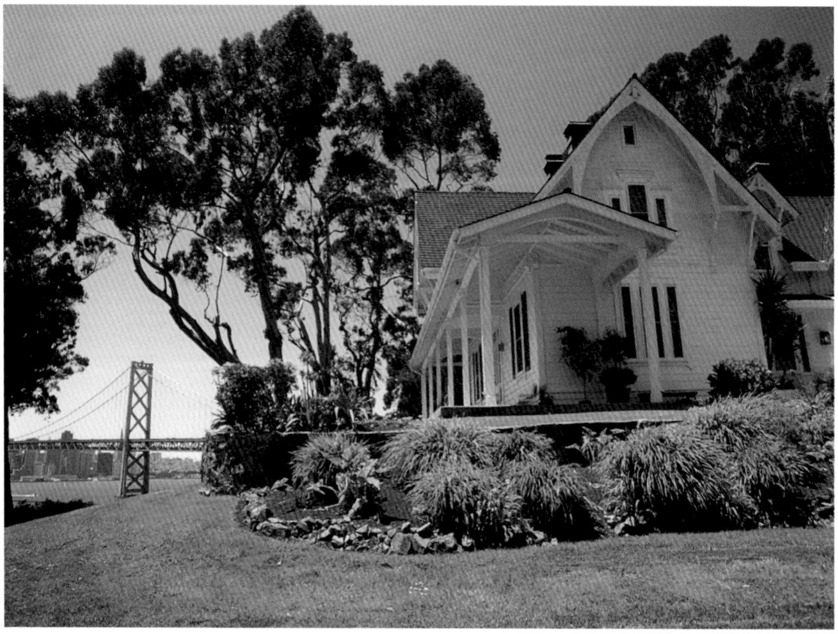

Left: **Yerba Buena Island lighthouse**
The head keeper, assistant, and their families shared this large Victorian residence barely 250 feet up a gentle lawn from the matching lighthouse and fog signal building. Beginning in 1873, the Lighthouse Service used the island as its supply depot. This lighthouse was completed in 1875.

Facing page: **Yerba Buena Island lighthouse**
Real estate brokers like to say location is everything. If that's the case, the lighthouse keeper on Yerba Buena Island in San Francisco Bay had everything. The twenty-six-foot-tall tower places the fixed but flashing light ninety-five feet above the waters.

Supplementing the Supply Ship

A lighthouse tender visited each station at least four times a year. In most cases the rule of thumb was "if the tender didn't bring it, you didn't need it." This adage worked well for supplies such as oil and replacement parts, but most families of lighthouse keepers were large and needed to add to their food rations.

Fishing and clamming were obvious and readily available choices. On Washington's Stuart Island, Turn Point lighthouse keeper L. A. Borchers was commended for putting up 311 cans of fish in a single season. He was able to harvest pink salmon, sardines, and salmon caviar, not bad for the waters of the San Juan Islands. U.S. Food Administrator Herbert Hoover praised Borchers and held him up as an example to other keepers: "The evidence which he has produced of what can be accomplished where raw material swims past the door is very unusual, in view of the amount of work which I know is necessary for a light keeper to perform in the course of his regular duties."

Supplementing rations with seafood worked to some extent but every mariner knows the value of vitamins from fresh vegetables. The family vegetable patch was a necessity and a point of pride at most lights. The biggest problem with coastal gardening was a lack of suitable soil. The *Lighthouse Service Bulletin* recommended that keepers "cart in soil from the timbered sections lying back of the drifting sand dunes, and spread this to a depth of about one inch on the surface of the sand." The *Bulletin* added that staking the ground with catch fencing will keep the shifting sands from encroaching on the seedlings.

At California's Point Sur, gardening soil was transported by bucket to the top of the 250-foot-high mountain. Nancy June Piland, whose father Wayne was a keeper from 1932 to 1959, wrote, "The only problem with the garden was gophers! The mountain was riddled with gopher holes. Growing a garden was a challenge between watching the wind blow topsoil away and the gophers pulling the shoots from below." Getting and keeping good soil kept families busy, but the long growing season on the West Coast made it worth the effort.

two years, career Lighthouse Service personnel and other knowledgeable civilians directed nine of the twelve districts. Their chief was George R. Putnam, appointed commissioner by President William Howard Taft. Putnam had served as Coast Survey director in the Philippines when Taft was regional governor.

Putnam was progressive and open-minded. Over the next thirty-five years, he brought electricity to lighthouses, adopted radio beacons as navigation aids, introduced electric buoys and fog signals, and advanced wireless radio communications between lighthouses and Coast Guard stations. Each improvement reduced Bureau expenses and personnel. In 1910, Putnam had inherited 11,713 navigational aids including lighthouses, lightships, range lights, harbor lights, and buoys. By 1924, that number surged to 16,888. Yet he reduced the number of employees 20 percent by using more automatic equipment than anywhere in the world, representing a huge cost savings to the government. He was, in fact, every bit as frugal as Stephen Pleasonton had been. And ironically, his miserliness had as serious and lasting an effect.

As historian Hans Christian Adamson wrote in *Keepers of the Lights*, "the old Lighthouse Bureau was not only dollar-conscious; it was actually penny-pinching. *Save, stretch and substitute* had become a policy and a creed. And if it had continued to rule the destinies of our aids to navigation, it might, in time, have affected the quality of the aids themselves. As it was, the penny-pinching supported mainly the supporting activities. . . . On many lights, sanitary facilities were early Victorian; in dwellings, the wives of keepers and their families still used kerosene for lighting and wood for fuel because electricity or gas was 'too expensive.'"

A retired keeper told Adamson that buildings and equipment were deteriorating because of the strict economy. "Sure, the lighthouses looked well enough," the man said, "because they were painted up to snuff. But underneath the paint, in many places, the wood was rotten and the foundation sagging."

There are countless stories of lighthouse inspectors demanding first-class upkeep from third-class equipment. They retrieved paint brushes out of trash bins with barely half-an-inch of bristles remaining and told the keeper it had one more good painting left in it—and then it could clean boots or scrub dishes. They admonished keepers' wives to recycle lens-polishing cloths that were tattered to lace, and to mend them and use them to patch keepers' shirts. An old joke described an ax used for thirty years at Point San Luis: "Of course, it's had three new heads and five new handles."

Putnam inaugurated the *Lighthouse Service Bulletin* in 1912. This journal offered not only official information and news to keepers but also everything from recipes for whitewash and fly poison to extraordinary reports from individual stations and monthly regional weather forecasts. Often issues included human-interest stories about station pets or projects and tales of heroic rescues at one light or tragedy at another.

This was a period when the work ethic was strong, and good value for wages received—and money spent—was a worker's highest motivation. Putnam's thriftiness forced sacrifice and hardship on the keepers and their families, but it also furthered the pride most of them already had in government service. They developed deep loyalty to their Commissioner. He repaid them in one generous way, winning them federal pensions for their retirement.

When he became Commissioner in 1910, Putnam found dozens of middle-aged employees who had joined the Lighthouse Service when Civil Service was inaugurated in 1896. These individuals, with earlier careers as

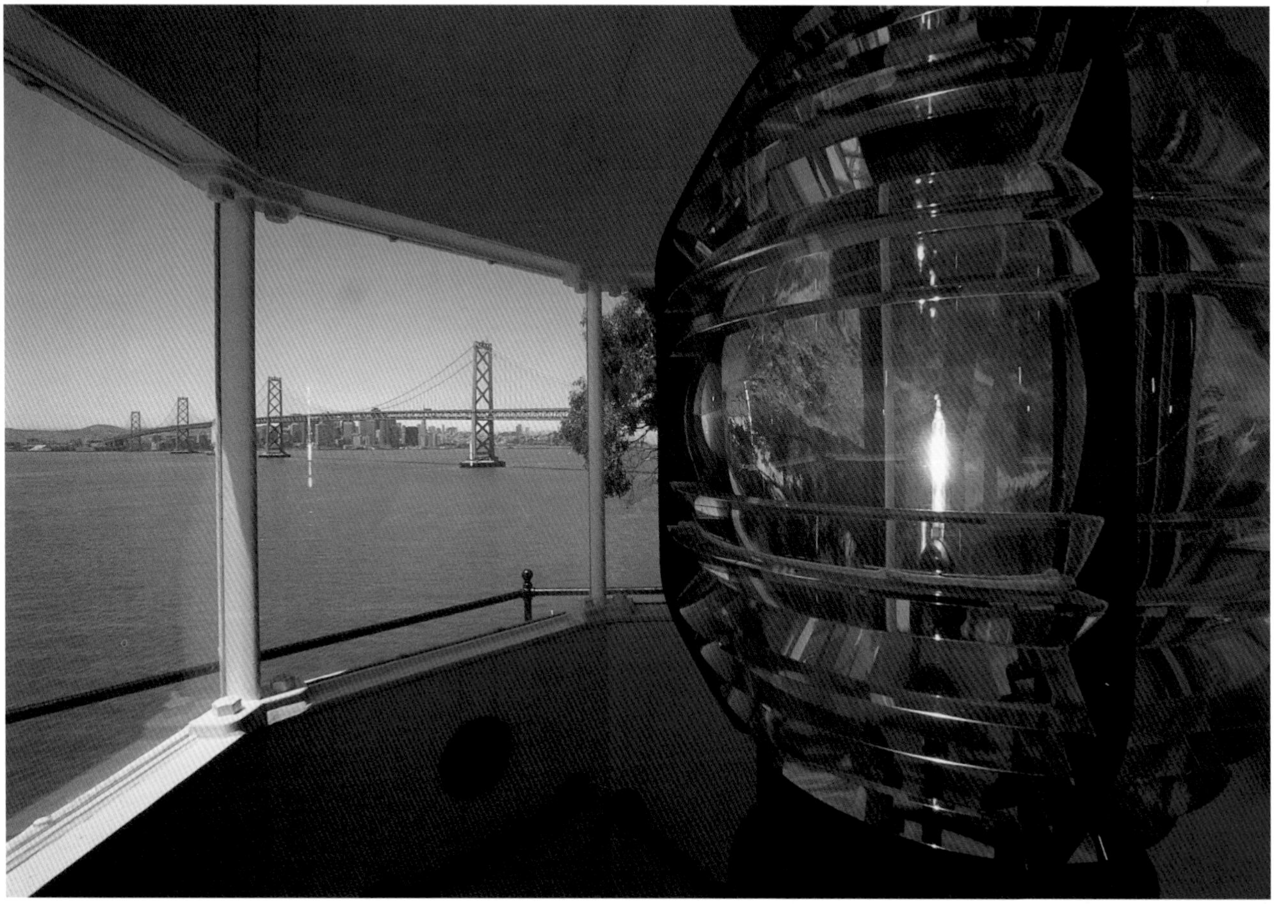

Yerba Buena Island lighthouse
The small, fourth-order Fresnel was produced in 1886 by Barbier & Fenestre of Paris. Inside, a 250-watt quartz bulb throws its light nearly fourteen miles at night, far beyond the Bay Bridge in the background. The original fifth-order lens, formerly the light at Oregon's Yaquina Bay lighthouse, was first lit here in 1875.

sea captains or sailors behind them, now had up to fifteen years experience. Some were growing too old or weak to meet the physical demands of their jobs. Yet without a pension plan, Putnam refused to force any of them out. He lobbied legislators and appealed to local mariners and publication officials serving the coasts who knew their keepers and families by name. Putnam recreated the groundswell of support that had brought in the orderliness of Civil Service. It worked, and by 1919, every Bureau employee was eligible for the same pension granted to other government workers.

"The Light-Keeper"

Keepers and the Lighthouse Service took their responsibilities seriously. The Service maintained that keepers played too important a role to be repeatedly distracted by visitors, yet regulations required keepers to be courteous to those who came calling. So long as it did not interrupt their duties, keepers were to provide tours and answer questions. They could not charge for their time or knowledge. The Service told keepers this was the public relations function of their job; it helped voters understand the Lighthouse Service's need for funds to keep the lights operating. This paradox never troubled the keepers who usually were glad for company.

Some visits contributed to America's literary wealth as well. Bruce Handy, a present-day Point Pinos lighthouse docent who dresses in an 1880s keeper's suit, greets visitors with a business-like but sincere welcome. He tells a story about Alan Luce, keeper at the light in 1879. One day a tall, slim traveler with a vaguely Scottish accent arrived unexpectedly and asked for a tour. The traveler was poet and novelist Robert Louis Stevenson, who was touring the West, researching his book on America, *Across the Plains*. Luce showed Stevenson the Fresnel, some arrowheads he'd found nearby, his ship models, and a handful of his amateurish paintings of Monterey sunsets. Luce even played piano as his young visitor took notes.

While Stevenson went on to write *Treasure Island*, *Kidnapped*, and *The Strange Case of Dr. Jekyll and Mr. Hyde*, it was his poem, "The Light-Keeper," that revealed what he thought of these individuals:

> This is the man
> Who gives up what is lovely in living
> For the means to live.

But Stevenson suggested a poet's responsibilities were different:

> Poetry cunningly guilds
> The life of the Light-Keeper,
> Held on high in the blackness
> In the burning kernal of night,
> The seaman sees and blesses him,
> The Poet, deep in a sonnet,
> Numbers his inky fingers
> Fitly to praise him. . . .

Pigeon Point light station
Its picture-perfect picket fence leads visitors to Pigeon Point's lighthouse office and workroom behind the tower. Originally known as Whale Point because migrating gray whales passed the rocky outcrop, it was renamed in 1853 when the clipper ship Carrier Pigeon *ran aground in fog, broke apart, and sank nearby.*

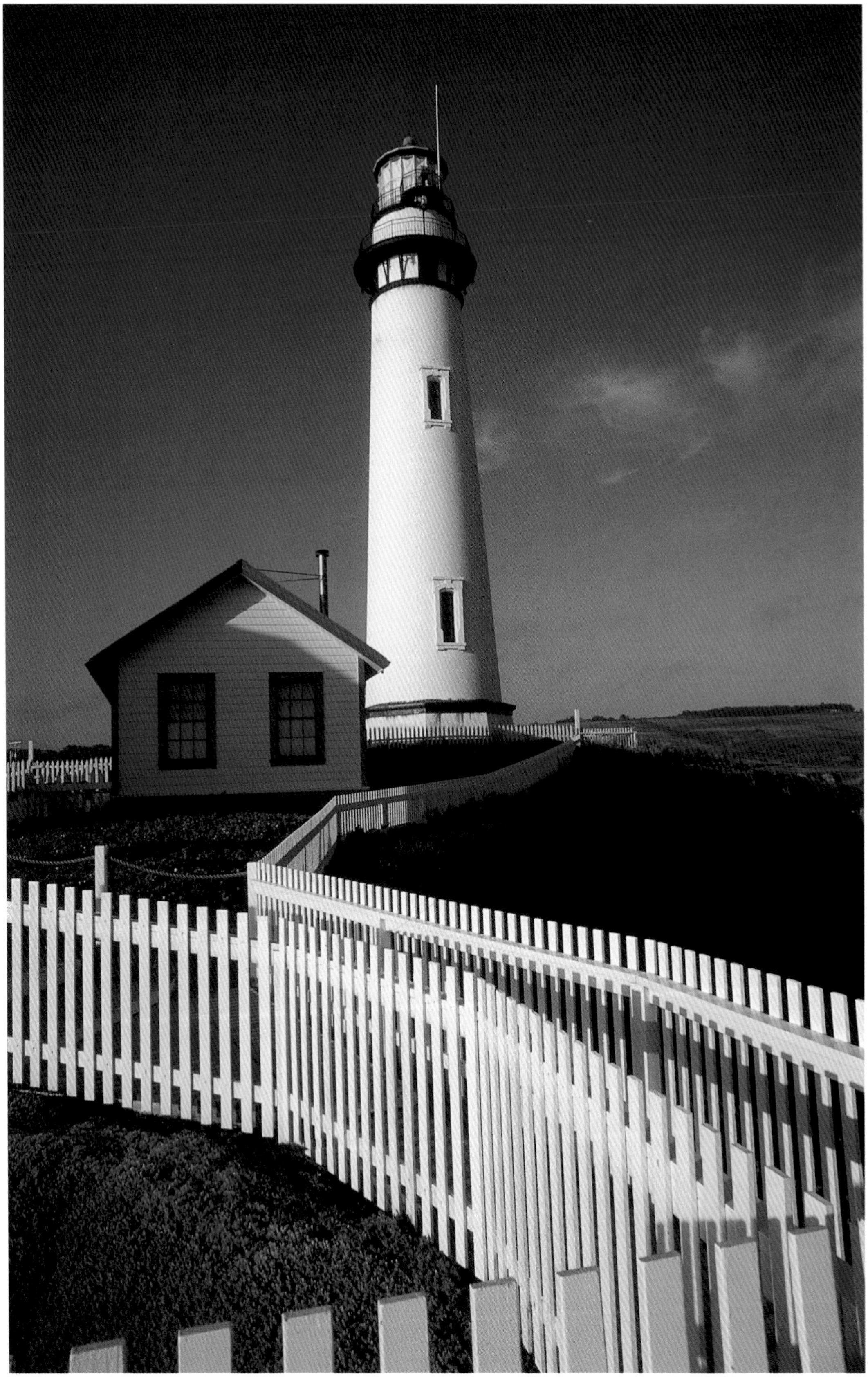

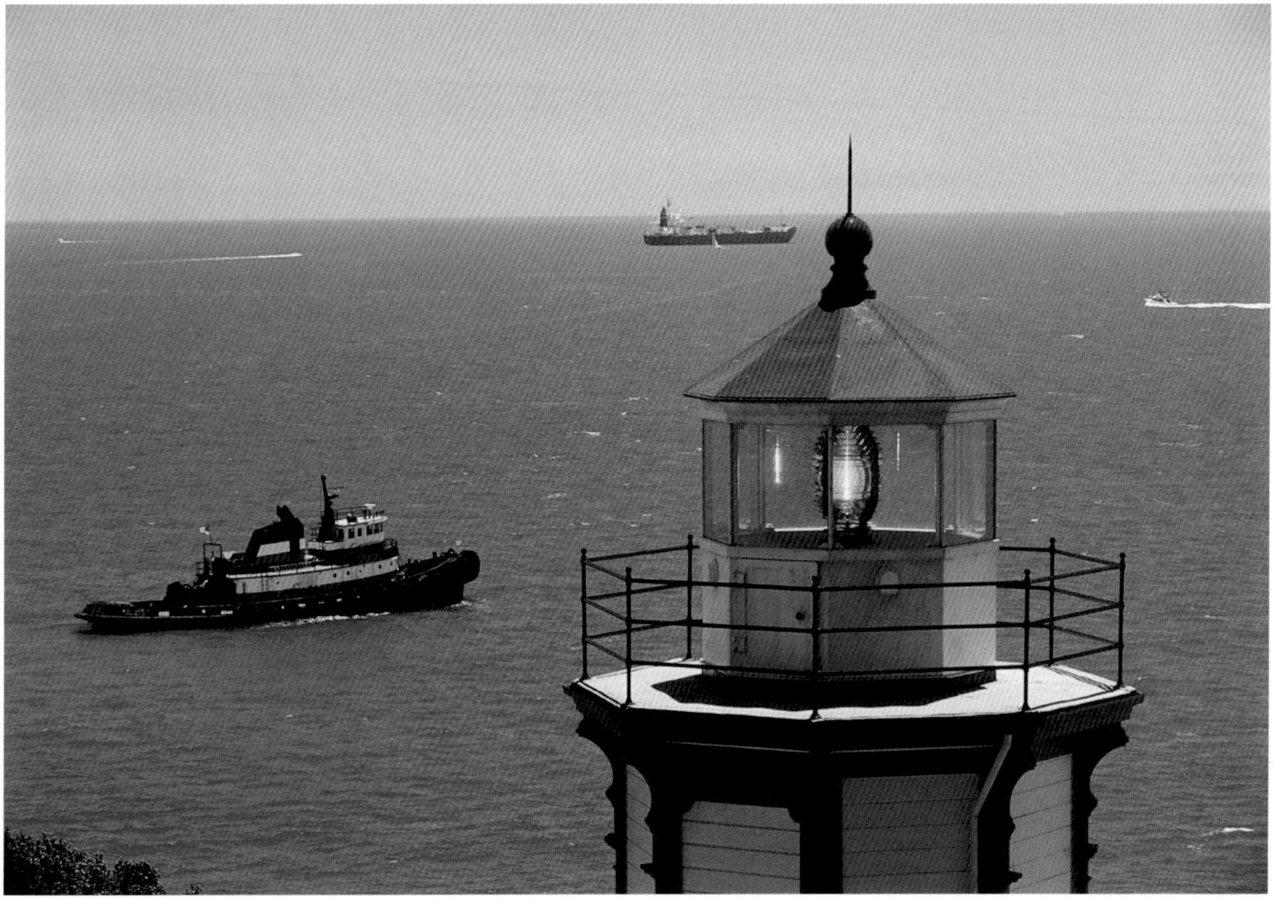

Yerba Buena Island lighthouse
The tiny octagonal tower flashes its light twenty-four hours every day. Lighthouses connected to local power grids operate around the clock, but have battery-power backup systems to continue service during power failures. Island lights, powered by batteries recharged by solar panels, are lit only during the dark.

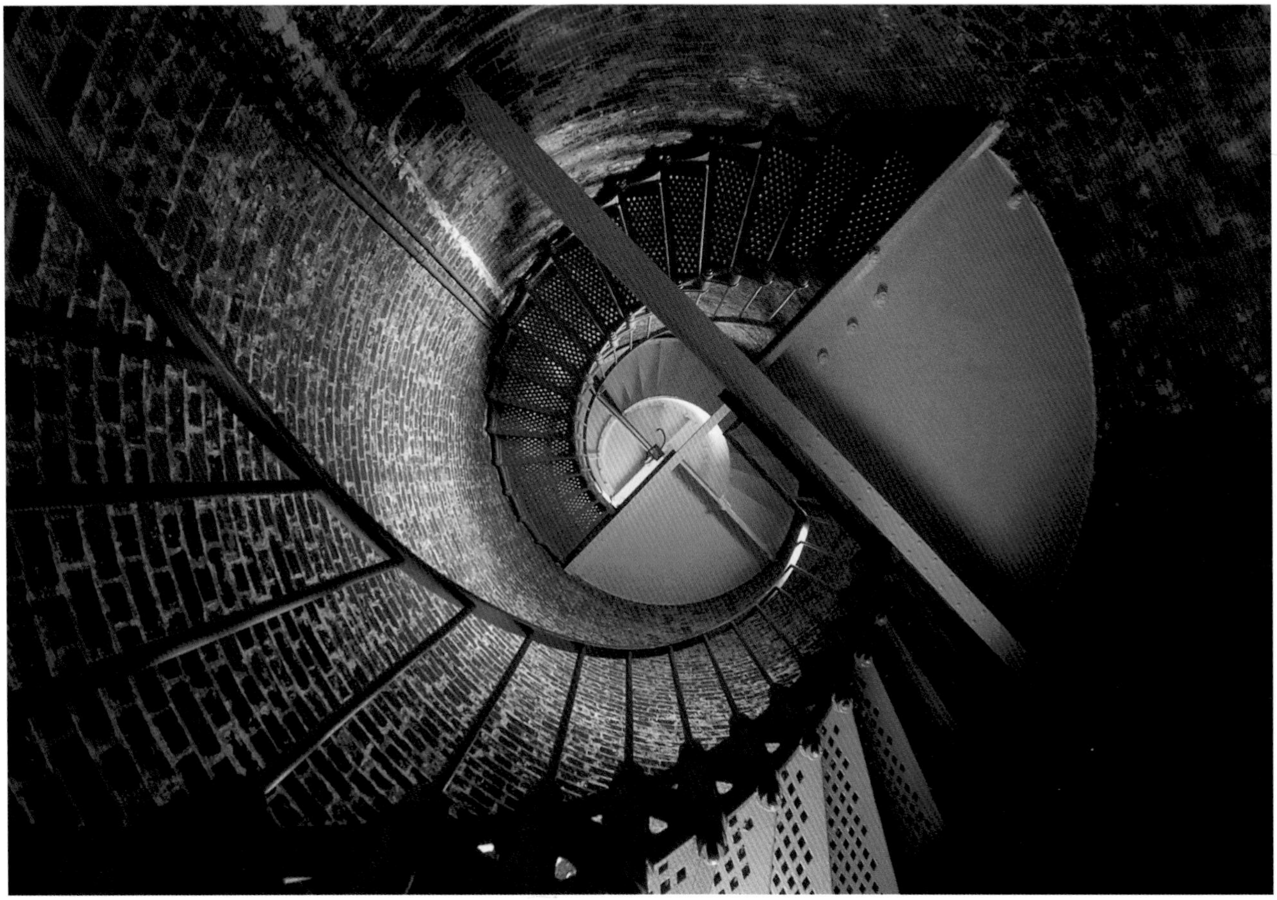

Cape Blanco light station

The lighthouse and attached workroom are constructed of 200,000 bricks that masons kilned on site. The interior originally had been painted white but restorers discovered moisture wicked through the mortar, and bubbled modern water-based paint. They removed the paint, making the interior more visually interesting at the same time.

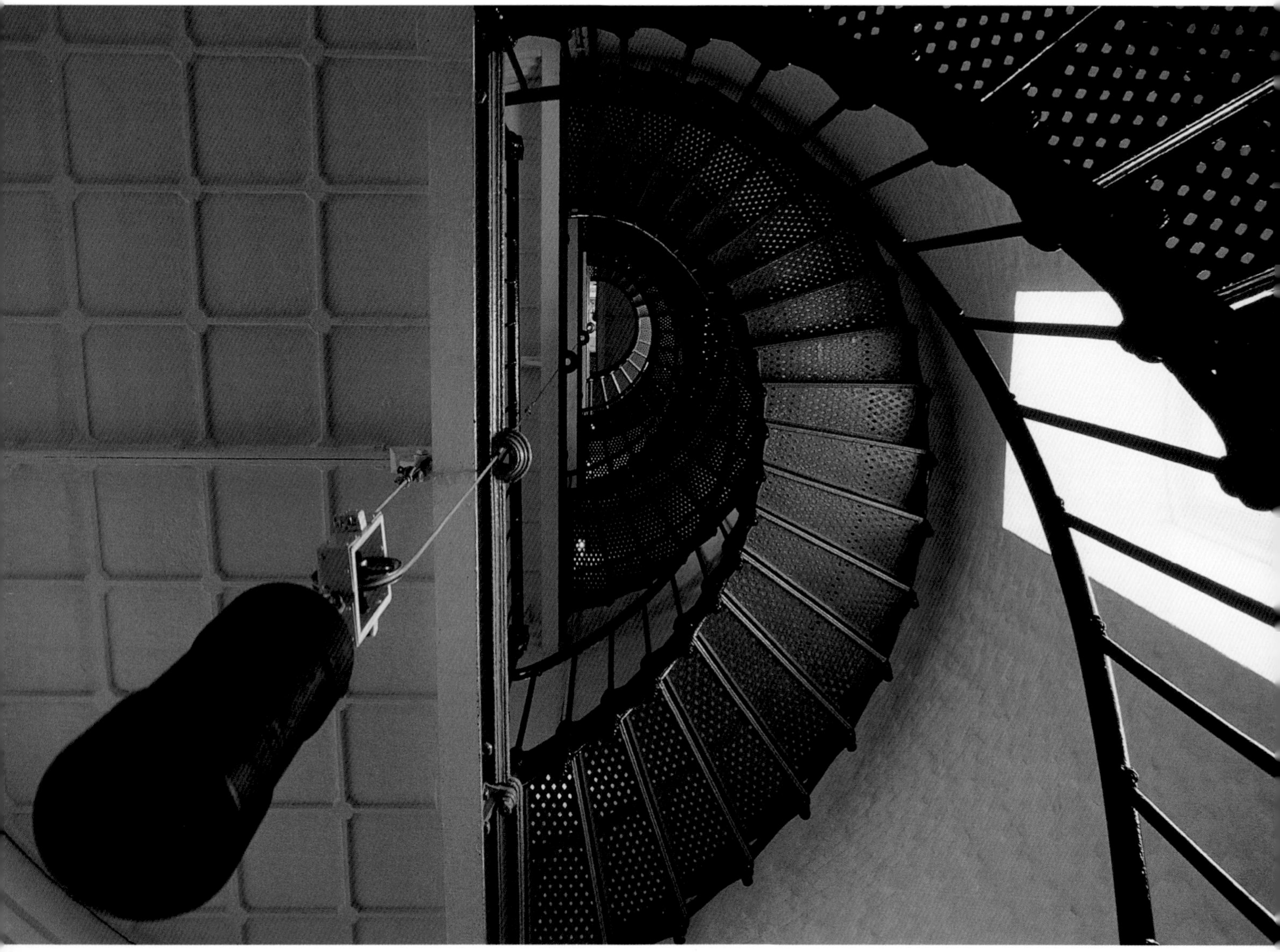

Pigeon Point light station
Lighthouse keepers spiraled up to the lantern room carrying twin five-gallon jugs of lantern fuel. Meanwhile the nearly 400-pound counterweight unwound toward the ground floor, working like a grandfather clock's mechanism to turn the lens. Keepers sometimes cranked up the weight twice during their overnight watches.

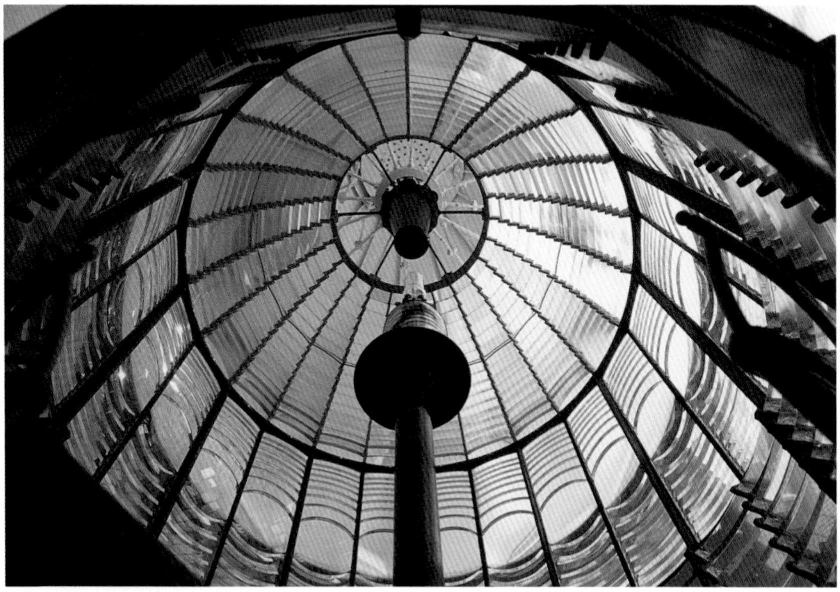

Pigeon Point light station
French lensmaker Henry LePaute produced most of the Fresnel lenses on the Pacific Coast. This first-order has 1,008 pieces of glass. Because so much lead and gold were incorporated into handblown glass in the eighteenth century, lighthouses shrouded the lenses to keep harsh sunlight from discoloring the crystal or to keep it from frying the lamp inside the lens.

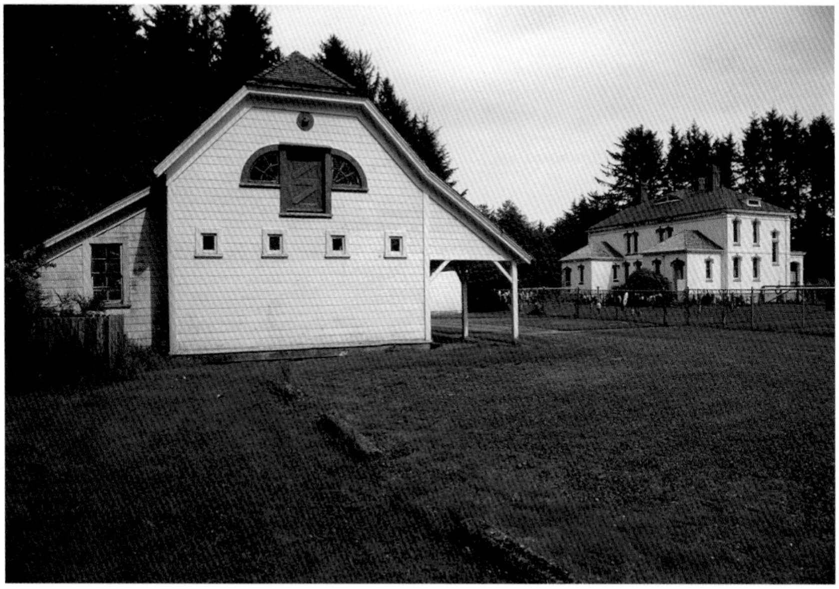

North Head light station
USLHE architect Carl Lieck designed not only North Head lighthouse but also the head keeper's residence, assistant's duplex (in the background), and this barn.

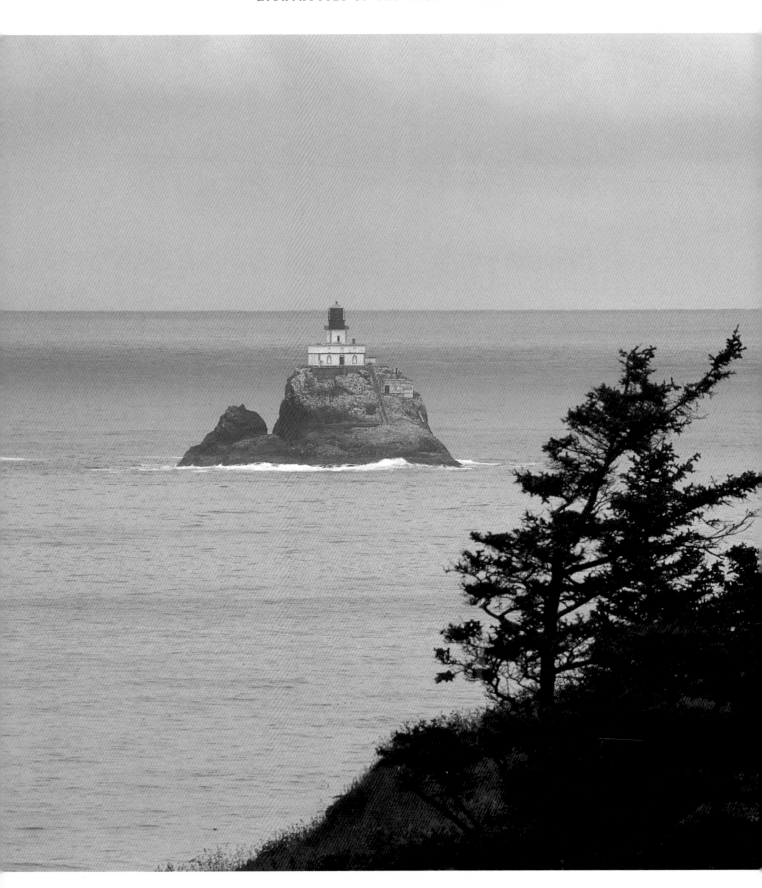

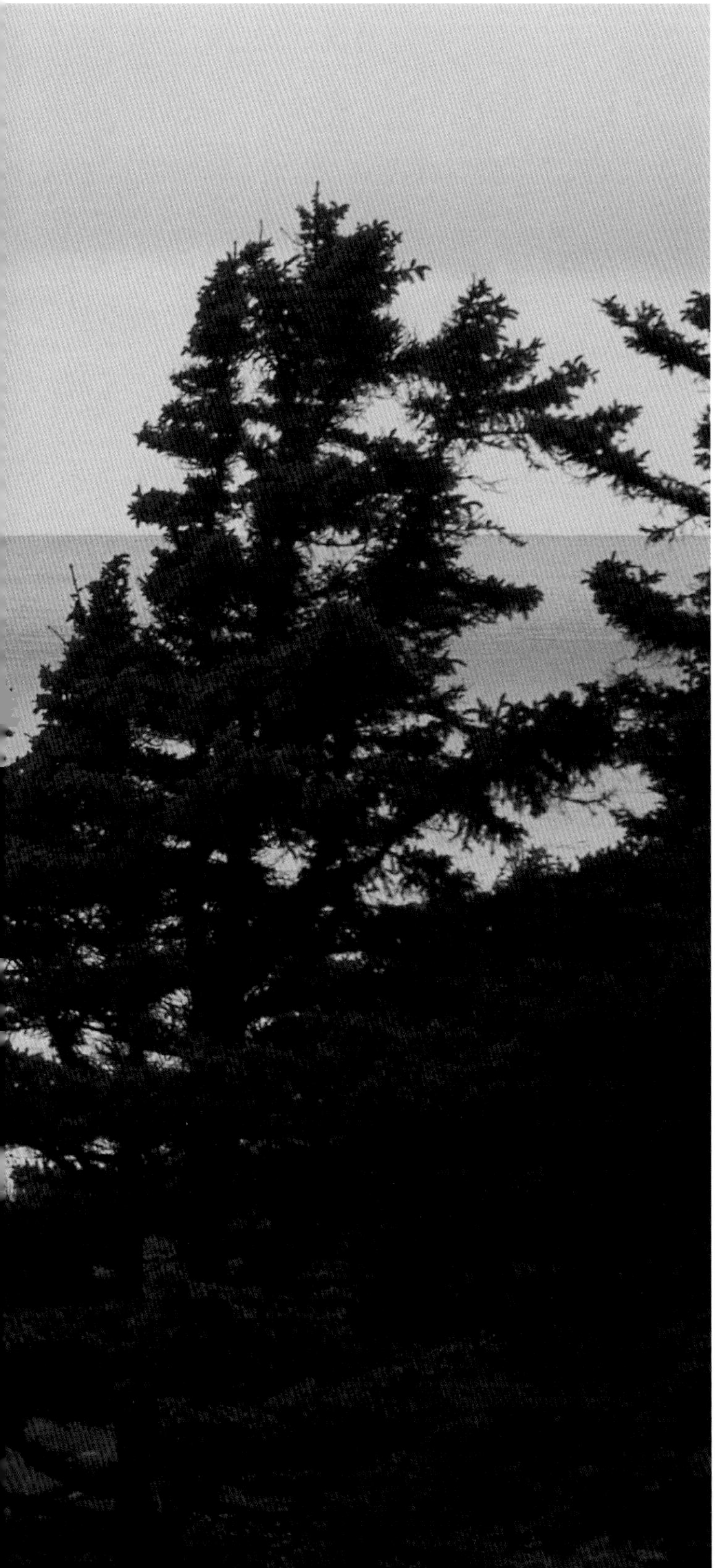

Tillamook Rock lighthouse
Looking deceptively benign, Tillamook Rock light has been known to drive its keepers mad. Builders constructed a 62-foot tower to house a first-order LePaute Fresnel. First lit in January 1881, it witnessed annual storms that put waves over the top of the lantern 133 feet above sea level. Deactivated in September 1957 as the most costly to operate, it later became the Eternity at Sea Columbarium, offering entombment for half a million mariners and other sea-lovers.

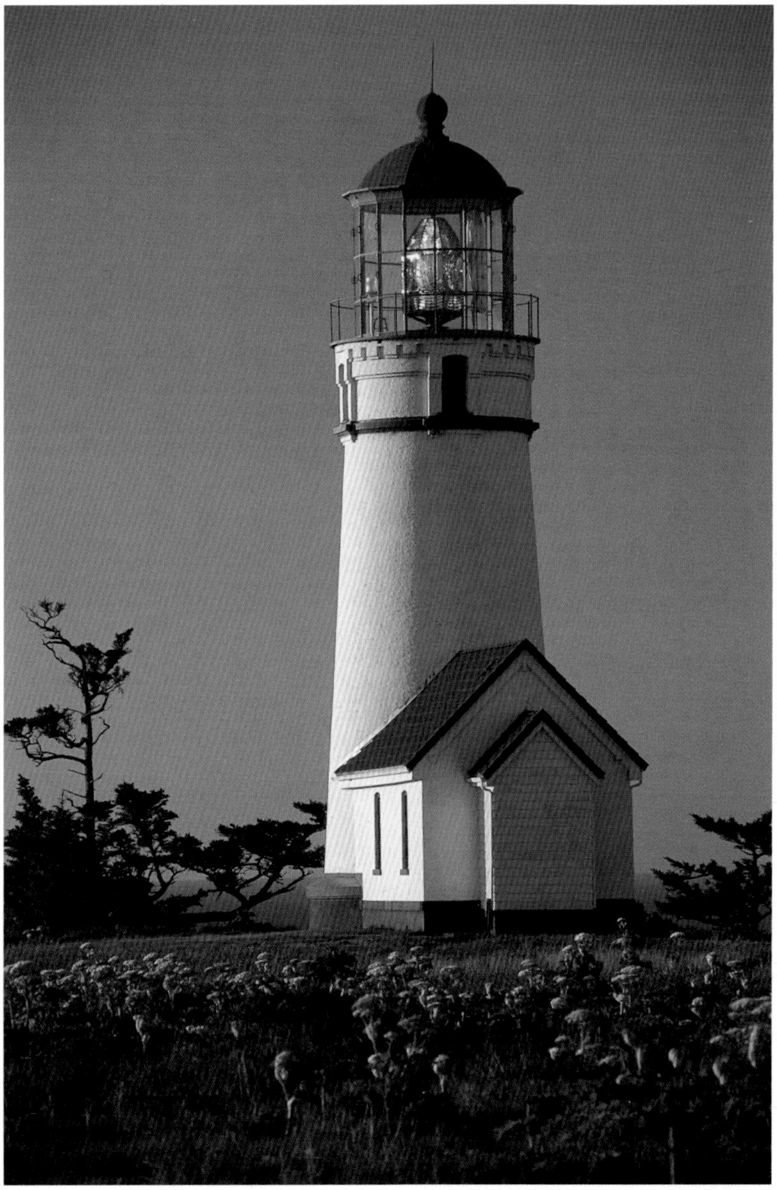

Cape Blanco light station
First lit in 1870, Cape Blanco was constructed by Lighthouse Service engineer R. S. Williamson. The 59-foot-tall light stands 245 feet above sea level. Its original LePaute first-order Fresnel was replaced in 1936 with this second-order lens manufactured in Paris by L. Sautter & Co.

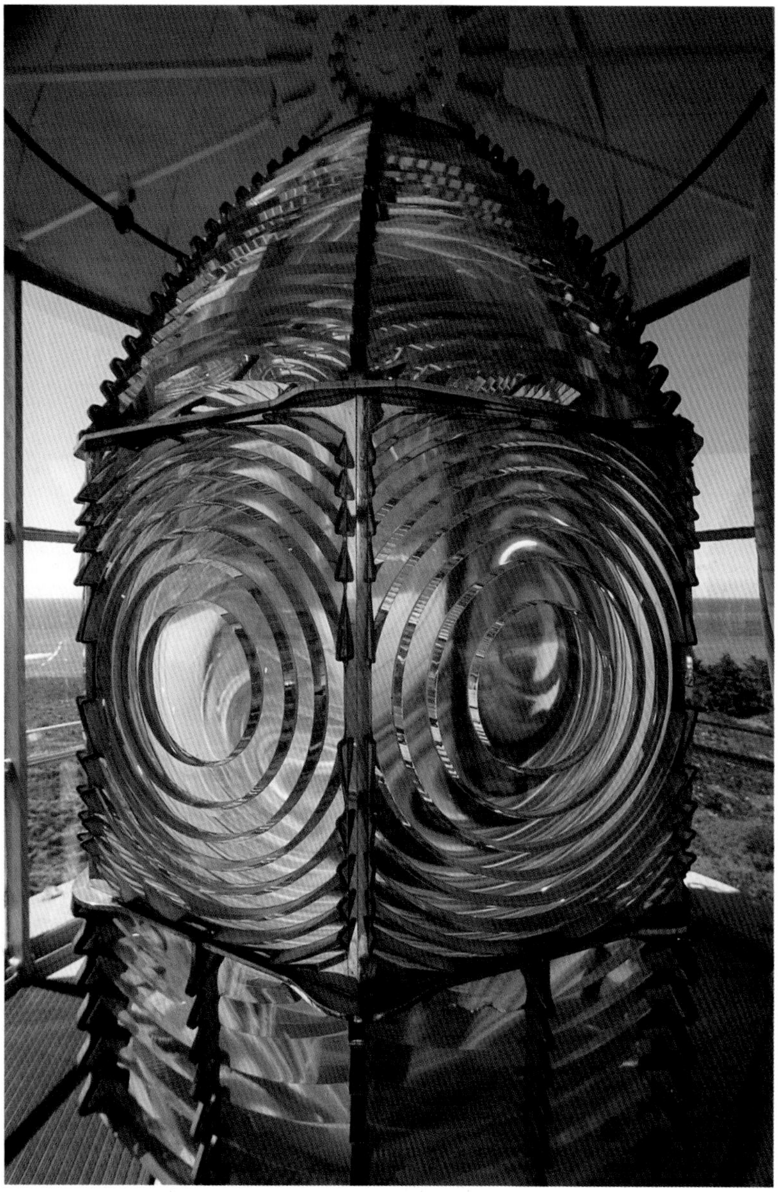

Cape Blanco light station
In 1992, vandals using a sledgehammer smashed several prisms and one of the eight bulls'-eye lenses. The vandals were caught, but the Coast Guard spent a year locating a glassmaker capable of this restoring the light. Hardin Optical in nearby Bandon, Oregon, worked another year to match perfectly the light transmission characteristics.

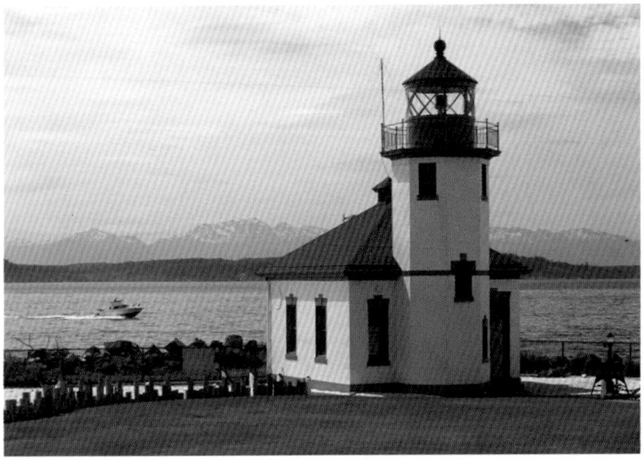

Above: **Alki Point light station**
Alki Point sits on Elliott Bay in West Seattle. This light, completed in 1913, stands just thirty-seven feet tall. By 1918, an electric bulb shined inside its fourth-order Fresnel. By this time lighthouse engineers knew vertical window frames interrupted the light, confusing mariners. They learned that light wrapped around diagonal braces.

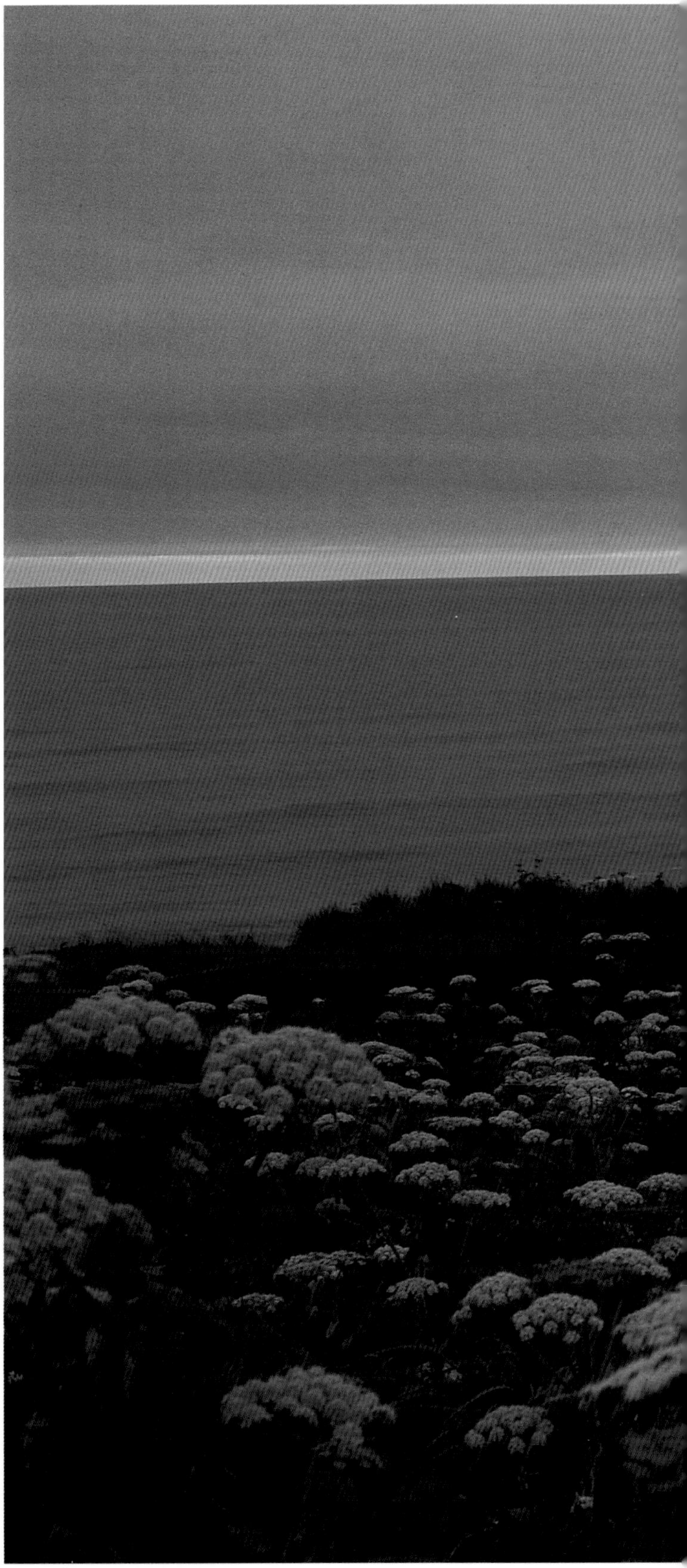

Right: **North Head light station**
North Head's large lantern room dwarfs the Vega Rotating Beacon atop the sixty-five-foot-tall tower. First lit in May 1898, the light accommodated the first-order Fresnel from nearby Cape Disappointment. Later, North Head housed a fourth-order Fresnel and then, following de-staffing in the early 1960s, two aero-beacons before getting this modern light. North Head gets pounded by winds reaching 150 mph. Builders set houses and outbuildings in the woods more than a quarter mile from the light and workroom.

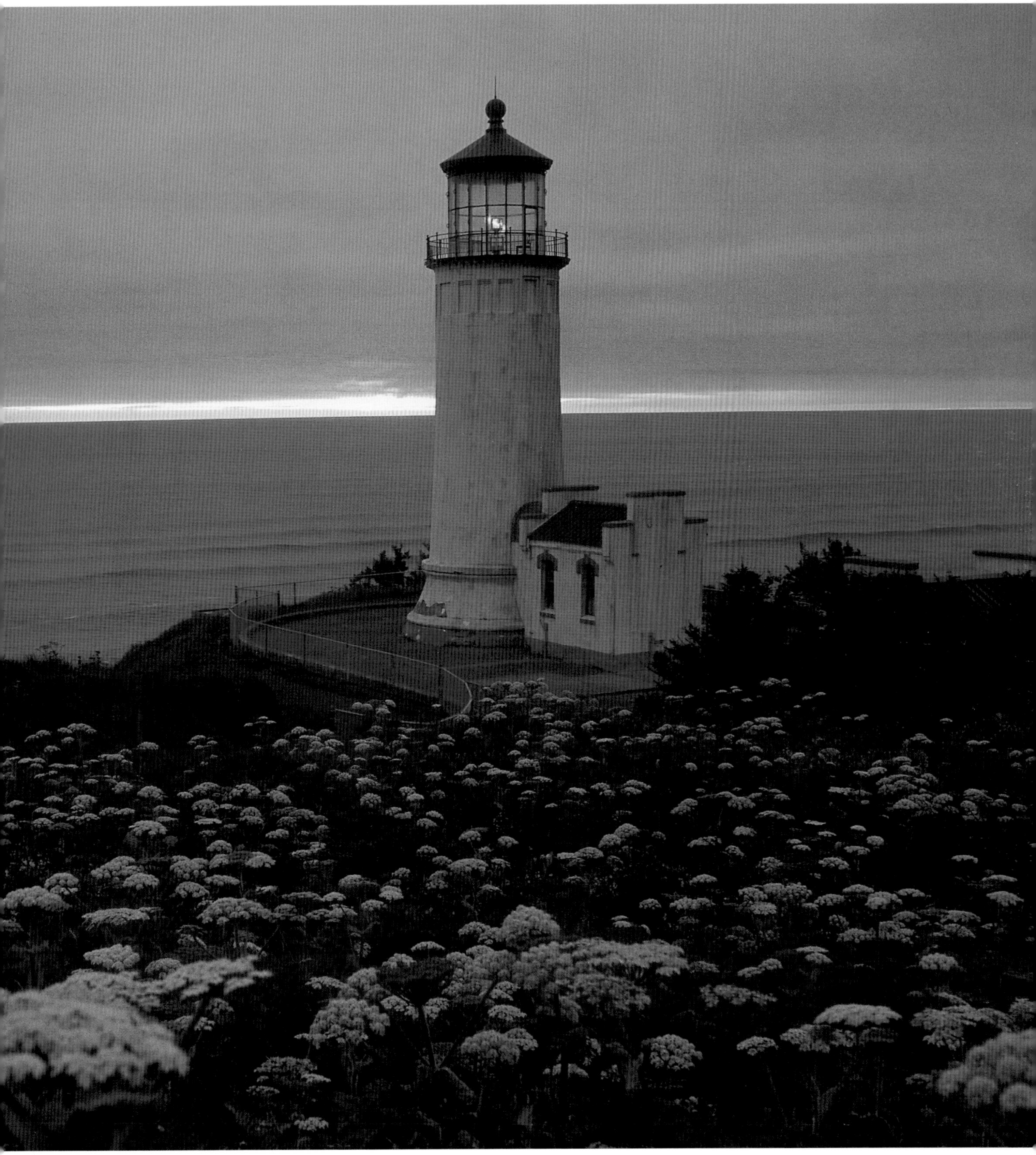

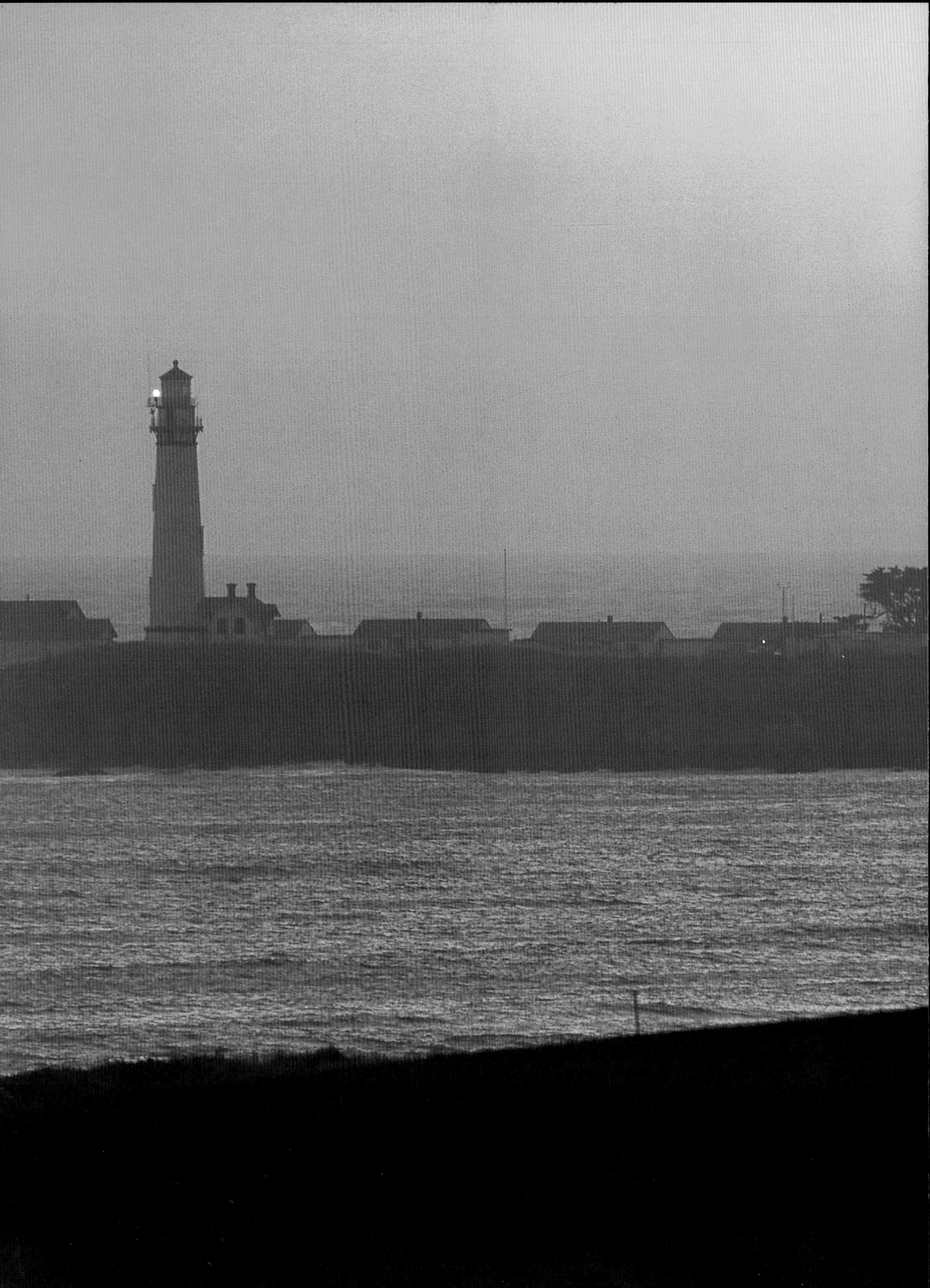

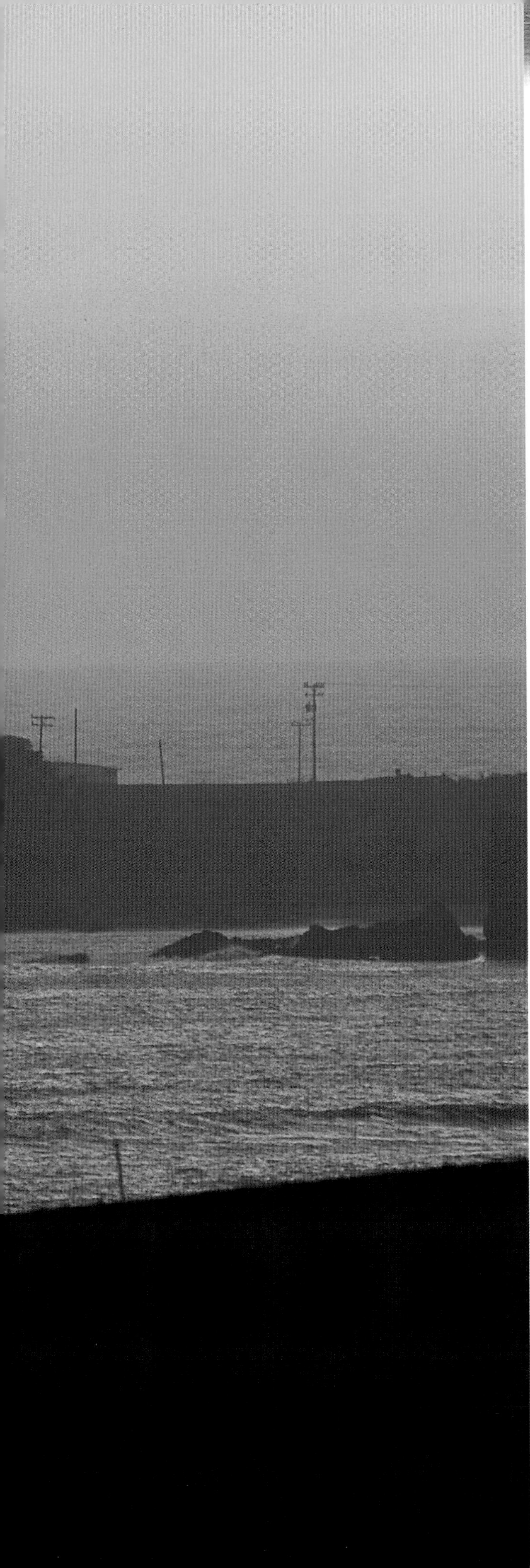

CHAPTER 4

The Role of Women Keepers

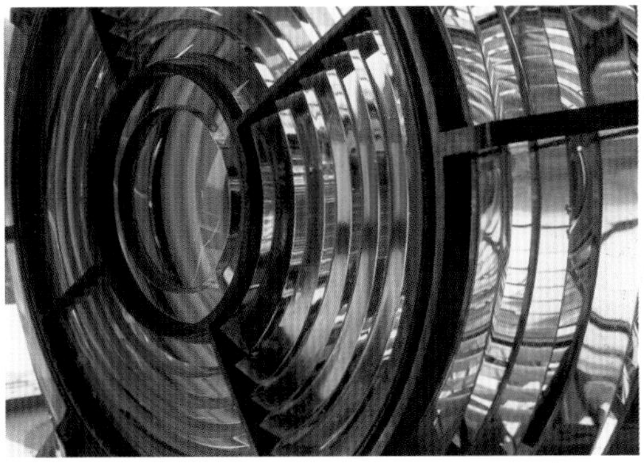

Left: PIGEON POINT LIGHT STATION
Augustin Fresnel's lenses gather light, reflecting and refracting the rays to project a point at a distance. Unlike these lenses, the earth's atmosphere defracts or scatters the setting sun through dust particles, airborne water vapor, and temperature layers, distorting the setting sun north of Pigeon Point on a summer evening.

Above: GRAYS HARBOR LIGHTHOUSE
Grays Harbor has a third-order "clamshell" Fresnel from Henry LePaute. It flashes red and white. Red glass cuts light transmission by as much as 90 percent, so LePaute made the red lens a first-order bull's-eye. The quality of his optics shows even on a gray day as the prisms break apart the light.

Head keeper Charles Layton, his wife Charlotte, and their four children moved into Point Pinos lighthouse near Monterey in August 1853. The Lighthouse Board encouraged married men with families to serve because wives and children often provided unpaid help to the keeper. Keepers had so many responsibilities that the USLHE, and later the Board, reasoned that wives and children could help out or even fill in if the keeper needed it—although the families did not receive more money unless members were officially appointed. This happened often on the Atlantic coast, and these families had shown dedication that sometimes defied belief.

Layton required his family's devoted assistance in October 1855, when he left Charlotte in charge of the light so he could join a local posse to capture the bandit Anastacio Garcia. Layton had served in both the British and U.S. Armies and had deep respect for right and wrong. In the mêlée, Garcia escaped but Layton was shot. He died on November 24, 1855, several days after returning home.

Charlotte kept the light going with help from assistant keeper Isaac Hitchcock. She wrote to new San Francisco Customs Collector Richard P. Hammond to tell him of Charles's death and to ask for his job. The USLHE and later the Board were among the first U.S. government agencies to recognize the skills and dedication of women and reward them with titles and pay identical to men. On January 4, 1856, the Board appointed Charlotte Layton as head keeper at Point Pinos. As the West Coast's first woman head keeper, she earned $1,000 a year.

Charlotte was the first of many woman head keepers on the West Coast. By the time she won her appointment, there already had been thirty women doing the same job on the East Coast. In 1860, Charlotte married her assistant keeper, George Harris, and a short time later, she left the Lighthouse Service.

Several decades after Charlotte left Point Pinos, the West Coast got another notable woman keeper, Laura Hecox, the ninth child of Santa Cruz keepers Adna and Margaret Hecox.

Throughout her childhood, Laura studied plants and creatures of coastal California, collecting unusual examples. She earned the head keeper job after her father died in 1883, by which time her collection had nearly filled the lighthouse office. She enthusiastically gave tours of the light and explained in detail the fossils, shells, and specimens she collected. In her fastidious manner, she demanded her visitors remove their shoes before climbing up to the lantern room.

Maria Israel was another collector who, while not head keeper, assisted her husband Robert at Point Loma. Assistant keeper Robert arrived with Maria in 1871. he became head keeper in 1873, remaining until 1891, when the Lighthouse Service replaced the often-fog-bound light with a steel tower built below the fog level. Maria kept a house that earned commendations at each inspection, but her artistry was more remarkable. She fashioned picture frames from seashells she found at the

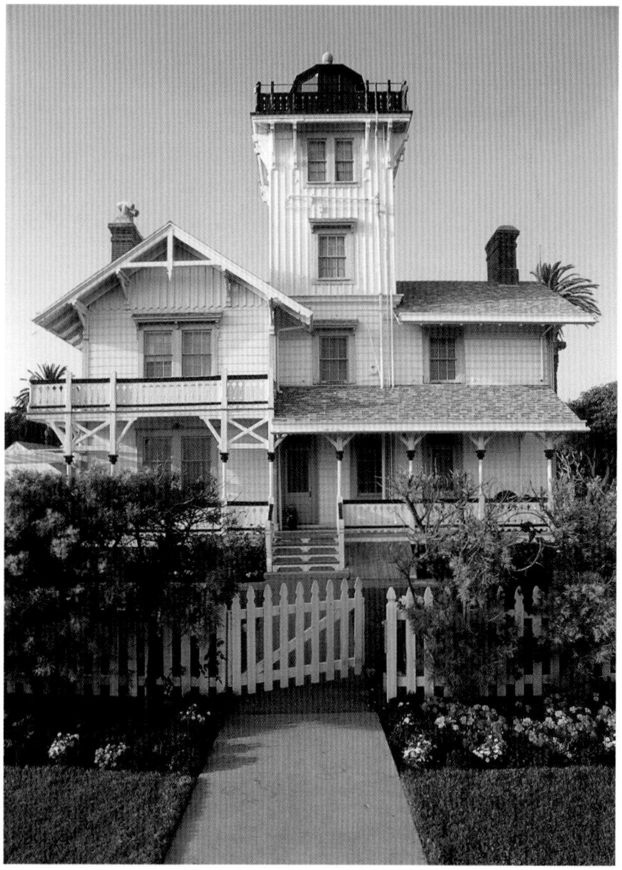

POINT FERMIN LIGHTHOUSE
Point Fermin's classic light was completed and first lit in December 1874. Built of Douglas fir for framing and California redwood for siding and trim, its first keepers were sisters Mary and Helen Smith, who resigned in 1882. The house, called Victorian, is more accurately called "Stick Style." This duplex provided separate entrances front and rear for head keeper and assistant. The Lighthouse Service operated the light until 1927, when the City of Los Angeles took over operating responsibility in exchange for use of the grounds as part of the new Point Fermin Park.

The First Wireless on the West Coast

Radio played an important role in lighthouses. Keepers supplemented their own intuition with radio weather reports, and in remote areas, evening broadcasts became a part of family entertainment. But radios also saved lives.

Perhaps the most celebrated early use of radio in an emergency occurred in 1912 when the *Titanic* struck an iceberg. Her SOS calls brought several ships to the aid of the sinking vessel; without these transmissions more passengers would have perished. Recognizing the role that radio played in saving lives, some *Titanic* survivors presented wireless radio inventor Guglielmo Marconi with a gold medal.

In 1896, Marconi received a patent for wireless communications. His devices sent electromagnetic waves from a transmitter to a receiver and antenna set. As Marconi experimented with new ideas and inventions, he expanded the distance between transmitter and receiver from a few yards to many miles. Marconi's wireless telegraph accomplished something scientists believed was impossible: A message was sent over the earth's horizon. People believed that a signal sent out parallel to the earth's surface continued to travel in a straight line forever. Marconi's signal bounced off the ionosphere and back to Earth, time and again following the planet's curvature. He established the Wireless Telegraph and Signal Company Ltd. to manufacture and sell wireless components.

By 1899, the wireless had reached the United States. The *San Francisco Call* newspaper purchased wireless equipment and tested it thoroughly. Electrical current in the city interfered with radio transmissions, however, so the *Call* asked for and received assistance from the Lighthouse Service.

The Service proposed that its new *Lightship San Francisco* No. 70 might be an ideal carrier for a transmitter, as it was anchored seven miles from the Golden Gate Bridge and carried electric lights and generators. The Marconi apparatus consisted of a temporary connection to the ship's electricity, telegraph key, Rhumkorff coil (a device used to create high voltage from low voltage through a copper-wire coil), and an antenna. The *Call* set up a receiving station at the Cliff House south of San Francisco.

The Spanish-American War had ended and San Francisco eagerly awaited the return of the troopship *Sherman* carrying soldiers from California. Announcing the ship's arrival into the Bay would be the first West Coast test of this new technology and a scoop for the paper. At 5:15 P.M. on August 23, 1899, the wireless operator transmitted the message "*Sherman* is sighted" repeatedly from the lightship to Cliff House. News of the returning ship and the success of the wireless message quickly spread.

One month later on September 21, 1899, Marconi arrived in New York to demonstrate his new technology during the America's Cup yacht race at Newport, Rhode Island. He set up a transmitter aboard the vessel *Ponce* and the Lighthouse Service approved a receiving station for New Jersey's Navesink lighthouse. The operator sent 2,500 words during the race, averaging 15 a minute. Navy officers, the Signal Corps, and the Lighthouse Service were all impressed by the devices.

Within months, Congress appropriated $25,000 to begin installing wireless apparatus on all lightships and at isolated lighthouses, bringing joy and peace of mind to many lighthouse keepers and their families for years to come.

base of the 460-foot-high peninsula on which their lighthouse was built. Some scenes she framed were produced using human hair, an artistic style widely practiced after the American Civil War.

Life at Point Pinos

Charlotte Layton, Laura Hecox, and Maria Israel paved the way for California's most famous keeper, Emily Maitland Fish, who followed Charlotte at Point Pinos thirty-three years after Charlotte left.

Maitland was born in 1843 in Albion, Michigan. When Emily was ten, her older sister, Juliet, married Dr. Melancthon Fish and moved to Shanghai, China, for six years where he was diplomatic counsel; Emily joined them in 1859. Unfortunately, Juliet died in childbirth. By the time Fish, Emily, and the baby, Juliet, came home in 1862, Emily and the doctor had married. They were accompanied by a Chinese servant, Que.

When they returned to the United States, they found that the Civil War had begun. Fish joined the Union Army and became medical director of the sixteenth Army Corps. Emily and Juliet followed him from one battle to the next, working with the predecessor of the American Red Cross. After the war, the Army transferred Fish and family to the Benecia Arsenal near Oakland, California. He soon set up private practice and moved to Oakland. In November 1888, daughter Juliet married Lieutenant Commander Henry E. Nichols, the Lighthouse Service's Twelfth District inspector.

After the doctor died in March 1891, Nichols and Juliet mentioned to Emily in 1893 that keeper Alan Luce planned to retire from Point Pinos. Emily announced that she'd like to apply for the job. Since this was before Civil Service examinations, it took only Nichols's recommendation to get the position.

Emily was intelligent and charming, tall and attractive, and had great style. She kept the small Cape Cod, its ninety-four-acre reserve, and her own life in the manner she learned in Shanghai and Oakland. Her thor-

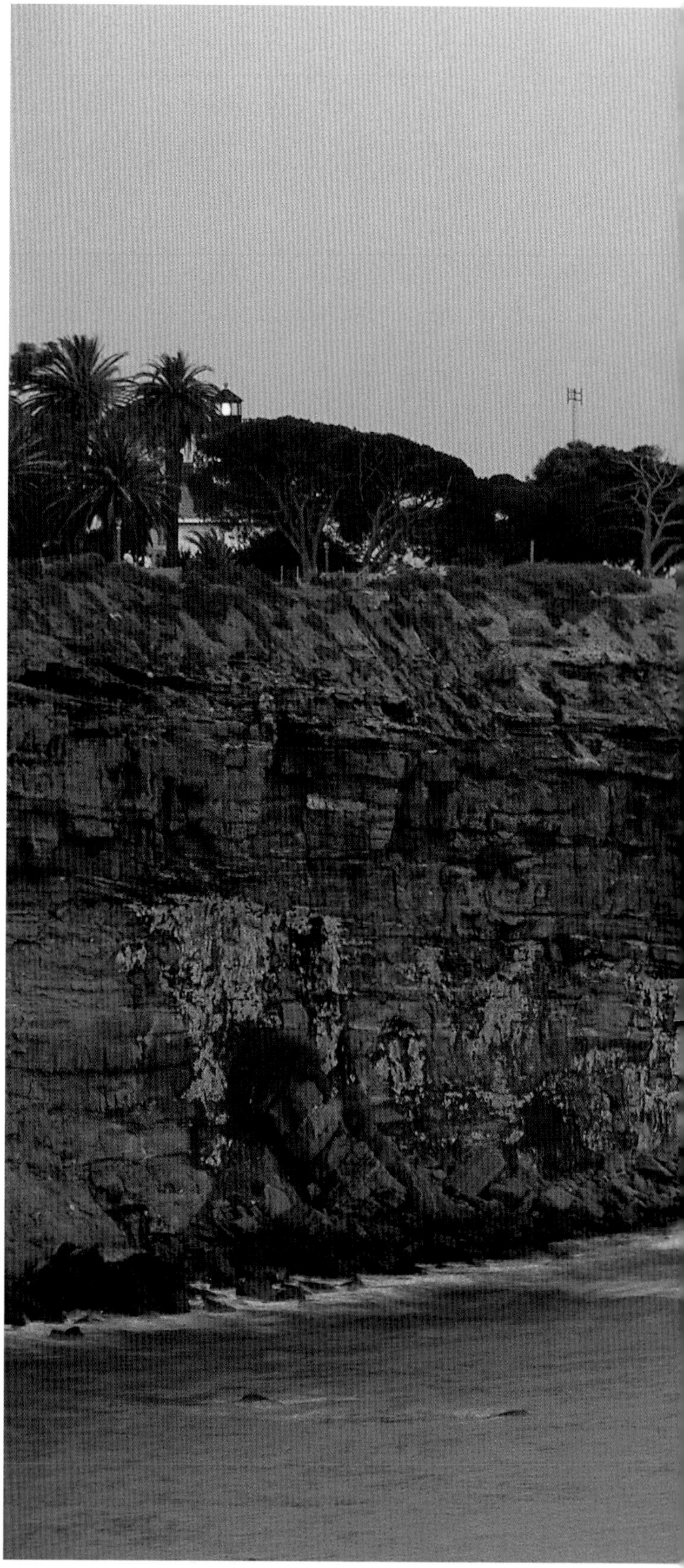

Point Fermin lighthouse
In December 1941, military personnel shut down the light. The lantern room gallery was then converted into an observation post to watch ships coming in and out of Los Angeles Harbor a mile east. A fourth-order Fresnel now shines at reduced power. The active navigation aid is behind a Coast Guard residence nearby.

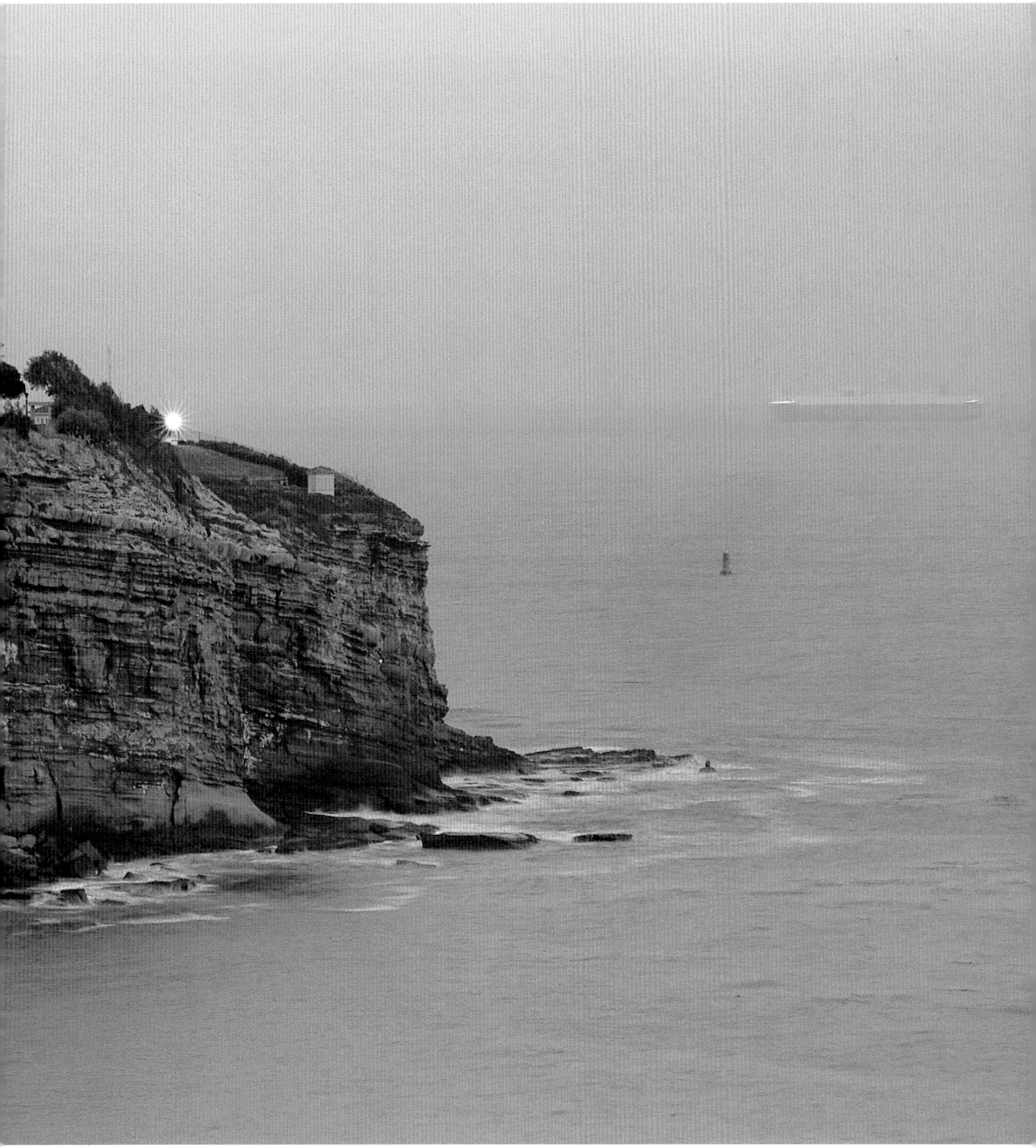

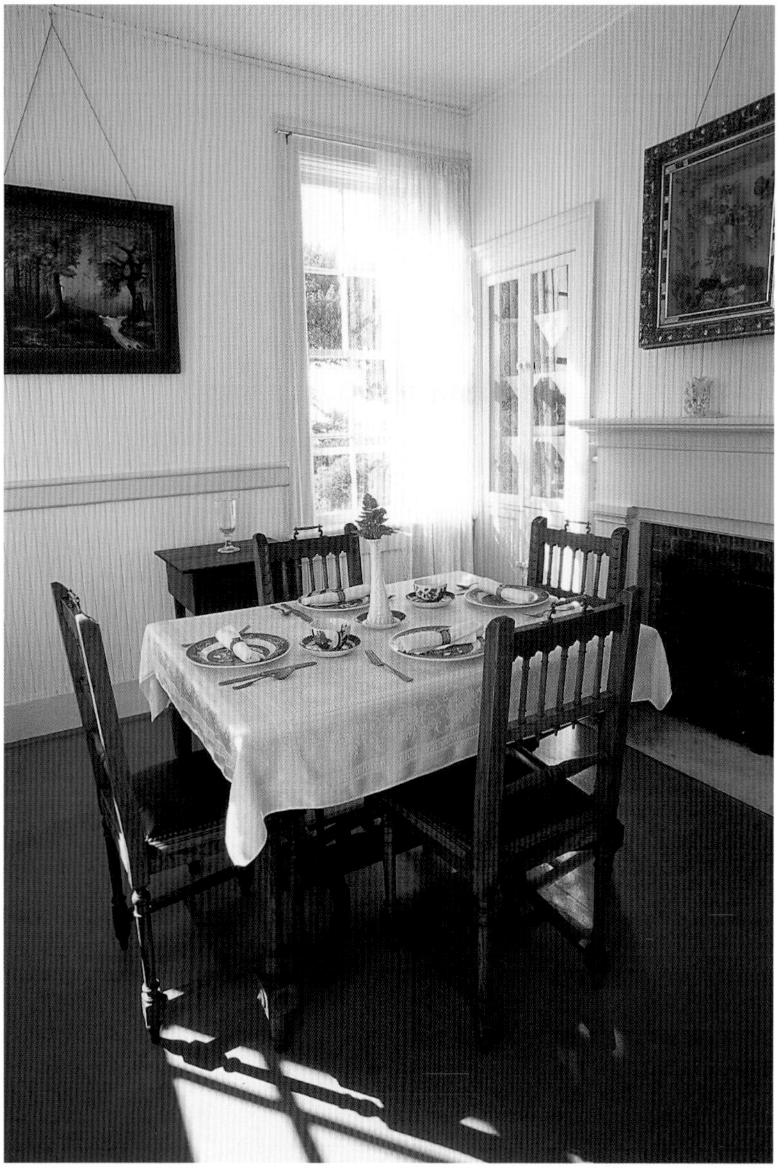

Yaquina Bay lighthouse
The lighthouse had only one keeper, Charles Pierce, plus his wife, Sarah, and seven of their nine children. A retired Army captain, Pierce, from Boston, and Sarah, from New York, served as keeper at Cape Blanco before and after their brief three-year service at Yaquina Bay. The Pierces took pride in their children's manners, and meals were formal.

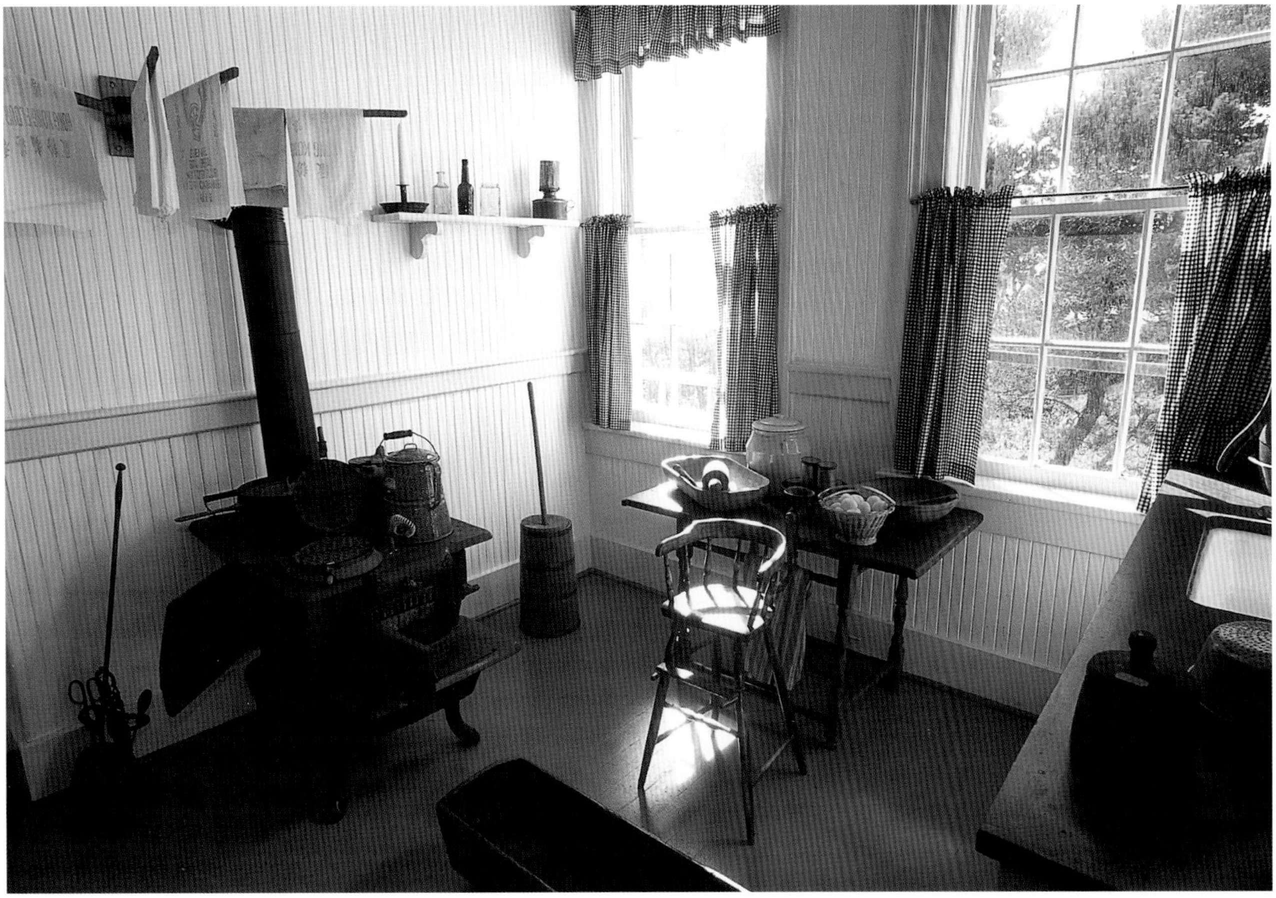

Above: **YAQUINA BAY LIGHTHOUSE**
The Pierces' kitchen was centered around a wood-burning stove. The light was scheduled for demolition regularly from 1946 until the Lincoln County Historical Society saved it.

Right: **YAQUINA BAY LIGHTHOUSE**
Yaquina Bay is an architectural gem, first lit in 1871. But beautiful as the house is, it proved to be badly located as a light, and the Lighthouse Service deactivated it in 1874. It was replaced with the Yaquina Head light four miles up the coast and closer to the ocean.

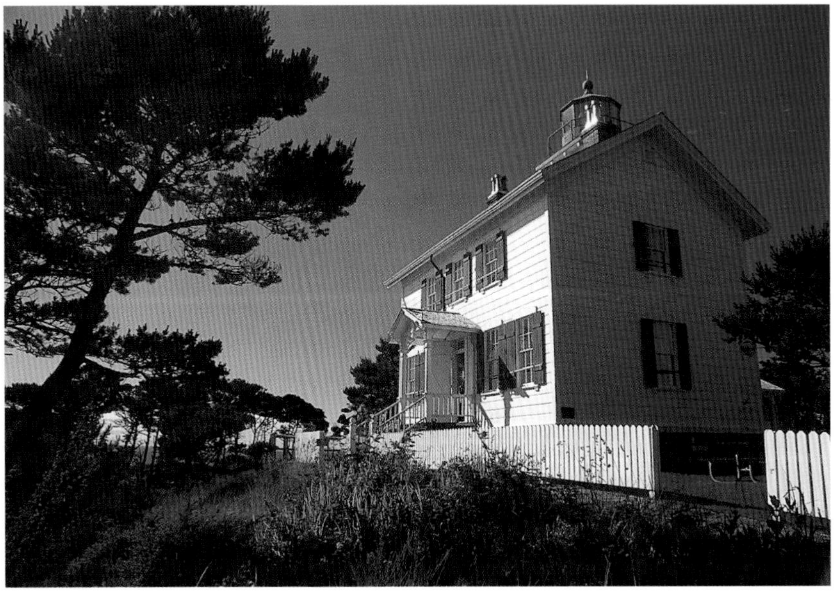

oughbred horses drew her carriage into Monterey. With help from two assistant keepers, she administered the light and a busy social schedule. Que assisted her with the gardens and livestock and helped tend party guests.

When her son-in-law came for routine inspections, Nichols treated Emily as he did keepers at Farallon or Point Bonita, and she earned commendations for the light's condition. Monterey and Carmel socialites who prized invitations to tea or dinner at the lighthouse envied her, and the communities surrounding the light were grateful to her when she helped form the Monterey–Pacific Grove American Red Cross.

After Nichols died in 1902, Juliet, inspired by her mother's life, applied for and became a keeper at San Francisco Bay's Angel Island lighthouse. She performed her job as conscientiously as Emily, and one time, she rang the fog bell by hand for more than twenty hours until visibility returned. When fog returned two days later, she spent the entire night pounding the bell with a hammer.

One of Emily Fish's most interesting log entries concerns the San Fransisco earthquake of April 18, 1906. "At 5:30 A.M. violent and continued earthquake shocks jarred the lens causing it to bend the connecting tube [from the oil reservoir] and loosened the lens, so it was unstable. . . ."

It had taken eighteen minutes for the shock waves to reach Pacific Grove from San Francisco where the infamous earthquake struck with what is now believed to be 8.3 Richter scale intensity. Ruptured gas lines burned for three days; there was no water to extinguish the blazes because water mains had also split. The quake and six hours of aftershocks killed some 3,000 people and destroyed 28,000 buildings. Up and down the coast, California's lighthouses rocked and reeled.

At Point Bonita, the wooden keepers' residences collapsed. Keepers lived in a large tent for a year before the Service could rebuild the houses. The Service had no disaster funds, and money was needed more urgently up at Point Arena where the quake severely cracked the tower, and it had to be razed. It took eleven months to get the funding to rebuild through Congress. The Service contracted with a San Francisco industrial-chimney builder for a new reinforced-concrete tower. The replacement lacked charm, but it has survived earthquakes since.

One lasting effect of the San Francisco earthquake was that the lighthouses that followed were constructed to resist the shaking. Another effect was that, as San Francisco began to rebuild and contractors sought wood from northern California's coast, new lighthouses were needed from Point Reyes up to Crescent City. Point Cabrillo light, completed in 1909, was constructed especially because of local lumber mill owners' shipping safety concerns.

"A Holy Shrine"

In 1925, Thelma Austin took over duties at Point Fermin light south of Los Angeles. Thelma, her sister, and five brothers grew up at Point Conception and Point Arena. After years of faithful duty, the Lighthouse Bureau rewarded her father with the Point Fermin head-keeper post. Yet within a short time of the family's arrival there, Thelma's mother died; her father took the loss hard. After he died, Thelma wrote the Bureau asking for his position: "Why, the sea and this lighthouse seem to me like a holy shrine, and I'm afraid it would break my heart to give it up. But no matter what happens, I will accept my fate with a brave heart, and just as cheerfully as my parents would have done. When you have been raised in the lighthouse atmosphere, as I have been, it is mighty difficult to change your mode of living and accept any other line of endeavor which does not offer romance and adventure." That seemed to be all the written examination that Bureau administrators needed to fill the Civil Service post. Thelma got the job, though to supplement the low salary, she worked part time as a dental assistant.

Electrification made Austin's job easier. Instead of hours each day spent cleaning soot, polishing the lens, and preparing oil and wicks, she passed a few moments each evening cleaning salt spray off the lantern room windows as she circled the widow's walk. Then she flipped a switch. She continued her dual life as dental hygienist and lighthouse keeper even after the Coast Guard assumed operation of all lighthouses in 1939.

Austin remained as civilian keeper until December 5, 1941. On that day, the Coast Guard deactivated Point Fermin lighthouse and replaced the Fresnel lens with a radar antenna. Lookouts with high-powered binoculars prowled Austin's widow's walk. Two days later, the Japanese bombed Pearl Harbor, and the role of lighthouses changed dramatically.

Fog Signals

California's coastal fog led to the undoing of more than a few keepers and eventually of two lighthouses as well. The lights at Point Bonita and Point Loma were lost in fog for weeks on end, due to their high elevation.

America's first lighthouse fog signal appeared at Boston Harbor on Great Brewster Island. Through the course of a murky but otherwise still night in 1719, John Hayes, Boston's second lighthouse keeper, heard several cutters firing small deck cannons; they were answered within moments by another ship as each one announced its location. Wise mariners dropped their sails and set anchors in fog, but strong tides and currents sometimes set them drifting. Hayes got a cannon for his station, and his assistant fired it at regular intervals when visibility was low.

When Point Bonita lighthouse went on duty high above the Pacific, technology hadn't advanced much. Some eastern stations experimented with bells; these ended up on the West Coast as well, but they weren't much better than the cannons that were still prevalent. Point Bonita's head keeper Edward Colston asked District Inspector Hartman Bache for something to warn ships away from his point. Bache acquired a ten-pound cannon from the Fort Benecia arsenal, and Colston installed it below the lighthouse tower on August 7, barely three months after first operating the light. Bache hired retired Army Sergeant Edward Maloney at first assistant keeper's wages to fire the cannon every thirty minutes in the fog.

Within a month, Maloney had his baptism. A thick cloud settled down onto the ocean and hung there for seventy-two hours. A day after it lifted, Maloney wrote San Francisco Customs Collector Richard Hammond: No one would relieve him, he complained, and he had grabbed only moments of sleep during the three days and nights he was on duty. Hammond sent Maloney an assistant, but no one anticipated the financial cost of this kind of signal.

By March 1857, the start of its foggiest year, Point Bonita cut back its signal to one blast hourly. By March 1858, however, Maloney and his colleague had fired the cannon 1,582 times. The 5,500 pounds of gunpowder they used cost more than \$2,000—twice a head keeper's salary. Eventually, they replaced the cannon with a bell. That worked little better than the cannon and was no less exhausting for the keepers.

This was one more frustration for Hartman Bache. His first job was to inspect and supervise his keepers. But his overarching concern—and his constant motivation—was to give navigational aid to mariners at sea. Fog bells that were rung by hammers soon replaced cannons at East and West Coast stations. There seemed to be a competition among districts for the largest bell. The Board, in 1860, installed a 3,150-pound bell at Ediz Hook light at Port Angeles, Washington; soon after, the Board placed the West Coast's largest—a 4,000-pound bell—at California's Trinidad Head. The Board experimented and discovered that certain mid-range metallic tones carried better across the water, and the tone's clarity and strength was proportional to the heft of the brass bells. Clockworks, similar to what spun the Fresnels, operated automatic striker mechanisms. But they often failed, requiring the keepers to break out their hammers.

By 1870, the Board adopted steam-operated diaphone horns. These blew compressed air through a diaphragm; the resulting noise resonated through a long, large megaphone. At South Farallon Island, Bache thought he had a clever idea after watching wave action in a small cave. As the water rushed in, it blasted air up a natural shaft that opened into the lighthouse yard. Bache capped the hole with a diaphragm-equipped trumpet. Although many of Bache's ideas worked well, this one backfired. While storm-tossed seas forced air through the horn perfectly, thick fog usually settled on calm seas with no wind, and the horn remained silent. A winter storm blew the entire apparatus down, and the station went to steam soon after.

To power the steam diaphones, coal-fired boilers consumed fuel at the rate of 140 pounds an hour. Point Reyes, north of San Francisco's Golden Gate, was often recorded as one of the foggiest stations in the United States; logbooks listed 2,100 hours of fog annually in several instances. One prolonged bout made the signal run 176 hours— seven days, and eight hours— nonstop. Keepers shoveled 24,640 pounds of coal in that week alone. Late summer and early fall months on San Francisco Bay have been described as sounding like giant bogs, the bay surrounded by enormous frogs that croaked in two tones.

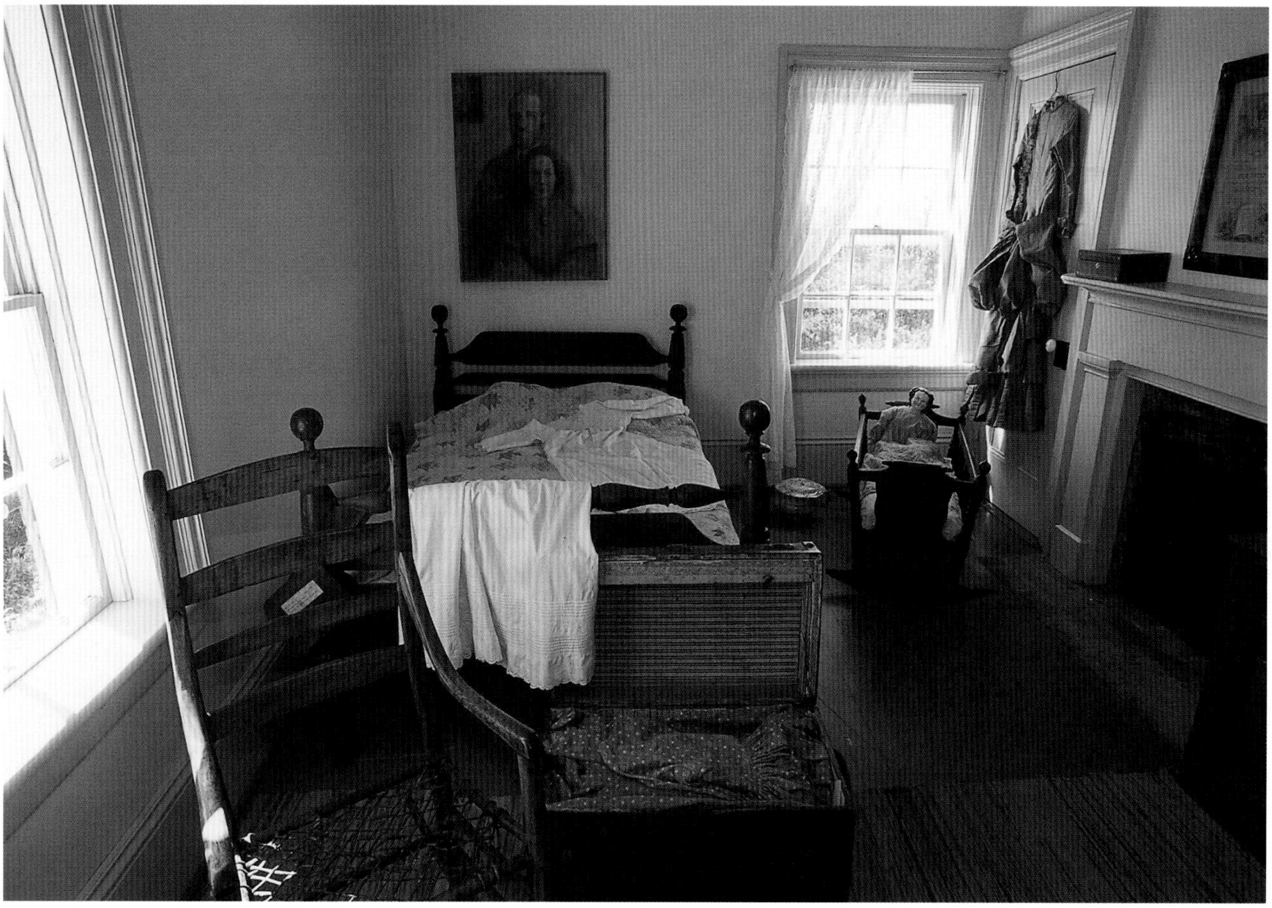

Yaquina Bay lighthouse
Charles and Sarah Pierce look out over their bed, beside the cradle for their ninth child, who was born at the lighthouse. Like most West Coast head keepers, Charles earned $1,000 a year. He and Sarah had a large garden and only a short walk into the town of Newport.

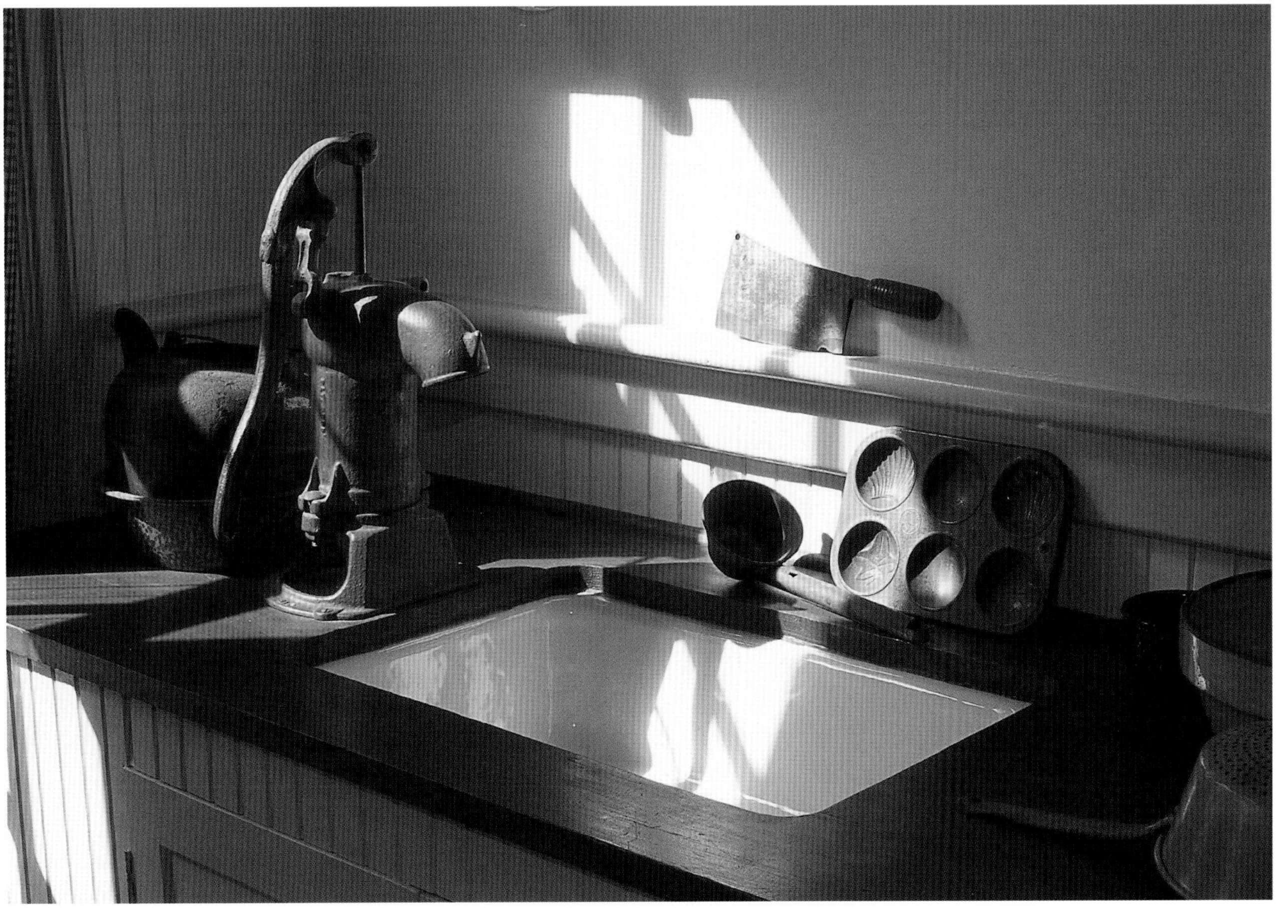

Yaquina Bay lighthouse
The house had running water in the kitchen. A rainwater-fed cistern supplied cooking, washing, and drinking needs for the Pierce family, and the subsequent jetty builders and Life Saving Service crews.

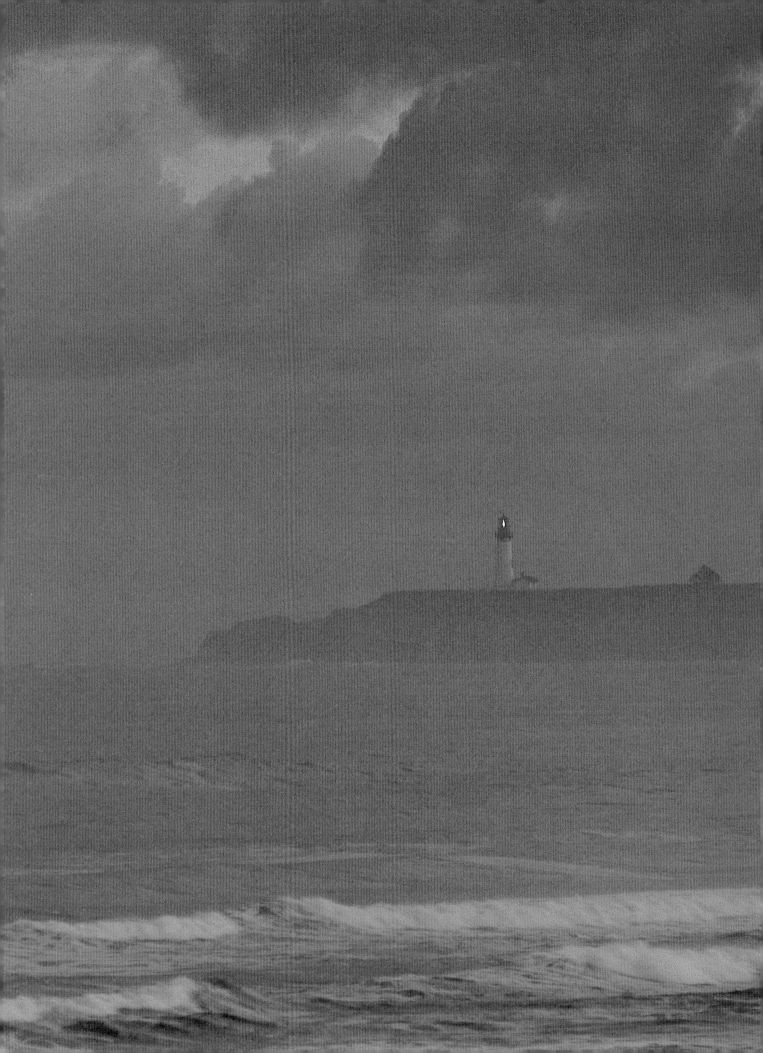

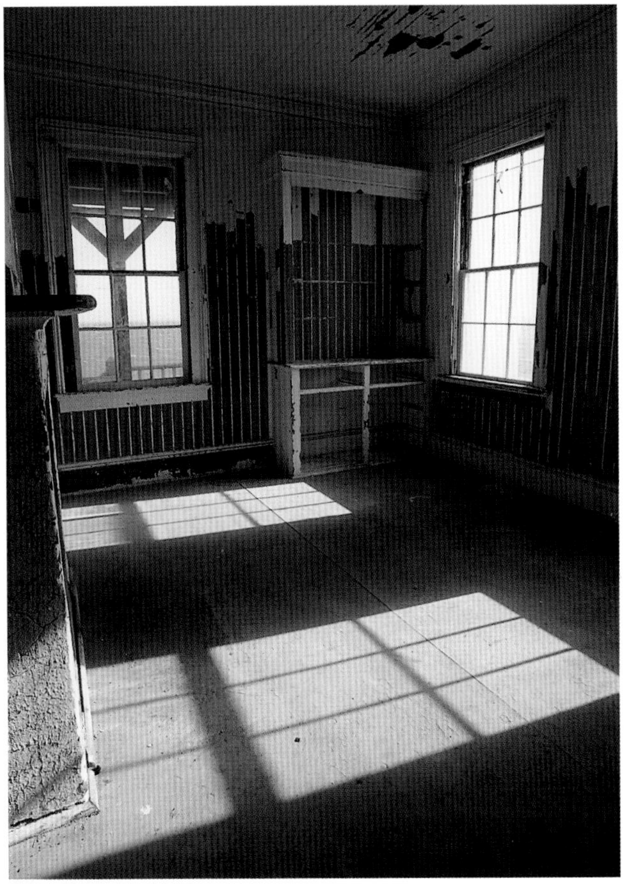

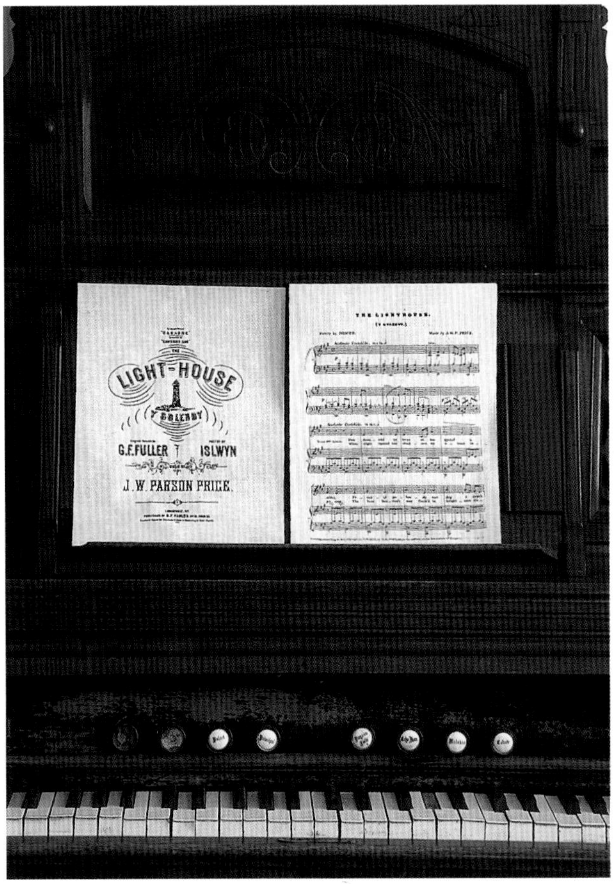

***Above, left*: Point San Luis light station**

The Coast Guard automated Point San Luis in 1975; soon afterwards the station was declared surplus. Now owned by the Point San Luis Harbor Commission, a local volunteer group, the Point San Luis Lighthouse Keepers are restoring the house. Once completed, this kitchen and other rooms will be open for visitors. The 1960s assistant keeper's duplex will become a visitors center.

***Above, right*: Yaquina Bay lighthouse**

Sheet music for "The Light-House," written in 1874, sits on the old J. J. Kimball pump organ. "When night spread her shadows on ocean reposing / The lone Beacon's star flash'd in brightness deposing / On the shore a grey lighthouse the dark clouds opposing / The heart of the sailor with gladness might leap / To see the bright rays shed abroad on the deep."

***Facing page*: Yaquina Head lighthouse**

Sunrise wisps the high clouds with subtle red as Yaquina Head light marks one of Oregon's more dangerous points. R. S. Stockton, the district Lighthouse Service engineer, opposed building Yaquina Bay light. He advocated that this, earlier known as "Cape Foulweather," was a better location.

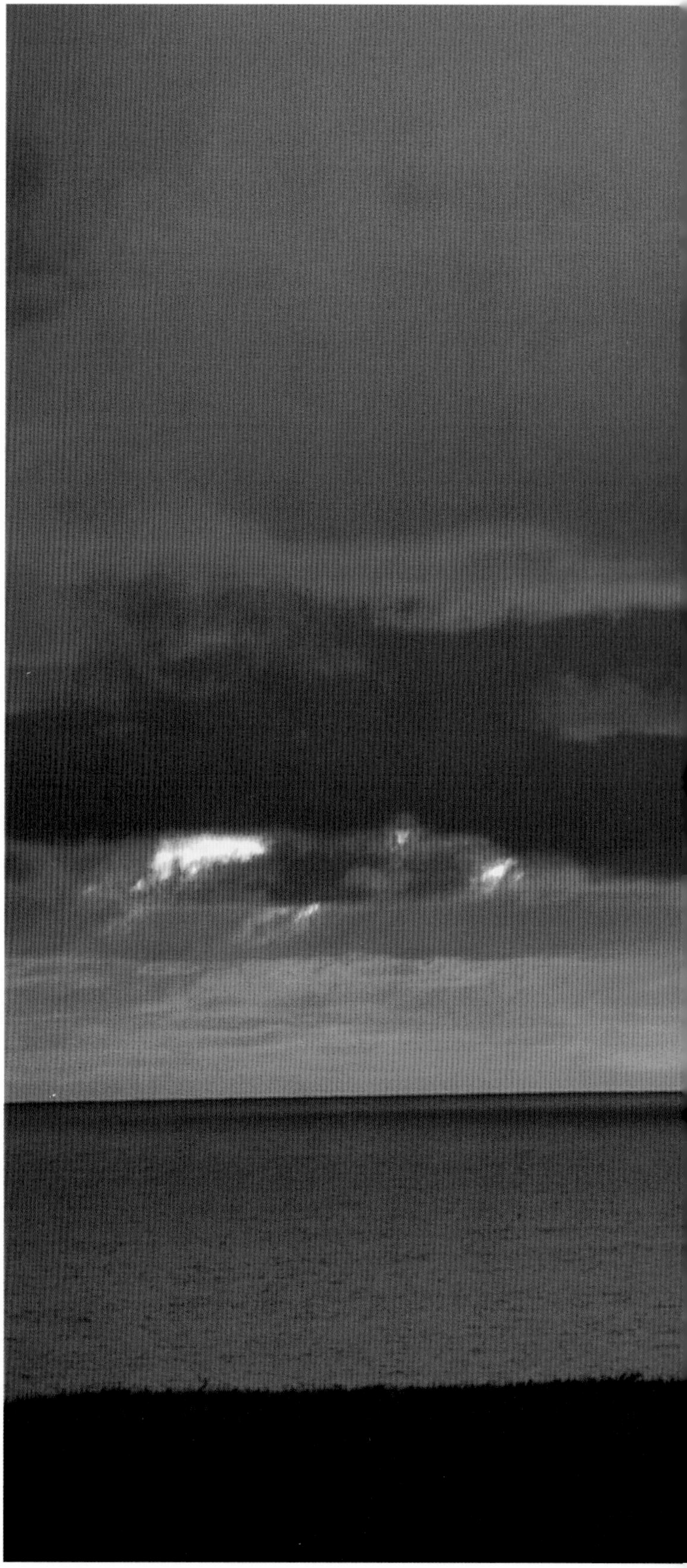

Yaquina Head lighthouse
Nearly twenty acres of land were acquired for this light in 1866, but service did not begin until August 1873. The ninety-three-foot tower, Oregon's tallest, and its workroom were built using 370,000 bricks. The first-order Fresnel, still in use, was manufactured by Barbier & Fenestre of Paris in 1868. The black panel at the back blocks light to the surrounding shoreline.

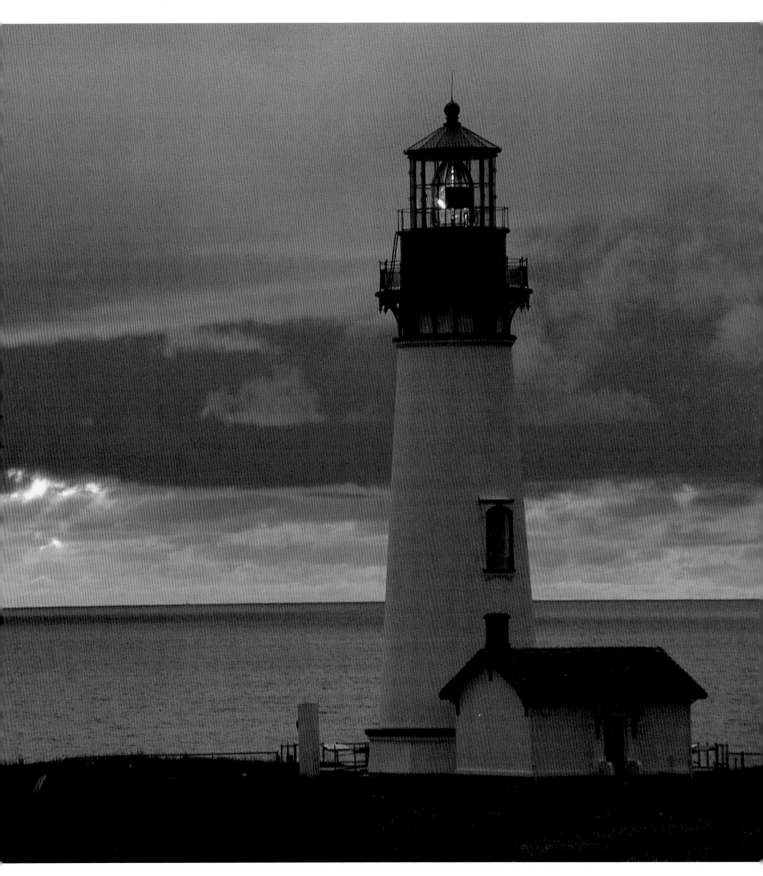

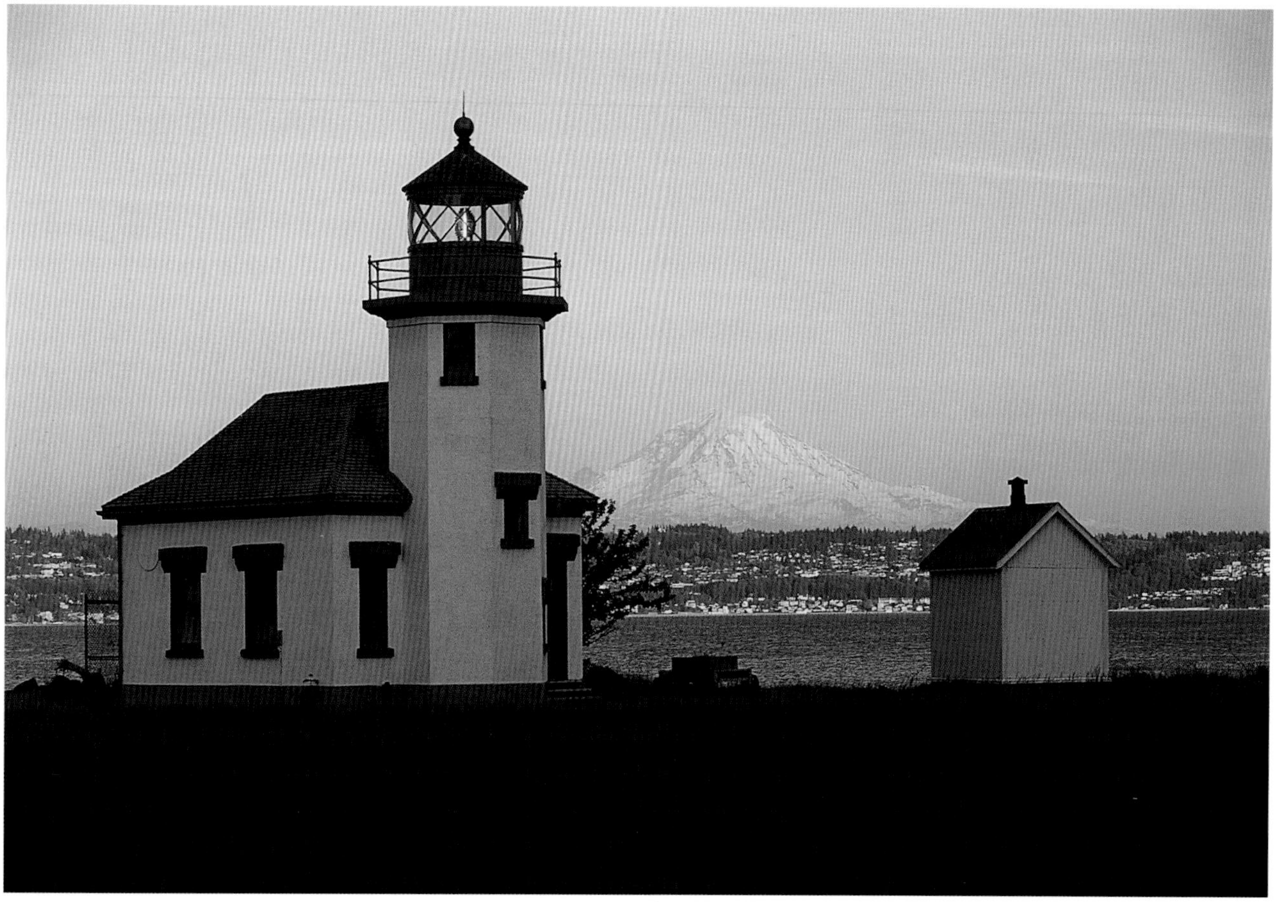

Point Robinson light station

Point Robinson light, on Maury Island across Puget Sound from Seattle, started life as a fog signal in 1885, nine years before the thirty-one-foot open tower showed a light. Similar to Seattle's Alki Point, this lantern room uses diagonal window braces. On a clear day, Washington's Mount Rainier, forty miles away, is easily visible.

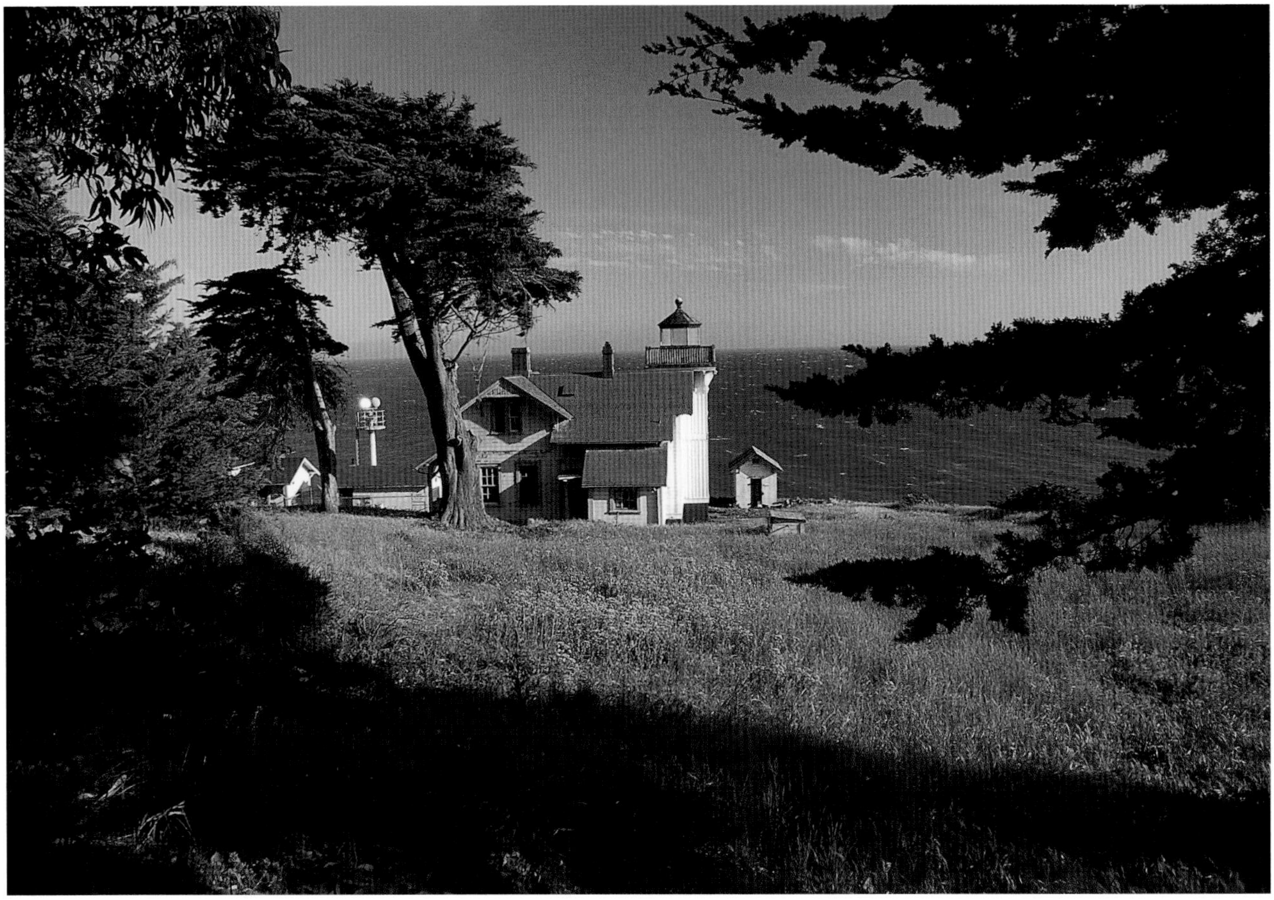

Point San Luis light station

Point San Luis light station was designed in the same Victorian Stick-Style as Los Angeles's Point Fermin light. Its 1878 fourth-order L. Sautter lens was first lit May 1890. The modern twin-aero beacon shines day and night. Rainwater was collected in two 10,000 gallon cisterns (left of the house). One was for household purposes and the other was for the steam fog signal. The Lighthouse Service constructed three identical lighthouses, one at San Luis, one at Humboldt Bay, and one at Ballast Point near San Diego. The latter two have been destroyed.

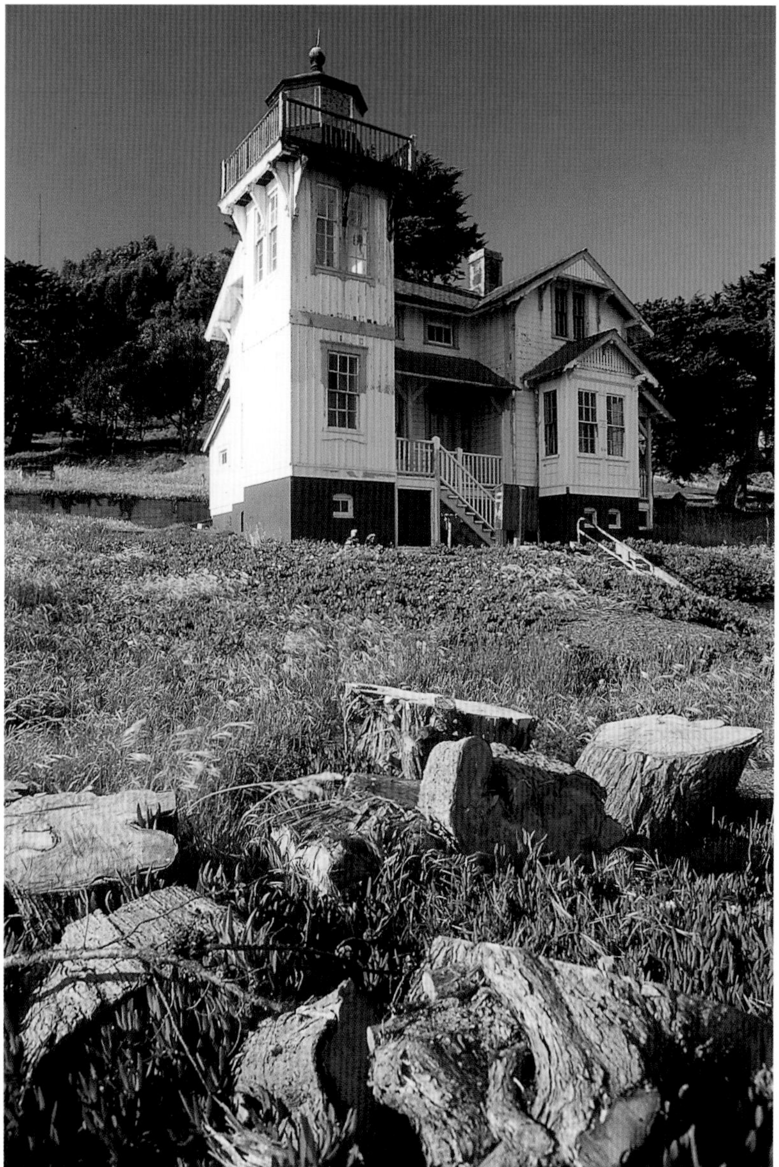

Point San Luis light station

The distinctive architecture of Point San Luis saved it from demolition. Though the light is difficult to reach (modern access passes through a neighboring nuclear power generating station), the Point San Luis Lighthouse Keepers volunteer organization is restoring all the structures. The original duplex was demolished in 1960.

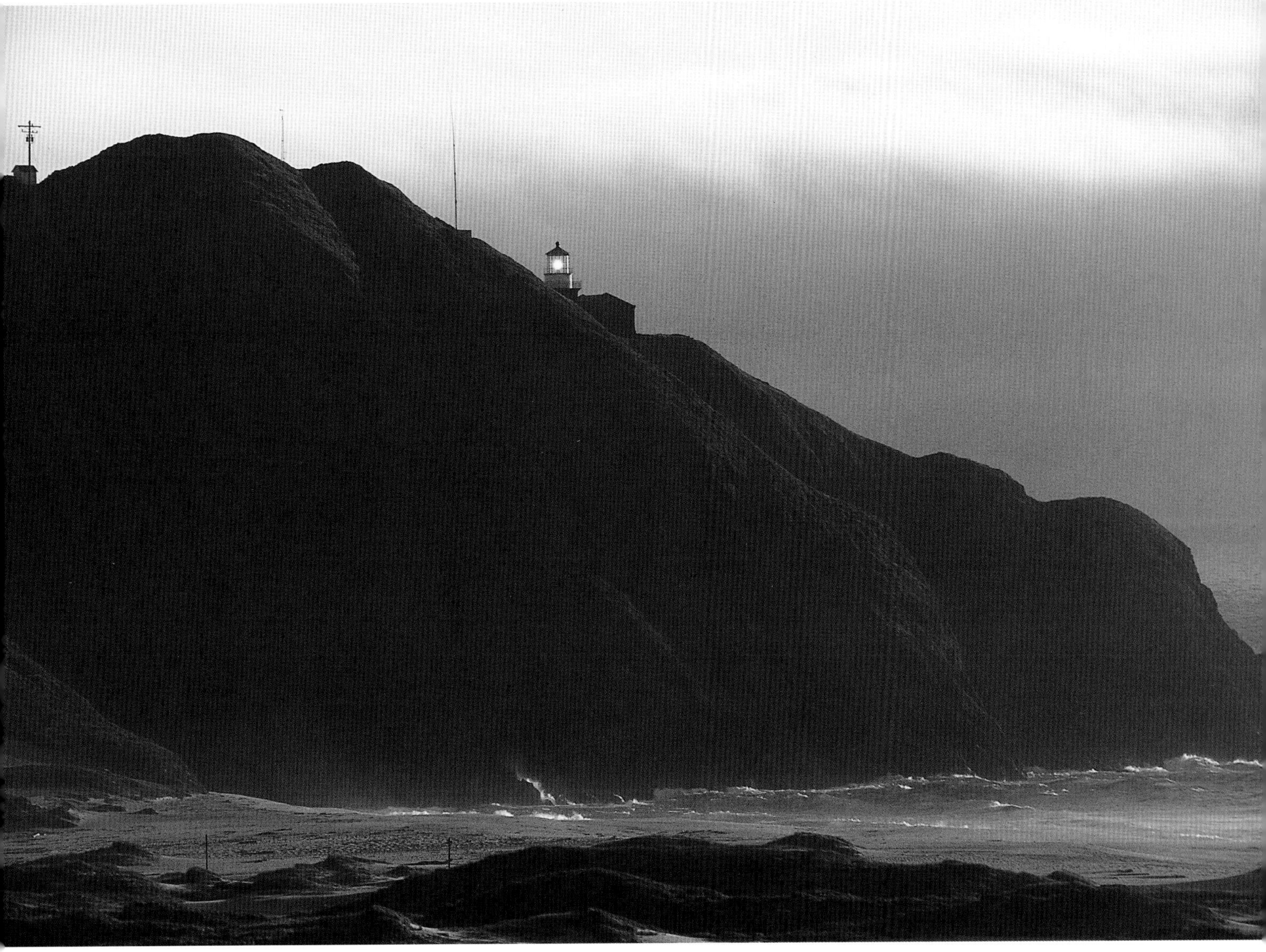

Point Sur light station
Point Sur light occupies most of the large rock at Big Sur, California. The light, originally a first-order Barbier & Fenestre Fresnel lens, sits 270 feet above sea level. After de-staffing the station in 1972, the entire rock was offered for sale in 1975 for $1 million. It is now a California State Historic Park.

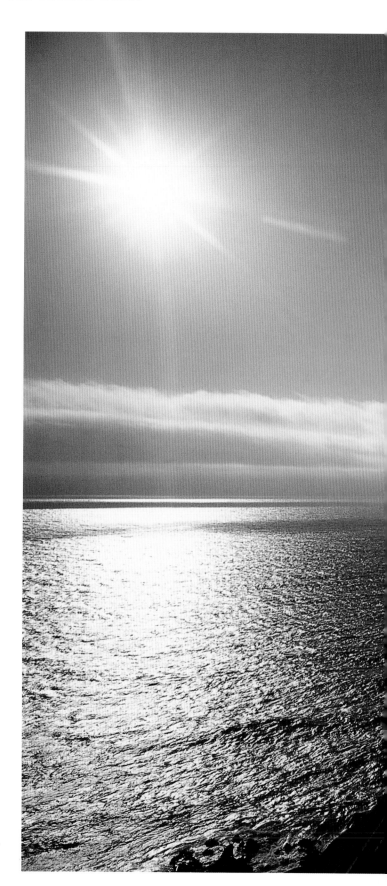

POINT SUR LIGHT STATION
While the rock is a state park, the Coast Guard still operates the rotating Carlisle & Finch twenty-four-inch aero beacons. The Central Coast Lighthouse Keepers volunteer organization maintains and restores the buildings atop 369-foot Point Sur Rock and operates tours. Point Sur was first lit in August 1889.

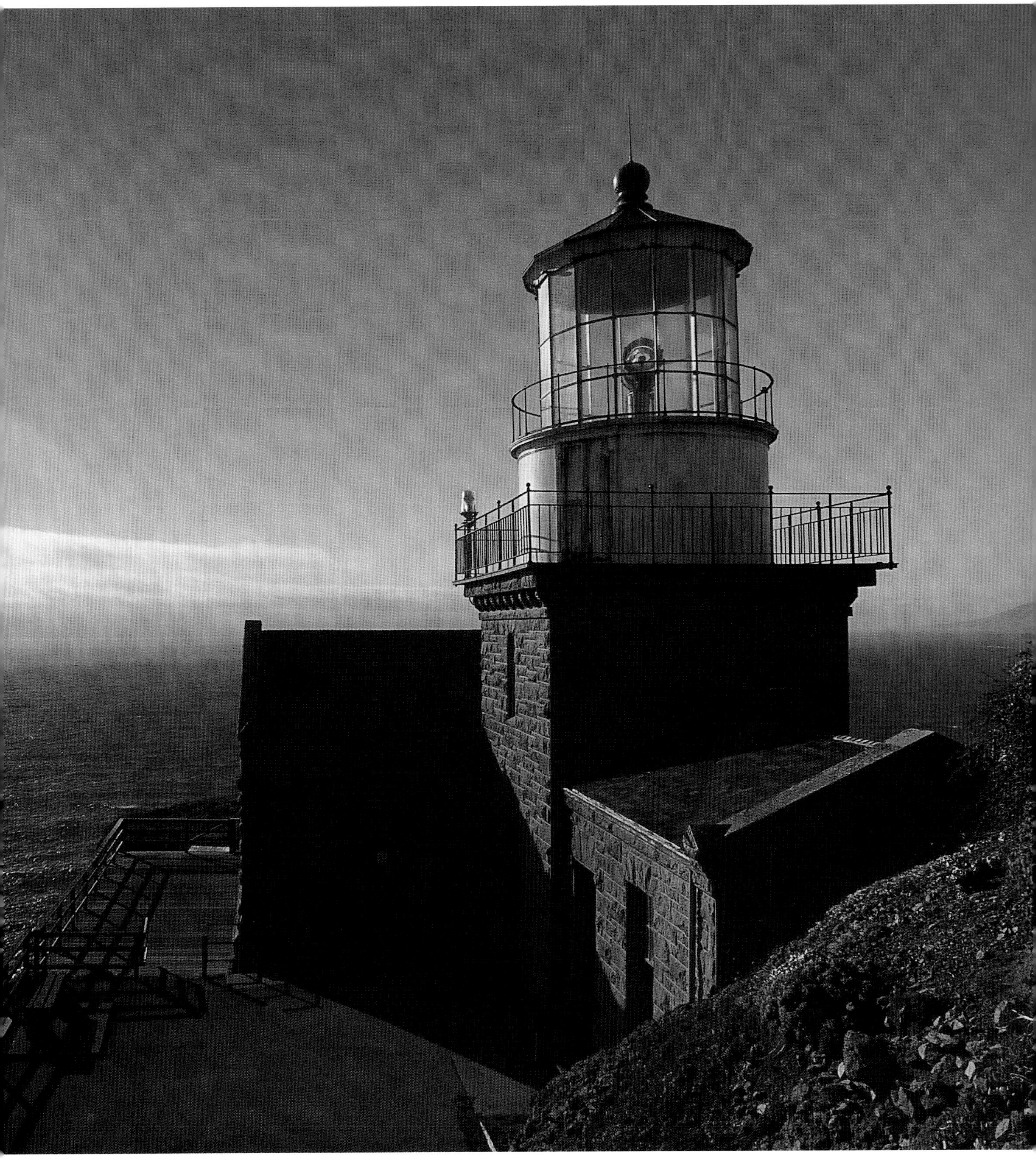

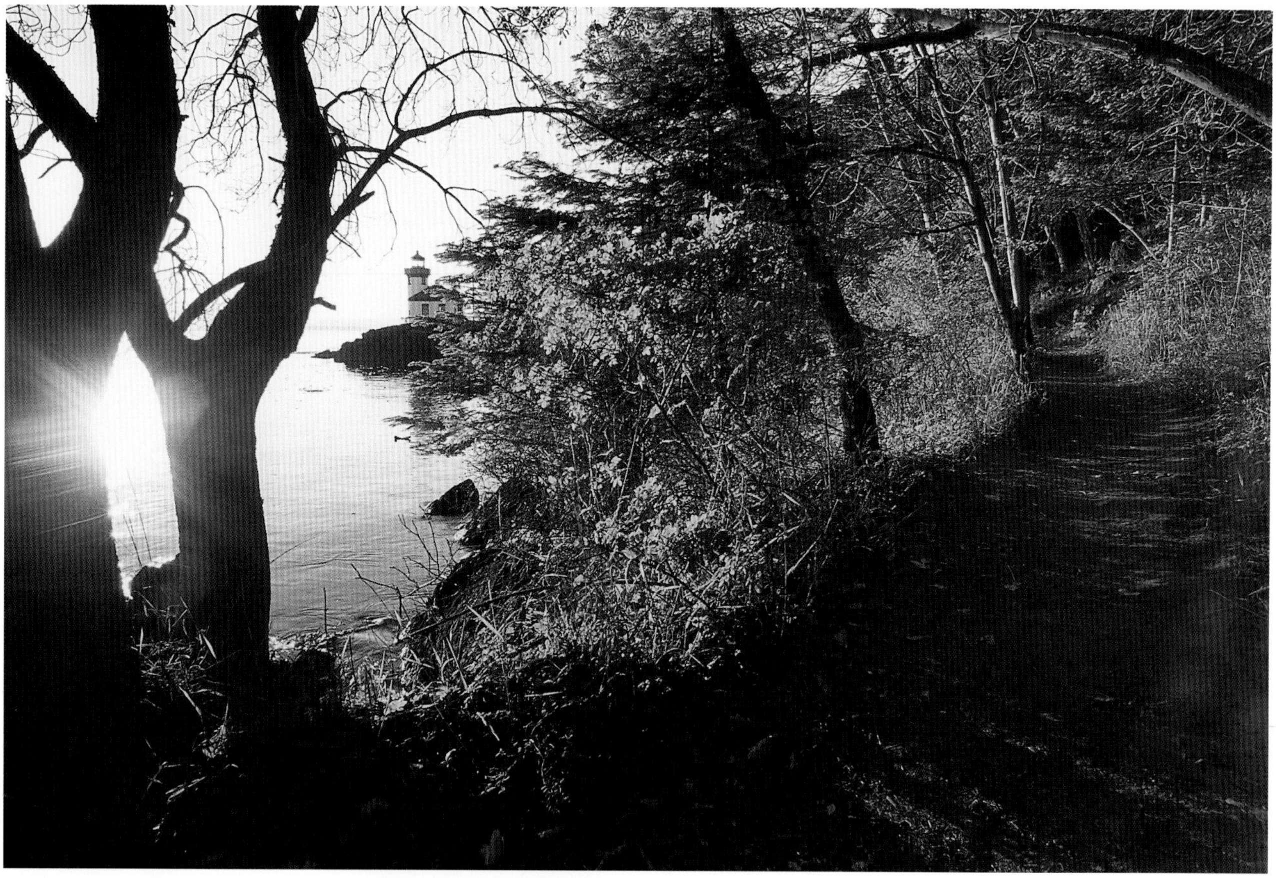

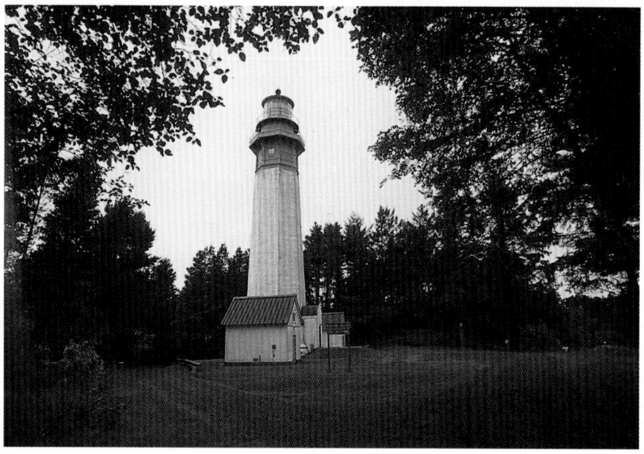

Above: **Lime Kiln light station**

Haro Strait veers off to the north from the Strait of Juan de Fuca, providing one shipping route to Vancouver, British Columbia. Lime Kiln light station, on San Juan Island, marks the route. Completed in 1919, it was the last lighthouse built in Washington and the last on the West Coast to receive electricity. Lime Kiln is similar architecturally to Washington's Mukilteo, Alki Point, and Point Robinson lights.

Left: **Grays Harbor lighthouse**

Architect Carl W. Lieck designed Grays Harbor light, the tallest in Washington at 107 feet. First lit in June 1898, it used a LePaute third-order clamshell lens that flashed red and white every five seconds. Built on a low bluff near the ocean, backfill and jetty development filled in the beach, and now the light sits 3,000 feet from the water.

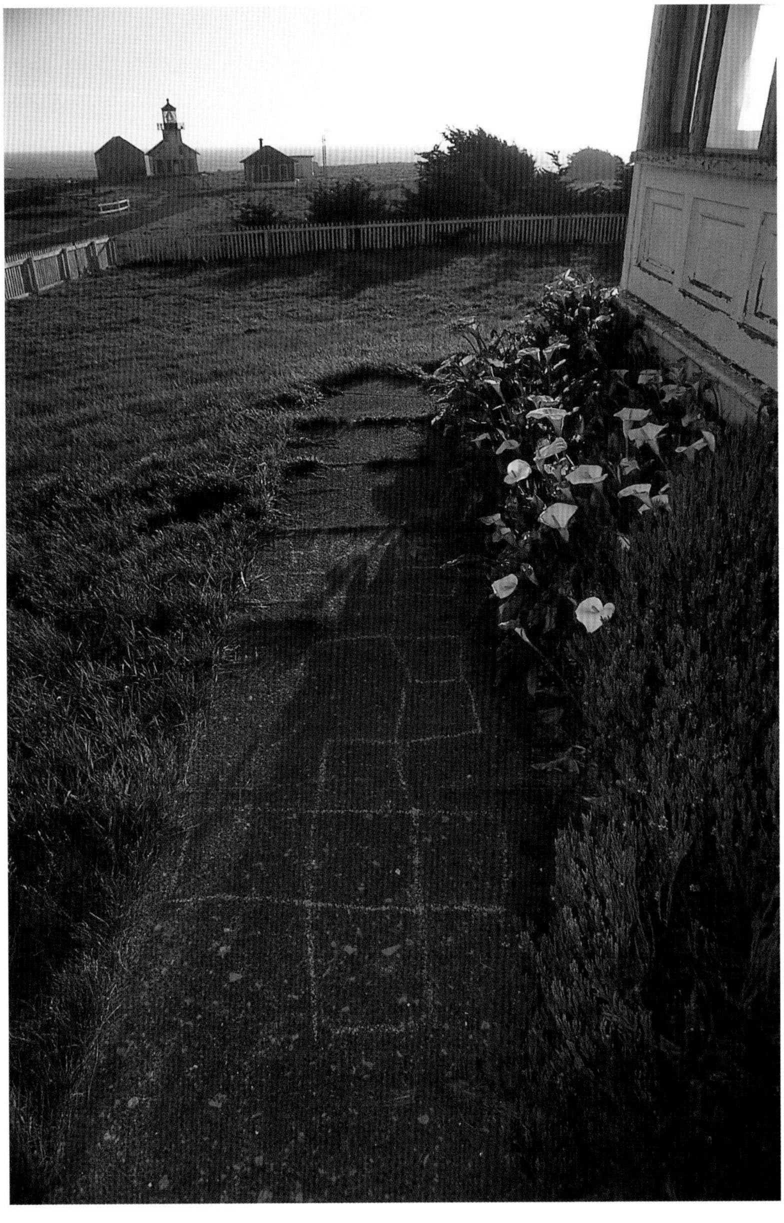

Point Cabrillo light station

Evidence of keepers' children past? Point Cabrillo light provided the head keeper and each assistant with a separate Craftsman-style dwelling. This second assistant's home was nearest the light—and the wind. First lit in June 1909, the station came into existence after San Francisco's earthquake made great demands on northern California's forests to rebuild the city.

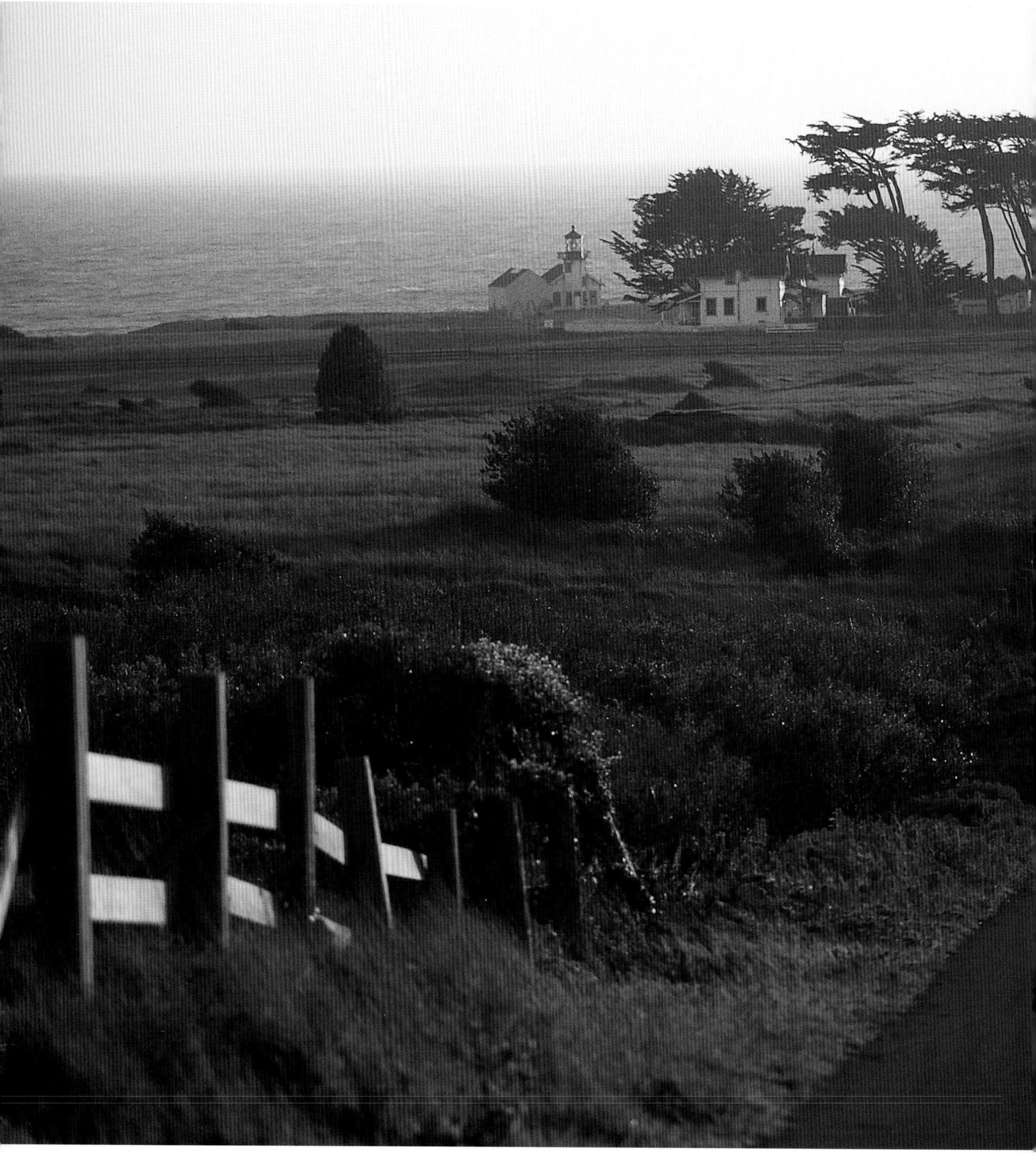

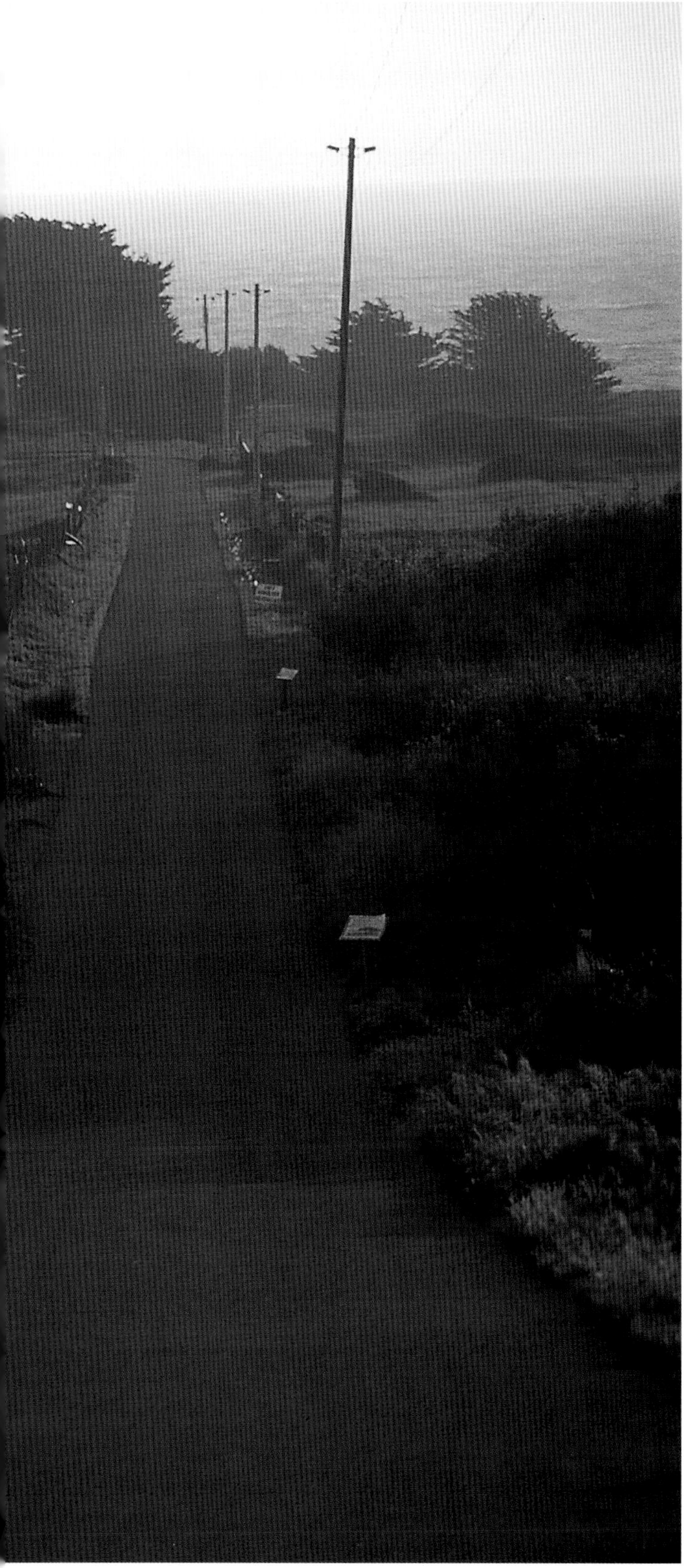

Point Cabrillo light station

Point Cabrillo was saved from real estate development by the California Coastal Commission, the State Coastal Conservancy, and the Coast Guard. The Point Cabrillo headland comprises 300 acres of history, natural resources, and wildlife for public use. Point Cabrillo light was the first lighthouse to be decommissioned—and then re-commissioned—using its original Fresnel. The Fresnel was produced by Chance Brothers of London, which manufactured just three lights for American lighthouses: this one, the lens at Heceta Head, and the optic at Staten Island, New York.

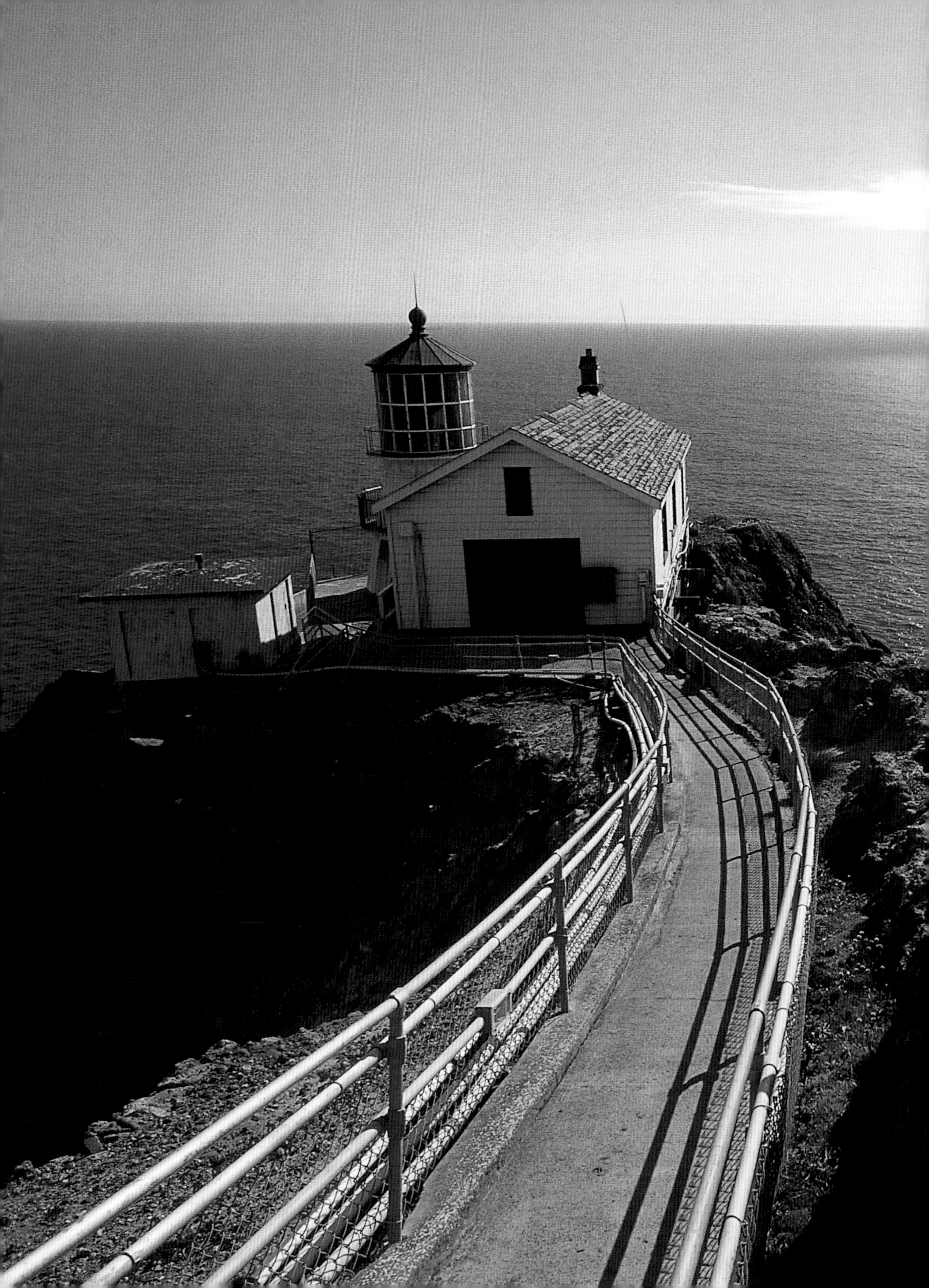

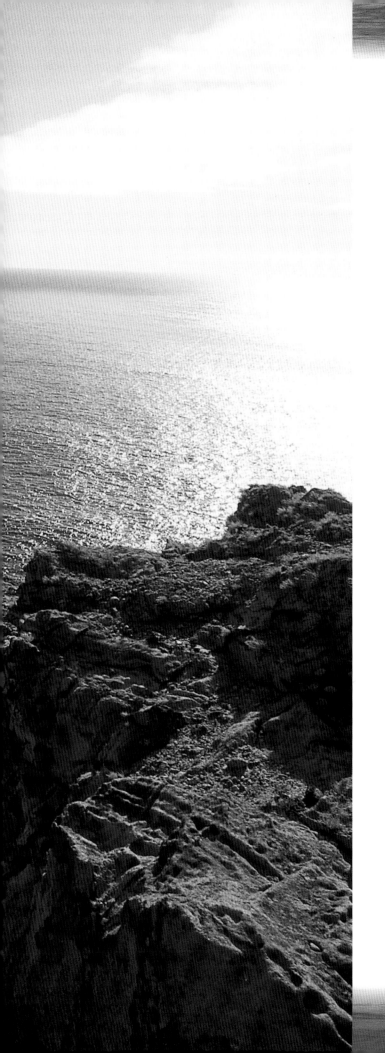

CHAPTER 5

Changing Times, Changing Roles

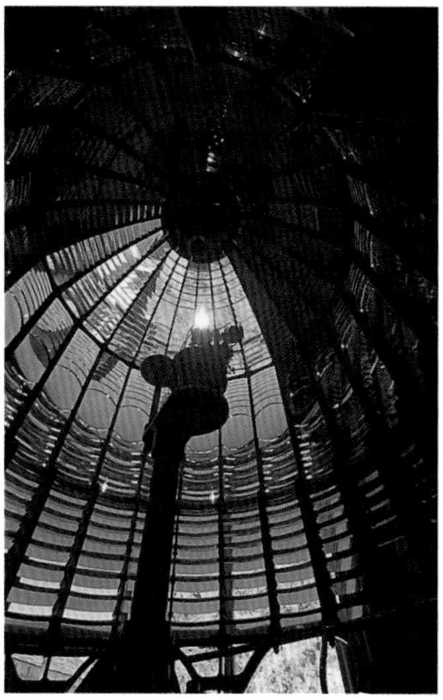

***Left*: Point Reyes light station**
Set thirty-five miles northwest of San Francisco, Point Reyes is normally one of the West Coast's windiest, foggiest spots. District Inspector Campbell Graham assigned construction to William Nagle in 1855, but land ownership squabbles delayed work for fifteen years. Now part of the Point Reyes National Seashore, visitors descend 308 steps to visit the light.

***Above*: Point Reyes light station**
Barbier & Fenestre's first-order Fresnel, completed in 1867, used 1,032 separate pieces of glass, including twenty-four bull's-eye lenses. National Park Service rangers keep the lead-crystal lens shrouded by curtains to prevent discoloration and limit the risk of a bull's-eye magnifying lens starting a fire.

Throughout the Great Depression, lighthouse keepers had jobs, paychecks, food, and a place to live. They received uniforms that, even though they paid for them, gave them a sense of pride through those hard times. With better times fairly certain to come, the Bureau of Lighthouses looked forward to its 150th anniversary on August 7, 1939.

Changes were looming, however. Waging war on the Depression, President Franklin Roosevelt sought to streamline government for efficiency. His Reorganization Act I of 1938 consolidated departments and saved the government money. Encouraged, he proposed Reorganization Act II in 1939, wherein his advisers examined the roles of the Coast Guard and Lighthouse Bureau. The President proposed to transfer administration of navigation aids from the Commerce Department back to the Treasury for consolidation into the Coast Guard. These lights protected our shores, he reasoned, as the did Coast Guard. Congress agreed, and on July 1, 1939, five weeks before the Bureau's 150th birthday, the transfer began.

Older keepers—and there were many in their seventies with thirty to fifty years of service—worried about their jobs and the few benefits they received. The dozens of women keepers like Thelma Austin questioned what it meant to become part of the military. Men wondered too; some already had military experience, having been drafted during World War I. A few men had served at their own lighthouses where they were part of military bases.

The Coast Guard's mandate was similar to the Bureau's: The preservation and safety of the lives of mariners at sea. Coast Guard Commandant Admiral Russell Waesche directed integration of lighthouse keepers into the Coast Guard. Waesche was familiar to many keepers, as he was the first lieutenant who supervised stringing radio wires to 139 lighthouses and lightships in 1919, connecting them for the first time with naval radio stations and the outside world. While lines often broke in stormy seas, his persistence earned him respect and admiration. As a commander in 1931, he was part of the board that reorganized the Coast Guard into districts and redefined its mission in a more humanitarian role. Following his promotion to commandant in 1936, he worked to improve relations between his enlisted men and officers in the field and the higher ranks at the Washington, D.C., headquarters.

Transferring properties, personnel, and responsibilities from the Lighthouse Bureau to the Coast Guard took only a week. The Bureau turned over more than 400 lighthouses, 30 lightships, and 64 tender ships as part of its total of about 30,000 navigation aids. The Coast Guard absorbed more than 4,100 civilian full-time keepers and nearly 1,200 part-time employees into a military organization more than double the Bureau's size. Sensitive to the keepers' experience and interests, Waesche offered them three choices: Remain as civilian employees; retire and take advantage of the Coast Guard Retirement Law's more generous terms; or join the organization. In all, 466 lighthouse keepers became Coast Guard chiefs or first class petty officers. In subsequent years, the Coast Guard replaced retiring civilians with its own personnel.

The Coast Guard reorganized its former divisions and the lighthouse regions into thirteen districts. Consolidation met Roosevelt's goal: By eliminating duplicate supplies and depots, the government saved $1 million in the first year by operating one service with 15,492 individuals on payroll.

The Role of the Lights in World War II

The evening after the Pearl Harbor attack on December 7, 1941, lighthouses on both coasts dimmed or went black. World War II had forced a new responsibility on the Coast Guard and its lighthouses.

The entire United States coastline came under the General Orders of February 3, 1941, which created ten Naval Coastal Frontiers. Eleven months later, Executive Order 8929 transferred the Coast Guard to the Navy until peace returned. The Coast Guard would patrol beaches to make observations, gather information, and guard the coast; the Army and Navy would repel invasion.

When four German saboteurs paddled ashore at

Point Reyes light station
The Fresnel lens was not only a light source but also it was the intricate 175-pound clockworks mechanism that rotated the light in perfect time. "Powered" by a 180-pound counterweight (visible through the works) that unwound cable from the drum, this system rotated the Fresnel. Mariners saw a flash of light every five seconds. A hand crank rewound the cable.

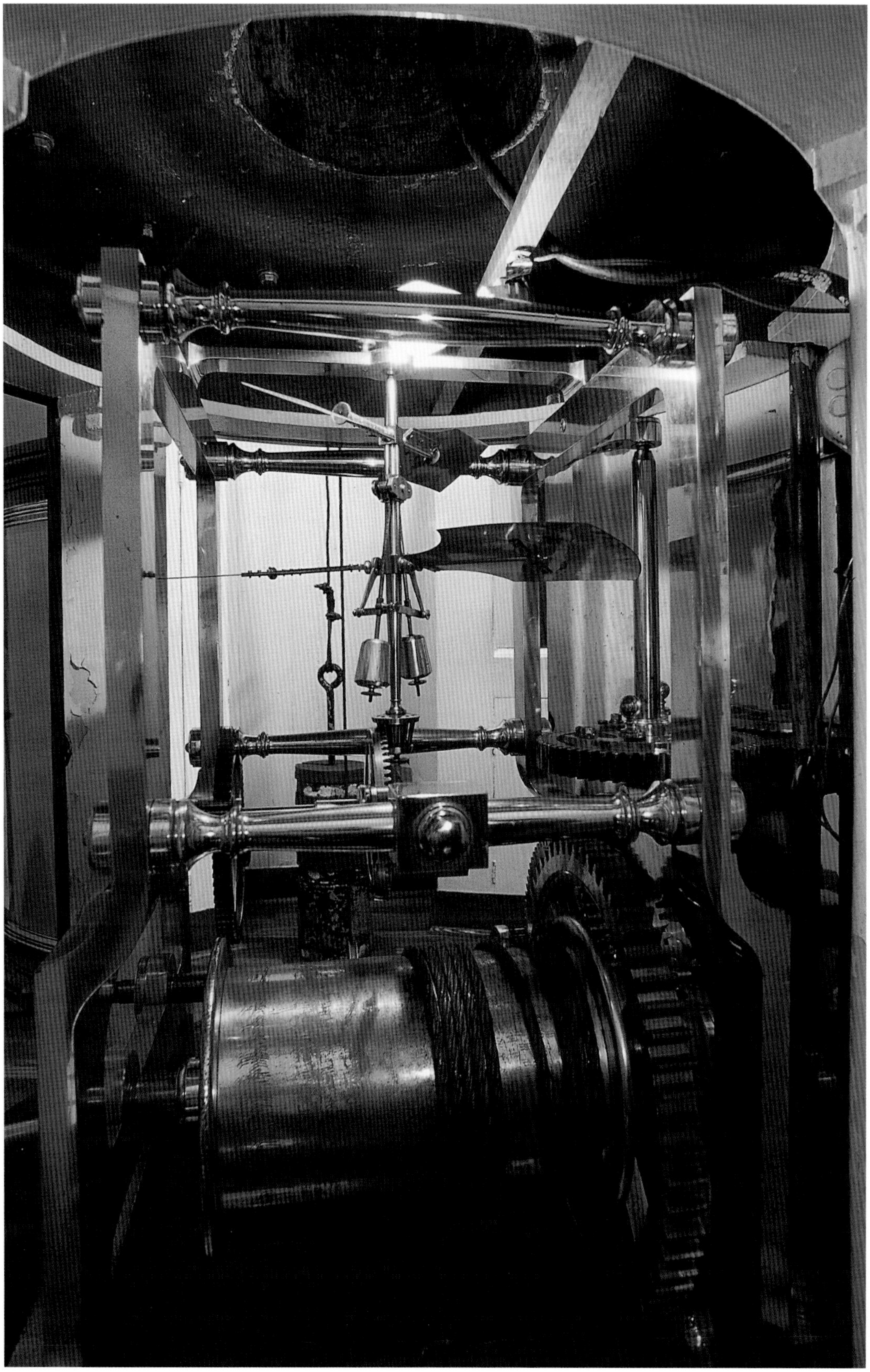

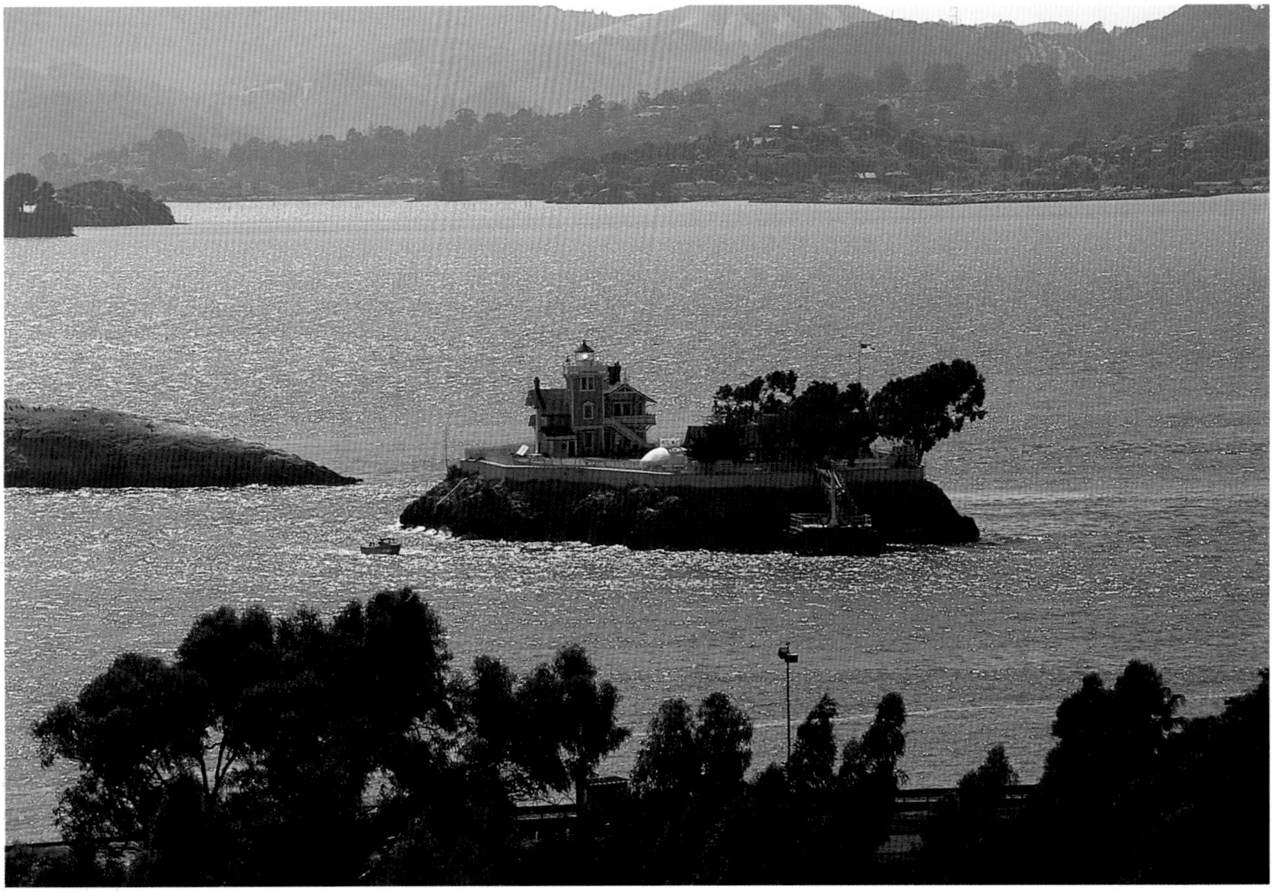

East Brother light station
Since 1980, East Brother light has operated as a non-profit inn, providing dinner, lodging, and breakfast five nights a week. Guests arrive and leave the seven-eighths-acre island on the inn's launch, seen rounding the island at left. The station went into service in March 1874.

Amagansett, New York, on April 13, 1942, they were intercepted by Coast Guard Bosun's Mate John Cullen, armed only with a flashlight. Four nights later another four reached the beach at Ponte Vedra, Florida, only to be captured. Many feared the Japanese might try something similar on the West Coast. U.S. shores had been violated, and the military turned up the heat on coastal protection.

On the West Coast, lights stayed out at gun emplacements such as Point Bonita, Point Loma, and Point Wilson lighthouse on the Army's Fort Worden near Port Townsend, Washington. The Army reopened Fort Casey where the Strait of Juan de Fuca met Puget Sound. The light there, Admiralty Head, had been deactivated in 1922, but the unusual lighthouse became officer housing and a wartime observation post. At the peak of World War II, the Coast Guard Beach Patrol counted 24,000 men patrolling 50,000 miles of shoreline on foot or horseback, generally with one of the Beach Patrol's 2,000 dogs. Most West Coast light stations housed a couple of dozen patrol personnel.

On December 21, 1941, the Japanese Navy torpedoed and sank the U.S. petroleum carrier *Emidio* near Blunts Reef, California. Two days later, just south of Piedras Blancas light station near Cambria, California, a Japanese submarine destroyed the Union Oil Company tanker *Montebello*. After the U.S. Navy sunk the Japanese sub *Sakuri* days later off Palos Verdes, near Point Vicente light, torpedo attacks stopped. The 6,000 miles between Japanese refueling bases and West Coast shipping was too great a distance for all but the longest-range subs.

Little enemy activity along the West Coast occurred again until later in 1942 when a Japanese sub fleet sank three more tankers between Cape Flattery and Cape Blanco, Oregon. After that, the Japanese needed their submarines closer to home.

By July 15, 1944, West Coast units began to demobilize, and most lights were turned back on by year end.

The Demise of the Keeper

As late as July 1969, there were still seven civilian keepers tending lighthouses. From the 1940s through the 1960s, technology engulfed older keepers unwilling to learn new tricks; the Coast Guard compassionately transferred them to stations operating with more familiar equipment. But by the 1970s, the Coast Guard replaced almost all keepers with batteries, sensors, and remote controls. The long legacy of the lighthouse keeper was coming to an end.

Some of this change resulted from Commissioner George Putnam. While he had supported his keepers in many ways, he neglected the structures and deferred maintenance to preserve budgets.

Starting in the late 1950s and continuing to this day, the Coast Guard faced major renovation and remodeling projects at many lights. Some buildings had deteriorated beyond which it was practical to repair them. The Coast Guard also listened to spouses of its enlistees and officers, and tore down aging, ailing wood structures and built modern concrete-block single-story duplexes such as those at Point Arena and Point San Luis. Lighthouse enthusiasts bemoan the passing of the wooden Victorians, but they never spent a windy, wet winter in one. In the extreme cases, it was most humane to remove keepers altogether. At stations like St. George Reef, Tillamook Rock, Destruction Island, Cape Flattery, and most stations in Alaska, physical discomforts of living in ailing buildings were second to psychological challenges of weather and isolation.

Everything about the old buildings was expensive. Remote light stations were costly not only in salaries and paid time off for each keeper, but the farther each of these was from San Francisco, Seattle, Juneau, or Honolulu supply depots, the more it took to regularly visit them. Extra supplies were necessary; some stations carried food, fuel, water, and other necessities for six or nine months should the tender not complete its quarterly delivery because of weather.

Maintenance expenses on lightships were similar to the remote lights, and duty on lightships was like that on St. George or Tillamook. There was only a steel bulkhead between the lightship keepers and the storms, and there was little to do during a blow except hunker down and wait. After the storms passed, keepers read, made repairs, and waited for the next storm. Some station chiefs let their crew set the tone and tempo of activity and exercise. Others took on this responsibility themselves.

The last chief aboard the lightship *Columbia*, anchored just west of the Columbia River mouth, was cre-

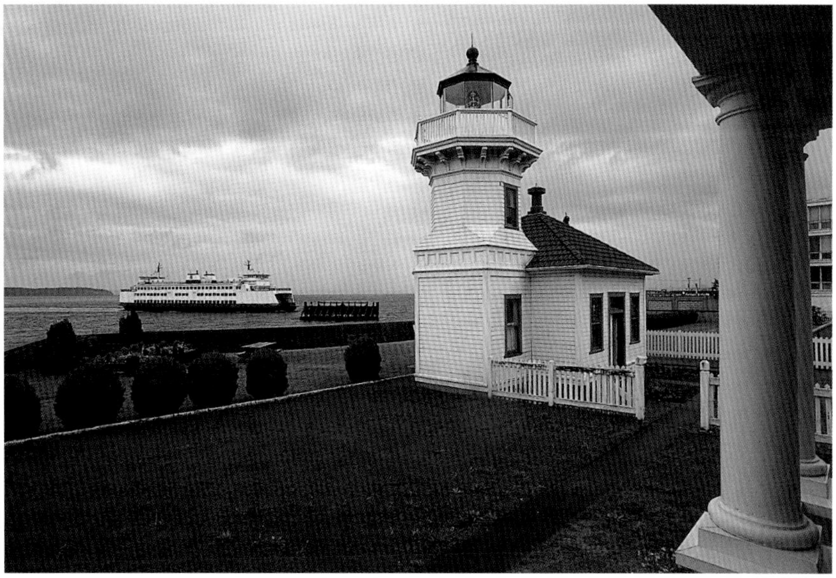

MUKILTEO LIGHT STATION
In 1901, the Lighthouse Board, noting increased lumber shipping in northern Puget Sound, authorized construction of Mukilteo light station. A small Victorian lighthouse and two keepers' residences were built at Mukilteo, all designed by Carl Lieck. The entire station cost $27,000 to build. Keeper Peter Christianson began service in March 1906.

ative. He devised two games to keep his crew amused and exercised. His most inventive idea aboard the ship was to stage automobile races. His crew lined up their toy automobile entries on the rolling deck and released them to careen from one weld seam to another. With each pitch and swell, the cars meandered from port to starboard. Chasing a car as it zoomed toward the sea kept the crew nimble. The chief's other exercise was a game of tag. Without warning, he would walk up to a crew member, tag him and run off.

Some civilian women continued to be in charge of stations after the Coast Guard took over in 1939. On March 22, 1980, the Coast Guard assigned its first woman as head keeper. Twenty-year-old Seaman Jeni Burr and her husband, Coast Guard radar technician Eric Burr, moved into New Dungeness Spit. They served there for three years, even though the Coast Guard had began to automate systems at New Dungeness in 1976. Burr acted equally as resident site manager and light keeper. Her duties included the public relations role of guide—explaining the light's function—and duties and responsibilities of a Coast Guard keeper.

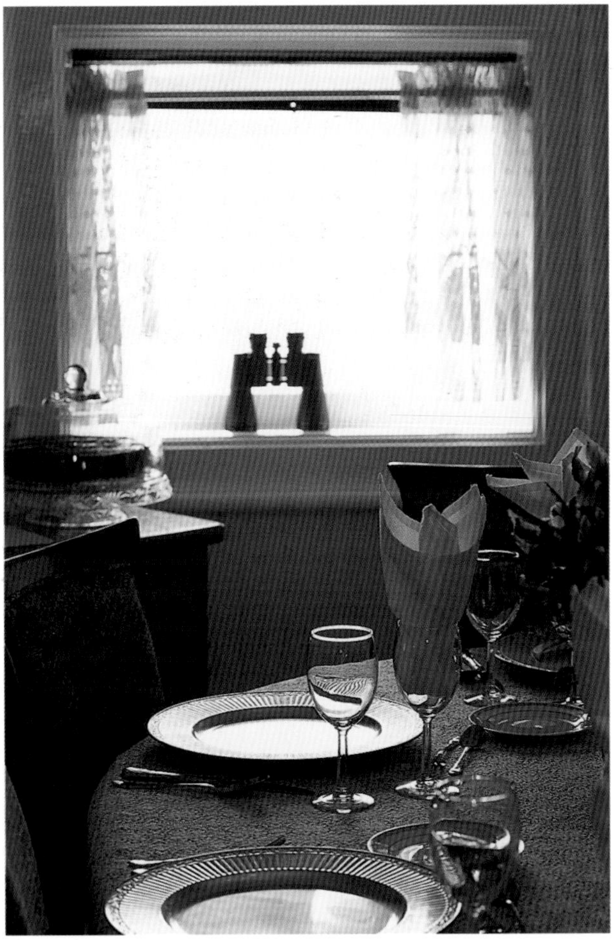

East Brother light station
Guests enjoy a champagne reception on arrival, a tour of the island, a five-course supper, hours afterward to relax and watch shipping activity, and a full, rich breakfast in the dining room. The Victorian house accommodates visitors in four restored rooms. The view from each window is always changing.

Automation and Robot Lights

The Coast Guard applied automation gradually. Long Beach Harbor light in southern California was the West Coast's earliest automated light (called a Robot Light), activated in 1947. It was a thirty-six-inch-diameter, airport-beacon-type lamp, accompanied by a fog signal and radio beacon, that required no staff at all.

The Coast Guard introduced its Lighthouse Automation and Modernization Project (LAMP) in 1968 to accelerate the automation process, but annual budgets and personnel commitments meant it was necessary to develop a reasoned policy of automation rather than take a steamroller approach. As special technology entered the lighthouses, personnel capable of installing, troubleshooting, and maintaining this new electronic equipment was required. In some instances, the Coast Guard was inventing equipment and electronics as it went along. To maintain these new devices, it developed its Aids-to-Navigation Teams.

The Coast Guard assigned keepers to stations as late as 1980, even after those stations had been automated. As outside contractors began producing devices that ultimately would eliminate the need to staff the station, such as optical sensors to turn on remote lights in the dark, manufacturers and the Coast Guard discovered that harsh environments exposed glitches in the new technology. They found that sometimes nice weather did too.

At Mukilteo Lighthouse north of Seattle, twenty-one-year-old Coast Guard Seaman Charles A. Milne was the only resident keeper at the station when the service installed a remote fog sensor in 1981. He lived in Quarters A, one of two small residences barely thirty feet from the light.

"There was no better duty than this," Milne said. "This was cream of the crop. I polished brass and cleaned sand from children's shoes when school groups came to visit.

"When the Coast Guard automated the light and

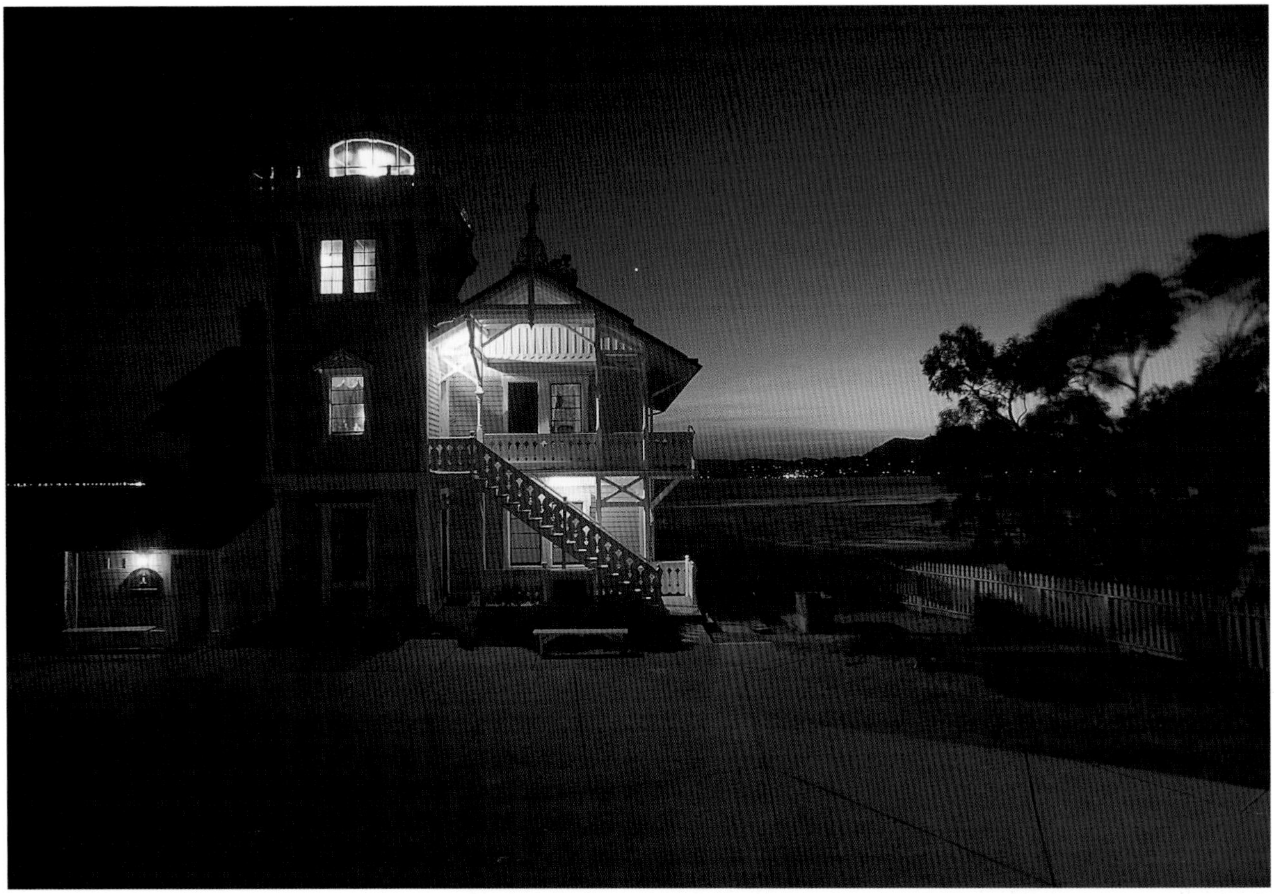

Above: East Brother light station
The light station duplex house and buildings were designed in 1872 by P. J. Pelz, chief draftsman of the Lighthouse Board. Pelz was under the supervision of George Elliott, Major of Engineers, U.S. Army, Engineer and Secretary of the Lighthouse Board. Scheduled for demolition in 1979, the East Brother Lighthouse Society saved it.

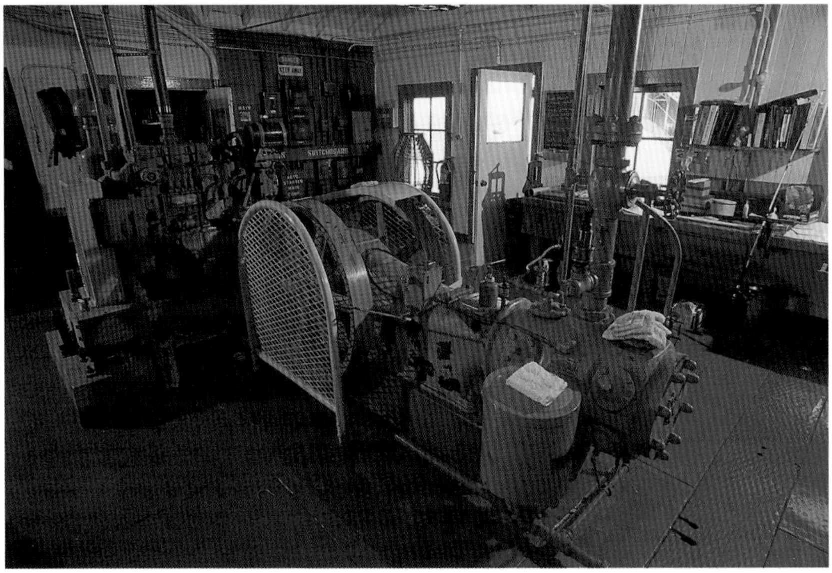

Right: East Brother light station
The fog-signal building and machinery shed are operational. East Brother remains an active navigation aid in the north end of San Francisco Bay. The Caterpillar diesel D3400 industrial engine runs an Ingersoll-Rand ER1 air compressor to blast the station's two diaphone fog signals. There are two generators as well.

The Airways Division

Airmail in the United States officially began May 15, 1918, as a joint project of the War Department and Post Office. What does this have to do with the Lighthouse Service?

Congress authorized $150,000 to set up airmail service, with the army providing airplanes and the Post Office preparing landing strips. The first airmail service ran between Belmont Park, New York, Long Island, and Bustleton, Pennsylvania. Flying, however, was risky business, and seven of the first ten airmail pilots died at work.

Neither snow nor hail nor dark of night, nor a 70 percent mortality rate would deter Assistant Postmaster General Otto Praeger from "getting the mail through." Although Praeger was not especially bothered by the human loss, Congress was. By February 1921, Congress had seen enough destruction and was set to discontinue airmail funding. Praeger had one last chance. He planned to impress Congress by opening the fastest coast-to-coast mail service yet. To accomplish this he would have to convince his pilots to do something virtually unheard of—fly at night.

Groups of volunteers would light lanterns and bonfires, much as early harbormasters did for incoming ships, to guide the four pilots across the country, following the proposed route. Two were to fly east to west and the others would go west to east. The four pilots left on February 22, 1921, and thirty hours, twenty minutes later, Jack Knight, the only to pilot to complete the trip, landed in San Francisco. Praeger got his funding.

Costs, delays, and disasters prompted Congress to pass the 1926 Contract Airmail Act, moving airmail delivery to contract carriers. Soon after, several of these mail carriers began passenger service; TWA, United, and American Airlines were among the first five airlines to gain government approval to operate commercially.

There were 9,475 miles of airways in operation by 1926, and in an effort to increase the viability of the airways, Congress passed the Air Commerce Act, providing for the "encouragement and use of aircraft in commerce." To expedite implementation, President Herbert Hoover placed the newly created job of Secretary of Commerce for Aeronautics and the Airways Division within the Lighthouse Service. The agency was divided into four departments: registration, research, airways, and information. Its goal was to "examine the airways, select emergency landing fields and beacon sites, erect structures, install the navigational aids, and thereafter maintain them."

Meanwhile, airlines recognized the need to establish express mail and passenger service, and the most efficient way to provide this service was to fly at night. To aid navigation, the Airways Division planned to establish 1,100 miles of lighted airways. The beacon of choice was a 1,000-watt, twenty-four-inch revolving searchlight of more than 2 million candlepower. The searchlights were mounted on fifty-foot-tall skeleton towers and, where available, they used commercial power. In rural areas where this was not available, the agency called on farm lighting equipment to generate electric current.

By 1933, the federal airways system comprised 18,000 miles of lighted airways containing 1,550 rotating beacons and 236 intermediate landing fields.

A year later, the Airways Division's job had outgrown the Lighthouse Service, and in July 1934, the Federal Aviation Administration's Aeronautics branch assumed full responsibility for constructing and maintaining the nation's airways.

the signal, they didn't provide much information for keepers," he said. "In the first four months of automation, fog signals everywhere went on all the time.

"Next to the station, developers had completed a new luxury condominium. A lot of wealthy people lived there. A couple of admirals moved in. They got pretty irked. At noon on a bright sunny day, the signal would go on. It went on one clear, moonlit night at about 12:30 A.M. Seattle [the supply depot thirty miles away] sent repair technicians up every three or four days for months."

The fog sensors send two beams of light out about half a mile into the sky. The distance is adjustable. If sensors pick up reflected light, they interpret that as fog and switch on the signal.

"There was a white seawall around the station, banked on the shore side to resist storm waves from Puget Sound. If the sun or moon reflected on that wall, it tricked the sensor and the fog signal went on. Once we figured that out, I painted the seawall black and the problems stopped completely."

One of the great dangers at any light station was, and still is, fire. At Victorian stations constructed of wood such as Point San Luis or Los Angeles's Point Fermin, a fire could mean the loss of the whole structure. Fire buckets filled with water or sand stood in every hallway in every building. It was the reason that flammable lantern fuel was always stored in separate buildings constructed of stone, concrete, or brick, and was never brought into the lighthouse until just before it was time to light the lamp. But recent events prove fire destruction can happen innocently and unexpectedly.

The National Wildlife Refuge at New Dungeness Spit was littered with salt-encrusted driftwood. During Fourth of July weekend in 1999, holiday revelers started a bonfire on the spit where the fire spread to encompass the light. The visiting keepers succeeded in putting that fire out. Small "hot spots" appeared over the next few days but the keepers caught them all as well. Or so they believed.

On July 11, a keeper was in the lantern room watching the sunset fade behind Victoria Island to the northwest. He looked southeast, down the spit, and saw what he later described as a forest fire on the ground, moving rapidly toward the station. He turned on lawn sprinklers that had run during the afternoon, and set them between the metal helicopter pad and barn, the first point fire would reach.

The keepers alerted the Coast Guard, Erik Henriksson of the U.S. Lighthouse Society's New Dungeness Chapter, and the Clallam County fire and sheriff departments. The Coast Guard, which had turned over the station to the Lighthouse Society in 1994, responded from nearby Port Angeles with a helicopter to pick up the eight keepers, but it had to land behind the house as the pad was surrounded by fire. The last keeper was evacuated at midnight when flames cut them off from the light.

Olympic National Park sent nineteen firefighters by boat; they corralled the fire, controlling its burn until it ran off the spit, a mile-and-a-half further northeast. The

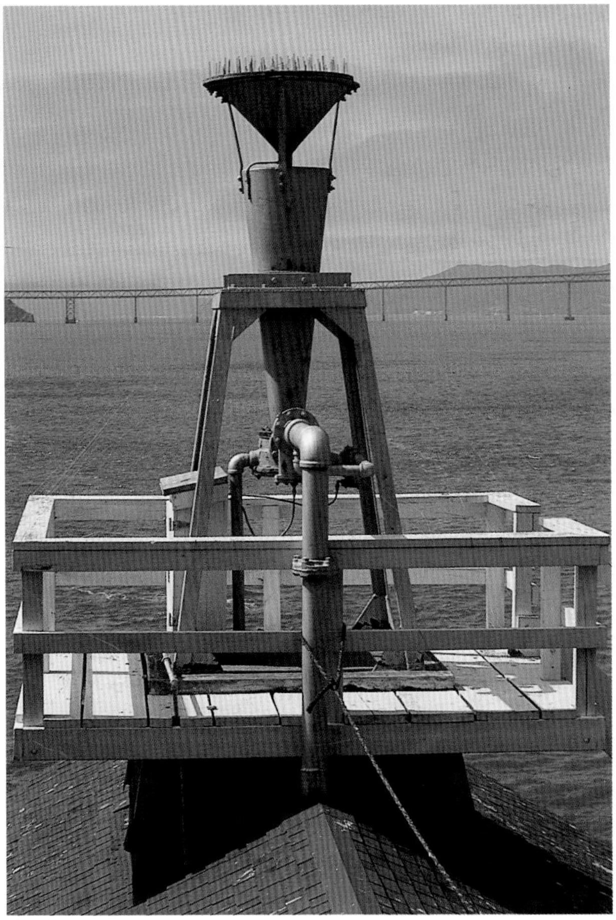

EAST BROTHER LIGHT STATION
The first fog signals were cannons, replaced by enormous trumpets sounded by steam. The most familiar sound, however, a two-tone deep bleet-blat, *came from these diaphone horns. Diesel engines and air-compressors replaced boilers to power the diaphones. East Brother features the only operating diaphone signals on the West Coast, sounded each day, briefly, just before supper.*

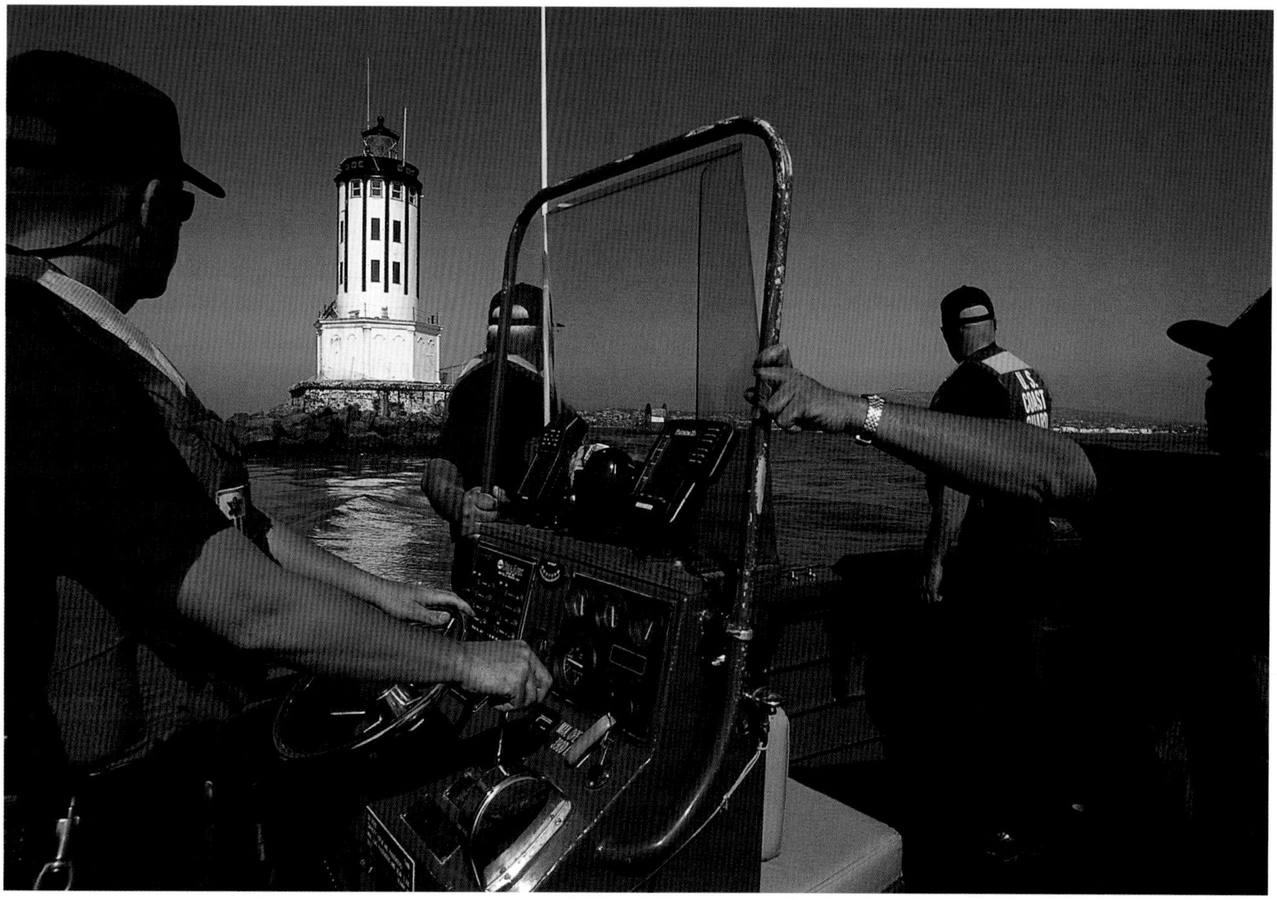

Los Angeles Harbor lighthouse

Petty Officer John Hurst heads toward L.A. Harbor light with his ANT team for routine service. Sometimes called Angel's Gate, its fourth-order Fresnel first shined with incandescent oil vapor (IOV) in March 1913. Keepers lived in pie-shaped quarters below the lantern until de-staffing in 1973.

sprinklers split the fire around the station, but it reconnected just forty feet east of the main keeper's house. There was smoke damage to every building, but none were lost.

After the Coast Guard de-staffed lighthouses, some fell into serious disrepair. In the past decade, people recognized the value and appeal of many sites, and the Coast Guard released some of its property to individuals and organizations. Cape Flattery and Yaquina Head light began to host University of Washington researchers who study marine life and shore birds in the 1970s.

At Cape Flattery, zoology professor emeritus Robert Paine has spent thirty years chronicling the dozens of animal species that thrive in tide pools. Biology professor Julia Parrish watches shorebird aggregations on the island, questioning "Why be a member of a group?" The common murres that she studies are the densest-nesting birds in the world, laying eggs shoulder to shoulder. Analogies to populous cities are easily drawn.

More than a hundred years earlier, in 1860, Smithsonian Institution researchers first tried similar research, asking several Texas keepers to gather shore- and seabird eggs for study. With the blessing of the Lighthouse Board, the keepers were happy to oblige, giving them a relaxing hobby when the light did not need tending or the fog signals sounding, and providing them contact with the outside world that often seemed far removed from their light station.

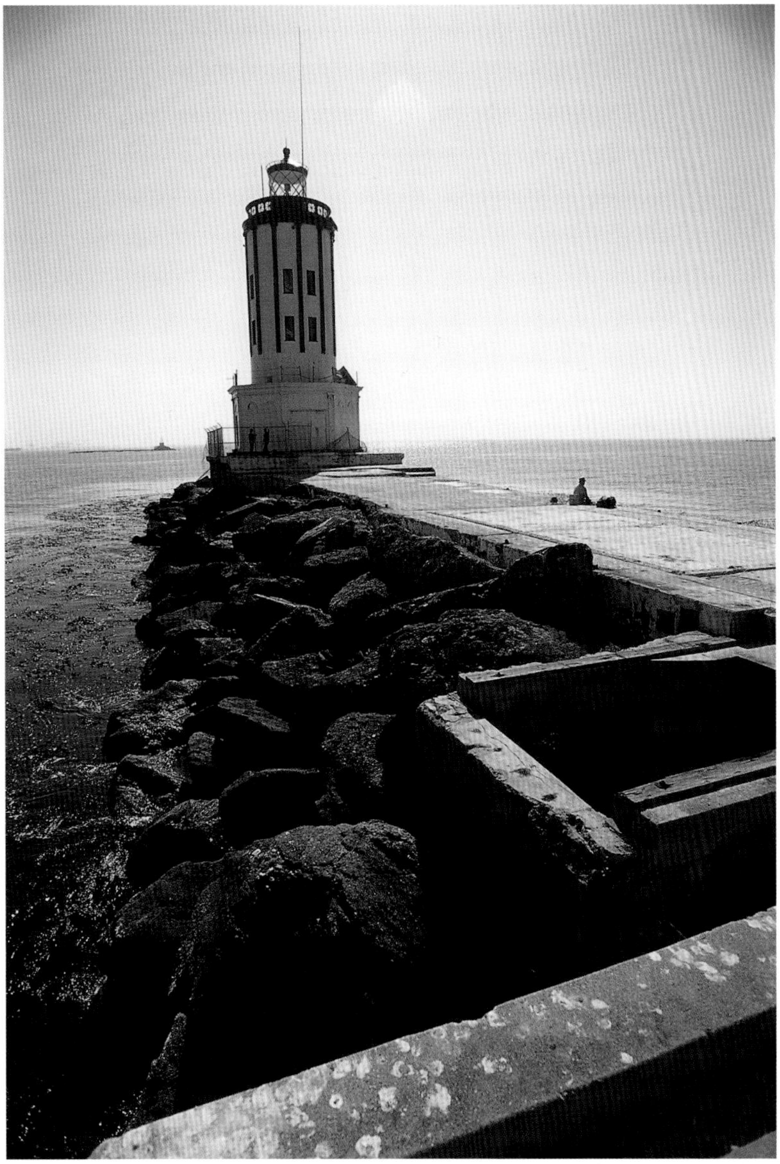

Los Angeles Harbor lighthouse
L.A. Harbor went to a green lens in the early 1930s to stand out from background distraction. To a mariner south of Long Beach and San Pedro, the clutter of industrial and harbor yellow or white lights made it difficult to locate the white Fresnel. Running on batteries, the modern Vega Rotating Beacon shines only from dusk to dawn.

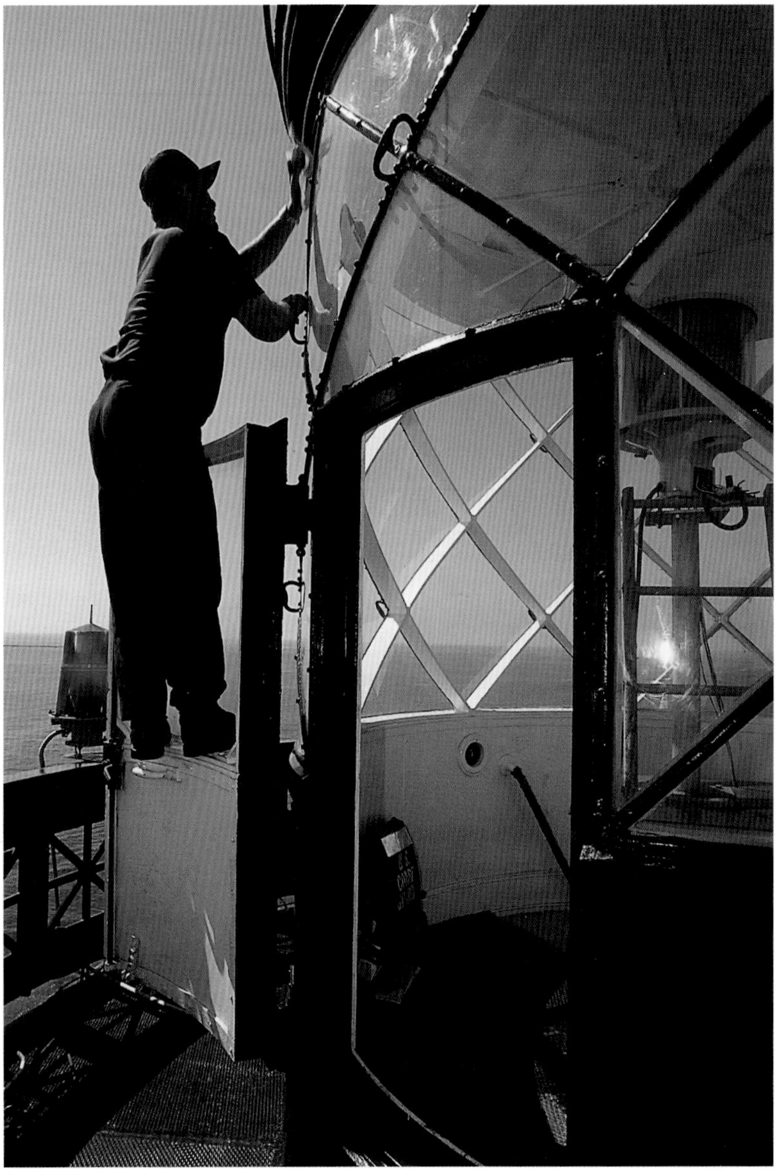

Los Angeles Harbor lighthouse

ANT team member Al Servin adopts a classic "Wickie" stance while cleaning the glass. The Coast Guard treats this light though it were an island light by using solar panels to recharge storage batteries, the first on the West Coast to use this system.

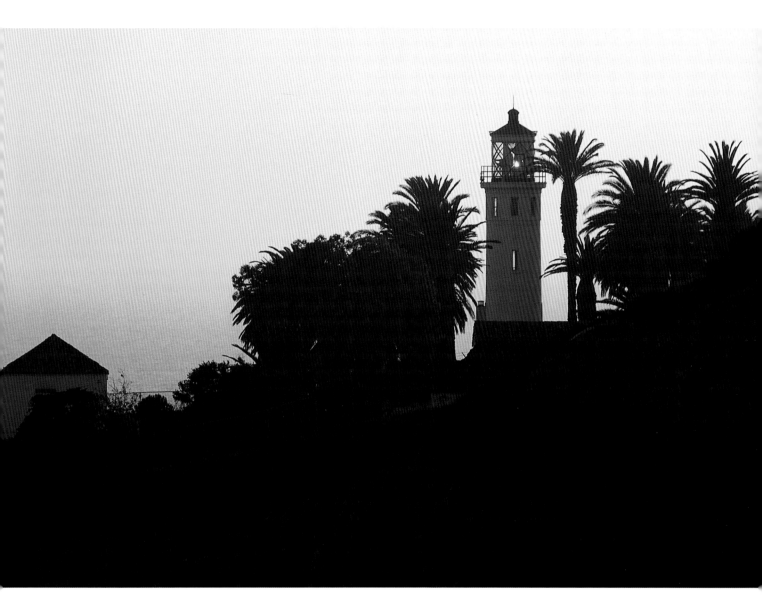

Point Vicente light station
The light station, proposed in 1914, encountered land acquisition difficulties like Point Reyes. Exclusive real estate developments were built on the point. The fifty-five-foot-tall light was not lit until early 1926. Wealthy neighbors complained about the light's glare, so the Coast Guard painted over shore-side gallery windows in 1944.

Lighthouse Getaways

Off the front porch, the lights of the town of Dungeness are barely visible. Behind the house, across the Strait of Juan de Fuca, the first landfall is Victoria, British Columbia. By 3:00 P.M., your last visitors have begun their nearly six-mile hike back across the sandy spit, and if you're lucky there will be enough time before dinner to polish the brass and sweep the stairs. Your week long "watch" at New Dungeness lighthouse is almost over; the truck will be out at low tide tomorrow to pick you up. You'll take away memories of peaceful mornings spent watching ships pass by or of afternoon fence painting.

Many people find a certain romance about staying in a lighthouse. On the West Coast, there are lighthouse vacations to suit all desires. For those on a budget or anyone interested in meeting new friends, California's Pigeon Point and Point Montara are International Youth Hostels. But don't let the title turn you away from these wonderful getaways. Point Montara rents out the fog-signal room, designed for a couple, and Pigeon Point has family rooms complete with private kitchens. Both locations have a private hot tub overlooking the ocean.

Groups or individuals in search of a great weekend place can try California's Point Arena or Washington's New Dungeness and North Head. At these locations you can rent a keeper's cottage. Most rentals are three-bedroom, one-bath affairs restored with modern conveniences. Reservations must be made at least eight months in advance.

For the ultimate pampered getaway, East Brother light near San Francisco and Oregon's Heceta Head light offer exclusive bed and breakfast opportunities. Occupancy is limited to between six and ten adults at each lighthouse. At East Brother, the package includes a champagne reception, four-course dinner, and a full breakfast. At Heceta Head, an evening reception precedes a private nighttime tour of the light; a multi-course breakfast in the morning caps off your visit. Both East Brother and Heceta Head have internet Websites for more information at www.elbs.org and www.HecetaLighthouse.com, respectively.

Point Vicente light station
This third-order Barbier, Bernard & Tirenne lens was manufactured in 1886 and used at Sitka, Alaska, for forty years before reassignment to Point Vicente. Its double bull's-eye opens for ease in cleaning the lens and servicing the 1,000-watt bulbs and automatic changer. Point Vicente has always been an electric station.

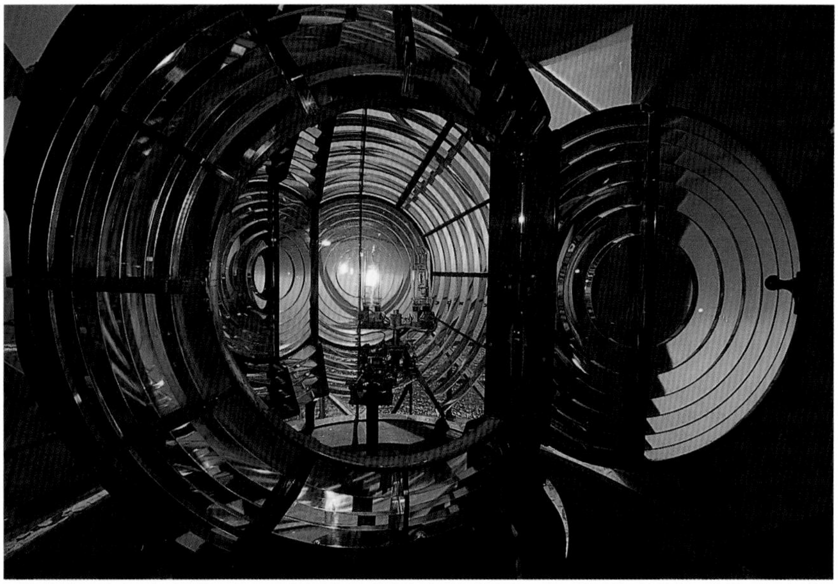

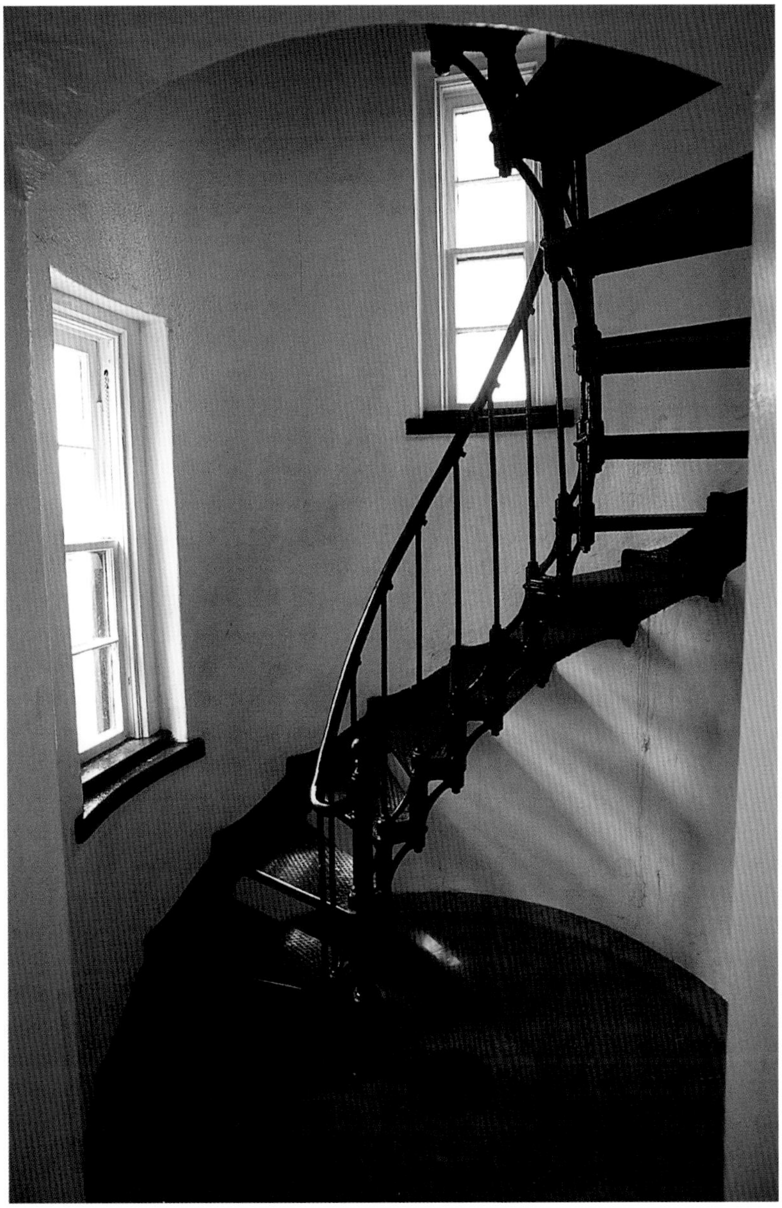

Admiralty Head lighthouse

Perhaps Lighthouse Board architect Carl Lieck's most beautiful lighthouse, this California Spanish-style residence not only incorporated the light into its structure, but it also provided an indoor bathroom and laundry, unusual for 1903. The walls of the tower are eighteen-inch-thick brick.

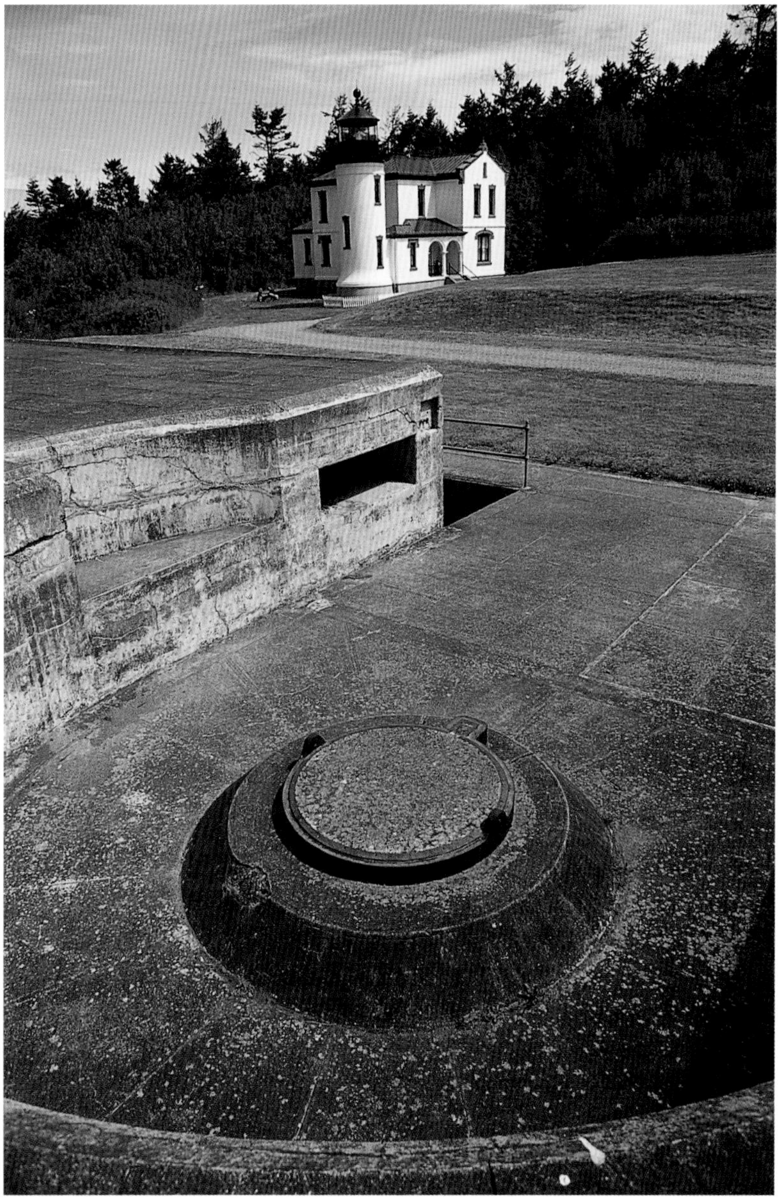

Admiralty Head lighthouse

The original lighthouse, a two-story wood frame structure located on a bluff overlooking Puget Sound, first shined in January 1861. Fort Casey needed the site for ten-inch gun emplacements in 1897, so the Lighthouse Board built a new structure, which it kept in service until 1922. During World War II, it housed Coast Guard Beach Patrol personnel and dogs.

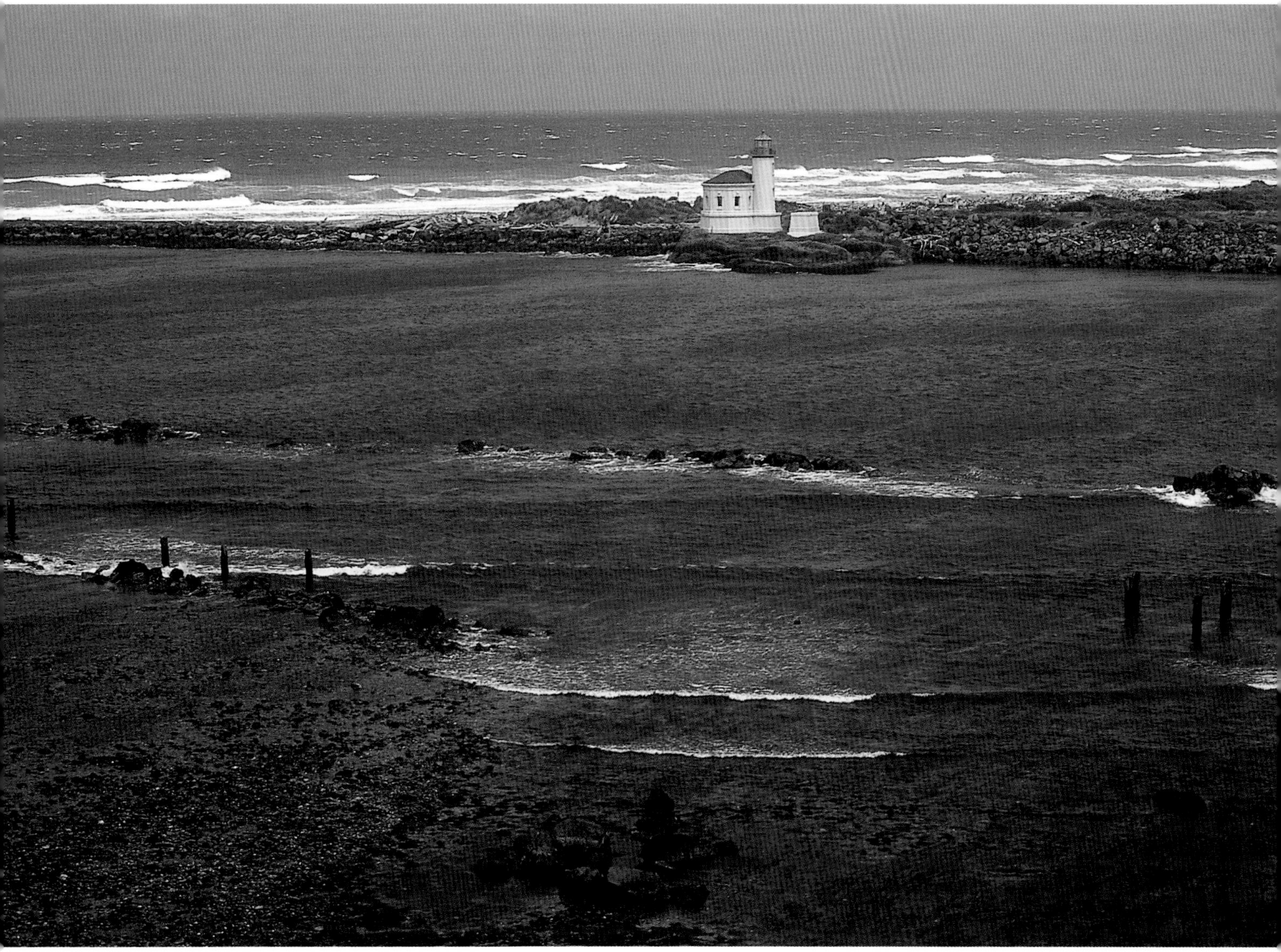

Coquille River lighthouse
This was the last lighthouse built on the Oregon coast, its fourth-order lens first lit in February 1896. It served both as ocean lighthouse and river marker for dozens of vessels heading into Bandon harbor just opposite the lighthouse. In 1939, the Coast Guard replaced the lighthouse with a post light on the jetty.

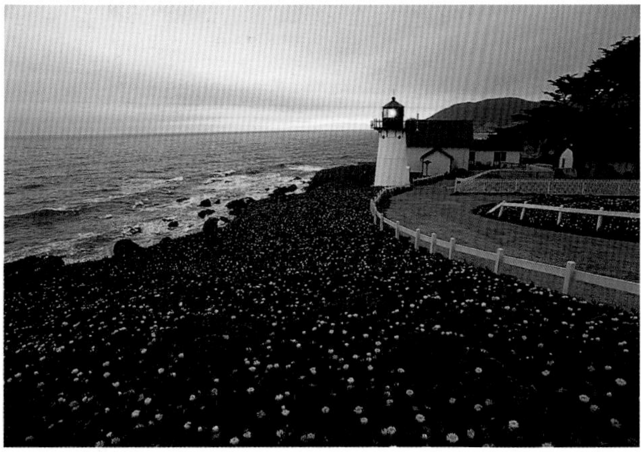

Above: **Point Montara light station**
Because this area twenty miles south of San Francisco actually had more fog than darkness, the Point Montara light was a fog signal as early as March 1875. Its red post lamp didn't appear until November 1900. The fourth-order Fresnel first shined in 1912 and was electrified in 1919. The entire station was automated in 1970.

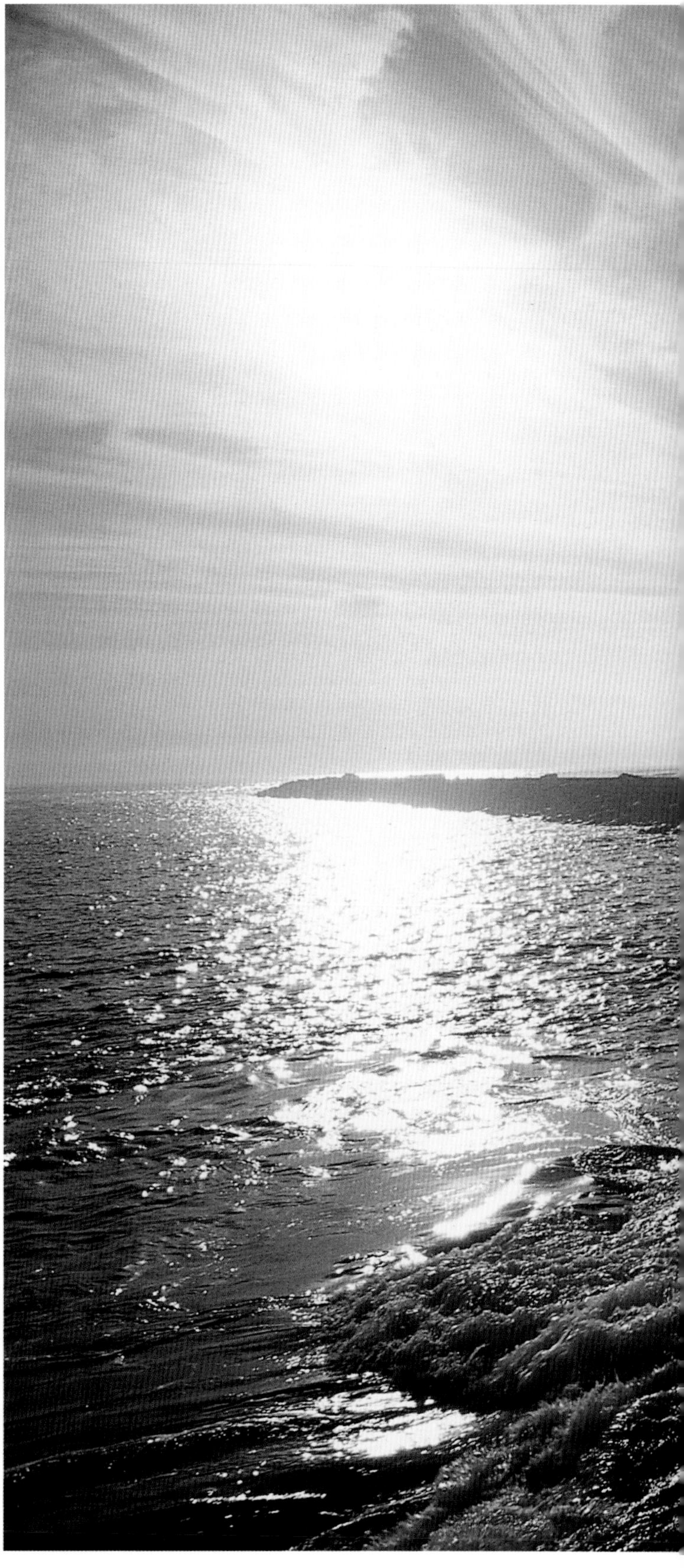

Right: **Coquille River lighthouse**
The lighthouse, minus keepers' residences and other structures, reopened in 1979 as a visitor attraction in the newly created Bullards Beach State Park.

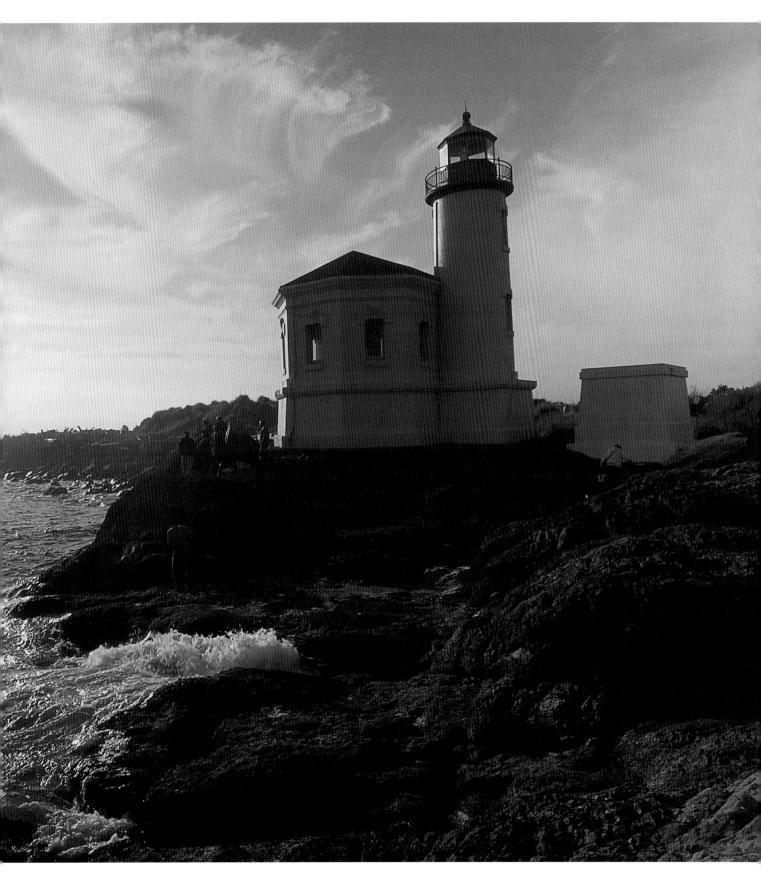

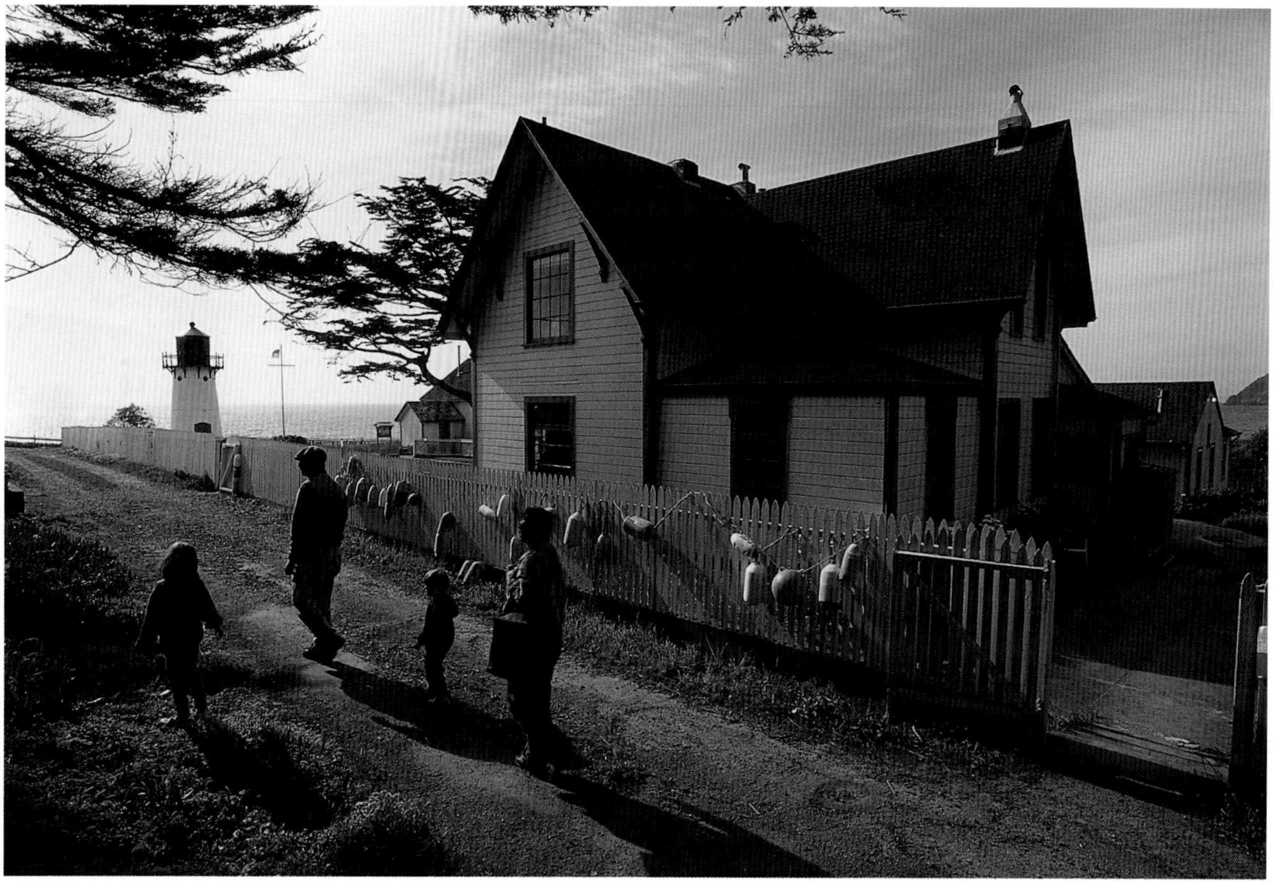

Point Montara light station

The original 1875 Victorian duplex keeper's house still stands. During World War II, the station housed Beach Patrol personnel. More modern Coast Guard housing, built in 1961, is now a youth hostel with reasonably priced overnight accommodations. Point Montara is part of the Golden Gate National Recreation Area.

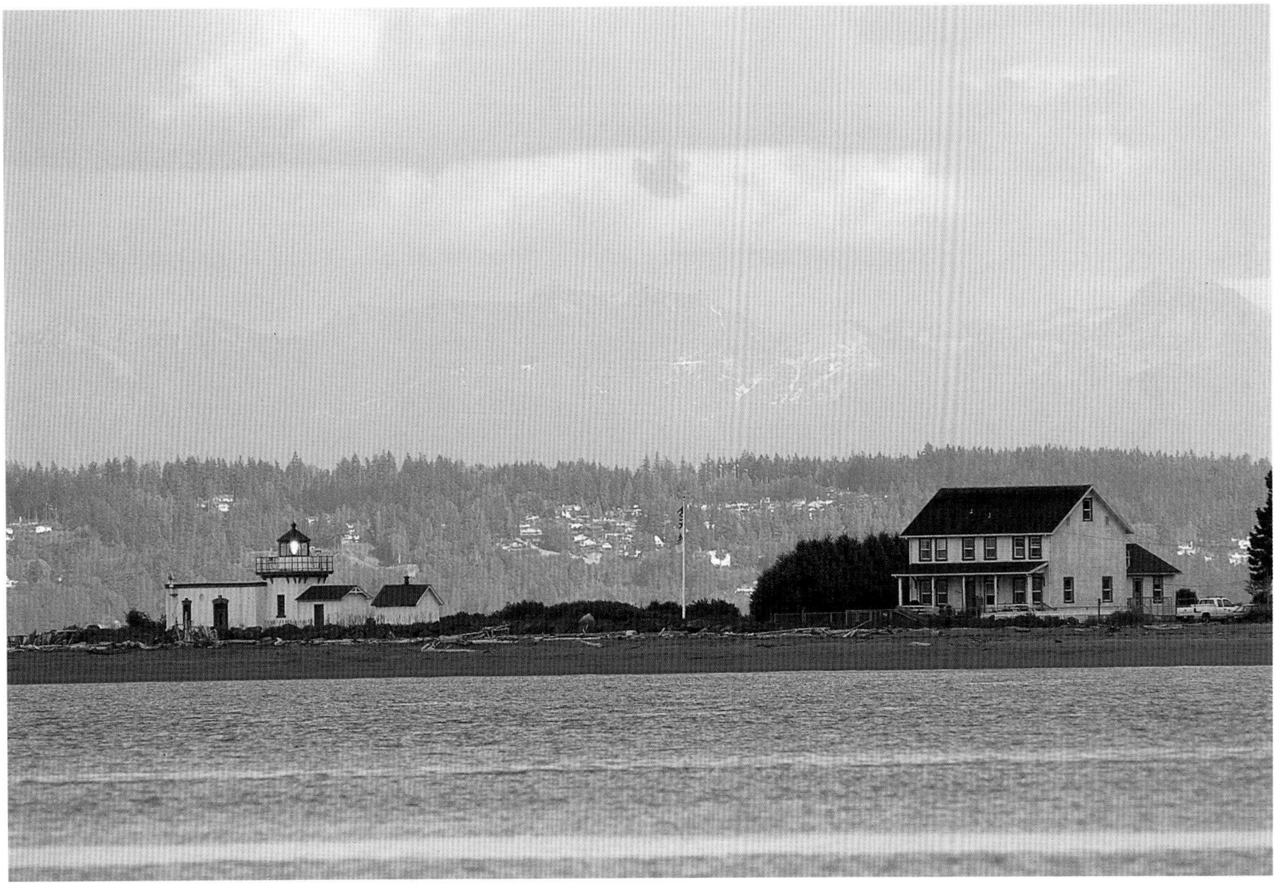

Point No Point light station
Lt. Charles Wilkes named this tiny spit in 1841, thinking from his ship it looked larger than it was. Its first light was no more consequential, simply a household kerosene lantern on a pole. By 1880, the Lighthouse Board installed a fifth-order Fresnel. It replaced this with a fourth-order lens in 1915. Lightning struck the tower in 1931, cracking a bull's-eye. This station is an architectural near-twin to West Point light across Puget Sound.

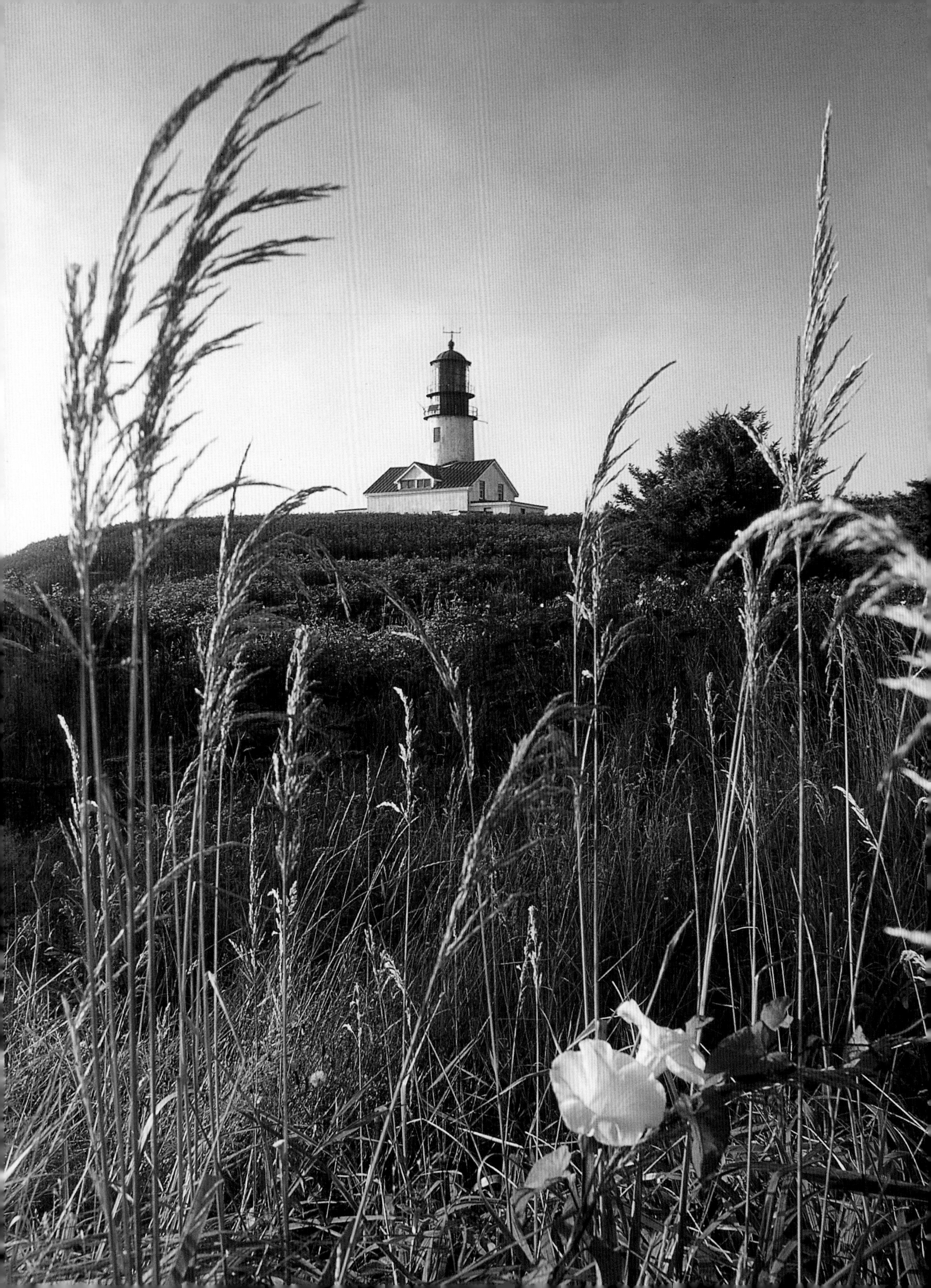

Lux Continua—Continuing Light

As the Aids-to-Navigation Team (ANT team) and civilian work crew left Tatoosh Island by helicopter 6003 in September 1999, they took one final look back at the Cape Flattery lighthouse where they had worked so hard. "It doesn't look any different from when I arrived," carpenter Garth Kuykendall said.

"What the Cape Flattery lighthouse needs," contractor Bob Allison had said when they arrived on the island to start their work, "is five hundred thousand dollars, which would stop all the problems and restore it to its original condition."

While true, and certainly desirable from the perspective of lighthouse enthusiasts and those who admire beautifully crafted old buildings, it begs a point: The money is not available, and is not a priority. The work that ANT teams did in the past as well as the civilian work done in September will protect Cape Flattery for another twenty years or longer. The United States is still a young country, and historical preservation is not ingrained in the national spirit.

The best thing that happened to U.S. lighthouses was Congress's reassignment of their operation to the Coast Guard in July 1939. Early in their sixty-year management of these navigation aids, the Coast Guard made some mistakes, acting with expediency rather than historical consciousness. However, in the past decade, priorities have shifted under direction from Coast Guard admirals all the way down to ANT-team chiefs such as J. Franklin, who supervised the work at Cape Flattery. The best evidence of this was Franklin's top priority of restoring the cemetary at Cape Flattery that week, and the care with which ANT-team members Erik Wiard, Jeb Wheeler, and Eric Arwood executed his request. It would be easy to let the cemetery at Cape Flattery fall into disrepair, like what happened at Heceta Head. But the ANT teams see their responsibility from a long-range viewpoint.

Wheeler's riddle symbolizes the philosophy: "An old man, sitting in his recliner in the dark, is watching television. Outside he hears a crash. He runs up the stairs, looks out, and says, 'Oh my God! I've killed them all.'"

Modern technology allows global positioning satellites to give mariners off Cape Flattery—or commuters in rush-hour traffic in Des Moines, Iowa—a fix on their location within six feet. Lighthouses are not really necessary, and there is no longer anyone sitting in recliners at U.S. light stations.

"But what if the satellites fail?" Jeb Wheeler asked one night as he watched the six spokes of Cape Flattery lighthouse's Vega beacon rotate overhead, slicing a white-and-red disk into the fog. There may be no one home at U.S. lighthouses any more, but the ANT teams will make sure the lights will still be on.

Cape Flattery light station
When the fog lifts, Cape Flattery reveals a seldom-seen face. After nearly fifty-five hours of work by six contractors and routine maintenance by three ANT team members, the light looked little changed but it was much improved. Darkness falls and the fog returns.

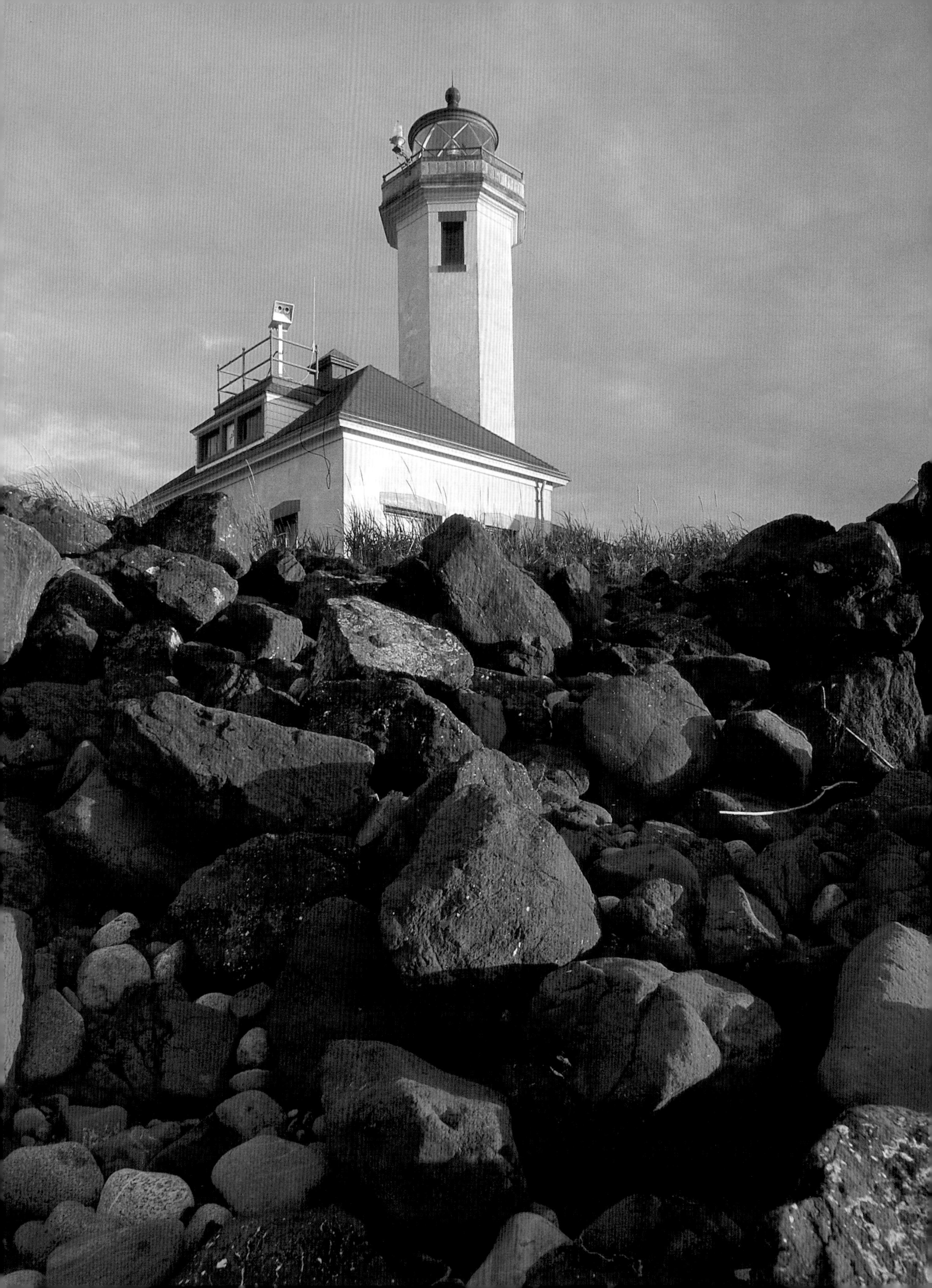

Guide to Pacific Coast Lighthouses

This appendix lists existing lights in California, Oregon, and Washington, but does not list lights that have been demolished.

As a note, the Coast Guard classifies a "light station" as having at least a light tower and one or more outbuildings; these usually include a barn, workshop, oil-storage shed, one or more assistant keepers' residences, and a fog-signal building. A "lighthouse" has only the light tower or a light as part of the keeper's residence, but it has no other outside buildings except for the oil-storage shed.

Admiralty Head Lighthouse

Whidbey Island, Washington
Date activated: 1861/1903
Latitude/longitude: 48°08'N/122°25.2'W

The first wooden lighthouse in Washington was completed at Admiralty Head in 1861. It was replaced in 1903 by the striking two-story C. W. Lieck–designed residence and tower within the confines of what became Fort Casey. Gun embankments surrounded the light, which was decommissioned in 1922. The original fourth-order Fresnel was transferred to New Dungeness light in 1927, and the lantern room has been dark since.

Directions: Located on Whidbey Island, Fort Casey is adjacent to the dock for the Port Townsend–Keystone Ferry, off Fort Casey Road just north of Washington State 20.

Alcatraz Island Lighthouse

San Francisco, California
Date activated: 1854
Latitude/longitude: 37°49.6'N/122°25.3'W

The West Coast's first navigation aid still operates in San Francisco Bay. Since 1973, the island has been part of the Golden Gate National Recreation Area, and self-guided audio tours of the famous prison are available. Visitors can see the lighthouse from various parts of the island but it is closed to the public.

Alki Point Light Station

Seattle, Washington
Date Activated: 1913
Latitude/longitude: 47°34.6'N/122°25.2'W

This light marks the south entrance to Seattle's Elliott Bay. Both the keeper's and assistant keeper's residences are now Coast Guard personnel housing, but the light is open to public visits on weekends from 12 P.M. to 4 P.M.

Directions: Take the Seattle Freeway west from either Highway 99 or I-5. Follow SW Admiral Way, then turn right onto Sixty-third Avenue SW. Turn left on Alki Avenue SW and look for signs directing visitors to the lighthouse.

Anacapa Island Light Station

Ventura, California
Date Activated: 1912/1932
Latitude/Longitude: 34°01.1'N/119°21.6'W

Commissioned in 1912, the structure was replaced in 1932. An active navigation aid, the lighthouse itself is closed. Travel to the island can be arranged through Channel Islands National Park's concessionaires.

POINT WILSON LIGHT STATION
Point Wilson was first lit in December 1879, but storms and tidal action undermined the tower. The Lighthouse Board reinforced the spit in 1904, but in 1914, it replaced the original with this structure further out on the point. It still uses its original fourth-order Fresnel. The assistant keeper's duplex stands close by.

Angel Island Point Blunt Lighthouse

San Francisco, California
***Date Activated:** 1886/1960*
***Latitude/Longitude:** 37°51.2'N/122°25.2'W*

Originally constructed in 1886, the structure at Point Knox was enlarged in 1939. However, after the Coast Guard completed the station at Point Blunt in 1960, the Point Knox station was razed. Located on San Francisco Bay's largest island, Angel Island, Point Blunt is an active Coast Guard station, and the light is not open to the public.

Battery Point Lighthouse

Crescent City, California
***Date Activated:** 1856*
***Latitude/Longitude:** 41°44.6'N/124°12.1'W*

Once known as Crescent City lighthouse, this private navigation aid sits inside the keeper's restored residence. Its fourth-order Fresnel is still in place and can be viewed by climbing a steep stairway and slipping through a slender trapdoor.

Directions: Take US 101 to Crescent City. Turn west onto Front Street, then south on A Street to reach the parking lot. It is a short walk to the light, which is open from 10 A.M. to 4 P.M. Wednesday through Sunday. Check the tide tables; the small island can be unreachable at high tide.

At the nearby Del Norte County Historical Museum at Sixth Avenue and H Street, the restored first-order light from the St. George Reef lighthouse is on display.

Browns Point Light Station

Tacoma, Washington
***Date Activated:** 1887/1933*
***Latitude/Longitude:** 47°18.4'N/122°26.6'W*

Opposite Commencement Bay from Tacoma, this lighthouse is an Art Deco structure whose vertical lines and edges form a sort of day marking. The new structure replaced the original lighthouse first lit in 1887. The residence, built with the first light, and the light are not open to visitors but the grounds, part of Tacoma City Parks, are open from sunrise to sunset year round.

Directions: From Tacoma on Interstate 5 take I-705 north to Washington 509. Follow 509 around the commercial piers as it becomes Marine View Drive, and continue to the park.

Burrows Island Lighthouse

Burrows Island, Washington
***Date Activated:** 1906*
***Latitude/Longitude:** 48°28.6'N/122°42.7'W*

This active navigation aid is located on the western tip of Burrows Island on Rosario Strait. Automated in 1972, it can be reached only by boat or helicopter but it is not open to the public.

Cape Arago Lighthouse

Charleston, Oregon
***Date Activated:** 1866*
***Latitude/Longitude:** 43°20.5'N/124°22.5'W*

An active navigation aid, the light is not open to the public. However, it can be seen from a pull-out one-quarter mile south at Cape Arago State Park off of Cape Arago Highway. The high bridge connecting the lighthouse island to shore can be seen as well as from Bastendorf Beach County Park about one-half mile north.

The original fourth-order Fresnel made by Barbier, Bernard & Turenne of Paris was in service from 1866 to 1993 when it was removed to Coast Guard Air Station North Bend. The fifty-three-piece lens is on display inside the main entrance.

Cape Blanco Light Station

Port Orford, Oregon
***Date Activated:** 1870*
***Latitude/Longitude:** 42°50.2'N/124°33.8'W*

Constructed in 1870 and still an active navigation aid, it is open from 11 A.M. to 3 P.M. Thursday through Monday. The lighthouse is located in Cape Blanco State Park.

Directions: Follow US 101 north from Port Orford. Turn west on Cape Blanco Highway and proceed about five miles to the end.

Cape Disappointment Lighthouse

Ilwaco, Washington
***Date Activated:** 1856*
***Latitude/Longitude:** 46°16.6'N/124°03.1'W*

This is the only West Coast light with painted day markings in the style of East Coast lights. It also is Washington's oldest. It marks the north shore of the Columbia River. The lighthouse is not open to the public but it can be reached by a hilly, one-half-mile-long hiking trail

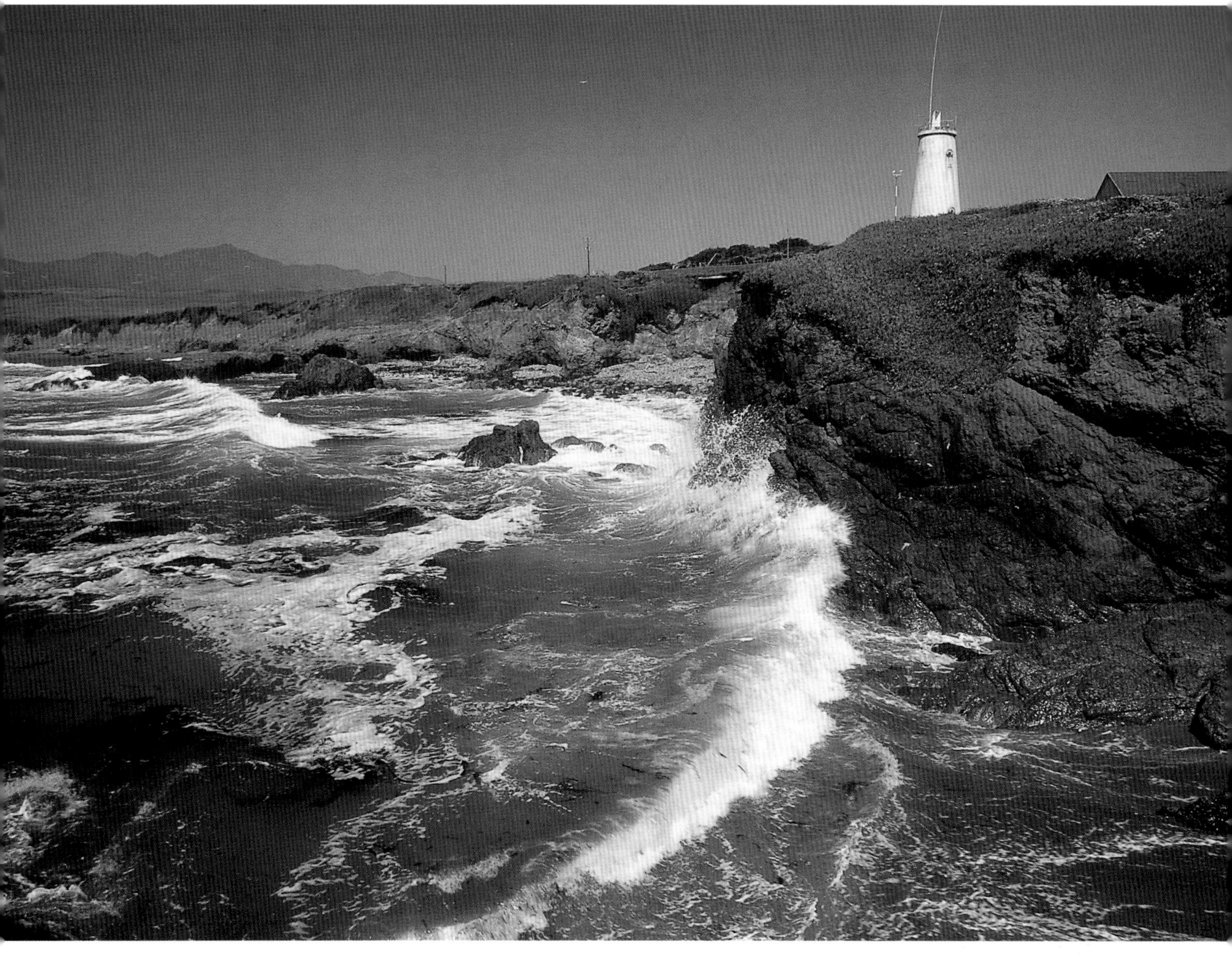

Piedras Blancas light station

First lit in February 1875, the first-order Fresnel sat atop a 115-foot tower. In 1949, a storm nearly destroyed the lantern room. The Coast Guard removed the Fresnel, capped the tower, and installed an aero beacon that has since been replaced with an even more compact light. At the base of the tower, the walls are five feet thick, though they taper to just eighteen inches at the top. For several years after its removal, the original Fresnel sat ignored, on the ground near the lighthouse. The Friends of the Piedras Blancas Lighthouse Lens rescued it and restored it, and now display it in nearby Cambria.

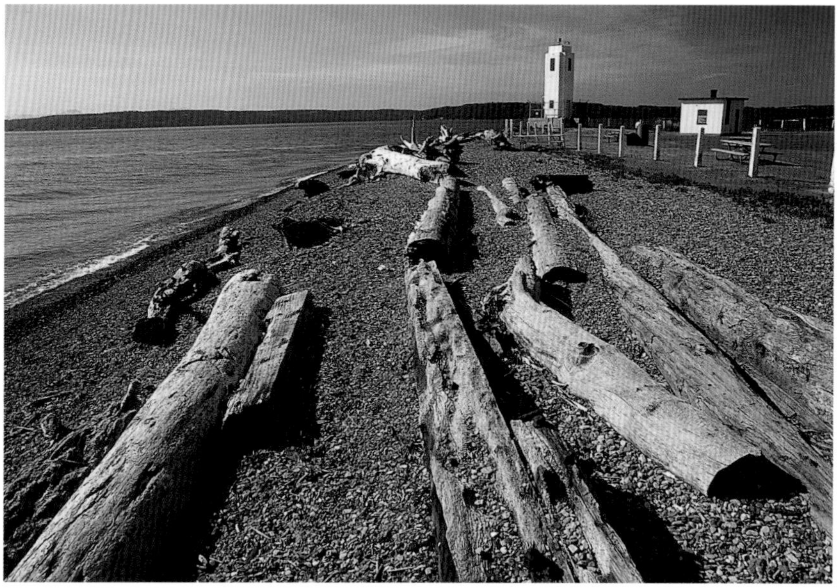

BROWNS POINT LIGHT STATION
At the entrance to Tacoma's Commencement Bay, Browns Point light first shined in December 1887. Then in 1933, the Lighthouse Board replaced the original wood structure with this Art Deco thirty-one-foot tower. The original keeper's residence and grounds are part of a city park.

from the parking lot at Fort Canby State Park. A great view is available from the Lewis & Clark Interpretive Center a short distance from the same parking lot.

Directions: From Ilwaco off US 101, head south on Second Street into Fort Canby State Park. Follow signs.

Cape Flattery Light Station

Tatoosh Island, Washington
***Date Activated:** 1857*
***Latitude/Longitude:** 48°23.5'N/124°44.1'W*

This is the farthest northwest light in the forty-eight contiguous states, and marks the entrance to the Strait of Juan de Fuca. Located on an island still owned by the Makah Indian nation, the light is reached only by helicopter and is closed to the public. However, the light can be viewed from an overlook on the Makah Indian Reservation. Contact the Makah Cultural and Research Center in Neah Bay for permission, directions, and further information.

Cape Meares Lighthouse

Tillamook, Oregon
***Date Activated:** 1890*
***Latitude/Longitude:** 45°25.2'N/123°58.6'W*

Summer hours are 11 A.M. to 4 P.M. daily, May through September. After October 1, it is open by special arrangement.

Directions: From US 101 in Tillamook, turn west on Third Street. Continue on toward Three Capes and Cape Meares State Park but follow the signs to Cape Meares Lighthouse. At the park, walk about 1,100 feet out to the light.

Cape Mendocino Lighthouse

Ferndale, California
***Date Activated:** 1868*
***Latitude/Longitude:** 40°26.4'N/124°24.4'W*

First lit in 1868, storms and earthquakes savaged the tower and first-order lens. The Coast Guard automated the light in 1951, then destroyed the outbuildings in 1960 and later placed a modern light on a white pole. A replica of the tower and the actual lens are visible at the Humboldt County fairgrounds in Ferndale.

Directions: Follow California 1 from US 101. Follow signs to the fairgrounds.

Cattle Point Lighthouse

San Juan Island, Washington
***Date Activated:** 1888/1935*
***Latitude/Longitude:** 48°27.1'N/122°57.7'W*

Cattle Point on the southern tip of San Juan Island was significant as one of the first radio beacon transmitter stations along the Strait of Juan de Fuca. Initiated by the U.S. Navy in 1921, signals from this station, Smith Island, and New Dungeness aided mariners in fog or darkness. By 1935, the Navy shut down the radio compass, and the Lighthouse Service replaced the original structure with a concrete tower.

Directions: The light tower is not open, but it can be seen from an interpretive center off Cattle Point Road. Follow signs from Friday Harbor to the San Juan Island National Historic Park (American Camp). The light is at the farthest southeast corner.

Lightship Columbia

Astoria, Oregon
***Date Activated:* 1950**
***Latitude/Longitude:* NA**

The *Lightship Columbia* is now permanently moored alongside the Columbia River Maritime Museum, which also has several displays relating to Tillamook Rock lighthouse. The museum is open 9:30 A.M. to 5 P.M. everyday except Christmas and Thanksgiving.

Directions: In Astoria, go east on Marine Drive along the river to the museum.

Coquille River Lighthouse

Bandon, Oregon
***Date Activated:* 1896**
***Latitude/Longitude:* 43°07.23'N/124°25.17'W**

Volunteers operate tours from 11 A.M. to 3 P.M. from Wednesday through Sunday. After dark, its three thirty-five-watt florescent lights shine toward Bandon, creating a green glow.

Directions: Located in Bullards Beach State Park just north of Bandon, follow signs along the road through the park to the lighthouse.

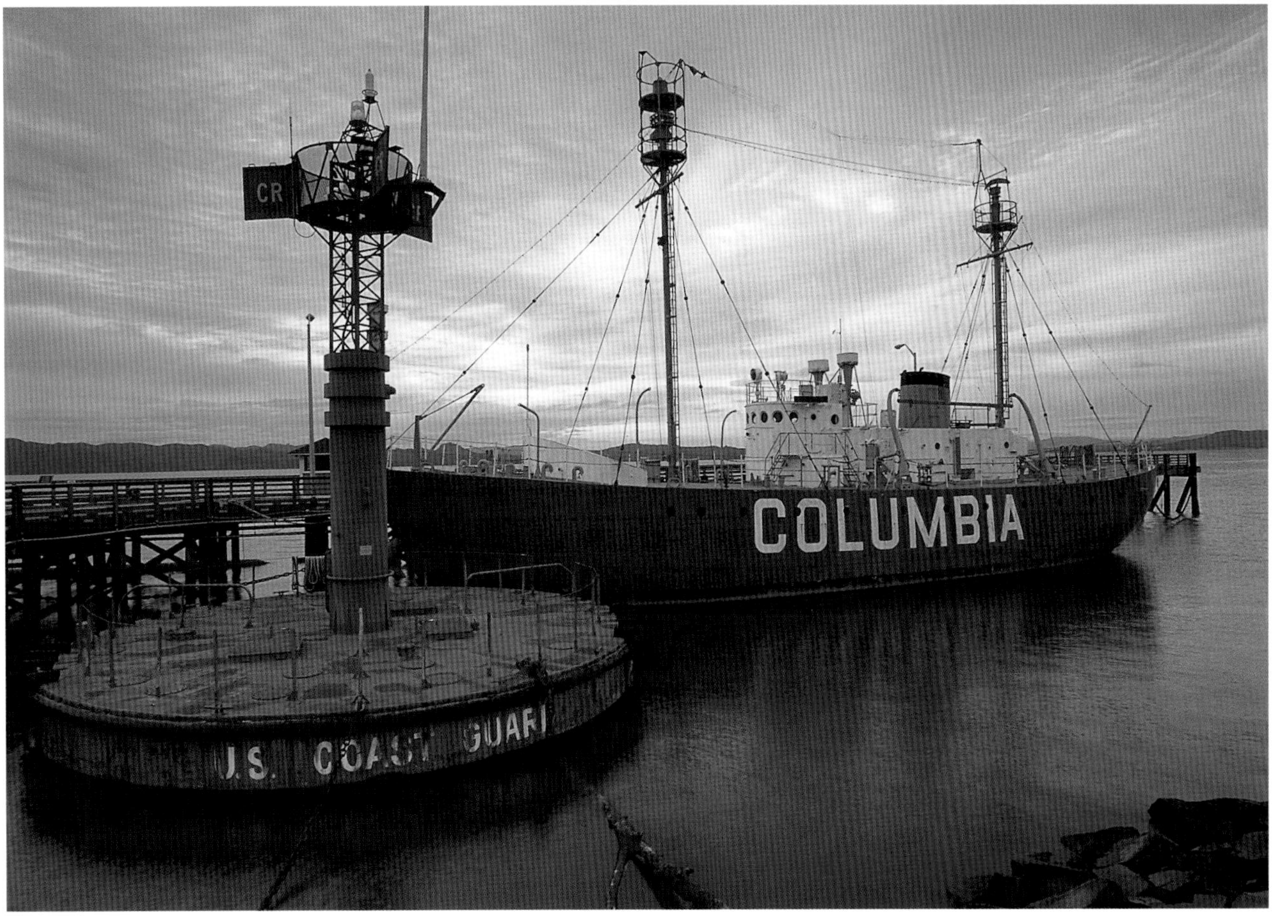

Lightship Columbia
Now permanently moored at the Columbia River Maritime Museum, the Columbia *was the West Coast's last active lightship, replaced in 1979 by a navigational buoy, also retired to the museum dock. The* Columbia's *375-mm "drum" light sat sixty-seven feet above the water, anchored 5.3 miles southwest of the Columbia River mouth.*

The Overland Trek of *Lightship Columbia*

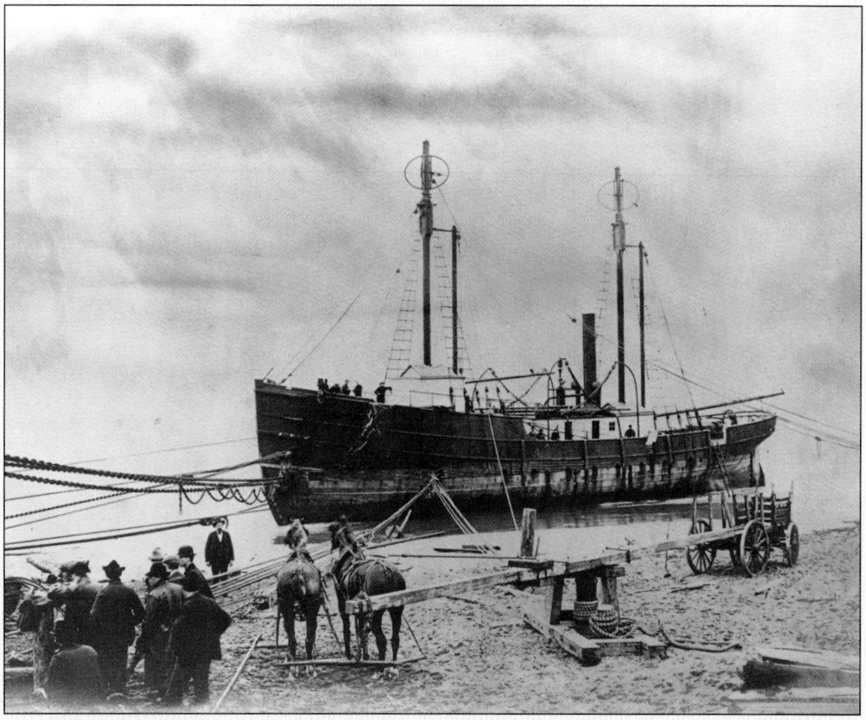

Lightship Columbia
In 1901, a team of forty men moved the Columbia *from the bar where it ran aground, over land, up a hill, and through a small forest. (Photo courtesy Columbia River Maritime Museum)*

On November 28, 1899, a raging storm tossed *Lightship Columbia* No. 50. As waves repeatedly broke over her bow and threatened to sink her, she pulled against her anchor chain and finally tore loose from her mooring at the mouth of Oregon's Columbia River. With no engine to drive her and emergency sails torn to shreds, No. 50 was at the mercy of the mad gods who rule the sea.

The first Pacific Coast lightship, *Columbia* was built at San Francisco's Union Iron Works. Launched in April 1892, the 112-foot-long, $80,000 vessel carried a crew of eight. Lightships were intended to be floating lighthouses, and as such, they did not have drive motors; the ship's two boilers supplied only enough steam for the fog whistles. Until that fateful night, No. 50 had stayed on station, just outside the Columbia River sand bar, ever since it had been towed out from San Francisco.

As the Columbia floated helplessly in the river mouth, the tugs *Wallula* and *Escort* and lighthouse tender *Manzanita* hurried to her aid. All three boats cast lines to the drifting ship but each time they parted. Early in the evening the ship went aground in a sandy bay near Cape Disappointment lighthouse. Lifesaving crews from Point Adams and Cape Disappointment, assisted by men from nearby Fort Canby, strung a breeches buoy and rescued all eight of the crew, including Captain Joseph H. Harriman. The only injury was to Anton Enberg, who suffered broken ribs after striking the ship's wheel.

Columbia lay grounded in the bay until January, when Captain Robert McIntosh got the contract to extract the boat from its precarious position. Although he had some success re-floating her, high tides and waves washed her back to shore. After six months of trying, McIntosh's contract was canceled and the Lighthouse Board sought a new round of bids. The shipbuilding firm of Wolff & Zwicker got approval to attempt to right the boat. By the end of October, eleven months after No. 50 washed ashore, Wolff & Zwicker gave up.

In a final attempt, the Board requested proposals to move the ship a half-mile overland and float her in Bakers Bay. Much to the surprise of the maritime community, the contract went to the Portland firm of Andrew Allen and J. H. Roberts—house movers.

They planned to lift the boat on jacks, place it in a specially designed wooden cradle, and pull it over the hill on a roadway built of railroad ties. For this engineering feat, Allen and Roberts would receive $17,500.

They began work on February 22, 1901, with a team of forty men. Moving a ship over land, up a hill, and through a small forest was not easy work but the contractors made steady progress. Ten weeks later, No. 50 completed the longest ship hike in the history of the Pacific Coast and was launched into Bakers Bay.

After completing repairs in Portland, she was towed back to her post at the mouth of the Columbia River. No. 50 continued to guard those treacherous waters until she was permanently relieved in 1909.

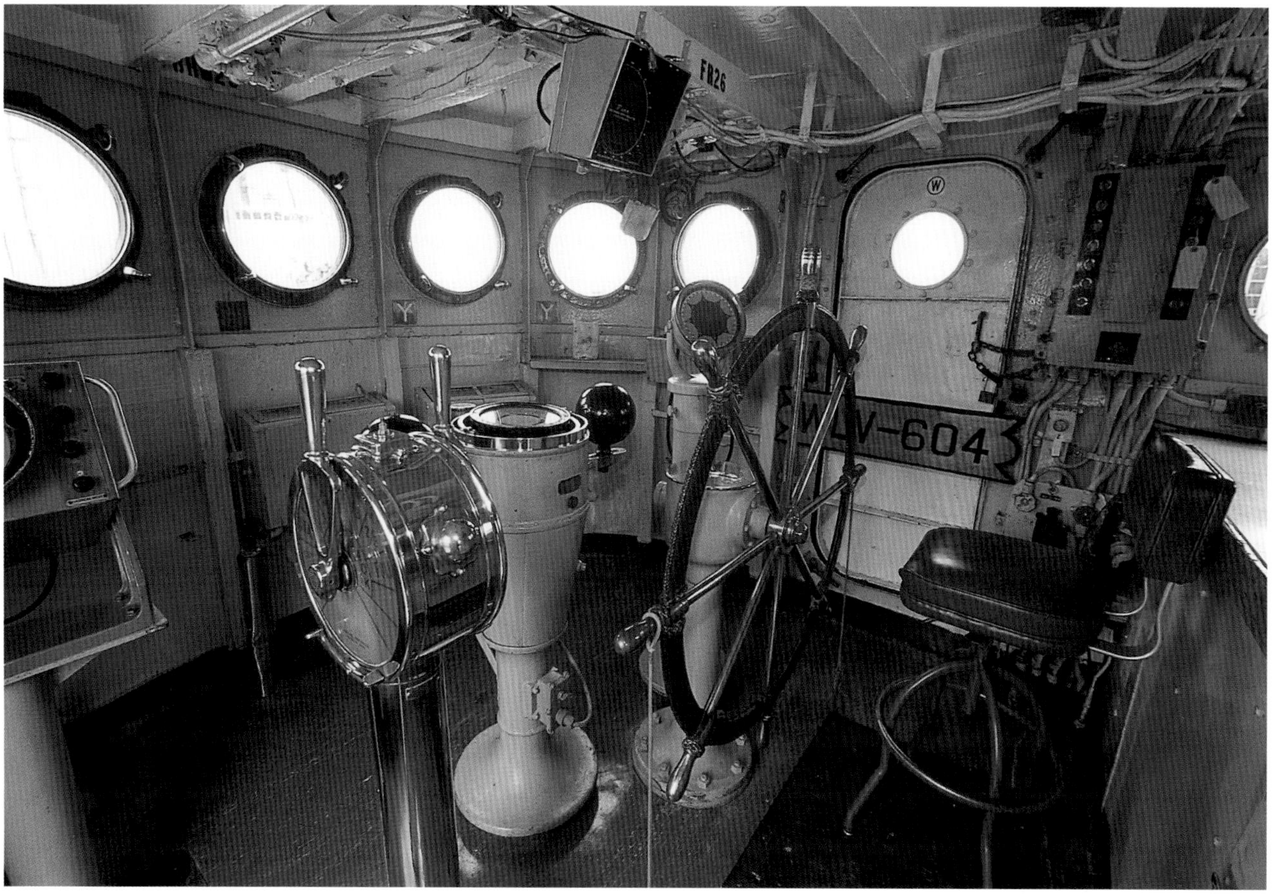

LIGHTSHIP COLUMBIA
Built in 1950 in Maine, the Columbia *was 128 feet long and powered by a 550-hp eight-cylinder diesel that worked with its 7,500-pound "mushroom" anchor to keep the ship in place regardless of weather. The wheelhouse was equipped with radar, depth indicator, compensating compass, and gyroscope. A crew of twelve lived aboard the ship, working twenty-eight days on, fourteen off.*

Destruction Island Light Station

Westport, Washington
Date Activated: 1891
Latitude/Longitude: 47°40.5'N/124°29.1'W

An active navigation aid on an island about three miles offshore, the light is automated and not open to the public. The Coast Guard replaced its original first-order Fresnel lens with a modern fixture and the original, completely restored, is displayed at the Westport Maritime Museum (see Grays Harbor lighthouse). The lighthouse can be seen from a parking area on US 101 about one mile south of Ruby Beach, about twenty miles south of LaPush.

East Brother Light Station

Richmond, California
Date Activated: 1874
Latitude/Longitude: 37°57.8'N/122°26.0'W

Named to the National Register of Historic Places in 1973, this Victorian light station now operates as a bed and breakfast. A fourth-order Fresnel, similar to what first operated at the station, is now on display in the fog-signal building. The light is visible from the short road to Port Richmond.

Accessible only by boat, reservations are required for overnight stays. Some daytime access is offered although none of the facilities are open.

Fort Point Lighthouse

San Francisco, California
Date Activated: 1864
Latitude/Longitude: 37°48.39'N/122°38.36'W
This third light at Fort Point, an iron tower, was built in 1864. Upon completion of the Golden Gate Bridge, which passes immediately overhead, the light was decommissioned in 1952. As a military fort, it is a National Historic Site.

Directions: Take Lincoln Boulevard to Long Avenue. Follow the signs. Open from 10 A.M. to 5 P.M. daily except major holidays.

Grays Harbor Lighthouse

Westport, Washington
Date Activated: 1898
Latitude/Longitude: 46°53.3'N/124°06.9'W
Often called the Westport lighthouse, it is located on Point Chehelis near Westport. It is Washington's tallest light. Its unusual clamshell third-order red-and-white Fresnel lens is no longer in use but can be seen when the lighthouse is open for tours.

The Westport Maritime Museum also is home to the completely restored and spectacularly displayed first-order Fresnel lens from the Destruction Island light. Visitor hours are from 10 A.M. to 4 P.M. from Memorial Day to Labor Day, and 12 P.M. to 4 P.M. Wednesday through Sunday the rest of the year.

Directions: Follow Washington 105 into Westport. The museum is located at 2201 Westhaven Drive, on the main street paralleling the marina and shops.

Heceta Head Light Station

Florence, Oregon
Date Activated: 1894
Latitude/Longitude: 44°08.3'N/124°07.6'W
The light is open to the public from 12 P.M. to 5 P.M. daily.

Directions: Follow US 101 north from Florence to Devils Elbow State Beach. Walk about ½ mile up to the light. If you stay at the Heceta Head Bed & Breakfast, in the former assistant keeper's residence, owners Carol and Mike Korgan take guests up for an afterdark tour.

Lime Kiln Light Station

San Juan Island, Washington
Date Activated: 1919
Latitude/Longitude: 48°31.0'N/123°09.1'W
Located on the west shore of San Juan Island and situated on Haro Strait, the light is also used as a whale-watching station. A powerpole stands just in front of the front door, reminding visitors this 1919 structure was the last lighthouse in Washington to receive electricity, in 1940. The Whale Museum in Friday Harbor houses some research personnel in the assistant keepers' residences. Lime Kiln Point State Park is open sunrise to sunset.

Long Beach Harbor Lighthouse

Long Beach, California
Date Activated: 1949
Latitude/Longitude: 33°43.4'N/118°11.2'W
This forty-two-foot-tall Art Deco structure stands on six pillars. The light was conceived and designed in 1949 as a fully automated light. Its functions are monitored from the nearby ANT team in L.A. Harbor. Its fog signal operates all the time.

Directions: The light sits at the end of Middle San Pedro Breakwater and is not accessible from shore. It is visible from several places along the shore.

Los Angeles Harbor Lighthouse

Los Angeles, California
Date Activated: 1913
Latitude/Longitude: 32°42.5'N/118°11.2'W
An active navigation aid, the lighthouse is located at the end of the two-mile-long San Pedro breakwater. It displays a green light illuminated only after dark. It is closed to the public. Also known as Angel's Gate lighthouse or San Pedro Harbor lighthouse, it can be viewed from Cabrillo Beach fishing pier.

Directions: Take I-110 south to Gaffey Street. Continue south to West Thirty-ninth Street. Turn east and go to Stephen M. White Street, down to the beach and pier.

The original fourth-order Fresnel lens was removed and is displayed at the Los Angeles Maritime Museum, located at Berth 84 at the foot of Sixth Street in San Pedro. The museum is open from 10 A.M. to 5 P.M. Tuesday through Sunday.

Marrowstone Point Light Station

Marrowstone Island, Washington
Date Activated: 1888

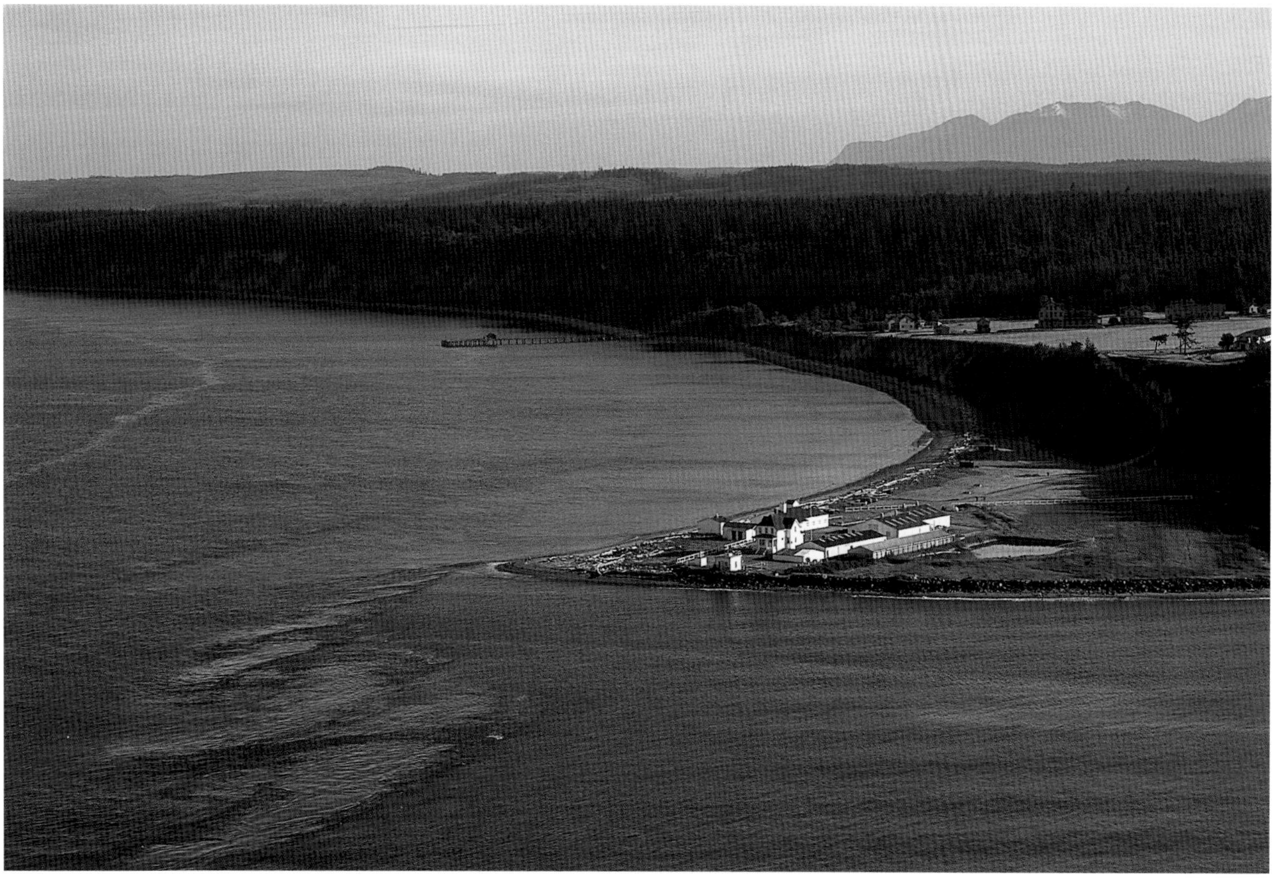

Marrowstone Point light station
Marking Admiralty Inlet, the seaway to Bremerton naval shipyard, this light has shown only a post light since October 1888. More important was its fog signal, first a bell, then later a succession of horns, guns, and diaphones. The point also denotes the north end of U.S. Army Fort Flagler, now a state park Environmental Learning Center.

***Latitude/Longitude:* 48°06.1'N/122°41.2'W**
Situated at the north end of Fort Flagler State Park, the post light, first used in 1888, now is activated only at night. Accompanied by a keeper's residence constructed in 1897, the entire compound currently houses the U.S. Fish & Wildlife Service National Fisheries Research Center. The residence is part of the Seattle-Marrowstone Field Station, and none of the facilities are open to the public, although visitors may view the modern optic by walking on the beach.

Directions: From Port Townsend, follow Washington 19 south to 116 east onto Marrowstone Island. Continue as it curves north. Follow signs to Fort Flagler State Park; inside the park, signs lead downhill to the lighthouse.

Mukilteo Light Station

Mukilteo, Washington
***Date Activated:* 1960**
***Latitude/Longitude:* 47°56.9'N/122°18.3'W**
The light is open from 12 P.M. until 5 P.M. on weekends. The lighthouse has its original fourth-order Sautter Fresnel lens in place. The historical society operates the light, a museum in the fog-signal building below the light, and the giftshop in the former Quarters B structure.

Directions: Follow Washington 525 north to Mukilteo State Park.

New Dungeness Light Station

Sequim, Washington
***Date Activated:* 1857**
***Latitude/Longitude:* 48°10.9'N/123°06.5'W**

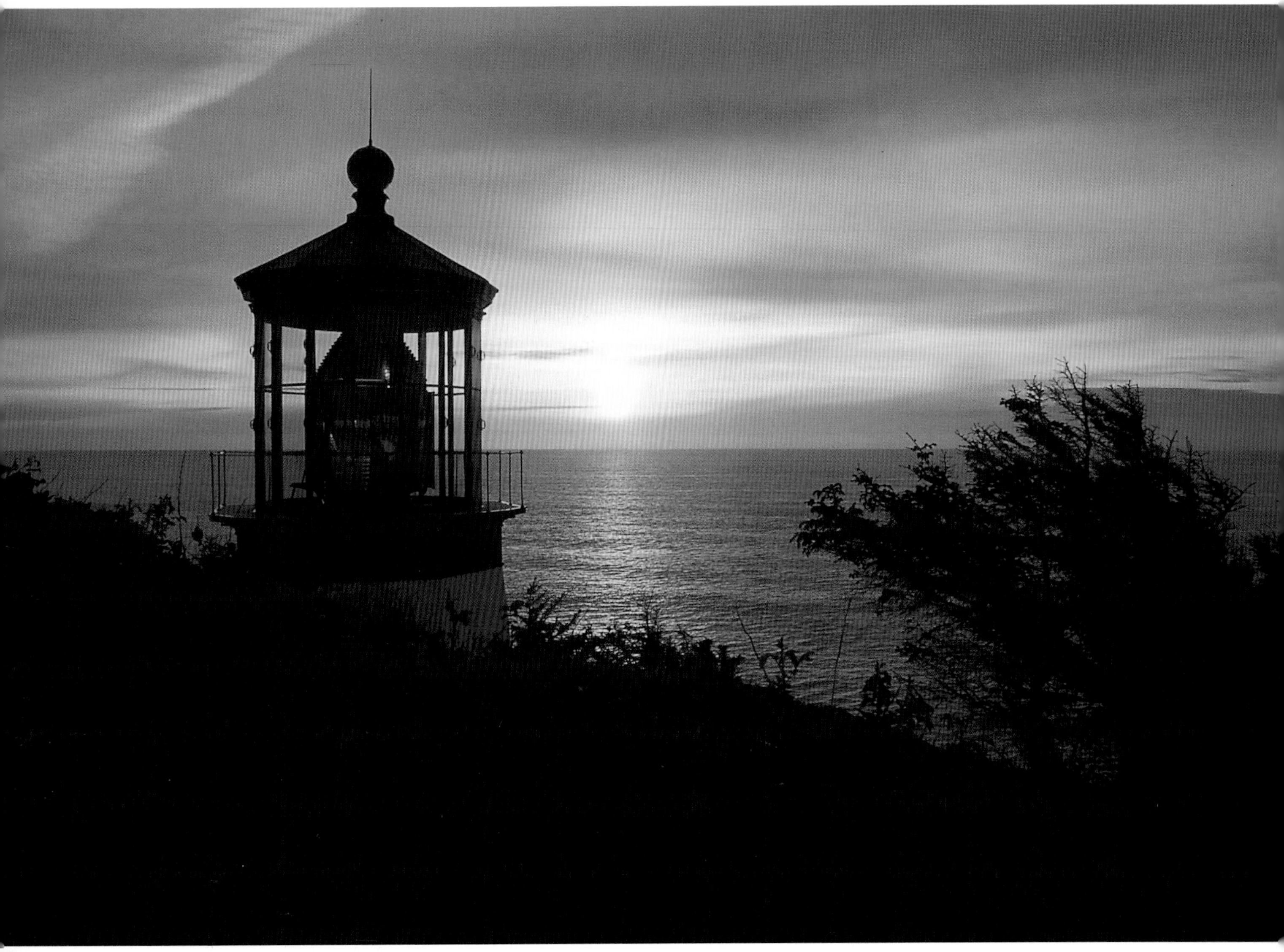

Cape Meares lighthouse
Cape Meares's LePaute eight-sided Fresnel is massive. This first-order optic is twelve feet tall, six feet wide, and weighs 2,000 pounds. First lit in January 1890, it's now missing several bull's eyes due to vandalism.

Situated near the end of a seven-mile-long spit north of Sequim, this active navigation aid is operated by the New Dungeness Chapter of the U.S. Lighthouse Society. Members have the opportunity to live at the light for a week, and they ride out in a USLS four-wheel drive at low tide on Saturdays.

Visitors who hike out to the spit or who travel by boat (there is a launch ramp at Cline Spit near the town of Dungeness) can tour the lighthouse from 10 A.M. to 5 P.M. Thursday through Monday. Check the tide tables before beginning this walk. The residence, constructed in 1905, is not open to the public.

Directions: From US 101 west of Sequim, turn north at Kitchen Road and follow signs to Dungeness Wildlife Area. From the parking lot, it is a six-and-one-half-mile walk.

North Head Light Station

Ilwaco, Washington
***Date Activated:** 1898*
***Latitude/Longitude:** 46°18.0'N/124°04.6'W*

This light supplemented Cape Disappointment by illuminating the coast to the north of the Columbia River. Located in Fort Canby State Park, it is open only at limited times for tours. Visitors can stay overnight in the restored head keeper's residence.

Directions: From Ilwaco, follow the signs to Fort Canby State Park and from there to the lighthouse.

Patos Island Lighthouse

Patos Island, Washington
***Date Activated:** 1893/1908*
***Latitude/Longitude:** 48°47.3'N/122°58.2'W*

About seventeen miles south of Point Roberts is 210-acre Patos Island. The light is located on the western tip, and its fourth-order Fresnel was first lit in 1893. The Lighthouse Service replaced the lighthouse in 1908, and the Coast Guard automated the facility in 1974. In 1984, it razed the residences and other structures that had been vandalized.

The island can be reached only by boat. It offers primitive camping. The light is not open to the public.

Piedras Blancas Light Station

Cambria, California
***Date Activated:** 1875*
***Latitude/Longitude:** 35°39.9'N/121°17.1'W*

An active navigation aid, the light displays the current Coast Guard rotating beacon. In 1949, the Coast Guard removed the original first-order Fresnel lens and the lantern room. The Cambria Lions Club rescued the lens, and in 1992, the Friends of Piedras Blancas Light began displaying it in an enclosure on Main Street, Cambria.

The existing light is closed to the public but can be seen from California 1, about one mile north of the visitor entrance to San Simeon.

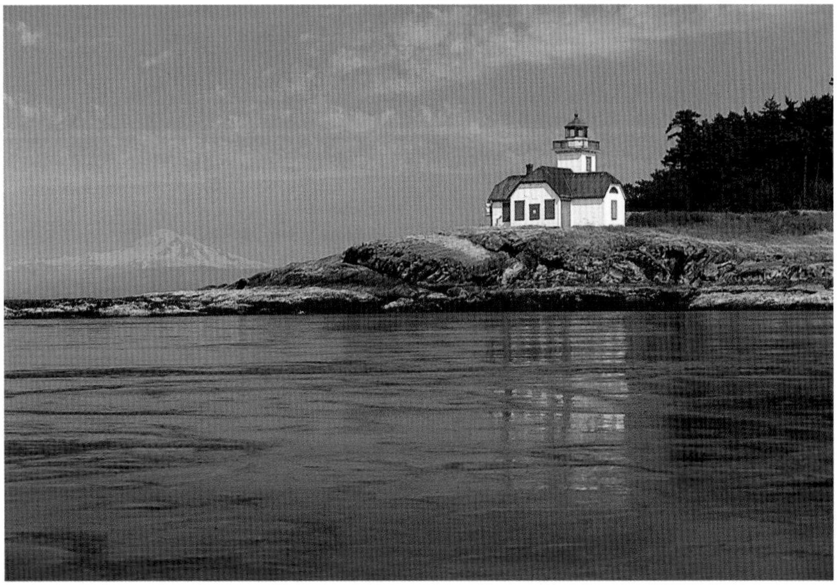

Patos Island lighthouse
This Washington Marine State Park encompasses the entire 210-acre island. Both Patos and Turn Point, along the route to Vancouver, were first lit in November 1893. The Coast Guard automated Patos in 1974, replacing its original fourth-order Fresnel with a battery-operated drum light. Mount Baker is about forty-five miles away in the background.

Pigeon Point Light Station

Pescadero, California
Date Activated: 1872
Latitude/Longitude: 37°10.9'N/122°23.6'W

The first-order Fresnel remains in place at the top of a 115-foot tower. The light was recently named a California State Historic Park. Docents lead visitors to the top of the tower between 12 P.M. and 4 P.M. Saturday and Sunday. The four 1960s Coast Guard bungalows adjoining the lighthouse are now operated by American Youth Hostels. The Youth Hostel grounds are open from 7:30 A.M. to 9:30 A.M. and again from 4:30 P.M. until 9:30 P.M. daily.

Directions: Take California 1 south nineteen miles from Half Moon Bay. Follow the signs.

Point Arena Light Station

Point Arena, California
Date Activated: 1870/1908
Latitude/Longitude: 38°57.3'N/123°44.4'W

This 1908 concrete tower replaced a masonry tower, which was built in 1870 but destroyed during the 1906 San Francisco earthquake. It remains today an active navigation aid with a 1977 aero-beacon. The first-order Fresnel is still in place at the top of the 115-foot-tall tower, and is open from 11 A.M. to 2:30 P.M. daily and from 10 A.M. to 3:30 P.M. summer weekends. Former Coast Guard keeper's quarters are available for overnight accommodations. Each unit has three bedrooms.

Directions: From California 1, turn west at Rollerville Junction just north of Point Arena, then take Lighthouse Road north.

Point Bonita Lighthouse

San Francisco, California
Date Activated: 1855
Latitude/Longitude: 37°48.9'N/122°31.8'W

Also part of the Golden Gate National Recreation Area, this lighthouse is an active navigation aid. The original second-order Fresnel lens is in place and operational. Tours, between 12:30 P.M. and 3:30 P.M. Saturday and Sunday, are led by National Park rangers.

Directions: From San Francisco, cross the Golden Gate Bridge northbound on US 101 and take the Alexander Avenue exit. Turn onto Conzelman Road and follow the signs to the lighthouse. The one-mile walk from the parking lot includes crossing a sturdy suspension bridge.

Point Cabrillo Light Station

Mendocino, California
Date Activated: 1909
Latitude/Longitude: 39°20.9'N/123°49.6'W

A privately operated navigation aid, the North Coast Interpretive Association reopened the lighthouse to visitors in 1999, following a complete restoration of its James Chance Fresnel lens made in England. The third-order light was first turned on in 1909, and was decommissioned in 1972.

Directions: Follow California 1 north from Mendocino or south from Fort Bragg. Signs clearly direct the way.

Point Conception Lighthouse

Point Conception, California
Date Activated: 1856
Latitude/Longitude: 34°26.9'N/120°28.2'W

An active navigation aid, this light uses its first-order Fresnel lens with a modern bulb. Located on Coast Guard property, the lighthouse is surrounded by private ranches and cannot be seen except from the ocean.

Point Fermin Lighthouse

Los Angeles, California
Date Activated: 1874
Latitude/Longitude: 33°42.3'N/118°17.6'W

The active navigation aid is opposite the old lighthouse listed on the National Register of Historic Places. It is closed to the public but can be viewed from grounds maintained by Los Angeles City Recreation and Park Department.

Directions: Follow I-110 south to Gaffey Street. Continue straight south to Point Fermin Park.

Port Hueneme Lighthouse

Port Hueneme California
Date Activated: 1874
Latitude/Longitude: 34°08.7'N/119°12.6'W

While not on U.S. Navy facility grounds, it is surrounded by Port Hueneme Naval Station. The Coast Guard replaced the original Victorian structure, built in 1874, with an Art Deco tower in 1941. Coast Guard Station Channel Islands has just completed a thorough restoration and there are proposals to open the light to visitors.

Point Loma Lighthouse (Old)

San Diego, California
***Date Activated:* 1855**
***Latitude/Longitude:* 32°39.9'N/117°14.5'W**

No longer an active navigation aid, its original third-order Fresnel lens is intact. The lighthouse is open daily 9 A.M. to 5 P.M. and until 6 P.M. July 4 through Labor Day.

Directions: Follow I-5 to Rosecrans Avenue exit, California 209. Then follow signs to Cabrillo National Monument.

Point Loma Light Station (New)

San Diego, California
***Date Activated:* 1891**
***Latitude/Longitude:* 32°39.9'N/117°14.6'W**

The iron tower supporting the third-order Fresnel is located inside a Coast Guard residential compound and is closed to the public. Visitors can see the light from a nearby tidepool parking area.

Directions: Take Cabrillo Road off Cabrillo Memorial Drive, inside Cabrillo National Monument.

Point Montara Light Station

Montara, California
***Date Activated:* 1875**
***Latitude/Longitude:* 37°32.2'N/122°31.2'W**

An active navigation aid, the light is also an American Youth Hostel–operated facility on California State Park grounds open from 7:30 A.M. to 9:30 A.M. and 4:30 P.M. to 9:30 P.M. There are no tours of the lighthouse, which operates a modern light. Point Montara's original fourth-order lens is displayed at the San Mateo County Historical Society Museum.

Directions: Point Montara is about twenty-five miles south of San Francisco, less than one-half mile north of Montara.

Point No Point Light Station

Hansville, Washington
***Date Activated:* 1879**
***Latitude/Longitude:* 47°54.7'N/122°31.5'W**

Completed in 1879, the light is an active navigation aid and the original keeper's duplex now houses Coast Guard personnel. The light is open for tours, however, operated by the Point No Point County Park, near Hansville. Parking at the lighthouse is extremely limited and there is no legal parking immediately outside the grounds.

Directions: Take Washington 305 north from Bainbridge Island to 307. Continue north to 104 east to Hansville Road. Turn north, and once in Hansville, follow the signs to the County Park and lighthouse.

Point Pinos Lighthouse

Monterey, California
***Date Activated:* 1855**
***Latitude/Longitude:* 36°38.1'N/121°56.0'W**

An active navigation aid, the light was licensed to the Pacific Grove Historical Society in 1975. Docents dressed in period costumes offer tours of the restored keeper's residence. The light is open 12 P.M. to 4 P.M. Saturday and Sunday. The third-order Fresnel lens with its 1,000-watt bulb shining day and night can be viewed easily from several locations nearby.

Directions: Take California 1 to 68 west toward Pacific Grove. Bear left onto Sunset Drive, then turn right onto Asilomar Avenue.

Point Reyes Light Station

Point Reyes, California
***Date Activated:* 1870**
***Latitude/Longitude:* 37°59.7'N/123°01.4'W**

The Point Reyes National Seashore offers tours of the lighthouse from 10 A.M. to 4:30 P.M. Thursday through Monday. Point Reyes is one of America's foggiest and windiest areas. The light is a 300-step descent. When winds are greater than 40 mph (a high of 133 mph has been recorded there) tours are canceled. The first-order Fresnel, still in place with its jewel-box-like mechanical gears, is worth the climb back up. Those steps are interrupted by three rest areas with large benches.

Directions: Take the Sir Francis Drake Boulevard exit from US 101 or from California 1. Continue west to the Point Reyes National Seashore Visitors Center. Follow the signs to the light from there, continuing on Sir Francis Drake Boulevard. Allow forty-five minutes travel time from the visitors center.

Point Roberts Lighthouse

Point Roberts, Washington
***Date Activated:* NA**
***Latitude/Longitude:* 48°58.1'N/123°04.7'W**

A post light only, this light can be viewed and reached only from Canada.

Directions: Take the ferry from Sydney, British

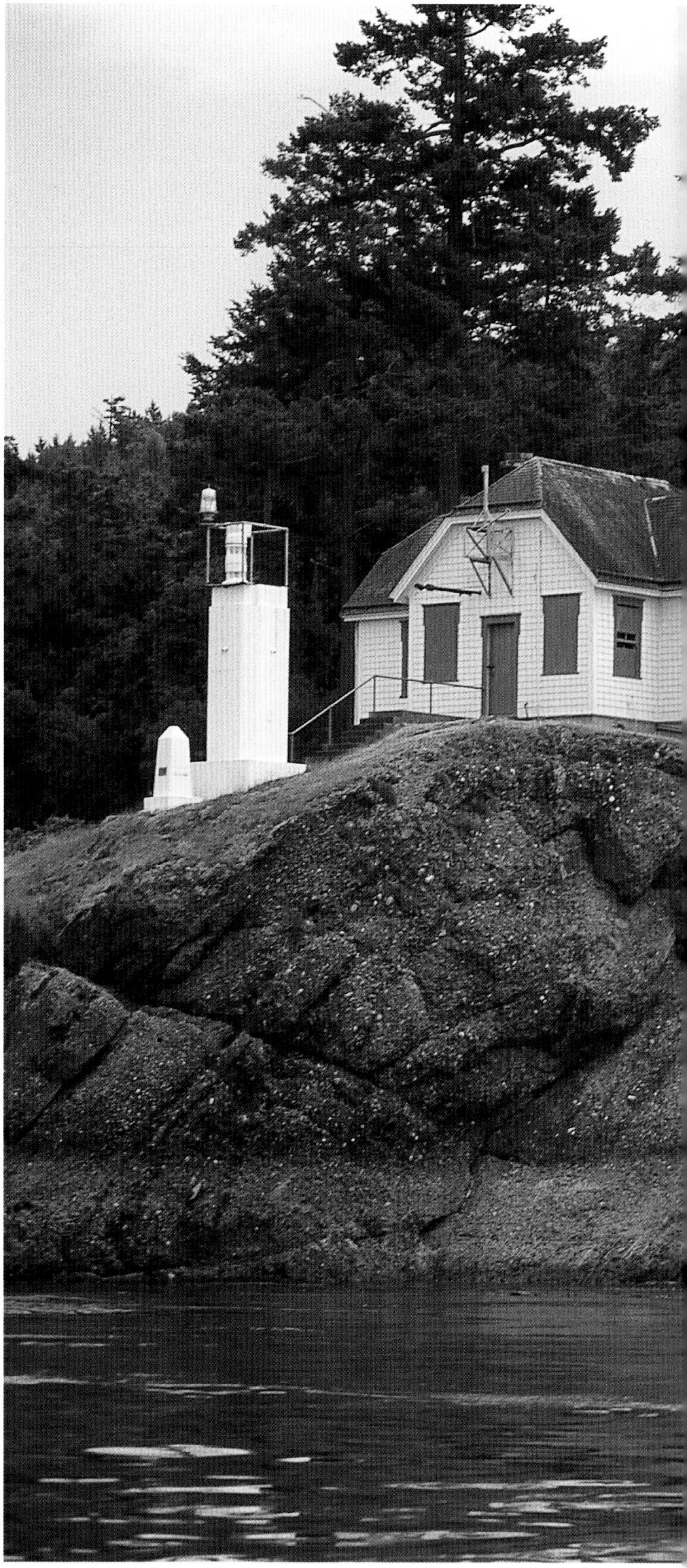

Turn Point light station

Stuart Island light is known as Turn Point for mariners navigating the Strait of Haro toward Vancouver. It's also the point where migrating orca whales turn south in early summer. During whale migration seasons, Washington University researchers live in the keeper's residence.

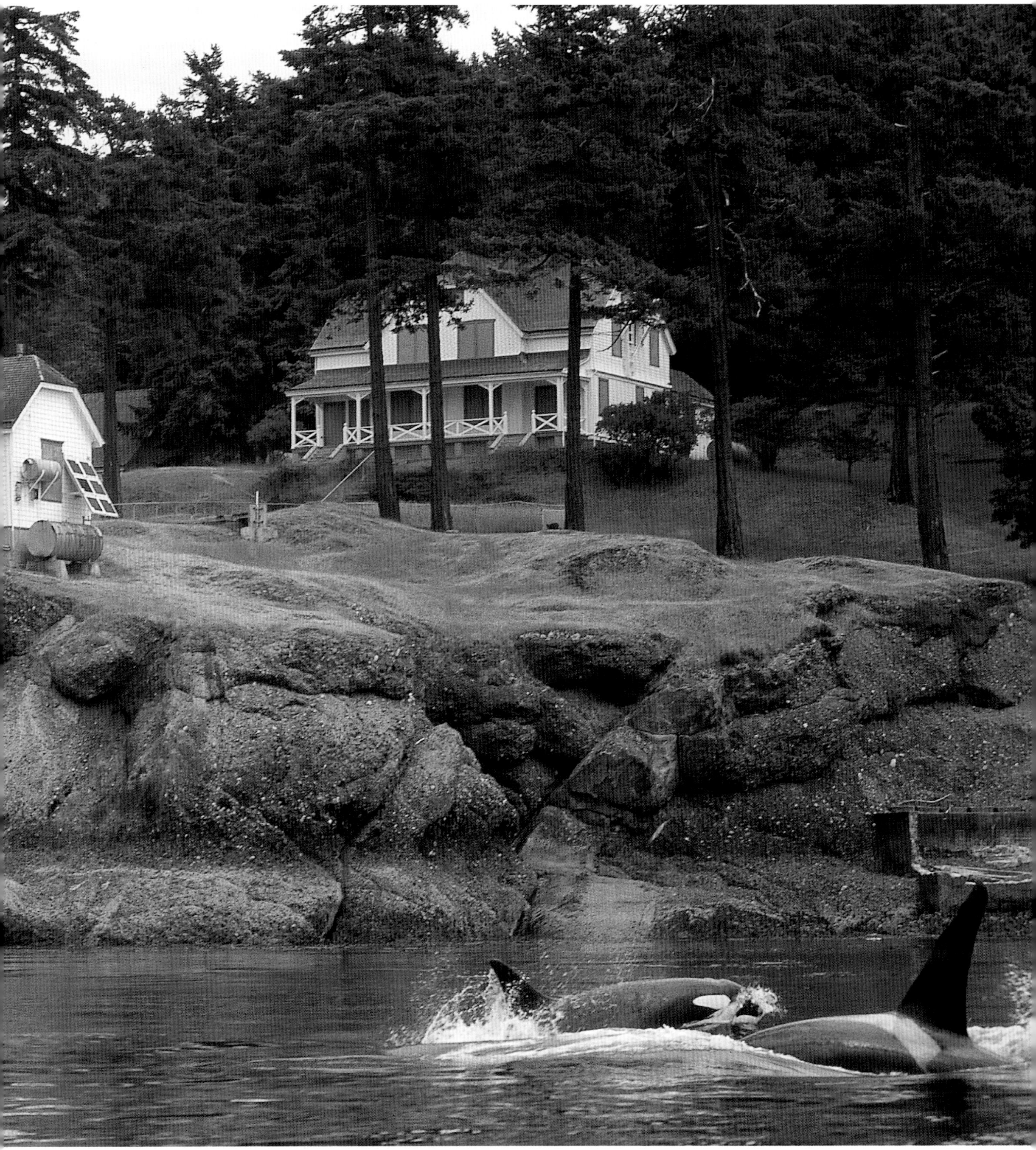

Columbia, across the Strait of Georgia to District of Delta, British Columbia, or drive south on British Columbia Route 17. View the light from the ferry dock at the end of 17.

Point Robinson Light Station

Maury Island, Washington
Date Activated: 1887/1915
Latitude/Longitude: 47°23.3'N/122°22.4'W

First lit in 1887, two years after the station started life as a fog signal only, Point Robinson continues as an active aid on Maury Island, a landmark for vessels from Seattle to Tacoma. The present lighthouse, built in 1915, is open for tours from 12 P.M. to 4 P.M. Saturday and Sunday year round except Christmas.

Directions: From Vashon Island take Vashon Highway SW to SW 240th. Turn east and follow around through Portage, onto Maury Island. Take Docton Road SW to Point Robinson Road and continue to the end of the road.

Point San Luis Light Station

Avila Beach, California
Date Activated: 1890
Latitude/Longitude: 30°09.6'N/118°24.6'W

The Point San Luis Preservation Society is restoring the lighthouse and its buildings. The station is surrounded by Pacific Gas & Electric's Diablo Canyon Power Station. It is accessible by docent-led weekend day hikes that run three-and-one-half miles over steep terrain.

The light's fourth-order Fresnel lens was removed and is on display at the San Luis Obispo County Historical Museum at 696 Monterey Street, San Luis Obispo. It is open from 10 A.M. to 4 P.M. Wednesday through Sunday.

Point Sur Light Station

Big Sur, California
Date Activated: 1889
Latitude/Longitude: 36°18.4'N/121°54.1'W

The Coast Guard operates an aero-beacon inside the tower as an active navigation aid. It also is a California State Historic Park. The tower and grounds, located about nineteen miles south of Carmel, are open to docent-led group hikes limited to forty people. Tours last three hours, including a one-half-mile hike up the 360-foot-high rock. In summer, tours are at 10 A.M. and 2 P.M. Saturday and Wednesday and 10 A.M. only Sunday and Monday, and are on a first-come-first-served basis. There are also monthly full-moon moonlight tours.

The original first-order Fresnel lens is displayed at the Maritime Museum of Monterey, Stanton Center, 5 Custom House Plaza, Monterey.

Point Vicente Light Station

Los Angeles, California
Date Activated: 1926
Latitude/Longitude: 33°44.5'N/118°24.6'W

An active navigation aid, the light is closed to visitors except by appointment. It can be viewed from the Interpretive Center at 31501 Palos Verdes Drive, Palos Verdes, which is open from 10 A.M. to 5 P.M. in winter and until 7 P.M. during summer.

Directions: Follow Hawthorne Boulevard (California Route 107) south off I-405 up and over the entire peninsula. At West Palos Verdes Drive, turn right and bear right to enter the Interpretive Center.

Point Wilson Light Station

Port Townsend, Washington
Date Activated: 1879
Latitude/Longitude: 48°08.7'N/122°45.2'W

Located in historic Fort Worden, which was constructed in 1896, this fourth-order Fresnel lighthouse was completed in 1879. The fort is now Fort Worden State Park, the grounds of which are open to the public from 6:30 A.M. until dusk from April 1 through October 15, and 8 A.M. until dusk the rest of the year. The keeper's residence is occupied by Coast Guard personnel, and the lighthouse is not open to the public except by special arrangement.

Directions: Signs in Port Townsend direct visitors to Fort Worden State Park.

Punta Gorda Lighthouse

Petrolia, California
Date Activated: 1912
Latitude/Longitude: 40°15.657'N/124°21.803'W

Located twelve miles south of Cape Mendocino, the twenty-seven-foot-tall light was decommissioned in 1951. The Coast Guard has removed and stored the original fourth-order light. It also destroyed the original keeper's residence to avoid further damage by squatters and vandals. Only the lighthouse and oil house remains.

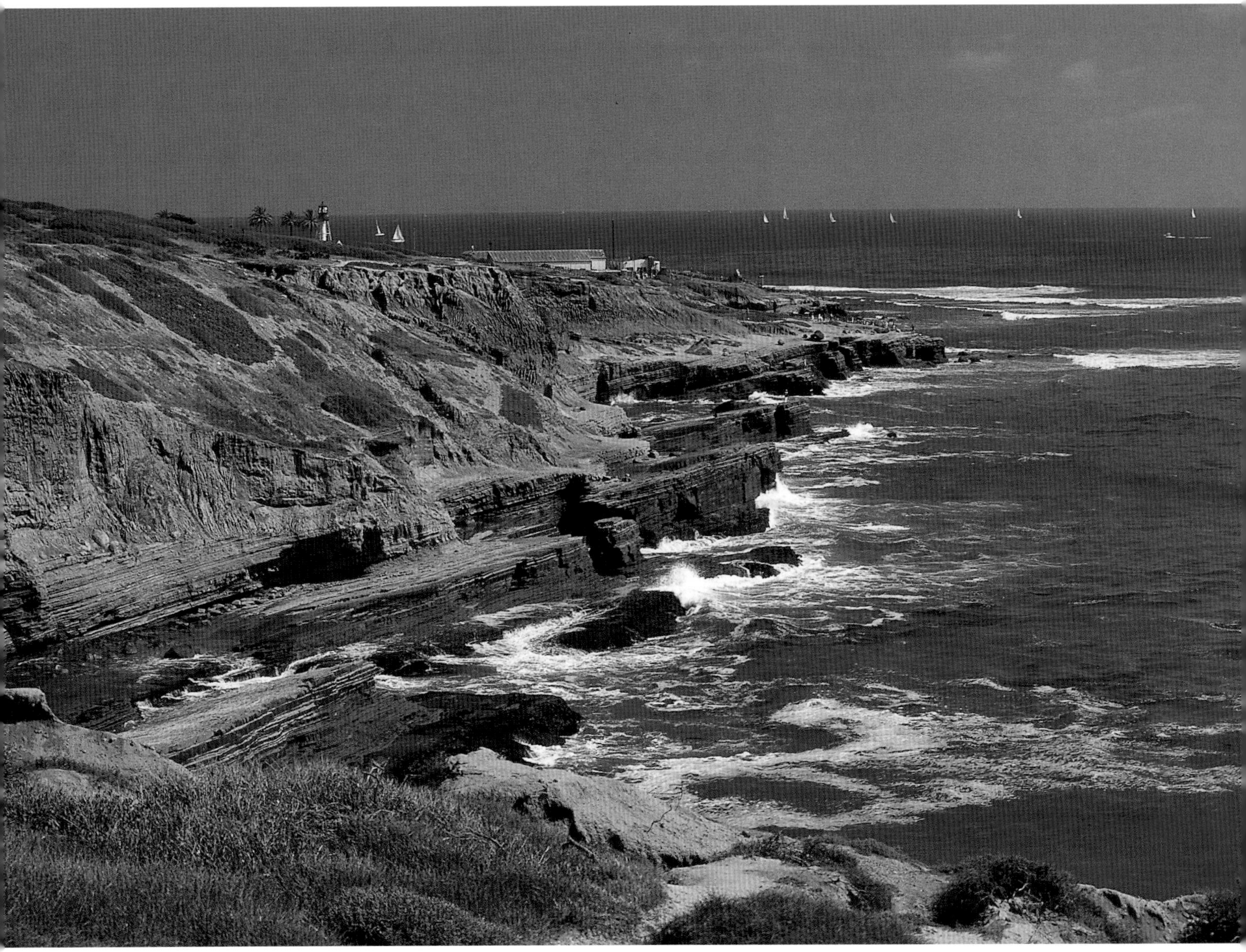

New Point Loma light station
Although the original Point Loma was the highest light in the nation at 462 feet above sea level, it was too often lost in fog. The new light, a skeleton-tower—the only one on the West Coast—first shined in March 1891. Its third-order LePaute Fresnel was used until a recent earthquake knocked it off center. Coast Guard families occupy the keepers' residences.

Directions: Take California 1 to Petrolia. Take Mattole Road up the hill, to the right, cross the Mattole River and turn right on Lighthouse Road. Continue to the beach. Park and walk south three-and-one-half miles along the beach to reach the lighthouse. Check the tide tables before you begin; at high tide, the beach is blocked and you can be stranded. It is a hard walk and the weather can be inhospitable.

St. George Reef Lighthouse

Crescent City, California
Date Activated: 1892
Latitude/Longitude: 41°50.14'N/124°22.29'W
The St. George Reef Preservation Society was formed in 1988 to save the most expensive light station ever built, costing $704,000 in 1892. Its first-order Fresnel lens, removed by the Coast Guard, is displayed at the Del Norte County Historical Museum in Crescent City. The St. George Reef lighthouse is located about six miles offshore, and while it is being restored by the society, it is not open to the public. The society travels by helicopter at about $3,000 a day, and visits are strictly limited to workers for the near future.

On clear days, the light station can be seen from the Battery Point lighthouse and from several points north along the coast. When restoration is complete, the preservation society plans to make helicopter visits available to the public for a more modest fee.

Santa Cruz Lighthouse

Santa Cruz, California
Date Activated: 1869/1967
Latitude/Longitude: 38°57.1'N/122°01.6'W
An active navigation aid, this reduced-scale lighthouse was built in 1967 as a family's monument to their son. It replaces a structure completed in 1869, decommissioned in 1941 and razed in 1948. It now houses the Santa Cruz Surfing Museum, open every day from 12 P.M. to 4 P.M., but closed on Tuesday.

Farallon Island Lighthouse

Farallon Islands, California
Date Activated: 1855
Latitude/Longitude: 37°41.9'N/123°00.1'W
The lighthouse is built on top of a 317-foot-tall rock twenty-three miles west of San Francisco. The Coast Guard replaced the first-order Fresnel with twin aerobeacons in 1972. The Farallon Islands are part of the Point Reyes Farallon Islands National Marine Sanctuary, and the light can be viewed only from their boats—fog permitting—on weekend tours between June and November arranged by the Oceanic Society Expeditions, San Francisco.

Table Bluff Lighthouse

Eureka, California
Date Activated: 1892
Latitude/Longitude: 40°41.72'N/124°16.58'W
The second light placed at the entrance to Humboldt Bay, this fourth-order lens in a twenty-one-foot-tall square tower was first lit in 1892. In 1953, the Coast Guard automated the station and stored its Fresnel at Point Loma. It abandoned the station in 1975. Local volunteers removed the tower from the original structure and restored it, relocating it in Woodley Island Marina in Eureka. The lens, returned from Point Loma, can be seen at the Humboldt Bay Maritime Museum, as well as an exhibit of lighthouses from Punta Gorda to St. George Reef.

Directions: Follow California 225 north from US 101 in Eureka to reach Woodley Island. Follow the signs to the marina. The museum is in new facilities at 423 First Street, in Old Town Eureka. It is open Tuesday through Saturday from 12 P.M. to 4 P.M.

Tillamook Rock Lighthouse

Tillamook, Oregon
Date Activated: 1881
Latitude/Longitude: 45°56.12'N/124°01.10'W
The first-order Fresnel first shone in 1881, but by 1957, the isolation of the station had made it the most costly to operate, and the Coast Guard decommissioned it. Following a period of real estate speculation, the rock became a columbarium in 1980. Since that time, mariners and others who love the sea have been interred there. Not open to visitors, it can easily be seen from Ecola State Park, near Seaside.

Trinidad Head Lighthouse

Trinidad, California
Date Activated: 1871
Latitude/Longitude: 41°03.1'N/124°09.1'W
The revolving fourth-order red Fresnel lens first shone from Trinidad Head in 1871. The Coast Guard replaced the Fresnel with a modern light in 1947 and, in the late 1960s, updated housing with a new structure. Still an

active navigation aid, the modern station is not open to the public but can be viewed from various places along US 101 south of Trinidad. The Trinidad Civic Club acquired the Fresnel and constructed a replica of the original tower at the bottom of Trinity Street, overlooking the waterfront.

Turn Point Light Station

Stuart Island, Washington
***Date Activated:** 1893/1936*
***Latitude/Longitude:** 48°41.3'N/123°14.2'W*

The station on Stuart Island was remodeled in 1936 with a new light and fog signal mounted on a concrete tower. The site is named Turn Point because mariners following Haro Strait to or from the Strait of Juan de Fuca from Vancouver make a sharp direction change just off the lighthouse, following the international boundary.

The station, on a sixty-nine-acre preserve, is part of Washington State Parks & Recreation Commission. The keeper's residence is frequently inhabited by University of Washington researchers studying orca whale migration. The house and light are not open to the public. Access to the island is by boat or private aircraft.

Umpqua River Light Station

Reedsport, Oregon
***Date Activated:** 1894*
***Latitude/Longitude:** 43°39.8'N/124°11.9'W*

An active navigation aid, the light is closed to the public. However, an historical and informational center is open from 10 A.M. to 5 P.M. Wednesday through Saturday and 1 P.M. to 5 P.M. Sunday.

Directions: Follow signs to Umpqua Lighthouse State Park from US 101, about six miles south of Reedsport. Stay until dark to see the red-and-white light shining across surrounding trees.

West Point Light Station

Seattle, Washington
***Date Activated:** 1881*
***Latitude/Longitude:** 47°39.7'N/122°226.1'W*

The light is located at the north entrance to Elliot Bay in Seattle's Discovery Park. On weekends, Discovery Park Visitors Center operates a shuttle bus to the beach. At low tide, visitors can walk around the lighthouse. There is no private car parking except at the visitor center.

Yaquina Bay Lighthouse

Newport, Oregon
***Date Activated:** 1871*
***Latitude/Longitude:** 44°37.374'N/124°03.811'W*

This restored light and residence was in use only until 1874. The state acquired the light and surrounding grounds in 1934, using the structure for park personnel housing until 1946. In 1974, state workers began restoration, furnishing it with period pieces from the Oregon State Historical Society. It is open daily from Memorial Day to September 30 from 11 A.M. to 5 P.M. The rest of the year, hours are 12 P.M. to 4 P.M. Saturday and Sunday.

Directions: From US. 101, follow signs to Yaquina Bay State Park & Historic Lighthouse, located at the end of Elizabeth Street, Newport.

Yaquina Head Lighthouse

Newport, Oregon
***Date Activated:** 1874*
***Latitude/Longitude:** 44°40.6'N/124°04.7'W*

This light replaced the Yaquina Bay structure in 1874. Still active today, it is open to visitors who can climb to the watchroom and glimpse the light's flashing first-order Fresnel. Hours are 10 A.M. to 4 P.M. daily from June through October and 12 P.M. to 4 P.M. the rest of the year.

The modest five-dollar admission fee covers the lighthouse as well as one of the finest interpretive centers on the West Coast. Numerous displays and several videos relate to this lighthouse and others, as well as the area's marine and bird life. The interpretive center is open June through October from 10 A.M. to 6 P.M. and the rest of the year from 10 A.M. to 4 P.M. The entire site, including fascinating tide pools, is open from dawn to dusk year round.

Directions: Turn off US 101 at Agate Beach.

Yerba Buena Island Lighthouse

Yerba Buena Island, near San Francisco, California
***Date Activated:** 1875*
***Latitude/Longitude:** 37°48.4'N/122°21.7'W*

The original fourth-order Fresnel still shines with a modern bulb. In 1958, the Coast Guard began lighting the outside of the tower to differentiate it from other structures. The nearby head keeper's residence is now home to a Coast Guard admiral. Neither are open to the public and may be seen only from the bay.

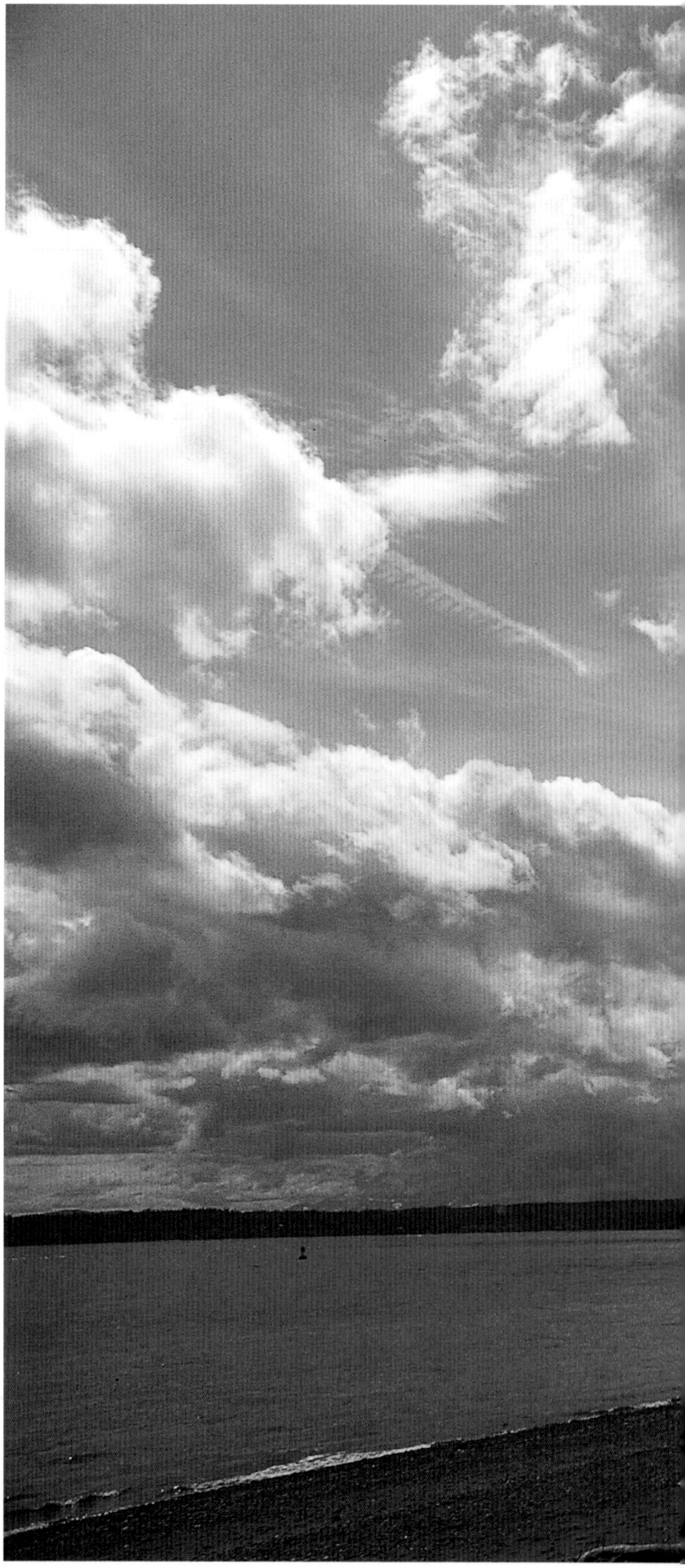

West Point light station
Rainstorms are sometimes called cloudbursts. This time, the sky burst open within a few moments of a heavy downpour, bringing visitors back to the rocky beach. The shipping traffic along Puget Sound relies on modern electronic and satellite navigation aids, but the visual and aural security of seeing the light and hearing the fog horn is indisputable.

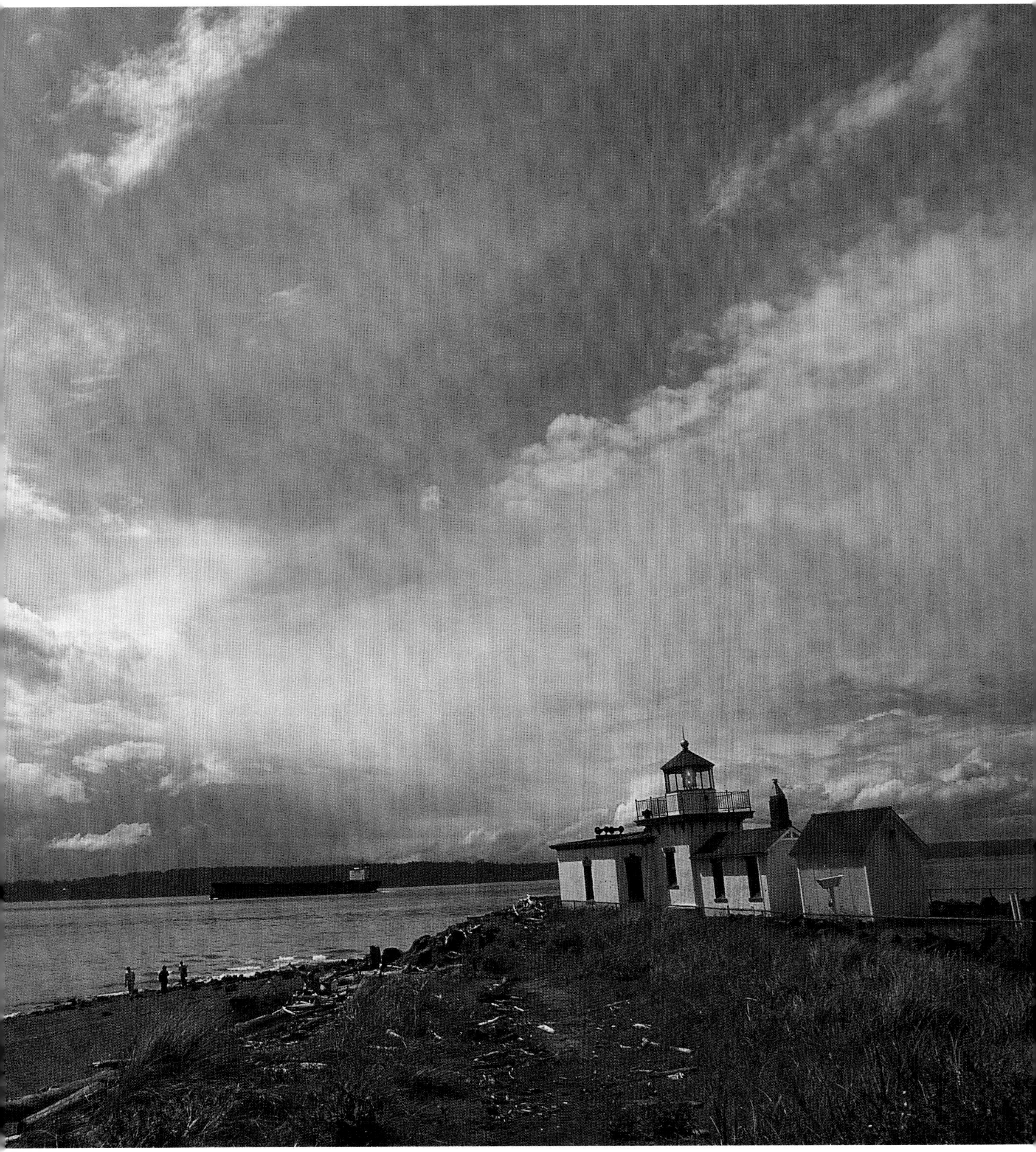

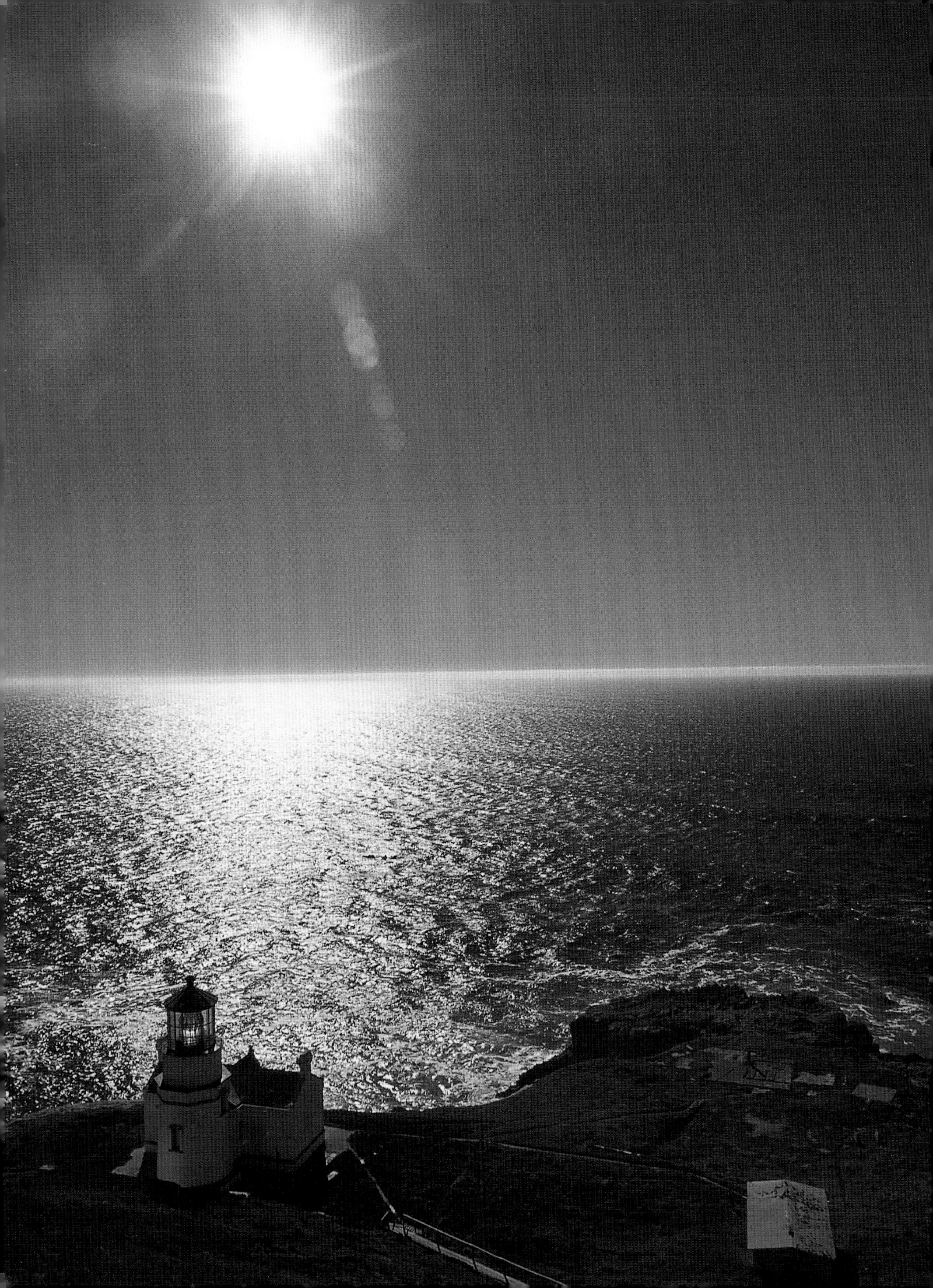

Bibliography

Adamson, Hans Christian. *Keepers of the Lights*. New York: Greenberg Publishers, 1955.

Bishop, Eleanor C. *Prints in the Sand: The U.S. Coast Guard Beach Patrol During World War II*. Missoula, MT: Pictorial Histories Publishing Company, 1989.

Bloomfield, Howard V. L. *The Compact History of the United States Coast Guard*. New York: Hawthorn Books, 1966.

Canney, Donald L. *U.S. Coast Guard and Revenue Cutters, 1790–1935*. Annapolis, MD: Naval Institute Press, 1995.

Clifford, Mary Louise, and Clifford, J. Candace. *Women Who Kept the Lights: An Illustrated History of Female Lighthouse Keepers*. Williamsburg, VA: Cypress Communications, 1993.

Congressional Record. Washington, D.C.: U.S. Government Printing Office.

De Wire, Elinor. *Guardians of the Lights: Stories of U.S. Lighthouse Keepers*. Sarasota, FL: Pineapple Press, 1995.

Ehlers, Chad; and Gibbs, Jim. *Sentinels of Solitude: West Coast Lighthouses*. San Luis Obispo, CA: EZ Nature Books, 1981.

Engle, Norma. *Three Beams of Light*. San Diego, CA: Tecolote Publications, 1986.

Fitch, James Marston. *American Building: The Forces That Shape It*. Boston, MA: Houghton Mifflin Company, 1948.

Gibbs, James. *West Coast Lighthouses: A Pictorial History of the Guiding Lights of the Sea*. Seattle, WA: Superior Publishing Co., 1974.

Gibbs, James. *Shipwrecks of the Pacific Coast*. Portland, OR: Binford and Morts, 1957.

Goodrich, Frank B. *Ocean's Story: Triumphs of Thirty Centuries; Achievements, Explorations, Discoveries and Inventions*. Philadelphia, PA: Hubbard Bros., 1873.

Holland, Francis Ross, Jr. *America's Lighthouses: An Illustrated History*. Brattleboro, VT: The Stephen Greene Press, 1972.

Johnson, Robert Erwin. *Guardians of the Sea: History of the United States Coast Guard 1915 to the Present*. Annapolis, MD: Naval Institute Press, 1987.

Kinder, Gary. *Ship of Gold*. New York: Vintage Books, 1998.

Lewis, Emmanuel Raymond. *Seacoast Fortifications of the United States*. Annapolis, MD: Naval Institute Press, 1970.

Lighthouse Board. *Annual Reports*. Washington, D.C.: Lighthouse Board, 1852–1910.

Noble, Dennis L. *Lighthouses & Keepers: The U.S. Lighthouse Service and its Legacy*. Annapolis, MD: Naval Institute Press, 1997.

Noble, Dennis L. *That Others Might Live: The U.S. Life-Saving Service, 1878–1915*. Annapolis, MD: Naval Institute Press, 1994.

Putnam, George R. *Sentinel of the Coasts*. New York: W.W. Norton Co., Inc., 1937.

Shanks, Ralph C., Jr., and Shanks, Janetta Thompson. *Lighthouses and Lifeboats on the Redwood Coast*. San Anselmo, CA: Costano Books, 1978.

United States Coast Guard. *Historically Famous Lighthouses*. Washington, D.C.: Department of Transportation, 1972.

United States Department of Commerce. *United States Coast Pilot: Pacific Coast—California, Oregon, and Washington. Sixth ed.* Washington, D.C.: U.S. Government Printing Office, 1942.

United States Department of Commerce and Labor. *United States Coast Pilot: Pacific Coast—California, Oregon, and Washington*. Washington, D.C.: U.S. Government Printing Office, 1909.

United States Department of Transportation. *Light List Pacific Coast and Pacific Islands. Volume VI*. Washington, D.C.: U.S. Government Printing Office, 1993.

Weiss, George. *The Lighthouse Service, Its History, Activities and Organization*. Baltimore, MD: The Johns Hopkins Press, 1926.

Witney, Dudley. *The Lighthouse*. Boston, MA: New York Graphic Society, 1975.

Point Conception lighthouse

Point Conception originally boasted a head keeper and three assistants, each with separate dwellings. A barn, washhouse, bunkhouse, carpenter shop, and storehouse were also located at the station. Two rainwater cisterns held 60,000 gallons each; they were also fed by a nearby spring.

Index

About the Authors

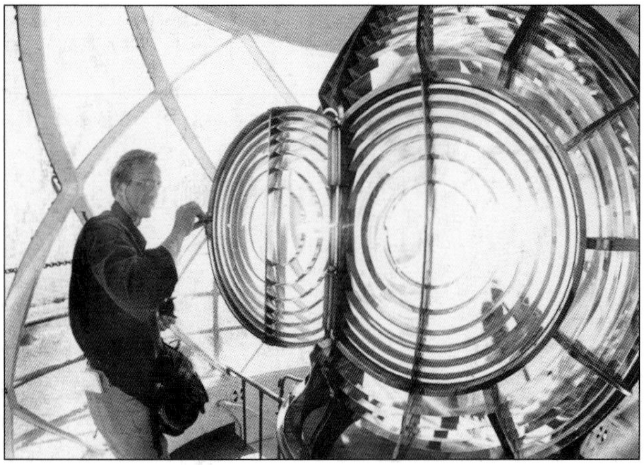

Photograph © Alastair Worden

Writer and photographer Randy Leffingwell lives in Ojai, California, although he was raised in the Chicago suburbs. He received a bachelor of science in Journalism from Kansas University in 1970. He worked two years for the Kansas City *Times* before joining the Chicago *Sun-Times*. He remained there for nine years, then worked a year as Associate Editor at *AutoWeek* magazine in Detroit. In 1984, he joined the staff of the Los Angeles *Times* as writer/photographer. While at the *Times*, he began writing and photographing non-fiction books on Americana, covering subjects as diverse as barns in America and Harley-Davidsons. He left the *Times* in 1995 to do books full time. This is his eighteenth book, his first with Voyageur Press, and his first with co-author Pamela Welty.

Author Pamela Welty lives in Orange County, California, but calls the San Lorenzo Valley in Northern California her hometown. She received a bachelor of science degree from California State University Dominguez Hills. While completing her masters degree at Massey University, Palmerston, North New Zealand, she wrote "These Hallowed Halls," a history and walking tour of the campus. Welty travels extensively gathering information for upcoming books and genealogical research. This is her first book with Voyageur Press and co-author Randy Leffingwell.

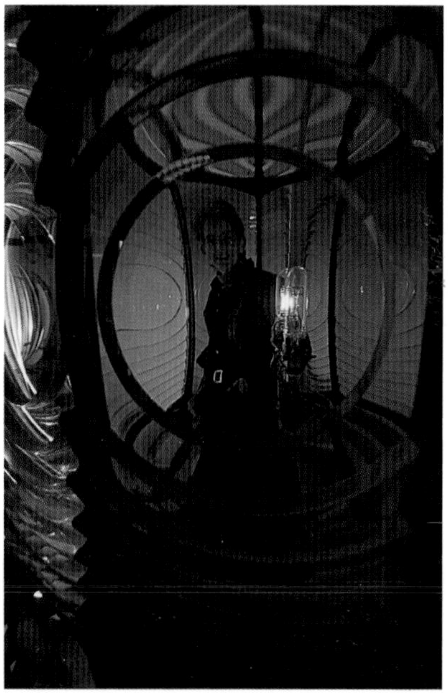